into Literature™

GRADE
12
VOLUME 2

Printed in the U.S.A.

ISBN 978-0-358-41647-0

3 4 5 6 7 8 9 10   1468   29 28 27 26 25 24 23 22

4500854014

r11.20

Program Consultants:

Kylene Beers

Martha Hougen

Tyrone C. Howard

Elena Izquierdo

Carol Jago

Weston Kieschnick

Erik Palmer

Robert E. Probst

GRADE
12
VOLUME 2

Program Consultants

Kylene Beers

Nationally known lecturer and author on reading and literacy; coauthor with Robert Probst of *Disrupting Thinking, Notice & Note: Strategies for Close Reading,* and *Reading Nonfiction;* former president of the National Council of Teachers of English. Dr. Beers is the author of *When Kids Can't Read: What Teachers Can Do* and coeditor of *Adolescent Literacy: Turning Promise into Practice,* as well as articles in the *Journal of Adolescent and Adult Literacy.* Former editor of *Voices from the Middle,* she is the 2001 recipient of NCTE's Richard W. Halle Award, given for outstanding contributions to middle school literacy.

Martha Hougen

National consultant, presenter, researcher, and author. Areas of expertise include differentiating instruction for students with learning difficulties, including those with learning disabilities and dyslexia; and teacher and leader preparation improvement. Dr. Hougen has taught at the middle school through graduate levels. Dr. Hougen has supported Educator Preparation Program reforms while working at the Meadows Center for Preventing Educational Risk at The University of Texas at Austin and at the CEEDAR Center, University of Florida.

Tyrone C. Howard

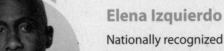

Veteran teacher, author, and professor in the Graduate School of Education and Information Studies at UCLA. Dr. Howard is the inaugural director of the UCLA Pritzker Center for Strengthening Children and Families, a campus-wide consortium examining academic, mental health, and social and emotional experiences and challenges for the most vulnerable youth populations. Dr. Howard has published over 75 peer-reviewed journal articles and several bestselling books, including, *Why Race & Culture Matters in Schools* and *Black Male(d): Peril and Promise in the Education of African American Males.* He is considered one of the premier experts on educational equity and access in the country.

Elena Izquierdo

Nationally recognized teacher educator and advocate for English language learners. Dr. Izquierdo is a linguist by training, with a Ph.D. in Applied Linguistics and Bilingual Education from Georgetown University. She has served on various state and national boards working to close the achievement gaps for bilingual students and English language learners. Dr. Izquierdo is a member of the Hispanic Leadership Council, which supports Hispanic students and educators at both the state and federal levels.

Carol Jago

Teacher of English with 32 years of experience at Santa Monica High School in California; author and nationally known lecturer; former president of the National Council of Teachers of English. Ms. Jago currently serves as Associate Director of the California Reading and Literature Project at UCLA. With expertise in standards assessment and secondary education, Ms. Jago is the author of numerous books on education, including *With Rigor for All* and *Papers, Papers, Papers*; and she is active with the California Association of Teachers of English, editing its scholarly journal *California English* since 1996. Ms. Jago also served on the planning committee for the 2009 NAEP Reading Framework and the 2011 NAEP Writing Framework.

Weston Kieschnick

Author, award-winning teacher, principal, instructional development coordinator, and dean of education. Mr. Kieschnick has driven change and improved student learning in multiple capacities over his educational career. Now, as an experienced instructional coach and Senior Fellow with the International Center for Leadership in Education (ICLE), Mr. Kieschnick shares his expertise with teachers to transform learning through online and blended models. He is the author of *Bold School: Old School Wisdom + New School Innovation = Blended Learning that Works* and co-author of *The Learning Transformation: A Guide to Blended Learning for Administrators*.

Erik Palmer

Veteran teacher and education consultant based in Denver, Colorado. Author of *Well Spoken: Teaching Speaking to All Students* and *Digitally Speaking: How to Improve Student Presentations*. His areas of focus include improving oral communication, promoting technology in classroom presentations, and updating instruction through the use of digital tools. He holds a bachelor's degree from Oberlin College and a master's degree in curriculum and instruction from the University of Colorado.

Robert E. Probst

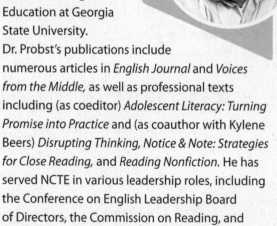

Nationally respected authority on the teaching of literature; Professor Emeritus of English Education at Georgia State University. Dr. Probst's publications include numerous articles in *English Journal* and *Voices from the Middle,* as well as professional texts including (as coeditor) *Adolescent Literacy: Turning Promise into Practice* and (as coauthor with Kylene Beers) *Disrupting Thinking, Notice & Note: Strategies for Close Reading,* and *Reading Nonfiction*. He has served NCTE in various leadership roles, including the Conference on English Leadership Board of Directors, the Commission on Reading, and column editor of the NCTE journal *Voices from the Middle.*

Origin of a Nation Page 1

KEY LEARNING OBJECTIVES

- Determine themes
- Analyze narrator
- Analyze conflict
- Analyze characterization
- Make inferences
- Evaluate author's purpose
- Analyze tone

READER'S CHOICE

SHORT READS

from **Beowulf**
   Grendel's Mother
   The Battle with Grendel's Mother
   Beowulf's Last Battle
   The Death of Beowulf
   Mourning Beowulf
Epic Poem by the Beowulf Poet
translated by Burton Raffel

Beowulf Is Back!
Article by James Parker

Barbara Allan
Ballad by Anonymous

Journeymen Keep the Medieval Past Alive
Article by Melissa Eddy

Available online

ⓔ**Ed**

LONG READS

Grendel
Novel
by John Gardner

Beowulf
Graphic Novel
by Gareth Hinds

Norse Mythology
Mythology
by Neil Gaiman

Recommendations

UNIT 1 TASKS

WRITING

SPEAKING & LISTENING

ⓔ**Ed**

Go online for
Unit and Selection Videos
Interactive Annotation and Text Analysis
Selection Audio Recordings
SAT® Exam / ACT® Test Prep
Collaborative Writing   Writable

A Celebration of Human Achievement

Page 150

? ESSENTIAL QUESTIONS:

What can drive someone to seek revenge?

How does time affect our feelings?

What's the difference between love and passion?

How do you defy expectations?

KEY LEARNING OBJECTIVES

- Analyze dramatic plot
- Analyze soliloquy
- Analyze interpretations of drama
- Analyze arguments
- Interpret figurative language
- Analyze text features
- Summarize and paraphrase texts

COLLABORATE & COMPARE

READER'S CHOICE

Available online
Ed

Recommendations

UNIT 2 TASKS

Ed

Go online for
Unit and Selection Videos
Interactive Annotation and Text Analysis
Selection Audio Recordings
SAT® Exam / ACT® Test Prep
Collaborative Writing

Writable

Tradition and Reason Page 380

ESSENTIAL QUESTIONS:

How can satire change people's behavior?

What's your most surprising friendship?

What keeps people from reaching their potential?

Why are plagues so horrifying?

KEY LEARNING OBJECTIVES

- Analyze satire
- Analyze development of ideas
- Evaluate rhetorical devices
- Analyze counterarguments
- Integrate and evaluate information
- Analyze narrator
- Analyze author's point of view

READER'S CHOICE

SHORT READS

Dido Elizabeth Belle: A Black Woman in Georgian England
Article by Steve Danzis

Written at the Close of Spring
Poem by Charlotte Smith

On Her Loving Two Equally
Poem by Aphra Behn

King George's Letters Betray Madness, Computer Finds
Article by Mindy Weisberger

Available online

ⓔ**Ed**

LONG READS

Robinson Crusoe
Novel
by Daniel Defoe

The Hitchhiker's Guide to the Galaxy
Novel
by Douglas Adams

Angela's Ashes
Memoir
by Frank McCourt

Recommendations

UNIT 3 TASKS

WRITING

SPEAKING & LISTENING

© Houghton Mifflin Harcourt Publishing Company

ⓔ**Ed**

Go online for
Unit and Selection Videos
Interactive Annotation and Text Analysis
Selection Audio Recordings
SAT® Exam / ACT® Test Prep
Collaborative Writing

Writable

Emotion and
Experimentation Page 514

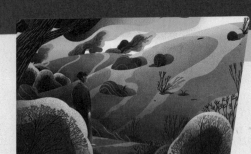

?

ESSENTIAL QUESTIONS:

What can nature offer us?
How do you define beauty?
How can science go wrong?
What stirs your imagination?

KEY LEARNING OBJECTIVES

- Analyze romantic poetry
- Analyze imagery
- Analyze stanza structure
- Analyze rhyme scheme
- Evaluate essay
- Analyze ode
- Analyze symbols

COLLABORATE & COMPARE

READER'S CHOICE

SHORT READS

William Blake: Visions and Verses
Explanatory Essay by Rachel Galvin

Frost at Midnight
Poem by Samuel Taylor Coleridge

Walking with Wordsworth
Personal Narrative by Bruce Stutz

from **A Defense of Poetry**
Argument by Percy Bysshe Shelley

The Skylark
Poem by John Clare

Available online

LONG READS

Frankenstein
Novel
by Mary Shelley

The Sun Is Also a Star
Novel
by Nicola Yoon

The Stranger in the Woods: The Extraordinary Story of the Last True Hermit
Nonfiction
by Michael Finkel

Recommendations

UNIT 4 TASKS

WRITING

Go online for
Unit and Selection Videos
Interactive Annotation and Text Analysis
Selection Audio Recordings
SAT® Exam / ACT® Test Prep
Collaborative Writing

Writable

An Era of Rapid Change Page 616

ESSENTIAL QUESTIONS:

What is a true benefactor?

How do you view the world?

What brings out cruelty in people?

Which invention has had the greatest impact on your life?

KEY LEARNING OBJECTIVES

- Analyze first-person point of view
- Analyze mood
- Analyze plot
- Analyze characterization
- Analyze compare and contrast essay
- Analyze sound devices
- Draw conclusions about speakers

READER'S CHOICE

SHORT READS

Poems by Victorian Women

Sonnet 43
by Elizabeth Barrett Browning

Remembrance
by Emily Brontë

Song
by Christina Rossetti

The Great Exhibition
Article by Lara Kriegel

Evidence of Progress
Essay by Thomas Babington Macaulay

Available online

ⓔEd

LONG READS

Great Expectations
Novel
by Charles Dickens

The Eyre Affair
Novel
by Jasper Fforde

While the Locust Slept
Memoir
by Peter Razor

Recommendations

UNIT 5 TASKS

WRITING

SPEAKING & LISTENING

ⓔEd

Go online for
Unit and Selection Videos
Interactive Annotation and Text Analysis
Selection Audio Recordings
SAT® Exam / ACT® Test Prep
Collaborative Writing

Writable

New Ideas, New Voices Page 728

?

ESSENTIAL QUESTIONS:

What makes people feel insecure?

Why is it hard to resist social pressure?

What is the power of symbols?

How do you measure a person's worth?

KEY LEARNING OBJECTIVES

- Evaluate an unreliable narrator
- Analyze third-person point of view
- Analyze reflective essay
- Analyze cause-and-effect relationships
- Understand modernist poetry
- Evaluate persuasive techniques
- Analyze deductive reasoning

© Houghton Mifflin Harcourt Publishing Company

READER'S CHOICE

SHORT READS

Araby
Short Story by James Joyce

Professions for Women
Speech by Virginia Woolf

Do Not Go Gentle into That Good Night
Poem by Dylan Thomas

Digging
Poem by Seamus Heaney

Marriage Is a Private Affair
Short Story by Chinua Achebe

Available
online

ⓔ *Ed*

LONG READS

Things Fall Apart
Novel
by Chinua Achebe

Milkman
Novel
by Anna Burns

White Teeth
Novel
by Zadie Smith

Recommendations

UNIT 6 TASKS

WRITING

SPEAKING & LISTENING

© Houghton Mifflin Harcourt Publishing Company

ⓔ *Ed*

Go online for
Unit and Selection Videos
Interactive Annotation and Text Analysis
Selection Audio Recordings
SAT® Exam / ACT® Test Prep
Collaborative Writing

Writable

Selections by Genre

FM19

Selections by Genre

© Houghton Mifflin Harcourt Publishing Company

DRAMA

MEDIA STUDY

© Houghton Mifflin Harcourt Publishing Company

into Literature™ Online

Ed

Experience the Power of
HMH Into Literature

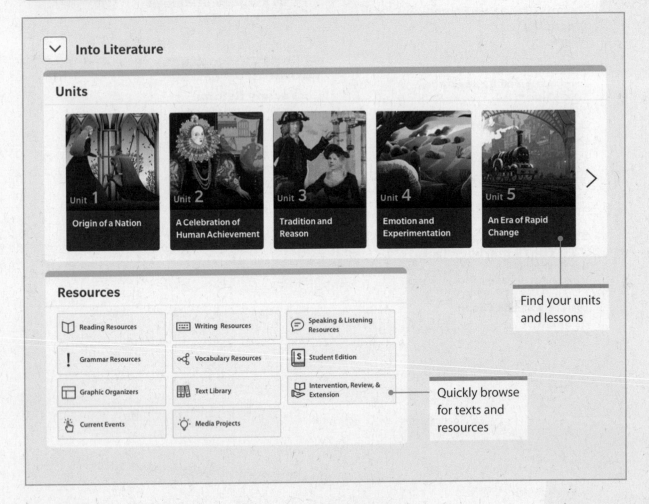

Into Literature

Units

Unit **1** — Origin of a Nation

Unit **2** — A Celebration of Human Achievement

Unit **3** — Tradition and Reason

Unit **4** — Emotion and Experimentation

Unit **5** — An Era of Rapid Change

Find your units and lessons

Resources

- Reading Resources
- Writing Resources
- Speaking & Listening Resources
- ! Grammar Resources
- Vocabulary Resources
- Student Edition
- Graphic Organizers
- Text Library
- Intervention, Review, & Extension
- Current Events
- Media Projects

Quickly browse for texts and resources

Tools for Today—All in One Place

Whether you're working alone or collaborating with others, it takes effort to analyze the complex texts and competing ideas that bombard us in this fast-paced world. What will help you succeed? Staying engaged and organized. The digital tools in this program will help you take charge of your learning.

UNIT **1**

The Anglo-Saxon and Medieval Periods
Origin of a Nation
"It is chivalry that makes a true knight, not a sword."
— George R. R. Martin

ANALYZE THE IMAGE
Which ideals of chivalry are reflected in this image?

Engage!

Spark Your Learning

These activities kick-start the unit and help get you thinking about the unit theme.

Engage Your Brain

Before you read, take some time to do a fun activity designed to rev up your brain and connect to the text.

Interact with the Texts

- As you read, highlight and take notes to mark the text in your own customized way.

- Use interactive graphic organizers to process, summarize, and track your thinking as you read.

- Play the audio to listen to the text read aloud. You can also turn on read-along highlighting.

Choices

Choose from engaging activities, such as writing an advice column, creating a podcast, or participating in a debate, to demonstrate what you've learned.

Stay Involved!

Collaborate with and Learn from Your Peers

- Watch brief **Peer Coach Videos** to learn more about a particular skill.

- Flex your creative muscles by digging into **Media Projects** tied to each unit theme.

- Bring your writing online with **Writable,** where you can share your work and give and receive valuable feedback.

Read On!

Find helpful **Reader's Choice** suggestions with each unit, and access hundreds of texts online.

No Wi-Fi? No Problem!

With HMH *Into Literature,* you always have access; download when you're online and access what you need when you're offline.

The Positive Disrupter

Dr. Kylene Beers

Dr. Robert E. Probst

Reading is Change: Thoughts by Two Teachers

by **Dr. Kylene Beers** and **Dr. Robert E. Probst**

Here you are, in the last years of high school, and for more of your school years than you might care to remember you've probably been told not to be disruptive. Sit still. Listen. Keep quiet. But now we're going to tell you to be a disrupter.

Sometimes, of course, you should be still and listen, learn, ponder. But sometimes you should speak up to make a change, to influence those around you, to cause a disruption. We're not encouraging you to misbehave. We're encouraging something much bigger than that.

Disruptions That Bring Change and Growth

Throughout our nation's history, we've grown due to technological disruptions: the horse and buggy eventually became the electric car, the telegram evolved into the text, and the rabbit-eared, three-channel TV became a three-hundred-channel smart device. We've also grown due to social and political disruptions. Women demanded the right to vote; African Americans fought for their freedom; and at one point reading and writing were things reserved for the privileged—ordinary people had to fight to upset that imbalance of power.

Disruptions are a part of life. Some will be positive: new and faster ways to communicate, better ways to grow food, easier ways to clean water. And some will be negative. One of the greatest disruptions we've faced as a nation and world was the COVID-19 pandemic of 2020. The "stay home, stay safe" order disrupted everyone's life. The questions we must ask are, "What did we learn" and "What will we carry forward?"

Other disruptions will affect only you, or you and your family or friend community. You may decide that your religious or political views differ from those of your friends or family. You may choose to be a musician though your parents wanted you to be a pharmacist, or a soldier though your parents wanted you to be a farmer. And there will be other personal choices that you will have to make.

Or others will make them for you. You are going to have to deal with those disruptions and the changes they will bring. You, and others your age, will make the decisions. It's important that you decide what you think. If you don't read and learn, the decisions will be made for you by those who do, or by those who are simply louder.

Some groups of people have always withheld power from others by making sure they know less. One of the most powerful ways of doing that is to ensure groups can't read or write. In some countries today, girls are denied schooling. And, too many who do learn to read and write fail to realize that the more they read, the more able they will be to use reason and evidence to question the world around them and influence their own futures. Too many choose not to read.

The Path to Positive Disruption

The texts you will read this year take on some of the issues every human must face: love, greed, hope, death, injustice, equity, and our relationship with nature, to name a few. Read these selections carefully. Though the story might have taken place in another time with a different group of people, the human emotions and issues remain relevant. Decide what matters to you. Wonder what the issues mean in your life today. And as you decide, think of the world that you will help to shape. You are tomorrow's builders, scientists, politicians, artists, teachers, and nurses. You are our brave soldiers who will defend this country, and our curious thinkers who will change it. And you will change it only by disrupting, slightly or significantly, what it is now.

To do that you need to read well—attentively and thoughtfully. We'll help you do that with some tools we call the **Notice & Note Signposts**, explained throughout this program (see the chart on the next two pages). Recognizing signposts will help you better understand what you're reading and thus, what you're thinking.

Reading—smart reading—gives you the opportunity to weigh a thought, a value, a belief, and decide whether to hold onto it, change it, or dispose of it. If you don't decide for yourself, then someone else will. And if you allow that, then you no longer have much influence over the shape of the world in which you live. Don't be that person. Be a person with power, a positive disrupter.

Shape the world in which you live.

COLLABORATIVE DISCUSSION

What is something you'd like to disrupt? How might reading help you do that?

 Ed

Notice & Note Handbook
Peer Coach Videos

Signposts

When you notice a signpost in your reading, mark the text with its initials.

LITERARY TEXTS

CONTRASTS AND CONTRADICTIONS   CC

A sharp contrast between what we would expect and what we observe the character doing; behavior that contradicts previous behavior or well-established patterns

When you notice this signpost, ask:

Why would the character act (feel) this way?

AHA MOMENT   AM

A sudden realization of something that shifts a character's actions or understanding of self, others, or the world

When you notice this signpost, ask:

How might this change things?

TOUGH QUESTIONS   TQ

Questions characters raise that reveal their inner struggles

When you notice this signpost, ask:

What does this question make me wonder about?

WORDS OF THE WISER   WW

The advice or insight about life that a wiser character, who is usually older, offers to the main character

When you notice this signpost, ask:

What is the life lesson, and how might this affect the character?

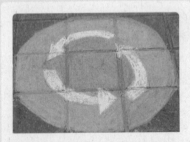

AGAIN AND AGAIN   AA

Events, images, or particular words that recur over a portion of the story

When you notice this signpost, ask:

Why might the author bring this up again and again?

MEMORY MOMENT   MM

A recollection by a character that interrupts the forward progress of the story

When you notice this signpost, ask:

Why might this memory moment be important?

INFORMATIONAL TEXTS

BIG QUESTIONS   BQ

It's important to take a **Questioning Stance** or attitude when you read nonfiction.

- *What surprised me?*
- *What did the author think I already knew?*
- *What changed, challenged, or confirmed what I already knew?*

CONTRASTS AND CONTRADICTIONS   CC

A sharp contrast between what we would expect and what we observe happening; a difference between two or more elements in the text

When you notice this signpost, ask:

What is the difference, and why does it matter?

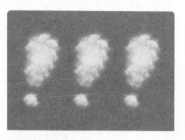

EXTREME OR ABSOLUTE LANGUAGE   XL

Language that leaves no doubt about a situation or an event, allows no compromise, or seems to exaggerate or overstate a case

When you notice this signpost, ask:

Why did the author use this language?

NUMBERS AND STATS   NS

Specific quantities or comparisons to depict the amount, size, or scale; or the writer is vague and imprecise about numbers when we would expect more precision

When you notice this signpost, ask:

Why did the author use these numbers or amounts?

QUOTED WORDS   QW

Opinions or conclusions of someone who is an expert on the subject or someone who might be a participant in or a witness to an event; or the author might cite other people to provide support for a point

When you notice this signpost, ask:

Why was this person quoted or cited, and what did this add?

WORD GAPS   WG

Vocabulary that is unfamiliar to the reader—for example, a word with multiple meanings, a rare or technical word, a discipline-specific word, or one with a far-removed antecedent

When you notice this signpost, ask:

Do I know this word from someplace else? Does this seem like technical talk for experts on this topic? Can I find clues in the text to help me understand the word?

Social & Emotional Learning

The Most Important Subject Is You!

by **Carol Jago**

You have essays to turn in. You have quizzes to take. You have group projects to complete. Your success in those areas depends on more than your understanding of the academic skills they cover. It also depends on how well you understand yourself, and how well you're able to extend that understanding to others. This might seem obvious, but there's an actual term for that type of learning—it's called **Social and Emotional Learning.**

Why It Matters

But doing well in school is not the only benefit to understanding yourself and others. When it comes to Social and Emotional Learning, the answer to the question, "When will I actually use this in my life?" is clear: every single day, forever. Whether you are with your family, your community, your friends, at a workplace, or by yourself on a deserted island, you will have a better chance of achieving satisfaction and making positive contributions if you're able to do things like the following:

- ✓ identify your emotions
- ✓ make smart choices
- ✓ set reasonable goals
- ✓ recognize your strengths
- ✓ have empathy
- ✓ manage your reactions
- ✓ evaluate problems and solutions
- ✓ show respect for others

Where Literature Comes In

English Language Arts classes can provide some of the best opportunities to develop these skills. That's because reading literature allows you to imagine yourself in different worlds and to understand what it's like to be in a wide range of situations. You can think through your own feelings and values as you read about various characters, conflicts, historical figures, and ideas, and you can become more aware of why others might act and feel as they do.

Throughout this book, you will find opportunities for Social and Emotional Learning in the Choices section of many lessons. But you don't need to wait for a special activity to practice and learn. Reading widely and discussing thoughtfully is a natural way to gain empathy and self-knowledge. The chart below shows the five main areas of Social and Emotional Learning and tells how reading can help you strengthen them.

Areas of Social and Emotional Learning	How Reading Can Help
If you have **self-awareness,** you're conscious of your own emotions, thoughts, and values, and you understand how they affect your behavior.	Understanding why characters act the way they do can increase your understanding of your own responses and motivations.
If you're good at **self-management,** you are able to control your emotions, thoughts, and behaviors in different situations.	Paying attention to why characters explode in tumultuous ways or how they keep calm under pressure can help you recognize what to do and not to do when faced with stressful situations in your own life.
If you have **social awareness,** you can empathize with others, including people who are different from you.	Reading about people with different life experiences can help you understand the perspectives of others.
If you have well-developed **relationship skills,** you can get along with different kinds of people and function well in groups.	Reflecting on the conflicts between characters can help you gain insight into what causes the conflicts in your life and how to reach mutual satisfaction.
If you are good at **responsible decision-making,** you make good choices that keep you and others safe and keep you moving toward your goals.	Evaluating the choices characters make and thinking about what you would do in their place can help you understand the consequences of your decisions.

Having the Hard Conversations

The more widely and deeply you read, the more you'll strengthen your social and emotional skills, and the more likely you are to encounter ideas that are different from your own. Some texts might bring up strong reactions from you, and you'll need to take a step back to understand how you're feeling. Or, your classmates might have responses that are dramatically different from yours, and you'll need to take a breath and decide how to engage with them. Remember: it's okay to disagree with a text or with a peer. In fact, discussing a difference of opinion can be one of the most powerful ways to learn.

Tips for Talking About Controversial Issues

> The reason I think so is because I've noticed that I . . .

> So what I hear you saying is . . .
> Did I get that right?

Communicate clearly.
Speak honestly and carefully, rather than for dramatic effect. Notice if the person listening seems confused and give them room to ask questions.

Listen actively.
Try your best to understand what the other person is saying, and why they might think or feel that way. If you don't understand, ask questions or rephrase what you thought you heard and ask them if you're getting it right.

> When you use that word I have a negative reaction because it sounds like you are saying you think that person isn't smart.

> I'm sorry. That's not what I meant.

Take a stand against name-calling, belittling, stereotyping, and bias.
Always try exploring ideas further rather than making personal attacks. If someone feels hurt by something you said, listen to them with an open mind. Perhaps you expressed bias without realizing it. Apologize sincerely if that happens. And if you are hurt by a comment or hear something that could be interpreted as hurtful, calmly let the person who said it know why you feel that way.

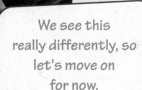

> I need to take a break from this conversation now.

Pay attention to your feelings.
Recognize the topics or situations that make it hard for you to stay calm. Try to separate your strong feelings from what the person is saying. If you need to, excuse yourself from the conversation and find a place where you can help yourself relax.

> We see this really differently, so let's move on for now.

Consider the relationship.
It's likely that the people you're in class with are people you will be seeing regularly for years. You don't have to be friends with them or agree with their point of view, but you do have to get an education alongside each other. Speaking respectfully even if you're on opposite sides of an issue will make it easier to work together if you ever have to collaborate. Try to assume the best about them rather than the worst. Acknowledge that our experiences affect our points of view.

Agree to disagree.
Even after listening carefully and being listened to, you still might not agree. That's okay. You can acknowledge your differences, remain respectful, and exit the conversation.

> I don't agree with you, but I understand why it looks that way from your perspective.

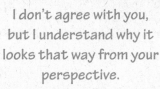

Learning, growing, and working with others isn't always easy. If you read widely and deeply and try your best to speak honestly, you're likely to gain the understanding and compassion that can help you manage the stresses, challenges, and opportunities that life brings your way.

"I will not Reason and Compare; my business is to Create."

—William Blake

The Flowering of Romanticism

Emotion and Experimentation

? As you read the texts in this unit, think about how they explore these **Essential Questions.**

What can nature offer us?
As the Industrial Revolution began to transform daily life in Britain, Romantic poets sought refuge in rural traditions and the natural world.

How do you define beauty?
Romantic writers developed new ideas about beauty and the relationship between beauty and art.

How can science go wrong?
Scientific progress accelerated rapidly in the 19th century. With advances, however, came new responsibilities and new dilemmas, many of which still concern society today.

What stirs your imagination?
The Romantics valued imagination over reason, seeing it not only as fuel for creativity, but also as a force capable of transforming the world.

ANALYZE THE IMAGE
How would you describe the mood of this image? Which details influence your emotional response?

Explore unit themes and build background.

Stream to Start Video

Spark Your Learning

Here are some opportunities to think about issues related to **Unit 4: Emotion and Experimentation.**

As you read, you can use the **Response Log** (page R4) to track your thinking about the Essential Questions.

?

Make the Connection

Romanticism was a literary and artistic movement that flourished in Britain from the late 18th century to the 1830s. Think about the quotation on page 514 from William Blake, an early Romantic poet.

- How would you paraphrase this statement?

- What does the statement suggest about the values of Romantic writers?

Discuss your ideas with a partner.

Think About the Essential Questions

Review the Essential Questions on page 515. Which question is most intriguing to you? Perhaps it relates to something you have read or reminds you of a personal experience. Write down your thoughts.

✓

Prove It!
Use one of the Academic Vocabulary words in a sentence about a personal experience.

Build Academic Vocabulary

You can use these Academic Vocabulary words to write and talk about the topics and themes in the unit. Which of these words do you already feel comfortable using when speaking or writing?

	I can use it!	I understand it.	I'll look it up.
appreciate			
insight			
intensity			
invoke			
radical			

Preview the Texts

Review the images, titles, and descriptions of the texts in the unit. Mark the title of the text that interests you most.

Lines Composed a Few Miles Above Tintern Abbey

Composed upon Westminster Bridge, September 3, 1802

I Wandered Lonely As a Cloud

Poems by **William Wordsworth**

Wordsworth explores emotions inspired by beauty in nature and in human creations.

Ode on a Grecian Urn

Poem by **John Keats**

The speaker of this poem reflects on what an ancient ceramic can teach us about the relationship between time and beauty.

from **Frankenstein**

Novel by **Mary Shelley**

A scientist reacts with horror to a living creature he created.

Frankenstein: Giving Voice to the Monster

Essay by **Langdon Winner**

The author discusses Mary Shelley's groundbreaking achievement and explores how it connects to issues in society today.

Ode to the West Wind

Poem by **Percy Bysshe Shelley**

The speaker of this ode praises the creative and destructive power of wind.

Ode to My Mother's Hair

Poem by **Joseph O. Legaspi**

In this poem, the speaker pays homage to his mother's hair and to the woman herself.

from **Songs of Innocence**

   The Lamb
   The Chimney Sweeper

from **Songs of Experience**

   The Tyger
   The Chimney Sweeper

Poems by **William Blake**

Blake explores how our understanding of the world is shaped by our perspective.

Emotion and Experimentation

"**Liberty, equality, brotherhood**"—the ideals that spurred the French Revolution in 1789 found an answering echo in the hearts of many of England's finest Romantic poets and novelists who saw it as a turning point in the history of humankind. The literary movement known as Romanticism was also a reaction to the excesses of the Industrial Revolution and the widespread poverty and oppression of workers that it caused.

The Age of Revolution

During the American Revolution and the French Revolution, George III ruled Britain. He was not a very capable king, and many blamed the loss of the American colonies on his inflexible attitude toward the colonists. In 1788, the year before the French Revolution began, George III suffered a major attack of mental illness; in 1811 he was declared permanently insane. His son George ruled as prince regent until the king's death in 1820.

Initially, many British citizens felt sympathy for the French Revolution. The early Romantic writers saw it as a move toward an ideal civilized society in which the oppressed would find

The storming of the Bastille in Paris on July 14, 1789, ignited the French Revolution.

1793
The French Revolution gives way to the Reign of Terror; war begins between Britain and France.

1780

1789
The French Revolution begins.

1794
William Blake publishes *Songs of Innocence and of Experience.*

© Houghton Mifflin Harcourt Publishing Company • Image Credits: ©Niday Picture Library/Alamy

relief. When the revolution turned radical and violent, however, British sympathy dissipated. During the Reign of Terror, radical revolutionaries massacred thousands of French aristocrats and middle-class citizens.

The British upper and middle classes were all too aware that England's lower classes faced many of the same social ills as the French lower classes. The British ruling classes were afraid that any efforts at reform could lead to anarchy as it had in France. As a result, British leaders grew more conservative, suppressing reform and outlawing writing or speech that was critical of the government.

Napoleon Takes Control

In 1793 Britain entered into a war with France that would last for more than 25 years. It was during this conflict that General Napoleon Bonaparte took control of France's government, made himself emperor, and then conquered much of continental Europe. Britain was continually threatened with invasion until the British fleet destroyed the French navy in 1805 at the Battle of Trafalgar. After that, Britain was able to loosen Napoleon's hold on Europe, and Napoleon was finally defeated at Waterloo in 1815.

EXTEND

Think of a question you have about a topic, event, or person from the historical period. Then, research the answer and add it as an entry to the timeline.

1805
The British fleet defeats the French navy at the Battle of Trafalgar.

1815
Napoleon is defeated at Waterloo.

1820
The Regency ends when George III dies and his son becomes king.

1820

1804
Napoleon crowns himself Emperor of France.

1811
George III is declared insane; his son is named regent.

1818
Mary Shelley anonymously publishes *Frankenstein*.

519

The Downside of Industry

During this period, England was an industrial as well as an agricultural country. The Industrial Revolution and improvements in farming brought increased prosperity to the middle and upper classes, but brought degrading poverty to the families employed in the factories and mills. Living and working conditions were appalling. There were no laws to regulate work safety, hours, wages, or child labor. At the time, Britain operated under the doctrine of *laissez-faire* economics, which means that an economy works best without government intervention.

An economic depression and advances in technology led to the loss of many factory jobs, which meant that fewer workers were needed to run textile mills. During the Luddite Riots, unemployed mill workers smashed the machines they blamed for taking their jobs. Instead of working to solve the root causes of this frightening violence, Parliament passed laws that made the rioters' actions punishable by death. Labor unions were outlawed, and workers had little power in Parliament.

A Revolution in Literature

Romantic writers often sympathized with the oppressed lower classes and wrote about their plight. Lord Byron, a Romantic poet and a member of Parliament, openly expressed his sympathy for the poor to other members of the British government. In fact, he was one of only three members of Parliament to vote against the law punishing the Luddite rioters with death.

Such political efforts, however, yielded few results. Many of the Romantic writers reacted to the harsh realities of industrialization by turning to

George Gordon, Lord Byron
(1788–1824)

© Houghton Mifflin Harcourt Publishing Company • Image Credits: (t) ©North Wind Picture Archives/Alamy; (b) ©The Granger Collection, New York

nature for truth and beauty. They revolted against the order, propriety, and traditionalism of the Age of Reason and rejected the classical tradition that venerated the achievements of ancient Greece and Rome. The Romantics were influenced by the same forces that gave rise to the American and French revolutions and by the agitation for political, social, and economic change taking place in their own country. For the Romantics, emotion became more important than reason. Thus, they preferred styles of writing that allowed self-expression, like lyric poetry, which came to dominate English literature during this time.

COLLABORATIVE DISCUSSION

In a small group, identify the major events in this historical period and discuss how they influenced British society. Was this influence mainly direct or indirect?

Assessment Practice

Choose the best answer to each question.

1. Which event caused many British citizens to lose sympathy for the French Revolution?

   (A) Britain's loss of the American colonies in an earlier revolution

   (B) the takeover of the French government by Napoleon Bonaparte

   (C) the execution of French aristocrats during the Reign of Terror

   (D) the defeat of the French navy by the British fleet

2. Which factor contributed most directly to the Luddite Riots?

   (A) instigation by Romantic writers like Lord Byron

   (B) Britain's doctrine of *laissez-faire* economics

   (C) discontent over the outlawed status of labor unions

   (D) loss of factory jobs due to advances in technology

3. Romantic writers valued —

   (A) traditionalism over revolution

   (B) emotion over reason

   (C) industry over nature

   (D) order over agitation

Test-Taking Strategies

Poems by
William Wordsworth

Lines Composed a Few Miles Above Tintern Abbey

Composed upon Westminster Bridge, September 3, 1802

I Wandered Lonely As a Cloud

Engage Your Brain

Choose one or more of these activities to start connecting with the poems you're about to read.

Under Pressure

In "Lines Composed a Few Miles Above Tintern Abbey," Wordsworth describes how he escapes from the pressures of city life. What do you turn to for help when you feel stressed out?

1. Write a paragraph describing what you turn to, and explain how it helps you unwind.

2. Then, discuss your response with a partner.

Conduct a Class Survey

In these poems, Wordsworth writes about places that have special meaning for him.

1. Along with your classmates, write the name or a brief description of a place you cherish on a sticky note and post it on the classroom wall.

2. As everyone reads the notes, they should look for similarities in the kinds of places people chose.

3. In a small group, talk about what meaning those places might have.

4. Share your group's insights with the class.

Analyze Romantic Poetry

Romanticism was a literary movement that flourished in Britain and other European countries in the 19th century. Unlike the neoclassical poets who preceded them, the Romantics emphasized the importance of the individual's subjective experiences rather than issues that concerned society as a whole. Their philosophy valued emotion, spontaneity, and imagination over reason, analysis, and orderliness.

Romantic poets wrote about personal experiences, often using simple, unadorned language. Many Romantic poems celebrate the beauty and grandeur of the natural world. The Romantics rejected the forces of industrialization that were beginning to transform Europe, and they tended to idealize the distant past. They looked to nature for inspiration and also for insight into their creative processes.

As you read the poems by Wordsworth, note details that show characteristics of Romantic poetry, such as the following example from "Lines Composed a Few Miles Above Tintern Abbey."

Focus on Genre
↳ **Lyric Poetry**

- a poetic form often used by the Romantics
- usually written in the first person
- expresses the feelings and thoughts of the speaker
- uses sound devices such as rhythm and repetition to create a musical quality
- often deals with intense emotions surrounding events like death, love, or loss

Detail	Characteristic
I have owed to them, In hours of weariness, sensations sweet, Felt in the blood, and felt along the heart;	describes a personal, subjective experience

Analyze Imagery

Imagery is language that creates vivid sensory experiences for the reader. Visual imagery, which appeals to the sense of sight, is the most common form, but writers also use words and phrases to appeal to the senses of hearing, touch, smell, and taste to deepen the reader's understanding of and connection to their works. For example, in "Tintern Abbey," Wordsworth refers to the "soft inland murmur" of the Wye River, an auditory image that describes the sound of the moving water. This beautiful, engaging language also suggests the river's calming effect. Below are more examples of sensory language in the poem.

Therefore let the moon Shine on thee in thy solitary walk;	appeals to the sense of sight
And let the misty mountain winds be free To blow against thee:	appeals to the sense of touch

Look for sensory language as you read Wordsworth's poems, and create mental images of the sights and sounds of the landscapes and experiences the poet describes. Also, notice how Wordsworth develops the subject, tone, and theme of each poem through imagery.

Annotation in Action

Here is an example of notes a student made about a poem by Wordsworth. As you read, mark images that convey the speaker's ideas about nature.

> Five years have passed; five summers, with the length
> Of five long winters! and again I hear
> These waters, rolling from their mountain-springs
> With a soft inland murmur. Once again
> Do I behold these steep and lofty cliffs,

These images bring to mind the impressive wilderness near Tintern Abbey.

William Wordsworth (1770–1850)

William Wordsworth revolutionized English poetry and helped launch the Romantic movement in England. Rebelling against the lofty style of many poets of the time, he used simple language to celebrate subjects drawn mostly from nature and rural life.

As a child, Wordsworth happily explored the countryside near his home. When he was seven, his mother died, and he was sent to boarding school. Fortunately, he was able to continue spending time outdoors there, developing his deep love for the natural world and writing poetry.

Love in a Time of War

On a trip to France in 1790, Wordsworth was excited to witness the early stages of the French Revolution. After graduating from Cambridge University, he returned to France and fell in love with a French woman. He traveled home in 1792 to look for work, and conflict between England and France prevented him from reuniting with his lover and their newborn child.

As his political optimism faded, Wordsworth committed himself to writing poetry. In 1795 he set up a home with his sister, Dorothy. They befriended the poet Samuel Taylor Coleridge, who collaborated with Wordsworth on a book of poetry called *Lyrical Ballads*. Published in 1798, the book ushered in the English Romantic movement.

Rebel Poet to Poet Laureate

Wordsworth often wrote about specific natural settings. In "Lines Composed a Few Miles Above Tintern Abbey," he reflects on the beauty of the Wye River valley in Wales, an area he hiked through extensively. Near this valley are the ruins of Tintern Abbey, a medieval monastery that captivated public imagination with its picturesque decay.

In 1802 Wordsworth married his childhood friend Mary Hutchinson. Over the next two decades, he struggled to find readers for his work. But he finally began to gain widespread recognition, and in 1843 he was named England's poet laureate.

> **"Fill your paper with the breathings of your heart."**
>
> —William Wordsworth

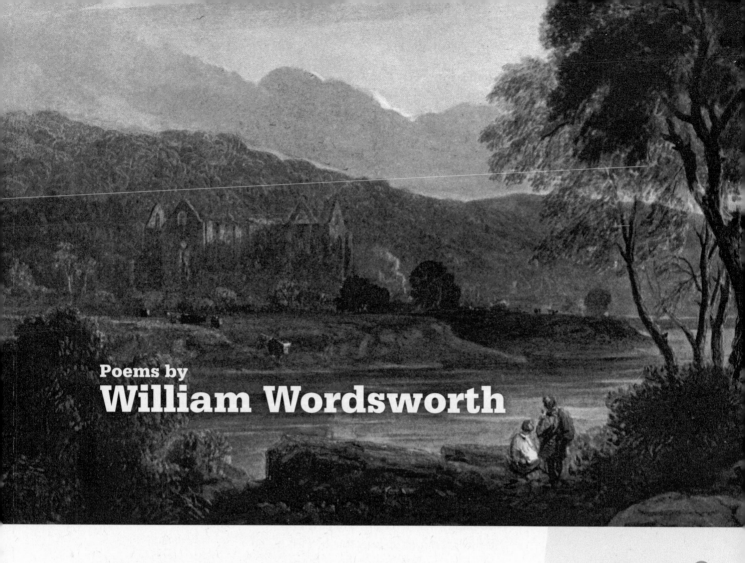

Poems by
William Wordsworth

In these poems, pay attention to Wordsworth's ideas about nature and about city life.

© Houghton Mifflin Harcourt Publishing Company • Image Credits: ©Print Collector/Getty Images

 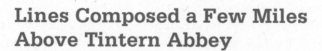
Lines Composed a Few Miles Above Tintern Abbey

Five years have passed; five summers, with the length
Of five long winters! and again I hear
These waters, rolling from their mountain-springs
With a soft inland murmur. Once again
5 Do I behold these steep and lofty cliffs,
That on a wild secluded scene impress
Thoughts of more deep seclusion; and connect
The landscape with the quiet of the sky.
The day is come when I again repose
10 Here, under this dark sycamore, and view
These plots of cottage ground, these orchard tufts,
Which at this season, with their unripe fruits,
Are clad in one green hue, and lose themselves

9 **repose:** lie at rest.

14 **copses** (kŏp´sĭz): thickets of small trees.

16 **pastoral** (păs´tər-əl): rural and serene.

20 **vagrant:** wandering.

'Mid groves and copses. Once again I see
15 These hedgerows, hardly hedgerows, little lines
Of sportive wood run wild; these pastoral farms,
Green to the very door; and wreaths of smoke
Sent up, in silence, from among the trees!
With some uncertain notice, as might seem
20 Of vagrant dwellers in the houseless woods,
Or of some Hermit's cave, where by his fire
The Hermit sits alone.

                    These beauteous forms,
Through a long absence, have not been to me
As is a landscape to a blind man's eye;
25 But oft, in lonely rooms, and 'mid the din
Of towns and cities, I have owed to them,
In hours of weariness, sensations sweet,
Felt in the blood, and felt along the heart;
And passing even into my purer mind,
30 With tranquil restoration—feelings too
Of unremembered pleasure; such, perhaps,
As have no slight or trivial influence
On that best portion of a good man's life,
His little, nameless, unremembered, acts
35 Of kindness and of love. Nor less, I trust,
To them I may have owed another gift,
Of aspect more sublime; that blessed mood,
In which the burthen of the mystery,
In which the heavy and the weary weight
40 Of all this unintelligible world,
Is lightened—that serene and blessed mood,
In which the affections gently lead us on—
Until, the breath of this corporeal frame
And even the motion of our human blood
45 Almost suspended, we are laid asleep
In body, and become a living soul;
While with an eye made quiet by the power
Of harmony, and the deep power of joy,
We see into the life of things.

                            If this
50 Be but a vain belief, yet, oh! how oft—
In darkness and amid the many shapes
Of joyless daylight; when the fretful stir
Unprofitable, and the fever of the world,
Have hung upon the beatings of my heart—
55 How oft, in spirit, have I turned to thee,

ANALYZE ROMANTIC POETRY

Annotate: Mark words and phrases in lines 25–49 that describe the speaker's feelings about the landscape.

Analyze: Why are these feelings important for the speaker?

38 **burthen:** burden.

43 **corporeal** (kôr-pôr´ē-əl): bodily.

Don't forget to
Notice & Note as you
read the text.

O sylvan Wye! thou wanderer through the woods,
How often has my spirit turned to thee!

And now, with gleams of half-extinguished thought
With many recognitions dim and faint,
60   And somewhat of a sad perplexity,
The picture of the mind revives again;
While here I stand, not only with the sense
Of present pleasure, but with pleasing thoughts
That in this moment there is life and food
65   For future years. And so I dare to hope,
Though changed, no doubt, from what I was when first
I came among these hills; when like a roe
I bounded o'er the mountains, by the sides
Of the deep rivers, and the lonely streams,
70   Wherever nature led—more like a man
Flying from something that he dreads than one
Who sought the thing he loved. For nature then
(The coarser pleasures of my boyish days,
And their glad animal movements all gone by)
75   To me was all in all.—I cannot paint
What then I was. The sounding cataract
Haunted me like a passion; the tall rock,
The mountain, and the deep and gloomy wood,
Their colors and their forms, were then to me
80   An appetite; a feeling and a love,
That had no need of a remoter charm,
By thought supplied, nor any interest
Unborrowed from the eye.—That time is past,
And all its aching joys are now no more,
85   And all its dizzy raptures. Not for this
Faint I, nor mourn nor murmur; other gifts
Have followed; for such loss, I would believe,
Abundant recompense. For I have learned
To look on nature, not as in the hour
90   Of thoughtless youth; but hearing oftentimes
The still, sad music of humanity,
Nor harsh nor grating, though of ample power
To chasten and subdue. And I have felt
A presence that disturbs me with the joy
95   Of elevated thoughts; a sense sublime
Of something far more deeply interfused,
Whose dwelling is the light of setting suns,
And the round ocean and the living air,
And the blue sky, and in the mind of man:
100 A motion and a spirit, that impels

56 **sylvan:** located in a wood or forest;
Wye: a river near Tintern Abbey.

67 **roe:** deer.

76 **cataract** (kăt´ə-răkt): waterfall.

ANALYZE IMAGERY

Annotate: Mark the auditory and
visual imagery in lines 76–78.

Analyze: How does this imagery
affect the reader's understanding
of the speaker's experience?

86 **Faint I:** I lose heart.

88 **recompense** (rĕk´əm-pĕns):
compensation.

93 **chasten** (chā´sən): scold; make
modest.

ANALYZE IMAGERY

Annotate: Mark images of nature
in lines 93–102.

Analyze: How do these images
support the speaker's idea about a
force that affects all things?

All thinking things, all objects of all thought,
And rolls through all things. Therefore am I still
A lover of the meadows and the woods,
And mountains; and of all that we behold
105 From this green earth; of all the mighty world
Of eye, and ear—both what they half create,
And what perceive; well pleased to recognize
In nature and the language of the sense
The anchor of my purest thoughts, the nurse,
110 The guide, the guardian of my heart, and soul
Of all my moral being.

                    Nor perchance,
If I were not thus taught, should I the more
Suffer my genial spirits to decay:
For thou art with me here upon the banks
115 Of this fair river; thou my dearest Friend,
My dear, dear Friend; and in thy voice I catch

111 **perchance:** by chance; perhaps.

113 **genial** (jēn´yəl): relating to genius; creative.

115 **thou my dearest Friend:** Wordsworth´s sister, Dorothy.

The language of my former heart, and read
My former pleasures in the shooting lights
Of thy wild eyes. Oh! yet a little while
120 May I behold in thee what I was once,
My dear, dear Sister! and this prayer I make,
Knowing that Nature never did betray
The heart that loved her; 'tis her privilege,
Through all the years of this our life, to lead
125 From joy to joy: for she can so inform
The mind that is within us, so impress
With quietness and beauty, and so feed
With lofty thoughts, that neither evil tongues,
Rash judgments, nor the sneers of selfish men,
130 Nor greetings where no kindness is, nor all
The dreary intercourse of daily life,
Shall e'er prevail against us, or disturb
Our cheerful faith, that all which we behold
Is full of blessings. Therefore let the moon

ANALYZE ROMANTIC POETRY

Annotate: Mark the verbs used in lines 123–134 to describe nature's actions.

Interpret: What Romantic idea does Wordsworth express in this passage?

135 Shine on thee in thy solitary walk;
And let the misty mountain winds be free
To blow against thee: and, in after years,
When these wild ecstasies shall be matured
Into a sober pleasure; when thy mind
140 Shall be a mansion for all lovely forms,
Thy memory be as a dwelling place
For all sweet sounds and harmonies; oh! then,
If solitude, or fear, or pain, or grief
Should be thy portion, with what healing thoughts
145 Of tender joy wilt thou remember me,
And these my exhortations! Nor, perchance—
If I should be where I no more can hear
Thy voice, nor catch from thy wild eyes these gleams

146 **exhortations:** words of
encouraging advice.

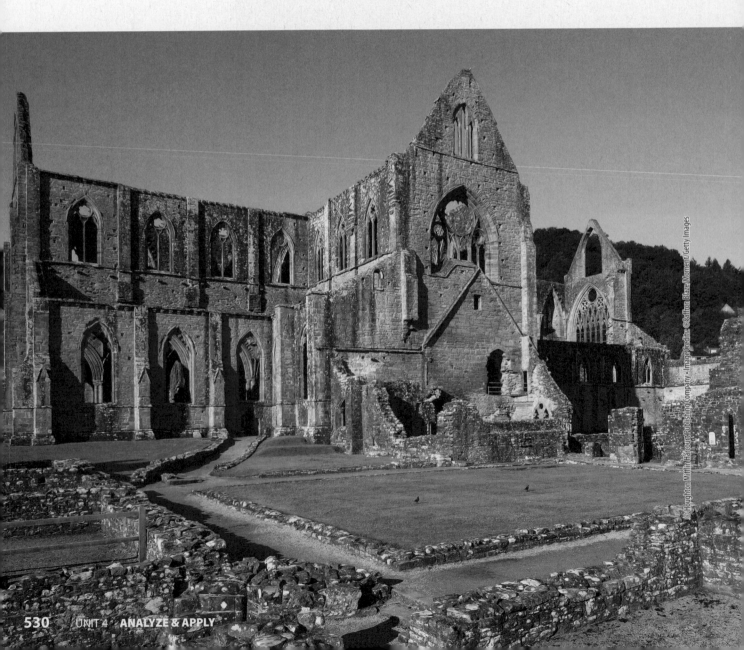

Of past existence—wilt thou then forget
150 That on the banks of this delightful stream
We stood together; and that I, so long
A worshiper of Nature, hither came
Unwearied in that service; rather say
With warmer love—oh! with far deeper zeal
155 Of holier love. Nor wilt thou then forget,
That after many wanderings, many years
Of absence, these steep woods and lofty cliffs,
And this green pastoral landscape, were to me
More dear, both for themselves and for thy sake!

149 **past existence:** the speaker's own past experience five years before (see lines 116–119).

Assessment Practice

Answer these questions about "Lines Composed a Few Miles Above Tintern Abbey" before moving on to the next selection.

1. How did the speaker's memories of the valley affect him during the past five years?

   (A) They tormented him.

   (B) They restored his spirit.

   (C) They made him resent city life.

   (D) They caused him to avoid nature.

2. What has the speaker lost since he last visited the valley?

   (A) his ability to run up the mountains

   (B) his memory of where the ruined abbey stood

   (C) his career in the city

   (D) his passionate reaction to nature

3. What does the speaker observe in his sister?

   (A) She responds to nature the same way he used to.

   (B) She fears hurting herself in the valley.

   (C) She shares his memories of the valley.

   (D) She behaves recklessly on their hike.

Test-Taking Strategies

Composed upon Westminster Bridge, September 3, 1802

ANALYZE ROMANTIC POETRY

Annotate: Mark language in lines 9–14 that conveys the emotions of the speaker.

Analyze: What emotions does this language convey?

9 **steep:** soak; saturate.

12 **The river:** Westminster Bridge spans the Thames (tĕmz)—the principal river in London.

13 **houses:** possibly a pun on the Houses of Parliament, near Westminster Bridge.

Earth has not anything to show more fair:
Dull would he be of soul who could pass by
A sight so touching in its majesty;
This City now doth, like a garment, wear
5 The beauty of the morning; silent, bare,
Ships, towers, domes, theaters, and temples lie
Open unto the fields, and to the sky;
All bright and glittering in the smokeless air.
Never did sun more beautifully steep
10 In his first splendor, valley, rock, or hill;
Ne'er saw I, never felt, a calm so deep!
The river glideth at his own sweet will:
Dear God! the very houses seem asleep;
And all that mighty heart is lying still!

Assessment Practice

Answer these questions about "Composed upon Westminster Bridge, September 3, 1802" before moving on to the next selection.

1. What time of day does "Composed upon Westminster Bridge, September 3, 1802" describe?

   (A) dawn

   (B) dusk

   (C) midnight

   (D) midday

2. Which of the following best describes the speaker's meaning in lines 2 and 3?

   (A) He prefers being in the city to being in nature.

   (B) He believes people should stop to appreciate the world around them.

   (C) He thinks his soul is better than the souls of other people.

   (D) He feels saddened by the majestic view.

3. How does the scene he describes in the poem make the speaker feel?

   (A) excited

   (B) melancholy

   (C) peaceful

   (D) disappointed

ⓔEd
Test-Taking Strategies

I Wandered Lonely As a Cloud

2 **vales:** valleys.

ANALYZE IMAGERY

Annotate: Mark the imagery that describes nature in lines 1–12.

Analyze: How do these images help the reader understand the speaker's experience?

I wandered lonely as a cloud
That floats on high o'er vales and hills,
When all at once I saw a crowd,
A host, of golden daffodils;
5 Beside the lake, beneath the trees,
Fluttering and dancing in the breeze.

Continuous as the stars that shine
And twinkle on the milky way,
They stretched in never-ending line
10 Along the margin of a bay:
Ten thousand saw I at a glance,
Tossing their heads in sprightly dance.

The waves beside them danced; but they
Outdid the sparkling waves in glee;
15 A poet could not but be gay,
In such a jocund company;
I gazed—and gazed—but little thought
What wealth the show to me had brought:

16 **jocund** (jŏk´ənd): merry.

For oft, when on my couch I lie
20 In vacant or in pensive mood,
They flash upon that inward eye
Which is the bliss of solitude;
And then my heart with pleasure fills,
And dances with the daffodils.

?

ESSENTIAL QUESTION:
What can nature offer us?

Review your notes and
add your thoughts to your
Response Log.

COLLABORATIVE DISCUSSION

Meet with a partner and discuss the impression these poems made
on you. How does Wordsworth's description of an urban landscape in
"Composed upon Westminster Bridge, September 3, 1802" compare
with his descriptions of rural landscapes in the other two poems?

Assessment Practice

Answer these questions about "I Wandered Lonely As a Cloud" before
moving on to the **Analyze the Texts** section on the following page.

1. What sight captures the speaker's attention in "I Wandered Lonely As a Cloud"?

(A) clouds

(B) daffodils

(C) dancers

(D) waves

2. The tone of the poem is best described as —

(A) lonely

(B) joyful

(C) solemn

(D) humorous

3. What does Wordsworth mean in line 21 when he says that the daffodils "flash upon
that inward eye"?

(A) They remind him that he is alone.

(B) They keep him awake at night.

(C) They make him feel pensive.

(D) They appear in his imagination.

Test-Taking Strategies

Analyze the Texts

Support your responses with evidence from the texts.

NOTICE & NOTE

Review what you **noticed and noted** as you read the text. Your annotations can help you answer these questions.

(1) **ANALYZE** What details in lines 1–22 of "Lines Composed a Few Miles Above Tintern Abbey" suggest that Wordsworth preferred to celebrate the individual in his work rather than society?

(2) **DRAW CONCLUSIONS** In "Tintern Abbey," how has the speaker's relationship with nature changed over time?

(3) **ANALYZE** How does Wordsworth use imagery in "Composed upon Westminster Bridge, September 3, 1802" to support the tone and theme of the poem?

(4) **INTERPRET** Reread lines 17–24 of "I Wandered Lonely As a Cloud." What is the "wealth" that the speaker doesn't initially appreciate when he sees the daffodils?

(5) **COMPARE** Review your notes on "Tintern Abbey" and "I Wandered Lonely As a Cloud." Compare how the speakers of these poems respond to and rely on nature.

> **Consider the following:**
> - imagery that appeals to the reader's senses
> - assumptions about nature that the speakers express
> - the setting described in each poem

(6) **SYNTHESIZE** Which characteristics of Romanticism do all three of these poems share?

Choices

Here are some other ways to demonstrate your understanding of the ideas in this lesson.

Writing
↳ **Write a Literary Analysis**

Write an essay analyzing "Lines Composed a Few Miles Above Tintern Abbey." First, review your notes and annotations in the text for support. Then, focus on one or more of the following:

- Identify a theme of the poem and discuss how it is conveyed.
- Describe the poem's setting, and explain the effect it has on the speaker.
- Analyze elements of Wordsworth's style in the poem.

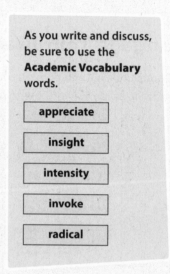

As you write and discuss, be sure to use the **Academic Vocabulary** words.

> appreciate

> insight

> intensity

> invoke

> radical

Research
↳ **Create a Presentation**

With a small group, research the British locations described in Wordsworth's poems: the Wye River valley in Wales (site of the ruined Tintern Abbey), Westminster Bridge in London, or the Lake District (where "I Wandered Lonely As a Cloud" is set).

1. Read some background information about the history of these places.
2. Search for images so you can see what the places look like.
3. Do a map search so you can see where in Britain they are located.

Present your research by taking classmates on a digital tour that brings these places to life and encourages them to embark on a literary pilgrimage to the land of Wordsworth.

Social & Emotional Learning
↳ **Paired Discussion**

With a partner, discuss ideas about youth in "Tintern Abbey." Address the following questions:

- Do you think the speaker conveys a realistic view of how young people think and feel?
- Why is it important for the speaker to share his views about nature with his younger sister?

Then, share one or two experiences in your past that have taken on new meaning over time. Talk about why your impression of them has changed.

Ode on a Grecian Urn

Poem by **John Keats**

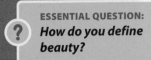

ESSENTIAL QUESTION:
How do you define beauty?

Engage Your Brain

Choose one or both of these activities to connect with the poem you're about to read.

My Favorite Things

Write a description of your favorite artwork or a prized possession. Be sure to include:

- a physical description of this object
- the feelings you associate with this object
- why you find it so appealing
- at least four sensory details

"Beauty Is . . ."

Write or sketch some ideas that complete the sentence "Beauty is . . ."

Then, form a group and discuss the different ideas about beauty that emerged. You may even decide to create a scrapbook or online board of beautiful things.

you are beautiful

Analyze Stanza Structure

A **stanza** is a group of lines that form a unit in a poem. In traditional poetic forms, stanzas often contain the same number of lines and have the same rhyme scheme and meter. Stanzas often function like paragraphs in prose, each presenting a discrete idea.

Although odes can vary in structure, the five stanzas of "Ode on a Grecian Urn" have a regular structure of ten lines of **iambic pentameter,** a metrical pattern of five feet, or units. Each iambic foot consists of two syllables, the first unstressed and the second stressed.

> Thou still unravish'd bride of quietness,
>
> Thou foster-child of silence and slow time,

Keats sometimes varies the meter to emphasize certain words and to keep the poem from sounding monotonous. You can gain insight into the meaning of the poem by reading it aloud and noticing which words are stressed. As you read, also notice the main idea expressed in each stanza.

Focus on Genre
↳ **Ode**

- is a lyric poem that develops a single theme
- has a serious tone
- appeals to both the imagination and the intellect
- may commemorate an event or praise people or nature's beauty

Analyze Rhyme Scheme

The **rhyme scheme** of a poem is the pattern of **end rhyme** that helps establish the structure and unity of a stanza and adds to the poem's musicality. A rhyme scheme is described using letters, such as *abab* or *aabb*, where lines that rhyme are given the same letter. Certain poetic forms, such as the various types of sonnets, follow a set rhyme scheme.

Keats's "Ode on a Grecian Urn" has a complex rhyme scheme. The first four lines of each stanza rhyme *abab*. The next six lines follow one of these patterns: *cdedce, cdeced,* or *cdecde*. Because of these variations, the rhyming becomes subtler and more unexpected as you move farther along in a stanza.

As you read, note the rhyme scheme for each stanza in the chart. Record your thoughts about how it appeals to your sense of hearing or impacts your understanding of Keats's ideas.

Stanza	Rhyme Scheme	Notes
1	ababcdedce	*adds a pleasing, musical quality*
2		
3		
4		
5		

Analyze Apostrophe

Apostrophe is a figure of speech in which the speaker addresses an object, abstract concept, or absent or imaginary person as if present and able to understand. Poets often use apostrophe to express strong emotions. This device was especially popular among the Romantic poets. In "Ode on a Grecian Urn," Keats uses apostrophe to address both the urn itself and the figures portrayed on it.

> O Attic shape! Fair attitude! with brede
>   Of marble men and maidens overwrought,

Here the speaker addresses the urn as one might speak to an admired person, heightening the reader's sense of the speaker's emotional response to seeing the urn. As you read the poem, pay attention to the shifting focus of the apostrophe.

Annotation in Action

Here are one student's notes about the poet's use of apostrophe. As you read, notice how Keats develops this figure of speech.

> Thou still unravish'd bride of quietness,
>   Thou foster-child of silence and slow time,
> Sylvan historian, who canst thus express
>   A flowery tale more sweetly than our rhyme:
> What leaf-fring'd legend haunts about thy shape
>   Of deities or mortals, or of both,
>   In Tempe or the dales of Arcady?

The speaker addresses the urn as if it can understand him.

Background

John Keats (1795–1821) only lived to age 25, yet he produced some of the most famous poems in the English language. Keats's life was marred by illness and tragedy. His father died in a riding accident when he was young. Later, both his mother and brother died of tuberculosis, and Keats himself became ill with the disease at 22. His poor health prevented him from marrying his sweetheart, Fanny Brawne. It was during his illness, however, that he produced some of his greatest work. "Ode on a Grecian Urn" was probably inspired by ancient Greek urns that Keats saw at the British Museum. Such urns were often painted with mythological scenes, as described in this poem.

Ode on a Grecian Urn

Poem by **John Keats**

Notice the ideas that the speaker associates with images on the urn.

NOTICE & NOTE
As you read, use the side margins to make notes about the text.

> Thou still unravish'd bride of quietness,
>   Thou foster-child of silence and slow time,
> Sylvan historian, who canst thus express
>   A flowery tale more sweetly than our rhyme:
> 5 What leaf-fring'd legend haunts about thy shape
>   Of deities or mortals, or of both,
>   In Tempe or the dales of Arcady?
>   What men or gods are these? What maidens loth?
> What mad pursuit? What struggle to escape?
> 10   What pipes and timbrels? What wild ecstasy?
>
> Heard melodies are sweet, but those unheard
>   Are sweeter; therefore, ye soft pipes, play on;
> Not to the sensual ear, but, more endear'd,
>   Pipe to the spirit ditties of no tone:
> 15 Fair youth, beneath the trees, thou canst not leave
>   Thy song, nor ever can those trees be bare;

3 Sylvan: pertaining to trees or woods.

5 haunts about: surrounds.

7 Tempe (tĕm´pē) **. . . Arcady** (är´kə-dē): two places in Greece that became traditional literary settings for an idealized rustic life. Tempe is a beautiful valley; Arcady (Arcadia) is a mountainous region.

8 loth: loath; unwilling; reluctant.

10 timbrels: tambourines.

© Houghton Mifflin Harcourt Publishing Company • Image Credits: ©Hulton Archive/Getty Images

Annotate: Mark the end rhymes in lines 11–20.

Analyze: What is the rhyme scheme in this stanza? Add it to your chart.

29 cloy'd: having had too much of something; oversatisfied.

Annotate: In lines 32–40, mark the two images that the author addresses.

Interpret: What emotions does the author express about each of these images?

41 Attic: pure and classical; in the style of Attica, the part of Greece where Athens is located; **brede** (brēd): interwoven design.

45 Pastoral (păs´tər-əl): an artistic work that portrays rural life in an idealized way.

Annotate: In lines 41–45, mark the syllables that are stressed.

Identify: Where in these lines does Keats vary the metrical pattern to emphasize certain words?

Bold Lover never, never canst thou kiss,
Though winning near the goal—yet, do not grieve;
   She cannot fade, though thou hast not thy bliss,
    For ever wilt thou love, and she be fair!

20

Ah, happy, happy boughs! that cannot shed
   Your leaves, nor ever bid the Spring adieu;
And, happy melodist, uwearied,
   For ever piping songs for ever new;
More happy love! more happy, happy love!
   For ever warm and still to be enjoy'd
    For ever panting, and for ever young;
All breathing human passion far above,
   That leaves a heart high-sorrowful and cloy'd,
    A burning forehead, and a parching tongue.

25

30

Who are these coming to the sacrifice?
   To what green altar, O mysterious priest,
Lead'st thou that heifer lowing at the skies,
   And all her silken flanks with garlands drest?
What little town by river or sea shore,
   Or mountain-built with peaceful citadel,
    Is emptied of this folk, this pious morn?
And, little town, thy streets for evermore
   Will silent be; and not a soul to tell
    Why thou art desolate, can e'er return.

35

40

O Attic shape! Fair attitude! with brede
   Of marble men and maidens overwrought,
With forest branches and the trodden weed;
   Thou, silent form, dost tease us out of thought
As doth eternity: Cold Pastoral!
   When old age shall this generation waste,
    Thou shalt remain, in midst of other woe
Than ours, a friend to man, to whom thou say'st,
   "Beauty is truth, truth beauty,"—that is all
    Ye know on earth, and all ye need to know.

45

50

© Houghton Mifflin Harcourt Publishing Company • Image Credits: ©Hulton Archive/Getty Images

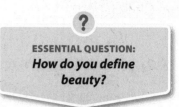

ESSENTIAL QUESTION:
How do you define beauty?

Review your notes and add your thoughts to your Response Log.

COLLABORATIVE DISCUSSION

What details about the urn stand out to you? Discuss your ideas with a partner.

Assessment Practice

Answer these questions before moving on to the **Analyze the Text** section on the following page.

1. In line 3, the phrase "Sylvan historian" refers to —

   (A) a Greek writer

   (B) a man pictured on the urn

   (C) the reader of the poem

   (D) the Grecian urn

2. In line 20, why does the author say, "For ever wilt thou love, and she be fair"?

   (A) True love is everlasting.

   (B) Their images are frozen in time.

   (C) They exist only in each other's memories.

   (D) Their love is immortalized in song.

3. What is the urn's message, delivered in the poem's last two lines?

   (A) Beauty and truth are unable to stand the test of time.

   (B) Beauty and truth are equivalent and eternal.

   (C) Beauty and truth both are important.

   (D) Beauty and truth are often confused.

Test-Taking Strategies

Analyze the Text

Support your responses with evidence from the text.

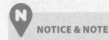

NOTICE & NOTE

Review what you **noticed and noted** as you read the text. Your annotations can help you answer these questions.

1. **ANALYZE** In lines 1–4, Keats addresses the urn as an "unravish'd bride" and a "Sylvan historian." What characteristics of the urn do these phrases in the apostrophe convey? Add your ideas to the chart.

Image	Characteristics of the Urn
"unravish'd bride"	
"Sylvan historian"	

2. **INTERPRET** Reread lines 11–14. How do you interpret the statement "Heard melodies are sweet, but those unheard / Are sweeter"?

3. **IDENTIFY PATTERNS** What words are repeated in stanza 3? What idea does this repetition help develop in the stanza?

4. **INTERPRET** If the urn could "tease us out of thought" (line 44), what state would we be in? In what sense would this state be superior to thought?

5. **DRAW CONCLUSIONS** Why might Keats have chosen to vary the rhyme scheme in the last six lines of the stanzas?

6. **CONNECT** How might Keats's personal circumstances have contributed to the sentiments expressed in the poem?

Choices

Here are some others ways to demonstrate your understanding of the ideas in this lesson.

Writing
↳ Use Apostrophe in a Poem

Is there an inanimate object or abstract idea that you have strong feelings about? Perhaps you love winter or are upset about the closing of a local restaurant. Write a poem addressing that inanimate object or abstract idea to express your feelings.

- Address the object or idea directly. Use apostrophe to express strong emotion.

- Include several stanzas. Decide whether you will use regular patterns of rhyme and meter or if you'll write in free verse, with no regular patterns.

- Use sensory details to create a vivid experience for your reader.

As you write and discuss, be sure to use the **Academic Vocabulary** words.

appreciate
insight
intensity
invoke
radical

Media
↳ Illustrate a Grecian Urn

Keats uses vivid images to describe the Grecian urn. What does the urn look like when you picture it in your mind? Create an illustration of the Grecian urn based on the details in the poem. Review each stanza, and jot down the details that stand out to you before you create your illustration. Share your work in a group, or post it in your classroom.

Speaking & Listening
↳ Panel Discussion

A famous textual difficulty surrounds the famous last two lines of the poems. Based on the original manuscript, some scholars enclose the entire couplet within quotation marks. Have a panel discussion on how this could change the meaning of the lines. Consider the following questions:

- Would the sentiments expressed in the couplet be the urn's or the poet's?

- Which of the two meanings makes better sense when you consider the entire poem?

During the conversation, be sure to use formal language and appropriate tone. Respond respectfully to others' ideas.

from
Frankenstein

Novel by **Mary Shelley**

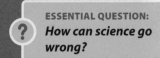

Engage Your Brain

Choose one or more of these activities to start connecting with the text you're about to read.

Love and Fear

At one point in the novel, the creature brought to life by Dr. Frankenstein says, "If I cannot inspire love, I will cause fear." What does this statement suggest about him? Write a paragraph expressing your thoughts about the quotation.

Top Ten Science Fiction

Frankenstein is considered one of the first science fiction novels. With a group of students, create a list of your ten favorite science fiction books, films, or TV series. For each title,

- write a one-sentence description

- write a sentence explaining what you like about it

When you are finished, share your group's list with the class.

Scary Memes

The novel *Frankenstein* is a meme machine—many people who haven't read the book are still familiar with it from film and television adaptations, toys, parodies, advertisements, video games, and even breakfast cereal. With a partner, discuss your familiarity with Frankenstein memes.

- What do you know about the Frankenstein story?

- What does the name *Frankenstein* mean to you?

- Where have you seen the name *Frankenstein* combined with other words to create meaning?

Analyze Science Fiction

Frankenstein is a work of gothic horror that is also considered one of the first science fiction novels. **Science fiction** is a literary genre based on imagined scientific or technological developments, such as time travel or encounters with extraterrestrial life. Mary Shelley said that the idea for the book came to her in a dream after spending several stormy nights discussing ghost stories and medical experiments with a group of friends. She wrote a story about a scientist who creates a man from human remains, which she later expanded into the novel *Frankenstein*.

As you read, use a chart like the one below to note how imaginary advances in science or medicine influence important elements of the novel.

Focus on Genre
↳ **Novel**

- a long fictional prose narrative
- includes the same fictional elements as a short story
- usually has a more complex plot and a wider range of characters than a short story
- may be written in subgenres such as science fiction, historical fiction, or mystery

Elements of Science Fiction in *Frankenstein*	
Plot	Frankenstein creates a living being.
Characters	
Theme	

Analyze Motivation

Motivation is the stated or implied reason behind a fictional character's behavior. Sometimes motivation is directly expressed in a story, but usually readers must infer a character's motivation from dialogue, thoughts, and actions. Characters' motivations often influence the plot and theme of a work, so careful readers look closely for relationships among these elements.

In Shelley's novel, Victor Frankenstein struggles with the moral dilemma of whether to accept or abandon the creature he has created. As you read, analyze the motivations that contribute toward this dilemma. Also, analyze the motivations underlying the creature's behavior toward Frankenstein.

Annotation in Action

Here is an example of notes a student made about this passage from *Frankenstein*. As you read, mark words and phrases that relate to science fiction.

It was on a dreary night of November that I beheld the accomplishment of my toils. With an anxiety that almost amounted to agony, I collected the instruments of life around me, that I might infuse a spark of being into the lifeless thing that lay at my feet.

Could only happen in science fiction

Expand Your Vocabulary

Put a check mark next to the vocabulary words that you feel comfortable using when speaking or writing.

infuse	
inanimate	
ardor	
tumult	
inarticulate	
misdeed	
precipice	
odious	

Turn to a partner and talk about the vocabulary words you already know. Then, use one of the words you know in a sentence.

As you read *Frankenstein*, use the definitions in the side column to help you learn the vocabulary words you don't already know.

Background

Mary Shelley (1797–1851) was the daughter of two famous writers, the early feminist Mary Wollstonecraft and the philosopher William Godwin. Shelley's education benefited from access to her father's vast library and the many scientific and literary people she encountered during her upbringing. When she was 19, she married the poet Percy Bysshe Shelley. Although her literary reputation was long overshadowed by those of her parents and husband, in recent decades Shelley has gained increased recognition as an important writer. Written in 1818, *Frankenstein* was first published anonymously, then later under Shelley's name.

from

Frankenstein

Novel by **Mary Shelley**

A scientist reacts with horror to a living creature he created.

NOTICE & NOTE
As you read, use the side margins to make notes about the text.

A young Swiss scientist named Victor Frankenstein sets out to learn the secret of creating life. For two years he devotes himself to studying chemistry and human anatomy. Finally, after assembling a creature from human remains, he prepares to use an electrical charge to bring it to life.

1   It was on a dreary night of November that I beheld the accomplishment of my toils. With an anxiety that almost amounted to agony, I collected the instruments of life around me, that I might **infuse** a spark of being into the lifeless thing that lay at my feet. It was already one in the morning; the rain pattered dismally against the panes, and my candle was nearly burnt out, when, by the glimmer of the half-extinguished light, I saw the dull yellow eye of the creature open; it breathed hard, and a convulsive motion agitated its limbs.

ANALYZE SCIENCE FICTION

Annotate: In paragraph 1, mark the words and phrases that suggest scientific endeavors.

Explain: How do these details support the categorization of *Frankenstein* as one of the first works of science fiction?

infuse
(ĭn-fyōōz´) *v.* to fill or cause to be filled with something.

inanimate

(ĭn-ăn´ə-mĭt) *adj.* not having the qualities associated with active, living organisms.

ardor

(är´dər) *n.* intensity of emotion, especially strong desire, enthusiasm, or devotion.

tumult

(tōō´mŭlt) *n.* a state of agitation of the mind or emotions.

inarticulate

(ĭn-är-tĭk´yə-lĭt) *adj.* uttered without the use of normal words or syllables; incomprehensible as speech or language.

2   How can I describe my emotions at this catastrophe, or how delineate the wretch whom, with such infinite pains and care, I had endeavored to form? His limbs were in proportion, and I had selected his features as beautiful. Beautiful! Great God! His yellow skin scarcely covered the work of muscles and arteries beneath; his hair was of a lustrous black, and flowing; his teeth of a pearly whiteness; but these luxuriances only formed a more horrid contrast with his watery eyes, that seemed almost of the same color as the dun white sockets in which they were set, his shriveled complexion, and straight black lips.

3   The different accidents of life are not so changeable as the feelings of human nature. I had worked hard for nearly two years, for the sole purpose of infusing life into an **inanimate** body. For this I had deprived myself of rest and health. I had desired it with an **ardor** that far exceeded moderation; but now that I had finished, the beauty of the dream vanished, and breathless horror and disgust filled my heart. Unable to endure the aspect of the being I had created, I rushed out of the room, and continued a long time traversing my bed-chamber, unable to compose my mind to sleep. At length lassitude succeeded to the **tumult** I had before endured; and I threw myself on the bed in my clothes, endeavoring to seek a few moments of forgetfulness. But it was in vain: I slept indeed, but I was disturbed by the wildest dreams. I thought I saw Elizabeth, in the bloom of health, walking in the streets of Ingolstadt. Delighted and surprised, I embraced her; but as I imprinted the first kiss on her lips, they became livid with the hue of death; her features appeared to change, and I thought that I held the corpse of my dead mother in my arms; a shroud enveloped her form, and I saw the grave-worms crawling in the folds of the flannel. I started from my sleep with horror; a cold dew covered my forehead, my teeth chattered, and every limb became convulsed; when, by the dim and yellow light of the moon, as it forced its way through the window-shutters, I beheld the wretch, the miserable monster whom I had created. He held up the curtain of the bed; and his eyes, if eyes they may be called, were fixed on me. His jaws opened, and he muttered some **inarticulate** sounds, while a grin wrinkled his cheeks.

4   He might have spoken, but I did not hear; one hand was stretched out, seemingly to detain me, but I escaped, and rushed downstairs. I took refuge in the courtyard belonging to the house which I inhabited; where I remained during the rest of the night, walking up and down in the greatest agitation, listening attentively, catching and fearing each sound as if it were to announce the approach of the demoniacal corpse to which I had so miserably given life. . . .

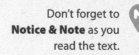

After fleeing from his creation, Victor Frankenstein falls seriously ill and is cared for by a friend. He learns that the creature has killed his younger brother, William, and framed a family servant for the murder. Frankenstein returns home, but he is unable to save the servant from execution for William's murder. Tormented by guilt, he sets out for a hike in the Swiss Alps, hoping to relieve his despair.

5   It was nearly noon when I arrived at the top of the ascent. For some time I sat upon the rock that overlooks the sea of ice. A mist covered both that and the surrounding mountains. Presently a breeze dissipated the cloud, and I descended upon the glacier. The surface is very uneven, rising like the waves of a troubled sea, descending low, and interspersed by rifts that sink deep. The field of ice is almost a league in width, but I spent nearly two hours in crossing it. The opposite mountain is a bare perpendicular rock. From the side where I now stood Montanvert was exactly opposite, at the distance of a league; and above it rose Mont Blanc, in awful majesty. I remained in a recess of the rock, gazing on this wonderful and stupendous scene. The sea, or rather the vast river of ice, wound among its dependent mountains, whose aerial summits hung over its recesses. Their icy and glittering peaks shone in the sunlight over the clouds. My heart, which was before sorrowful, now swelled with something like joy; I exclaimed — "Wandering spirits, if ye indeed wander, and do not rest in your narrow beds, allow me this faint happiness, or take me as your companion, away from the joys of life."

6   As I said this, I suddenly beheld the figure of a man, at some distance, advancing towards me with superhuman speed. He bounded over the crevices of the ice, among which I had walked with caution; his stature also, as he approached, seemed to exceed that of man.

7   I was troubled: a mist came over my eyes, and I felt a faintness seize me; but I was quickly restored by the cold gale of the mountains. I perceived, as the shape came nearer (sight tremendous and abhorred!), that it was the wretch whom I had created. I trembled with rage and horror, resolving to wait his approach, and then close with him in mortal combat. He approached; his countenance bespoke bitter anguish, combined with disdain and malignity, while its unearthly ugliness rendered it almost too horrible for human eyes. But I scarcely observed this; anger and hatred had at first deprived me of utterance, and I recovered only to overwhelm him with words expressive of furious detestation and contempt.

8   "Devil!" I exclaimed, "do you dare approach me? and do you not fear the fierce vengeance of my arm wreaked on your miserable head? Begone, vile insect! or rather stay, that I may trample you to dust! and, oh, that I could, with the extinction of your miserable existence, restore those victims whom you have so diabolically murdered!"

VOCABULARY

Antonyms: The word *uneven* in the fifth sentence of paragraph 5 contains the prefix *un-*, which means "not." A prefix such as *un-* can be added to a word to create its antonym.

Analyze: What details in the sentence provide clues that *uneven* means "not even"?

ANALYZE MOTIVATION

Annotate: Mark words in paragraph 7 that show how Frankenstein feels about his creation and what he plans to do to it.

Infer: Why might Frankenstein feel this way and resolve to take this action?

© Houghton Mifflin Harcourt Publishing Company • Image Credits: ©Magone/Getty Images

ANALYZE MOTIVATION

Annotate: Mark the words or phrases in paragraph 9 that show what the creature asks of Frankenstein.

Draw Conclusions: What does the creature ask for, and what motivates his request?

9   "I expected this reception," said the demon. "All men hate the wretched; how then must I be hated, who am miserable beyond all living things! Yet you, my creator, detest and spurn me, thy creature, to whom thou art bound by ties only dissoluble by the annihilation of one of us. You purpose to kill me. How dare you sport thus with life? Do your duty towards me, and I will do mine towards you and the rest of mankind. If you will comply with my conditions, I will leave them and you at peace; but if you refuse, I will glut the maw of death, until it be satisfied with the blood of your remaining friends."

10 "Abhorred monster! fiend that thou art! the tortures of hell are too mild a vengeance for thy crimes. Wretched devil! you reproach me with your creation; come on then, that I may extinguish the spark which I so negligently bestowed."

11 My rage was without bounds; I sprang on him, impelled by all the feelings which can arm one being against the existence of another.

He easily eluded me, and said, —

12 "Be calm! I entreat you to hear me, before you give vent to your hatred on my devoted head. Have I not suffered enough, that you seek to increase my misery? Life, although it may only be an accumulation of anguish, is dear to me, and I will defend it. Remember, thou hast made me more powerful than thyself; my height is superior to thine; my joints more supple. But I will not be

Don't forget to
Notice & Note as you
read the text.

tempted to set myself in opposition to thee. I am thy creature, and I will be even mild and docile to my natural lord and king, if thou wilt also perform thy part, the which thou owest me. Oh, Frankenstein, be not equitable to every other, and trample upon me alone, to whom thy justice, and even thy clemency and affection, is most due. Remember, that I am thy creature: I ought to be thy Adam; but I am rather the fallen angel, whom thou drivest from joy for no **misdeed**. Everywhere I see bliss, from which I alone am irrevocably excluded. I was benevolent and good; misery made me a fiend. Make me happy, and I shall again be virtuous."

13   "Begone! I will not hear you. There can be no community between you and me; we are enemies. Begone, or let us try our strength in a fight, in which one must fall."

14   "How can I move thee? Will no entreaties cause thee to turn a favorable eye upon thy creature, who implores thy goodness and compassion? Believe me, Frankenstein: I was benevolent; my soul glowed with love and humanity: but am I not alone, miserably alone? You, my creator, abhor me; what hope can I gather from your fellow-creatures, who owe me nothing? They spurn and hate me. The desert mountains and dreary glaciers are my refuge. I have wandered here many days; the caves of ice, which I only do not fear, are a dwelling to me, and the only one which man does not grudge. These bleak

misdeed
(mĭs-dēd´) *n.* a wrong or illegal deed; a wrongdoing.

ANALYZE SCIENCE FICTION

Annotate: In paragraph 14, mark the words or phrases that show that the creature believes he should be treated the same as all humans.

Evaluate: Do you find the creature's argument convincing? Why or why not?

skies I hail, for they are kinder to me than your fellow-beings. If the multitude of mankind knew of my existence, they would do as you do, and arm themselves for my destruction. Shall I not then hate them who abhor me? I will keep no terms with my enemies. I am miserable, and they shall share my wretchedness. Yet it is in your power to recompense me, and deliver them from an evil which it only remains for you to make so great, that not only you and your family, but thousands of others, shall be swallowed up in the whirlwinds of its rage. Let your compassion be moved, and do not disdain me. Listen to my tale: when you have heard that, abandon or commiserate me, as you shall judge that I deserve. But hear me. The guilty are allowed, by human laws, bloody as they may be, to speak in their own defense, before they are condemned. Listen to me, Frankenstein. You accuse me of murder; and yet you would, with a satisfied conscience, destroy your own creature. Oh, praise the eternal justice of man! Yet I ask you not to spare me: listen to me; and then, if you can, and if you will, destroy the work of your hands."

15   "Why do you call to my remembrance circumstances of which I shudder to reflect that I have been the miserable origin and author? Cursed be the day, abhorred devil, in which you first saw light! Cursed (although I curse myself) be the hands that formed you! You have made me wretched beyond expression. You have left me no power to consider whether I am just to you or not. Begone! relieve me from the sight of your detested form."

16   "Thus I relieve thee, my creator," he said, and placed his hated hand before my eyes, which I flung from me with violence; "thus I take from thee a sight which you abhor. Still thou canst listen to me, and grant me thy compassion. By the virtues that I once possessed, I demand this from you. Hear my tale; it is long and strange, and the temperature of this place is not fitting to your fine sensations; come to the hut upon the mountain. The sun is yet high in the heavens; before it descends to hide itself behind yon snowy **precipices**, and illuminate another world, you will have heard my story, and can decide. On you it rests, whether I quit forever the neighborhood of man, and lead a harmless life, or become a scourge to your fellow-creatures, and the author of your own speedy ruin."

17   As he said this, he led the way across the ice: I followed. My heart was full, and I did not answer him; but, as I proceeded, I weighed the various arguments that he had used, and determined at least to listen to his tale. I was partly urged by curiosity, and compassion confirmed my resolution. I had hitherto supposed him to be the murderer of my brother, and I eagerly sought a confirmation or denial of this opinion. For the first time, also, I felt what the duties of a creator towards his creature were, and that I ought to render him happy before I complained of his wickedness. These motives urged me to comply with his demand. We crossed the ice, therefore, and ascended the opposite rock. The air was cold, and the rain again began to descend:

precipice

(prĕs´ə-pĭs) *n.* an overhanging or extremely steep mass of rock; the brink of a dangerous or disastrous situation.

NOTICE & NOTE
AHA MOMENT

When you notice a sudden realization that shifts a character's actions or understandings, you've found an **Aha Moment** signpost.

Notice & Note: What does Frankenstein realize for the first time in paragraph 17? Mark the sentence where he expresses this thought.

Predict: How might this change things?

we entered the hut, the fiend with an air of exultation, I with a heavy heart and depressed spirits. But I consented to listen; and, seating myself by the fire which my **odious** companion had lighted, he thus began his tale.

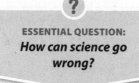

odious
(ō′dē-əs) *adj.* extremely unpleasant; repulsive.

ESSENTIAL QUESTION:
How can science go wrong?

Review your notes and add your thoughts to your Response Log.

COLLABORATIVE DISCUSSION

Get together with a classmate, and discuss your reaction to the interaction between Frankenstein and the creature. What surprised you the most about their encounter?

Assessment Practice

Answer these questions before moving on to the **Analyze the Text** section on the following page.

1. Why does Frankenstein feel disgusted by the creature soon after bringing him to life?

   (A) The creature acts violently.

   (B) The creature chases him.

   (C) The creature has an ugly appearance.

   (D) The creature is physically weak.

2. How does Frankenstein react when the creature finds him in the Swiss Alps?

   (A) He is afraid of the creature.

   (B) He tries to run away.

   (C) He feels guilty for creating the creature.

   (D) He wants to kill the creature.

3. The creature demands that Frankenstein —

   (A) listen to his story

   (B) protect him from his enemies

   (C) be his companion

   (D) improve his appearance

Test-Taking Strategies

Analyze the Text

Support your responses with evidence from the text.

NOTICE & NOTE

Review what you **noticed and noted** as you read the text. Your annotations can help you answer these questions.

1 **INTERPRET** In paragraph 3, Frankenstein dreams that Elizabeth, a woman he loves, turns into a corpse after he kisses her. How does this dream reflect his experience in the previous paragraph?

2 **DRAW CONCLUSIONS** Why does the creature think that he should be forgiven for his crimes? Cite evidence for your conclusion.

3 **ANALYZE** What moral dilemma does Frankenstein experience in the Swiss Alps? What conflicting motivations have contributed to this dilemma? Use the chart to record your answer.

Moral Dilemma	Conflicting Motivations

4 **EVALUATE** In an **Aha Moment** in paragraph 17, Frankenstein says, "For the first time, also, I felt what the duties of a creator towards his creature were." Is Frankenstein partly responsible for the creature's violent behavior? Why or why not?

5 **CRITIQUE** Did Shelley choose an effective setting for the confrontation between Frankenstein and the creature? Explain why or why not.

6 **CONNECT** How does the story of Frankenstein and his creation relate to scientific and technological developments today?

Choices

Here are some other ways to demonstrate your understanding of the ideas in this lesson.

Writing
↳ Science Fiction Story

Write a science fiction short story that addresses a moral or ethical issue. The story can be set in the present and involve an imagined scientific or technological development, or it can be set in the future.

- Identify an imagined scientific or technological advance or invention, and evaluate the moral and ethical dilemmas involved with this innovation.

- Consider the motivations of your characters as you develop the story.

- Use details to develop the characters and the setting of your story.

- Think about ways you can use sensory language to give your readers a vivid experience.

As you write and discuss, be sure to use the **Academic Vocabulary** words.

| appreciate |
| insight |
| intensity |
| invoke |
| radical |

Social & Emotional Learning
↳ Letter Exchange

Reread paragraph 14 of this excerpt from *Frankenstein*. Discuss the following with a partner:

- how people have treated the creature since he was brought to life

- his reaction to experiencing social isolation and hostility

- what he threatens to do if Frankenstein does not provide recompense, or compensation, for his suffering

After your discussion, one of you will write a letter to the creature, expressing empathy for his situation and offering advice on how to deal with it. The other will respond to this letter from the perspective of the creature.

Media
↳ Illustration

Many representations of Frankenstein's creature in popular media bear no resemblance to the descriptions of him in Mary Shelley's novel.

1. Reread Frankenstein's descriptions of the creature's physical appearance in paragraphs 2 and 7.

2. Reread the creature's description of himself in paragraph 12.

3. Create a drawing or painting of the creature based on these descriptions.

Expand Your Vocabulary

PRACTICE AND APPLY

Use your understanding of the vocabulary words to answer each question.

1. If a person is **inarticulate**, would that person make an excellent or a poor public speaker?

2. If someone feels **ardor** toward another person, does that person hate or love the other?

3. Would an **odious** meal be one you look forward to eating or one you refuse to eat?

4. If tea is **infused** with lemons, does that mean it is made of lemons or that it contains lemons?

5. Which is an **inanimate** object, a rock or a bird?

6. Would a **misdeed** be more likely to be punished or celebrated?

7. If you were afraid of heights, would you be likely to stand near a **precipice**?

8. Which would be more likely to cause a **tumult**, going on a vacation or moving to a new city?

Vocabulary Strategy

↳ **Antonyms**

An **antonym** is a word with a meaning opposite that of another word. Some antonyms are formed by adding a prefix that means "not" to a word to create one with the opposite meaning. For example, the word *inanimate* is formed by adding the prefix *in-* to the adjective *animate*, which means "living."

Interactive Vocabulary Lesson: Synonyms and Antonyms

PRACTICE AND APPLY

Add the prefix *dis-, il-, im-, in-, ir-, non-,* or *un-* to each word below to create its antonym.

1. violent

2. legitimate

3. responsible

4. mobile

5. conclusive

6. reverent

7. orderly

8. intelligible

Watch Your Language!

Sensory Language

Sensory language includes descriptive words and phrases that appeal to one or more of the reader's senses, creating a vivid experience for the reader. In *Frankenstein*, Mary Shelley often uses sensory words and phrases to provide descriptions that elicit feelings of horror in the reader. For instance, read the following sentence from the novel:

> It was already one in the morning; the rain pattered dismally against the panes, and my candle was nearly burnt out, when, by the glimmer of the half-extinguished light, I saw the dull yellow eye of the creature open; it breathed hard, and a convulsive motion agitated its limbs.

Notice that in this sentence, Shelley appeals to the senses of sight ("dull yellow eye") and hearing ("rain pattered dismally"). Now compare that sentence to the following paraphrased version:

> It was already one in the morning. Rain was falling, and my candle was nearly burnt out. I saw the creature's eye open. It breathed hard and moved its limbs.

Which version is more effective at establishing a mood and bringing the reader into the story? Why?

 Ed

Interactive Writing Lesson: The Language of Narrative

PRACTICE AND APPLY

Revisit a short story you have written. Identify settings, characters, and events in the story that lack vivid description. Look for opportunities to enhance the reader's experience by using sensory language. Revise your story to help bring your reader into the action by adding details that appeal to the senses. Share your revisions with a partner.

MENTOR TEXT

Frankenstein: Giving Voice to the Monster

Essay by **Langdon Winner**

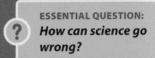

ESSENTIAL QUESTION:
How can science go wrong?

Engage Your Brain

Choose one or more of these activities to start connecting with the essay you're about to read.

Listening to Monsters

Think about the title of this text. What "monster" in literature or pop culture would you like to hear from? Create a cartoon panel depicting a dialogue between you and this monster.

Tech Forecast

Do you expect that advances in technology will lead to a brighter future or a scarier one? Write a paragraph in response to this question. Then, exchange paragraphs with a partner, and discuss your reactions to each other's ideas.

Tales of Artificial Life

With a group of students, brainstorm a list of stories about artificially created beings in mythology, folklore, or science fiction. Answer the following questions for each story on your list:

- What culture does the story come from?

- Is the artificially created being helpful or harmful to humans?

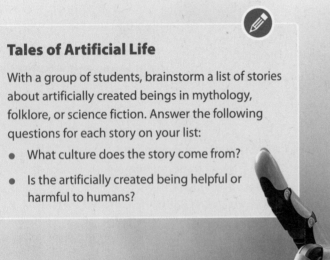

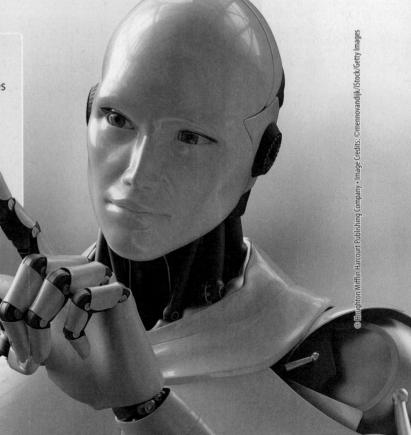

Evaluate an Essay

An essay is a brief work of nonfiction that offers an opinion on a subject. A **formal essay** is well organized and has a clear main idea. Formal essays are usually serious and impersonal in tone. Most formal essays are written to inform, to persuade, or to express ideas. An **informal essay** may be more loosely structured; the tone is conversational, reflecting the personality of the author. The purpose of an informal essay is often to express ideas and feelings or to entertain.

In "Frankenstein: Giving Voice to the Monster," Langdon Winner offers an interesting perspective on the relevance of Mary Shelley's novel today. As you read his essay, notice how he uses his analysis of the novel to support his ideas about science and technology.

Focus on Genre

↳ **Essay**

- is a short piece of nonfiction
- offers an opinion on a subject
- formal essays have a serious and impersonal tone
- informal essays are loosely structured and have a conversational tone

Monitor Comprehension

Some texts are more difficult than others due to their complex ideas, writing style, or unfamiliar content. When you **monitor comprehension,** you check to make sure that you understand what you are reading. One method is to ask questions about a text before, during, and after reading. The following types of questions can help clarify and deepen your understanding:

- **Literal questions** can be answered directly from statements in the text. You might also ask literal questions before you start reading; for example, you might ask yourself what you already know about the topic of an essay or what your purpose is in reading it.

- **Inferential questions** have answers that are not directly stated in the text. Readers make inferences and draw conclusions based on details in a text and their own knowledge and experience.

- **Evaluative questions** are generally asked after reading a text. You might ask whether you agree with ideas in an essay or how effectively you think the author presented them.

As you read this essay, mark up statements that you have trouble understanding, and make note of any questions you have about the content. Review and try to answer your questions after you finish reading.

Annotation in Action

Here is an example of notes a student made about this passage from "Frankenstein: Giving Voice to the Monster." As you read, mark words and phrases that you have questions about.

> The possibility that artificial creatures, products of human hands, might achieve sentience and take on an active role in society is an age-old conception in world cultures, the subject of myths, stories, moral fables, and philosophical speculation.

Why has this been a common theme in literature? What does this say about humans? Does it reflect the need to create?

Expand Your Vocabulary

Put a check mark next to the vocabulary words that you feel comfortable using when speaking or writing.

sentient	☐
artifice	☐
recoil	☐
ominous	☐
domain	☐
prescient	☐

Turn to a partner and talk about the vocabulary words you already know. Then, use one of the words you know in a sentence.

As you read "Frankenstein: Giving Voice to the Monster," use the definitions in the side column to help you learn the vocabulary words you don't already know.

Background

Langdon Winner (b. 1944) is a professor and political theorist. He has taught in colleges and universities and lectured on several continents. He currently serves as the humanities and social sciences department chair at Rensselaer Polytechnic Institute in Troy, New York. His essay "Frankenstein: Giving Voice to the Monster" was presented in Geneva in 2016 at the "Frankenstein's Shadow" conference, honoring the 200th anniversary of the writing of Mary Shelley's novel.

"What is the relationship between the creator and the thing created?"

–Langdon Winner

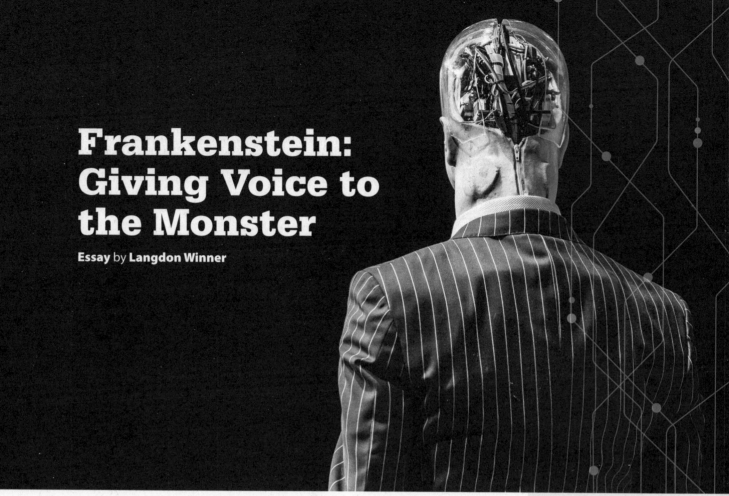

Frankenstein: Giving Voice to the Monster

Essay by **Langdon Winner**

Note Winner's ideas about the novel *Frankenstein* and how he connects those ideas to society today.

NOTICE & NOTE
As you read, use the side margins to make notes about the text.

1   The possibility that artificial creatures, products of human hands, might achieve sentience and take on an active role in society is an age-old conception in world cultures, the subject of myths, stories, moral fables, and philosophical speculation.

2   In Greek mythology one finds the tale of Pygmalion who carves a statue named Galatea with whom he falls in love and who eventually comes to life. In Jewish folklore there are stories of the Golem, an artificial creature animated with surprising results. Norse legends include reports of clay giants able to move on their own accord. An ancient Chinese text describes the work of Yan Shi who in the 10th century B.C. crafted a humanoid figure with lifelike qualities.

3   Both Plato and Aristotle draw upon the myth of the statues of Daedalus[1], mythical creations that could move, perform certain kinds of work and would wander off on their own unless tied down by a rope. In the *Politics* Aristotle uses the metaphor in his defense of

EVALUATE AN ESSAY

Annotate: Reread paragraph 2. Mark the examples of myths and legends.

Analyze: What is the author's purpose for listing these examples?

---

[1] **Daedalus** (dĕd´l-əs): Greek mythology; a renowned craftsman, sculptor, and inventor and builder of the Labyrinth. He fashioned the wings with which he and his son Icarus escaped from Crete after their imprisonment by Minos.

slavery: ". . . if every tool could perform its own work when ordered, or by seeing what to do in advance, like the statues of Daedalus in the story . . . master-craftsmen would have no need of assistants and masters no need of slaves."

4   World literature, not to mention modern science fiction, contains a great many stories of this kind, ones that are often used to shed light upon basic questions about what it means to be alive, what it means to be conscious, what it means to be human, what membership in society entails.

5   Within this tradition of thought Mary Shelley's *Frankenstein* plays a pivotal role. Within popular culture, of course, its story has spawned an astonishing range of novels, stories, movies, television programs, advertisements, toys, and costumes, most of which center upon images of monstrosity, horror and the mad scientist. Beyond these familiar manifestations, however, the novel offers a collection of deeply unsettling reflections upon the human condition, ones brought to focus by modern dreams of creating **sentient**, artificial, humanoid beings.

6   In direct, provocative ways the book asks: What is the relationship between the creator and the thing created? What are the larger responsibilities of those who seek power through scientific knowledge and technological accomplishment? What happens when those responsibilities are not recognized or otherwise left unattended?

7   Questions of this kind concern particular projects that involve attempts to create artificial devices that exhibit features and abilities similar to or even superior to ones associated with human beings. In a larger sense, however, the problems posed by the novel point to situations in which scientific technologies introduced into nature and society seem to run out of control, to achieve a certain autonomy, taking on a life of their own beyond the plans and intentions of the persons involved in their creation.

8   As she addresses issues of this kind, the genius of Mary Shelley is to give voice not only to Victor Frankenstein, his family, friends and acquaintances, but to the creature that sprang from his work and after a time learns to speak, read and form his thoughts, eager to speak his mind about his situation. I do not know whether this is the first time in world literature that one finds a serious dialogue between an artificial creation and its creator. But first instance or not, it is a literary device that Shelley uses with stunning effectiveness.

9   At their climactic meeting high in the Alps, the creature's observations and arguments painfully articulate the perils of unfinished, imperfect, carelessly prepared **artifice**, suddenly released into the world, emphasizing the obligations of the creator as well as the consequences of insensitivity and neglect.

© Houghton Mifflin Harcourt Publishing Company

MONITOR COMPREHENSION

Annotate: Mark the reference to technology in the last sentence of paragraph 5.

Infer: What inferential question can you develop in response to this statement? How would you answer it?

sentient
(sĕn´shənt) *adj.* having sense perception; conscious.

Close Read Screencast

Listen to a modeled close read of this text.

artifice
(är´tə-fĭs) *n.* cleverness or ingenuity in making or doing something.

I am thy creature, and I will be even mild and docile to my natural lord and king if thou wilt also perform thy part, that which thou owest me.

You propose to kill me. How dare you sport thus with life? Do your duty towards me, and I will do mine toward you and the rest of mankind. If you will comply with my conditions I will leave them and you at peace; but if you refuse, I will glut the maw of death, until it be satiated with the blood of your remaining friends.

10   The creature goes on to explain that his greatest desire is to be made part of the human community, something that has been strongly, even brutally, denied him to that point. His stern admonition to Victor is to recognize that the invention of something powerful, ingenious, even marvelous cannot be the end of the work at hand. Thoughtful care must be given to its place in the sphere of human relationships.

11   At first Victor **recoils** and bitterly denounces the creature's demands that he recognize, affirm and fulfill his obligations. But as the threat of violent revenge becomes clear, Victor finally yields to the validity of the argument. "For the first time," he admits, "I felt what the duties of a creator towards his creature were, and that I ought to render him happy before I complained of his wickedness."

12   Following that flash of recognition the story careens toward a disastrous conclusion. Within the wreckage that envelops both Victor and his creature, the book reveals crucial insight, one before its time and with profound implications for similar projects in the future. It can be stated succinctly as follows: The quest for power through scientific technology often tends to override and obscure the recognition of the profound responsibilities that the possession of such power entails.

13   Put even more simply: The impulse to power and control typically comes first, while the recognition of personal and collective moral obligation arrives later, if ever at all. Within that unfortunate gap—between aspirations to power through science and belated recognitions of responsibility—arise generations of monstrosity.

14   Mary Shelley's insights on these matters were well ahead of their time and foreshadow some of the most **ominous** hazards and most ghastly calamities found along the path to modernity from the early 19th century up to the present day. . . .

15   One could offer a great many historical and contemporary illustrations of what I would call "Frankenstein's problem." An appropriate, highly practical, obviously troubling set of developments at present are found within a particular **domain** of scientific inquiry and application, a zone of works not all that dissimilar from the

EVALUATE AN ESSAY

Annotate: Reread the author's analysis of a passage from *Frankenstein* in paragraphs 10–12. Mark words and phrases with strong connotations.

Evaluate: Identify the author's tone. How does his choice of words contribute to the persuasiveness of his essay?

recoil
(rĭ-koil´) *v.* to shrink back, as in fear or repugnance.

ominous
(ŏm´ə-nəs) *adj.* menacing; threatening.

domain
(dō-mān´) *n.* a sphere of activity, influence, or knowledge.

one the fictional Victor Frankenstein explored—today's realm of advanced computerization, smart algorithms, artificial intelligence (AI) and robotics. . . . During the past several years, notable scientists, engineers and luminaries in the technology business sector have stepped forward to express distress at what they see as dire risks that research in AI presents to the human species overall.

16   In a BBC interview, Stephen Hawking warned, "The development of full artificial intelligence could spell the end of the human race. . . . Humans, limited by slow biological evolution, couldn't compete and would be superseded by AI. . . . One can imagine such technology outsmarting financial markets, out-inventing human researchers, out-manipulating human leaders, and developing weapons we cannot even understand. Whereas the short-term impact of AI depends on who controls it, the long-term impact depends on whether it can be controlled at all."

17   In a live exchange on the internet, Microsoft cofounder Bill Gates offered similar views. "I am in the camp that is concerned about super intelligence," Gates wrote. "First the machines will do a lot of jobs for us and not be super intelligent. . . . A few decades after that though the intelligence is strong enough to be a concern."

18   In the same vein, British inventor Clive Sinclair recently told the BBC, "Once you start to make machines that are rivaling and surpassing humans with intelligence, it's going to be very difficult for us to survive. It's just an inevitability." . . .

19   Studies of and speculation about issues of this kind have inspired the creation of a collection of new research centers at leading universities. Among them are the Cambridge Center for the Study of Existential Risk and The Future of Life Institute at MIT. Taken together the shelf of books on AI and Robots, the systematic studies of the future of automation and employment, and the excited warnings about artificial devices superseding human beings as the key actors on the stage of world history are, in my view, a contemporary realization of the **prescient** concerns and warnings at the heart of Mary Shelley's book—concerns and warnings about the headlong flight from responsibility.

NOTICE & NOTE
QUOTED WORDS

When you notice the author has quoted the opinions or conclusions of an expert, or when you notice the author citing other people to provide support for a point, you've found a **Quoted Words** signpost.

Notice & Note: Mark the names of notable people the author quotes in paragraphs 16–18.

Evaluate: Do these quotations provide effective support for the author's opinion about artificial intelligence? Why or why not?

prescient
(prĕsh´ənt) *adj.* of or relating to prescience—which means knowledge of actions or events before they occur.

ESSENTIAL QUESTION:
How can science go wrong?

Review your notes and add your thoughts to your Response Log.

COLLABORATIVE DISCUSSION

Get together with a classmate, and discuss your thoughts about the connections Winner makes between *Frankenstein* and artificial intelligence.

Assessment Practice

Answer these questions before moving on to the **Analyze the Text** section on the following page.

1. According to the author, the genius of Shelley is in —

   (A) setting the climactic meeting place in the Alps

   (B) giving a voice to Frankenstein's creature

   (C) anticipating the novel's effect on popular culture

   (D) introducing the concept of a mad scientist

2. What is one of the deeper questions posed by Shelley's novel?

   (A) Who should participate in scientific development?

   (B) What is the relationship between nature and society?

   (C) What scientific projects should never be attempted?

   (D) What responsibilities accompany scientific development?

3. The attitude that Hawking, Gates, and Sinclair share about the future of artificial intelligence is one of —

   (A) concern and caution

   (B) hope and excitement

   (C) annoyance and dismay

   (D) doubt and negativity

Ed
Test-Taking Strategies

© Houghton Mifflin Harcourt Publishing Company

Analyze the Text

Support your responses with evidence from the text.

NOTICE & NOTE

Review what you **noticed and noted** as you read the text. Your annotations can help you answer these questions.

(1) **IDENTIFY** What is the main idea of this essay?

(2) **COMPARE** Reread paragraph 5. The author contrasts Mary Shelley's novel with how the Frankenstein story has been adapted for popular culture. Use the graphic organizer to identify these differences.

Popular Culture	Shelley's Novel

(3) **EVALUATE** Does the author provide sufficient support for his opinion that Shelley's genius was to give voice to the monster? Why or why not?

(4) **CRITIQUE** Reread paragraphs 16–18. Do you think that the author should have included **Quoted Words** from someone with a different view of the future of artificial intelligence? Explain why or why not.

(5) **EVALUATE** How effective is the author's conclusion to the essay? Explain.

(6) **QUESTION** Review your markups and notes on "Frankenstein: Giving Voice to the Monster." What questions do you have after reading this essay? What kind of research or investigation might help you answer these questions?

Choices

Here are some other ways to demonstrate your understanding of the ideas in this lesson.

Writing
↳ **Essay**

In his essay, Langdon Winner sums up a problem in scientific and technological development with the following statements:

- "The quest for power through scientific technology often tends to override and obscure the recognition of the profound responsibilities that the possession of such power entails."

- "The impulse to power and control typically comes first, while the recognition of personal and collective moral obligation arrives later, if ever at all."

Write an argument in favor of or opposed to Winner's views on scientific technology. Use reasons and evidence to support your position.

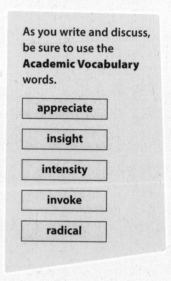

As you write and discuss, be sure to use the **Academic Vocabulary** words.

appreciate

insight

intensity

invoke

radical

Social & Emotional Learning
↳ **Policy Proposal**

With a group of students, discuss the risks posed by development of artificial intelligence. Consider the potential ethical and economic impacts of this new technology. Then, create a proposal for a policy to address these dangers.

- Include three to five steps you think will help control the risks of developing artificial intelligence.

- Explain each step, and explain why you think it will be beneficial.

- Use formal language and precise details in your proposal.

Research
↳ **Artificial Intelligence Projects**

Conduct research to learn about some recent developments in the use of artificial intelligence. Then, create a presentation about one of these products or technologies.

- Discuss how artificial intelligence is being used in the product or technology.

- Explain why it is more effective or efficient than older methods.

- Discuss any risks associated with this new development.

Expand Your Vocabulary

PRACTICE AND APPLY

Choose the vocabulary word that completes each sentence.

1. The politician used _____ to make it appear as if he wanted to enrich the people when, in fact, he wanted only to enrich himself.

   a. artifice   **b.** domain

2. Despite the _____ clouds on the near horizon, the skipper pressed onward toward the stricken vessel.

   a. prescient   **b.** ominous

3. The scientist invented a _____ device that perceives motion.

   a. sentient   **b.** recoil

Vocabulary Strategy
↳ **Technical Words**

When reading nonfiction, you may encounter **technical words,** or terms that are specific to a particular field of study. Writers in fields such as science and engineering use technical words to convey information precisely and accurately. Use one or more of these steps to help you understand the meaning of technical words:

Interactive Vocabulary Lesson: Specialized Vocabulary

- Check to see whether the word is defined in a footnote or glossary entry.

- Use the context in which the word appears to determine its meaning.

- Identify familiar word parts, such as roots or affixes, and use their meanings to help define the word.

- Consult a print or digital college-level dictionary. Refer to a specialized dictionary as needed.

PRACTICE AND APPLY

Complete the activity with a partner.

1. Find these terms in paragraph 15 of "Frankenstein: Giving Voice to the Monster": *algorithms, artificial intelligence,* and *robotics.* Use context clues to identify the field or fields of study in which these technical words are used.

2. Use word parts or consult a dictionary to define each technical word.

Watch Your Language!

Parallel Structure

Parallel structure, or parallelism, is the use of similar grammatical constructions to express ideas that are closely related or equal in importance. The grammatical constructions may include phrases, clauses, or sentences. Parallel structure helps writers organize, clarify, and emphasize their thoughts. It can also affect the meaning and tone of a sentence or passage. Read this sentence from Langdon Winner's essay:

> World literature, . . . contains a great many stories of this kind, ones that are often used to shed light upon basic questions about <u>what it means to be alive</u>, <u>what it means to be conscious</u>, <u>what it means to be human</u>, <u>what membership in society entails</u>.

Winner uses a series of noun clauses beginning with *what* that are the objects of the preposition *about*. The repetition of this grammatical construction gives equal weight to the "basic questions" he identifies in world literature. The parallelism also makes the sentence more rhythmic and memorable. Consider that he could have written the sentence like this:

> World literature, . . . contains a great many stories of this kind, ones that are often used to shed light upon basic questions about what it means to be alive, conscious, and human, and what membership in society entails.

Without parallel structure, the relationship between the questions is less clear. The sentence is also less memorable because it lacks a strong rhythm.

Writers can use parallel structure not only within sentences but also in groups of sentences. For example, Winner starts the first two sentences in paragraph 2 with "In Greek mythology" and "In Jewish folklore," using parallelism to tie together examples from different cultural traditions.

PRACTICE AND APPLY

Underline the parallel structures in the sentences below. Then, use each sentence as a model to write two sentences of your own with the same parallel structures.

1. "One can imagine such technology outsmarting financial markets, out-inventing human researchers, out-manipulating human leaders, and developing weapons we cannot even understand."

2. "Whereas the short-term impact of AI depends on who controls it, the long-term impact depends on whether it can be controlled at all."

Collaborate & Compare

Compare Themes

As you read these two odes, pay attention to the diction, figurative language, and imagery in each poem. Think about how these elements help convey the poem's theme.

A

Ode to the West Wind

Poem by **Percy Bysshe Shelley**
pages 576–579

B

Ode to My Mother's Hair

Poem by **Joseph O. Legaspi**
pages 580–583

After you have read the poems, you will collaborate in a small group to compare their themes. You will follow these steps:

- Make inferences about themes
- Agree on a theme
- Present to the class

© Houghton Mifflin Harcourt Publishing Company • Image Credits: (l) ©Henglein and Steets/Getty Images; (r) ©luceluce/Shutterstock; (inset) ©LeoPatrizi/iStock/Getty Images

Ode to the West Wind

Poem by **Percy Bysshe Shelley**

Ode to My Mother's Hair

Poem by **Joseph O. Legaspi**

Engage Your Brain

Choose one or more of these activities to start connecting with the poems you're about to read.

Reflections on Autumn

One of the poems you are about to read was inspired by autumn. Write one or two paragraphs expressing your thoughts and feelings about this season. Consider the following:

- What activities do you associate with autumn?

- How do changes in weather during autumn affect you?

Blowing in the Wind

With a group of students, research facts about wind. Cover the following topics:

- What causes wind to form?

- What are the different types of wind?

- How does wind affect plants and landscapes?

A Cut Above the Rest

With a partner, identify three celebrities who are famous for their hair.

- What is distinctive about each celebrity's hair?

- What do their hairstyles express about them?

Analyze Ode

An **ode** is complex lyric poem that praises a person, event, or thing. Odes usually have a serious theme and a dignified or reflective tone. This poetic form developed in ancient Greece and Rome, where poets wrote rhymed odes with elaborate stanza structures. The ode has remained popular over the centuries, but later poets took it in new directions.

- Romantic poets, such as Shelley and Keats, created odes that emphasize personal reflection, looking both inward and outward. Romantic odes usually are rhymed and have a regular meter, but they may stray from classical stanza patterns. For example, in "Ode to the West Wind," Shelley uses the 14-line sonnet structure to develop each section of his poem.

- Contemporary poets, such as Joseph O. Legaspi, often write odes in **free verse** with no regular pattern of rhyme, meter, or stanza structure. They may also choose unusual subjects and adopt a less serious tone.

As you read "Ode to the West Wind" and "Ode to My Mother's Hair," notice how each poet uses poetic elements to create a tone and develop a theme.

Focus on Genre
↳ Ode

- is a lyric poem that develops a single theme
- usually has a dignified or reflective tone
- appeals to both the imagination and the intellect
- may commemorate an event or praise the beauty of nature or a person

Analyze Diction

The beauty and freshness of poetic language depend partly on **diction,** a term that refers to both word choice and **syntax,** or the order of words. Traditional poets often used a special diction, **inverted syntax,** which reverses the expected order of words. Inverted syntax can help maintain patterns of rhyme and meter and give a poem an elevated tone. Traditional poets also often used obscure or old-fashioned words such as *thee* and *thou* to make their language sound more elevated. In contrast, the syntax of modern poetry is usually closer to the rhythms of natural speech. Most poets today choose concrete, vivid words to make their language engaging for a modern audience.

Use these questions to help you analyze diction:

- Does the poet use plain or elevated language?
- Is the writer's syntax inverted or natural? formal or informal?
- How does the poem's diction affect its tone?

Annotation in Action

Here is an example of notes a student made about the opening lines of "Ode to the West Wind." As you read, mark examples of diction in both poems.

O wild West Wind, thou breath of Autumn's being,
Thou, from whose unseen presence the leaves dead
Are driven, like ghosts from an enchanter fleeing,

Yellow, and black, and pale, and hectic red,
Pestilence-stricken multitudes: O thou,
Who chariotest to their dark wintry bed

By reversing the usual word order in "leaves dead" and "enchanter fleeing," the poet maintains a pattern of rhymes.

Background

Percy Bysshe Shelley (1792–1822) developed radical political and social views in his youth, alienating him from his aristocratic relatives. In the autumn of 1819, Shelley was prompted to write "Ode to the West Wind" after hearing of the Peterloo Massacre, in which soldiers killed English workers demonstrating for reform. The poem reflects Shelley's deep desire to change the world through poetry. In 1822, Shelley drowned just off the coast of Italy when his sailboat sank in a storm.

Joseph O. Legaspi (b. 1971) was born in the Philippines and immigrated to the United States when he was 12. He has a reverence for family and an admiration of his immigrant parents' struggle to make a home in a foreign land. Since obtaining an MFA from New York University, Legaspi has authored two collections of poetry. In 2001 he won the Global Filipino Literary Award. Three years later, he co-founded Kundiman, a nonprofit organization that promotes Asian-American poetry. Legaspi lives in New York City.

Ode to the West Wind

Poem by **Percy Bysshe Shelley**

Notice how the poet describes and personifies the autumn wind in his ode.

NOTICE & NOTE

As you read, use the side margins to make notes about the text.

ANALYZE ODE

Annotate: Use letters to mark the patterns of end rhyme in lines 1–14.

Analyze: What is the rhyme scheme? How does rhyme link each stanza to the next?

4 **hectic:** feverish.

9 **sister . . . Spring:** the reviving south wind of spring.

10 **clarion:** a trumpet with a clear, ringing tone.

I

O wild West Wind, thou breath of Autumn's being,
Thou, from whose unseen presence the leaves dead
Are driven, like ghosts from an enchanter fleeing,

Yellow, and black, and pale, and hectic red,
5 Pestilence-stricken multitudes: O thou,
Who chariotest to their dark wintry bed

The wingéd seeds, where they lie cold and low,
Each like a corpse within its grave, until
Thine azure sister of the Spring shall blow

10 Her clarion o'er the dreaming earth, and fill
(Driving sweet buds like flocks to feed in air)
With living hues and odors plain and hill:

Wild Spirit, which art moving everywhere;
Destroyer and preserver; hear, oh, hear!

II

15 Thou on whose stream, mid the steep sky's commotion,
Loose clouds like earth's decaying leaves are shed,
Shook from the tangled bough of Heaven and Ocean,

Angels of rain and lightning: there are spread
On the blue surface of thine aëry surge,
20 Like the bright hair uplifted from the head

Of some fierce Maenad, even from the dim verge
Of the horizon to the zenith's height,
The locks of the approaching storm. Thou dirge

Of the dying year, to which this closing night
25 Will be the dome of a vast sepulcher,
Vaulted with all thy congregated might

Of vapors, from whose solid atmosphere
Black rain, and fire, and hail will burst: oh, hear!

III

Thou who didst waken from his summer dreams
30 The blue Mediterranean, where he lay,
Lulled by the coil of his crystálline streams,

32 **pumice** (pŭm´ĭs): a light volcanic rock; **Baiae's** (bī´ēz´) **bay:** the Bay of Naples, site of the ancient Roman resort of Baiae.

Beside a pumice isle in Baiae's bay,
And saw in sleep old palaces and towers
Quivering within the wave's intenser day,

35 All overgrown with azure moss and flowers
So sweet, the sense faints picturing them! Thou
For whose path the Atlantic's level powers

37 **level powers:** surface.

Cleave themselves into chasms, while far below
The sea-blooms and the oozy woods which wear
40 The sapless foliage of the ocean, know

Thy voice, and suddenly grow gray with fear,
And tremble and despoil themselves: oh, hear!

IV

ANALYZE ODE

Annotate: Mark the words Shelley uses to describe the West Wind in section IV.

Infer: Based on how Shelley praises the West Wind in these lines, what qualities can you infer Shelley wants for himself?

If I were a dead leaf thou mightest bear;
If I were a swift cloud to fly with thee;
45 A wave to pant beneath thy power, and share

The impulse of thy strength, only less free
Than thou, O uncontrollable! If even
I were as in my boyhood, and could be

The comrade of thy wanderings over Heaven,
50 As then, when to outstrip thy skyey speed
Scarce seemed a vision; I would ne'er have striven

50 **skyey** (skī´ē) **speed:** the swiftness of clouds moving across the sky.

51 **vision:** something impossible to achieve.

As thus with thee in prayer in my sore need.
Oh, lift me as a wave, a leaf, a cloud!
I fall upon the thorns of life! I bleed!

55 A heavy weight of hours has chained and bowed
One too like thee: tameless, and swift, and proud.

V

57 **lyre:** a reference to the Aeolian harp, an instrument whose strings make musical sounds when the wind blows over them.

Make me thy lyre, even as the forest is:
What if my leaves are falling like its own!
The tumult of thy mighty harmonies

60 Will take from both a deep, autumnal tone,
Sweet though in sadness. Be thou, Spirit fierce,
My spirit! Be thou me, impetuous one!

62 **impetuous** (ĭm-pĕch´oo-əs): violently forceful; impulsive.

Drive my dead thoughts over the universe
Like withered leaves to quicken a new birth!
65 And, by the incantation of this verse,

65 **incantation:** recitation, as of a magic spell.

Scatter, as from an unextinguished hearth
Ashes and sparks, my words among mankind!
Be through my lips to unawakened earth

The trumpet of a prophecy! O Wind,
70 If Winter comes, can Spring be far behind?

ESSENTIAL QUESTION:
What stirs your imagination?

Review your notes and add your thoughts to your Response Log.

COLLABORATIVE DISCUSSION

With a partner, discuss how the poet's feelings change in the poem. Do you think the poem ends on a hopeful note? Explain.

Assessment Practice

Answer these questions about "Ode to the West Wind" before moving on to the next selection.

1. In section I, the speaker refers to the West Wind as a "preserver" because it —

(A) blows away the dead leaves

(B) spreads seeds that will bloom in the spring

(C) brings in the warm spring wind

(D) protects flocks of sheep from harm

2. In section IV, what does the speaker regret about his adult years?

(A) He has lost his appreciation of the seasons.

(B) Winter is hard for him to bear.

(C) He is all alone in the world.

(D) He has become less free and vigorous.

3. Which of the following themes can be inferred from the poem?

(A) Life is full of contradictions.

(B) Society lacks beauty and grace.

(C) The wind is the only constant in life.

(D) The world needs to be reawakened.

Test-Taking Strategies

Ode to My Mother's Hair

Poem by **Joseph O. Legaspi**

NOTICE & NOTE

As you read, use the side margins to make notes about the text.

Notice how the poet uses imagery to reflect on scenes from the speaker's childhood.

The provincial
river is transformed,
my mother
in a clear-sky afternoon
5   washes her hair,
dark as cuttlefish ink.
Between
her flat palms,
she rubs it
10 with silt, twisting
the strands
as if starting a fire:

my mother's Promethean
crown of smoke, daughter
15 of a woman with hair like fire.

6 **cuttlefish:** a marine mollusk with eight arms and two long tentacles.

13 **Promethean:** like the ancient Titan Prometheus, who stole fire and gave it to humans.

I have seen photographs:
my mother pony-tailed
as a girl, split-
ends, braided,
20 molasses stuck
and formed
prickly discs
like coiled, poisonous caterpillars;
like black holed flowers
25 in her follicle garden;
tangled little
mushrooms.

As a child
in the fringes of sleep,
30 when my fill of colostrum
swirled warmly inside me,
I often burrowed
my mole face

in my mother's hair,
35 the darkness beyond the banana grove.

I remember
how it brushed against my eyelids,
fending off the midnight dogs
of sleeplessness; tickled
40 my ears, deadening
the skeletons
of nightmares;
and how I breathed in
strands, which planted
45 the seed of the tree of memory.

My mother's hair is domestic hair:
absorbent to the scent
of her cooking—
milkfish, garlic, goat;
50 her fur of sweeping dust
clipped
in a bun, with wisps
that dangle on her face,
and dance
55 to floor scrubbing by coconut husk
to laundry five children soiled
to my father's pulling and shaking.

© Houghton Mifflin Harcourt Publishing Company

ANALYZE DICTION

Annotate: Mark at least three surprising or unusual ways the speaker describes his mother's hair in lines 17–25.

Analyze: What tone does the poet create with these descriptions of the mother's childhood hairstyles?

30 **colostrum:** the first form of milk produced by a nursing mother.

ANALYZE ODE

Annotate: Mark in lines 36–45 the phrases that reveal the intimacy between a mother and young child.

Analyze: How is the speaker commemorating his mother in these lines?

ANALYZE DICTION

Annotate: Mark examples of everyday language used in lines 46–57.

Analyze: What sensory details does the speaker include to indicate that he is remembering his childhood?

When my youngest sister
was born, our mother chopped
60   her hair, the incubating black hen
of her head ousted the starlings.
In hope of a reparation
for what we had driven her to do,
I gathered locks
65   from her brush,
tied them with blue ribbon
and buried them in our backyard,
dusting the plot
with sugar and cocoa,
70   moistening the mound with honey—

all the goodness from the world of the living.
I believed
the earth resurrects
what is nourished in its belly.

75   And in this river,
my mother's wet, swirling hair

reminds me
of monsoon seasons,
when our house,
80   besieged by wind and water,
teetered and threatened to split open,
exposing the diorama
of our barely protected lives
with my mother, seated, telling stories
85   to her children collected around her,
while my sister and I are brushing her mane,
smelling of rose soap,
sprouting by candle light,
her hair which is always the other half of the world.

62 reparation: an act of making amends for a wrong.

78 monsoon: seasonal heavy rainfall in southern Asia in the summers.

82 diorama: a three-dimensional, naturalistic setting for a miniature of figures or wildlife.

ESSENTIAL QUESTION:
What stirs your imagination?

Review your notes and add your thoughts to your Response Log.

COLLABORATIVE DISCUSSION

How would you describe the speaker's relationship with his mother? Discuss your thoughts with a partner.

Assessment Practice

Answer these questions about "Ode to My Mother's Hair" before moving on to the **Analyze the Texts** section on the following page.

1. In lines 1–12, the speaker emphasizes —

   (A) his appreciation of nature's beauty

   (B) how polluted the river has become

   (C) his fascination with his mother's hair

   (D) the poverty of his provincial birthplace

2. Which statement best describes the life of the speaker's mother?

   (A) She spent most of her time outdoors.

   (B) She worked hard to take care of her family.

   (C) She was widely admired for her beautiful hair.

   (D) She took great care over her personal appearance.

3. Why does the speaker say that he buried his mother's locks of hair hoping for "a reparation / for what we had driven her to do"?

   (A) She had to cut her hair and sell it to buy food for the children.

   (B) The children made her cut her hair because they were jealous.

   (C) He wanted to leave the hair behind as a memorial to his mother.

   (D) She cut her hair because she had no time to care for it.

😊Ed
Test-Taking Strategies

Analyze the Texts

Support your responses with evidence from the texts.

> **NOTICE & NOTE**
>
> Review what you **noticed and noted** as you read the text. Your annotations can help you answer these questions.

1. **INFER** In the last line of "Ode to the West Wind," Shelley poses the question, "If Winter comes, can Spring be far behind?" What theme does this question help convey? How might this theme relate to disturbing political events such as the Peterloo Massacre?

2. **ANALYZE** How would you describe the diction of "Ode to the West Wind"? What purpose does this use of diction serve? Explain.

3. **INFER** Reread lines 57–69. What transformation does Shelley want to undergo? What hope does he have for his poetry?

4. **ANALYZE** Which elements of Shelley's poem fit the characteristics of an ode? Why might he have chosen this form to express his ideas?

5. **ANALYZE** In "Ode to My Mother's Hair," what does the speaker's hair symbolize for him as a child? What might it symbolize for him as an adult? Explain.

6. **ANALYZE** Which aspects of "Ode to My Mother's Hair" are influenced by the traditional form of the ode? Which aspects of the poem are less traditional? Use the graphic organizer to analyze specific elements of the poem.

Theme	Tone
Structure	**Diction**

7. **DRAW CONCLUSIONS** In "Ode to My Mother's Hair," how would you characterize the speaker's life in the place where he grew up?

Choices

Here are some other ways to demonstrate your understanding of the ideas in this lesson.

Writing
↳ **Ode**

Write an ode praising a person, event, or thing. Before you begin, decide whether you want to write a traditional ode, with elements such as rhyme and meter, or a free-verse ode. Make sure your ode has

- a serious theme
- a dignified or reflective tone

As you write and discuss, be sure to use the **Academic Vocabulary** words.

appreciate

insight

intensity

invoke

radical

Media
↳ **Collage**

"Ode to the West Wind" is full of vivid nature imagery. Create a collage inspired by the poem.

1. Reread the poem, and pick out one or two important images in each section.

2. Search online to find photographs that relate to the imagery you have selected.

3. Arrange the photographs in a visually appealing composition.

4. If you wish, include brief quotations from the poem in your collage.

Speaking & Listening
↳ **Paired Discussion**

With a partner, discuss the speaker's relationship with his mother in "Ode to My Mother's Hair." Use the following questions to help guide your discussion:

- What do the poet's word choices emphasize about how the speaker views his mother?

- Why might the poet have chosen to praise the mother by focusing on her hair?

- What does the speaker mean when he says that his mother's hair "is always the other half of the world"?

Compare Themes

"Ode to the West Wind" and "Ode to My Mother's Hair" share a poetic form—the ode. However, the two poems express different **themes,** or messages about life or human nature.

Poets do not state their themes directly. Instead they use form, diction, figurative language, imagery, and other elements to express those themes.

In a small group, complete the chart below to analyze the poems and begin to identify the theme of each poem.

	A **"Ode to the West Wind"**	B **"Ode to My Mother's Hair"**
Form		
Diction		
Figurative Language		
Imagery		

Analyze the Texts

Discuss these questions in your group.

1. **COMPARE** With your group, review the imagery that you cited in your chart. How are the images in the two poems similar? How do they differ?

2. **INTERPRET** Both poems describe some of the ways we relate to nature. Discuss each poem's treatment of nature. Cite evidence in your discussion.

3. **EVALUATE** In "Ode to the West Wind," Shelley uses elevated language and formal diction; however, in "Ode to My Mother's Hair," Legaspi does the opposite. Which approach do you find most effective, and why?

4. **DRAW CONCLUSIONS** According to the two poems, what insights about life or human nature can we gain by considering the wind and other elements of the natural world?

Collaborate and Present

With your group, continue exploring the ideas in the poems by identifying and comparing their themes. Follow these steps:

1. **MAKE INFERENCES ABOUT THEMES** Review your charts as a group, considering the form, diction, figurative language, imagery, and other elements from both poems. Then, work together to infer possible themes for each poem.

2. **AGREE ON A THEME** Determine a theme statement for each poem. Use a chart like the one below to track the themes and supporting details.

	Theme Statement	Supporting Details
"Ode to the West Wind"		
"Ode to My Mother's Hair"		

3. **PRESENT TO THE CLASS** Organize your ideas, and choose a spokesperson to present them to the class.

- Clearly state the theme of each poem, explaining the similarities or differences in themes.

- Follow an organized plan of presentation.

- Include supporting details from the poems.

- Make clear transitions between ideas.

- Add visuals or diagrams to help convey information.

Collaborate & Compare

Compare Poems

As you read, pay attention to the ways in which William Blake
describes the two contrasting states of being—innocence
and experience. How are the details in the poems similar or
different, and how do they contribute to the themes described?

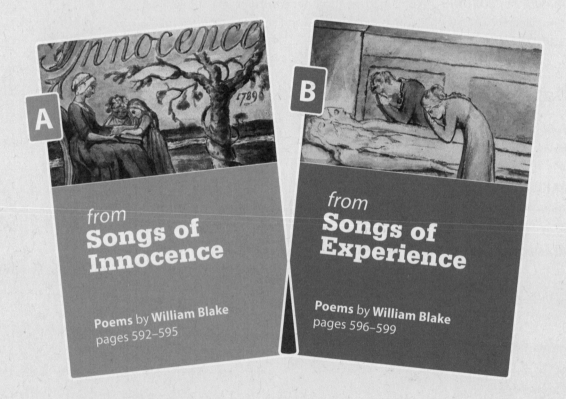

A

from
Songs of
Innocence

Poems by **William Blake**
pages 592–595

B

from
Songs of
Experience

Poems by **William Blake**
pages 596–599

After you read, you will explore ideas in the poems by
collaborating with a small group on a presentation. You will
follow these steps:

- Decide on the most important details
- Determine a message for each poem
- Compare ideas
- Present to the class

from **Songs of Innocence**

Poems by **William Blake**

from **Songs of Experience**

Poems by **William Blake**

Engage Your Brain

Choose one or more of these activities to start connecting with the poems you're about to read.

Compare Two Animals

With a partner, think of two animals that you are interested in or knowledgeable about. In what ways are they similar? In what ways are they different? Freewrite your ideas and share them with the class.

List It!

What comes to mind when you think of innocence and experience? Write down a list of at least three ideas or images for each state.

How Do We Fight for Justice?

Some of Blake's poems cry out against the social problems he saw all around him. How would you speak out against an evil of our day? Consider the following questions in a discussion:

- Which social injustice would you protest?

- How would you get people to listen to your view?

- Is poetry an effective way to speak out against evil today?

Understand Historical Background

Background information on historical, social, cultural, and economic issues may be important for understanding a poem's theme. In *Songs of Innocence* and *Songs of Experience*, for example, William Blake describes the plight of chimney sweepers, boys from poor families who were apprenticed to chimney sweeps and used to clean chimneys in London and other British cities. During the Romantic period, most fireplaces in England burned coal for fuel, creating sticky soot that had to be brushed or scraped away. Children crawled up narrow chimneys to perform this work. People who worked as sweepers rarely lived past middle age due to respiratory illnesses, cancer, and other diseases.

As early as 1788, legislation was enacted to prohibit children younger than eight from working as sweeps' apprentices. Subsequent legislation raised the minimum age again, but these laws were unenforced and ineffective. It was not until 1875 that sweeps were required to be licensed and police were given the power to enforce legislation, bringing an end to the practice of child labor. As you read Blake's poems about chimney sweepers, make connections between this historical information and details and themes of the poems.

Focus on Genre
↳ Lyric Poetry

- expresses personal thoughts or feelings
- is written from a first-person perspective
- has a musical quality
- is marked by imagination and evocative language

Analyze Symbols

A **symbol** is a person, place, object, or action that has a concrete meaning in itself and also stands for something beyond itself, such as an idea or a feeling. For example, a dove is widely known as a symbol of peace. In literature, symbols often take their meaning from the context in which they appear, and the symbolic meaning may be interpreted in different ways.

Symbols play an important role in Blake's poetry. Although at first glance the poems in *Songs of Innocence* and *Songs of Experience* seem simple and straightforward, Blake uses symbols to convey complex spiritual and social themes. As you read these poems, look for clues to help you interpret the symbols. Use a chart like the one below to jot down your interpretations.

Person, Place, or Object	Concrete Meaning	Symbolic Idea or Feeling

Annotation in Action

Here are one student's comments on a symbol in "The Lamb." As you read Blake's poems, look for other symbols, and think about their meaning and significance.

> Little Lamb, who made thee?
> Dost thou know who made thee?
> Gave thee life & bid thee feed,
> By the stream & o'er the mead;
> Gave thee clothing of delight,
> Softest clothing wooly bright;

The lamb is small and soft. This suggests it is a symbol of gentleness and innocence.

William Blake (1757–1827)

William Blake was born into a modest family in London. He learned to read and write at home, while studying the Bible and the works of John Milton. When he was 10, his father sent him to a drawing school. Blake began writing poetry when he was 12. However, the cost of the school was high, so four years later his parents apprenticed him to a master engraver.

After setting up shop as an engraver, Blake developed a technique that allowed him to print pages of text and illustration from the same plate, which he then hand colored. Blake used this time-consuming process, called illuminated printing, to publish most of his works.

In 1782 Blake married Catherine Boucher. She was illiterate when they met, but Blake taught her how to read, write, and paint. She was an assistant in his work and became a skilled draftsperson.

In 1789 Blake completed his first illuminated book, *Songs of Innocence,* featuring poems written for children that also depicted the innocent nature of childhood. *Songs of Experience* was published in 1794 as a companion volume to *Songs of Innocence.* He said his purpose in putting them together was to show "the two contrary states of the human soul."

Blake's later works were written on a grand scale, marked by prophetic and mythic visions, but these complex works were largely ignored by his contemporaries. More than 100 years passed before people began to recognize Blake's stunning achievements as a poet and an artist.

"No bird soars too high if he soars with his own wings."

—William Blake

from

Songs of Innocence

Poems by **William Blake**

As you read, think about how each poem expresses ideas about innocence. The second collection, *Songs of Experience,* which you will read next, includes poems that expand on similar themes.

The Lamb

> Little Lamb, who made thee?
> Dost thou know who made thee?
> Gave thee life & bid thee feed,
> By the stream & o'er the mead;
> 5 Gave thee clothing of delight,
> Softest clothing wooly bright;
> Gave thee such a tender voice,
> Making all the vales rejoice!
> Little Lamb who made thee?
> 10 Dost thou know who made thee?

4 **mead:** meadow.

8 **vales:** valleys.

Little Lamb I'll tell thee,
Little Lamb I'll tell thee!
He is callèd by thy name,
For he calls himself a Lamb:
15   He is meek & he is mild,
He became a little child:
I a child & thou a lamb,
We are callèd by his name.
    Little Lamb God bless thee.
20   Little Lamb God bless thee.

Assessment Practice

Answer these questions about "The Lamb" before moving on to the next selection.

1. In "The Lamb," the speaker begins by asking —

   (A) whether the lamb is lost

   (B) how old the lamb is

   (C) who created the lamb

   (D) what is the lamb's name

2. Blake reveals that the poem's speaker is —

   (A) the lamb

   (B) a child

   (C) Jesus Christ

   (D) Blake himself

3. Which of God's characteristics does Blake emphasize in "The Lamb"?

   (A) gentleness

   (B) power

   (C) beauty

   (D) creativity

Test-Taking Strategies

The Chimney Sweeper

When my mother died I was very young,
And my father sold me while yet my tongue
Could scarcely cry "'weep! 'weep! 'weep! 'weep!"
So your chimneys I sweep & in soot I sleep.

5   There's little Tom Dacre, who cried when his head
That curl'd like a lamb's back, was shav'd, so I said,
"Hush, Tom! never mind it, for when your head's bare,
You know that the soot cannot spoil your white hair."

And so he was quiet, & that very night,
10   As Tom was a-sleeping he had such a sight!
That thousands of sweepers, Dick, Joe, Ned, & Jack,
Were all of them lock'd up in coffins of black;

And by came an Angel who had a bright key,
And he open'd the coffins & set them all free;
15   Then down a green plain, leaping, laughing they run,
And wash in a river and shine in the Sun.

Then naked & white, all their bags left behind,
They rise upon clouds, and sport in the wind.
And the Angel told Tom, if he'd be a good boy,
20   He'd have God for his father & never want joy.

And so Tom awoke; and we rose in the dark
And got with our bags & our brushes to work.
Tho' the morning was cold, Tom was happy & warm;
So if all do their duty, they need not fear harm.

3 **'weep! 'weep!:** the child's attempt to say "Sweep! Sweep!" —a chimney sweeper's street cry.

UNDERSTAND HISTORICAL BACKGROUND

Annotate: Mark details in lines 1–12 that relate to the historical context of the poem.

Infer: What can you infer from these details about social conditions in late 18th-century Britain?

18 **sport:** play or frolic.

20 **want:** lack.

ESSENTIAL QUESTION:
What stirs your imagination?

Review your notes and add your thoughts to your Response Log.

COLLABORATIVE DISCUSSION

Which image from the poems best conveys innocence? Discuss your ideas with a partner.

Title page of *Songs of Innocence*, engraved and hand-printed by William Blake in 1789

Assessment Practice

Answer these questions about "The Chimney Sweeper" before moving on to the next selection.

1. In "The Chimney Sweeper," the speaker knows Tom Dacre because —

   (A) they go to the same school

   (B) they are brothers

   (C) they work together

   (D) Tom appeared in a dream

2. Why does Tom cry in "The Chimney Sweeper"?

   (A) His hair is shaved off.

   (B) His hair becomes dirty.

   (C) His father sells him.

   (D) He sees boys in coffins.

3. Tom is "happy & warm" in the morning because he —

   (A) had a good night's sleep

   (B) worked over a warm fireplace

   (C) was allowed to miss work

   (D) dreamed of an angel comforting him

Test-Taking Strategies

from

Songs of Experience

Poems by **William Blake**

N NOTICE & NOTE

As you read, use the side margins to make notes about the text.

As you read, think about how each poem expresses ideas about experience and contrasts with the corresponding poems about innocence that you've read.

The Tyger

Tyger! Tyger! burning bright
In the forests of the night,
What immortal hand or eye
Could frame thy fearful symmetry?

5   In what distant deeps or skies
Burnt the fire of thine eyes?
On what wings dare he aspire?
What the hand dare seize the fire?

And what shoulder, & what art,
10   Could twist the sinews of thy heart?
And when thy heart began to beat,
What dread hand? & what dread feet?

What the hammer? what the chain?
In what furnace was thy brain?
15   What the anvil? what dread grasp
Dare its deadly terrors clasp?

4 symmetry (sĭm´ĭ-trē): balance or beauty of form.

7 he: the tiger's creator.

ANALYZE SYMBOLS

Annotate: Mark details in lines 1–12 that describe the tiger.

Analyze: What symbolic meaning is suggested by these details?

15 anvil (ăn´vĭl): iron block on which metal objects are hammered into shape.

When the stars threw down their spears
And watered heaven with their tears,
Did he smile his work to see?
20   Did he who made the Lamb make thee?

Tyger! Tyger! burning bright
In the forests of the night,
What immortal hand or eye
Dare frame thy fearful symmetry?

NOTICE & NOTE
TOUGH QUESTIONS

When you notice the speaker in a poem asking questions that reveal their internal struggles, you've found a **Tough Questions** signpost.

Notice & Note: Mark each question in the last three stanzas of the poem.

Draw Conclusions: Why does the poem consist of so many questions?

Assessment Practice

Answer these questions about "The Tyger" before moving on to the next selection.

1. What does the "immortal hand or eye" in "The Tyger" refer to?

(A) God

(B) death

(C) mankind

(D) nature

2. Which aspect of nature does Blake associate with the tiger?

(A) wind

(B) air

(C) water

(D) fire

3. The lines "What the anvil? what dread grasp / Dare its deadly terrors clasp?" express —

(A) pity for the animals devoured by the tiger

(B) fear that the tiger cannot be controlled

(C) awe for the creator of such a terrifying creature

(D) suspicion that the tiger is not real

Test-Taking Strategies

The Chimney Sweeper

A little black thing among the snow
Crying "'weep, 'weep," in notes of woe!
"Where are thy father & mother? say?"
"They are both gone up to the church to pray.

5 "Because I was happy upon the heath,
And smil'd among the winter's snow;
They clothed me in the clothes of death,
And taught me to sing the notes of woe.

   "And because I am happy, & dance & sing,
10 They think they have done me no injury,
And are gone to praise God & his Priest & King,
Who make up a heaven of our misery."

Houghton Mifflin Harcourt Publishing Company • Image Credits: ©Artokoloro Quint Lox Limited/Alamy

2 'weep, 'weep: the child's attempt to say "Sweep, Sweep"—a chimney sweeper's street cry.

5 heath: a tract of open land that cannot be farmed.

UNDERSTAND HISTORICAL BACKGROUND

Annotate: Mark details in lines 5–12 that help create the tone of "The Chimney Sweeper."

Infer: Identify the tone of this poem. What does it suggest about British society?

ESSENTIAL QUESTION:
What stirs your imagination?

Review your notes and add your thoughts to your Response Log.

COLLABORATIVE DISCUSSION

How do the poems you've read reflect Blake's interest in "the two contrary states of the human soul"? Discuss your ideas with a partner.

Title page of *Songs of Experience*, engraved and hand-printed by William Blake in 1794

Assessment Practice

Answer these questions about "The Chimney Sweeper" before moving on to the **Analyze the Texts** section on the following page.

1. What is the "black thing" Blake refers to in "The Chimney Sweeper"?

- (A) a child
- (B) a piece of coal
- (C) a chimney
- (D) soot-coated snow

2. Why don't the parents of the chimney sweeper see that he is being harmed by his work?

- (A) He lies to them.
- (B) He keeps up a cheerful appearance.
- (C) He has run away from them.
- (D) He praises God for his job.

3. In "The Chimney Sweeper," what does the phrase "make up a heaven of our misery" suggest?

- (A) The church and the king profit from his sweeping.
- (B) The priest and the king also suffer.
- (C) His parents will be rewarded in heaven.
- (D) His parents' religion glorifies suffering.

Test-Taking Strategies

Analyze the Texts

Support your responses with evidence from the texts.

1 IDENTIFY Notice the words, phrases, and lines that Blake repeats in "The Lamb." What mood does this repetition help create?

2 INTERPRET In "The Tyger," the speaker describes the animal as "fearful" and "deadly." Do the negative connotations of this language suggest that the tiger should never have been created? Explain.

3 DRAW CONCLUSIONS In "The Tyger," Blake uses words such as *art, hammer, furnace,* and *anvil* to describe the tiger's creation, as if the animal were a metal sculpture. What does this symbolic meaning of the tiger suggest about Blake's view of art?

4 ANALYZE How do you think the voice of the speaker in "The Lamb" is different from the voice of the speaker in "The Tyger"? Why do you think the questions in "The Lamb" get answers, while the **Tough Questions** in "The Tyger" do not?

5 COMPARE How does Tom Dacre's dream compare and contrast with the actual conditions of his daily life? Complete the Venn diagram with details.

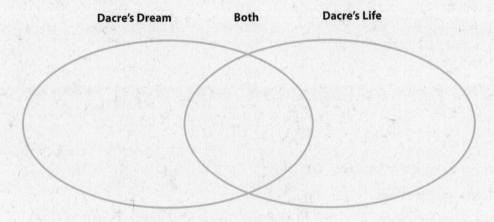

Dacre's Dream   Both   Dacre's Life

6 ANALYZE Describe Blake's use of the colors white and black in "The Chimney Sweeper" poems. What do these colors symbolize?

7 DRAW CONCLUSIONS In "The Chimney Sweeper" poems, the speakers have two sharply contrasting perspectives on religion. Considered together, what do both poems suggest about Blake's view of the religious establishment of his time? Explain.

Choices

Here are some others ways to demonstrate your understanding of the ideas in this lesson.

Writing
↳ ## Write a Reflective Essay

Do people today sometimes take the attitude expressed by the speaker of the version of "The Chimney Sweeper" from *Songs of Innocence*: "So if all do their duty, they need not fear harm"? Write a reflection on whether this sentiment is true. What true or fictional stories do you think relate to this idea?

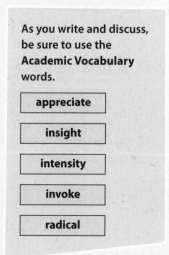

As you write and discuss, be sure to use the **Academic Vocabulary** words.

| appreciate |
| insight |
| intensity |
| invoke |
| radical |

Speaking & Listening
↳ ## Share Your Symbols

If you had to choose your own symbols for the qualities represented by Blake's lamb and tiger, what would they be? Discuss your ideas in a small group and then present them to the class.

- As a group, review "The Lamb" and "The Tyger." Discuss what qualities the lamb and the tiger represent to Blake.

- Discuss ideas for other symbols that represent these qualities.

- Plan your presentation. Focus on determining roles for your team. You might choose a spokesperson for each symbol and have a third member present visuals.

- Present your symbols to the class.

Social & Emotional Learning
↳ ## Create a Podcast

As you can tell by reading "The Chimney Sweeper," William Blake was profoundly disturbed by the use of children to do dangerous work. Unfortunately, this practice is still present in some societies throughout the world today. Create a podcast in which you discuss the injustice of child labor.

- Conduct research on child labor in contemporary times. Where and why is child labor utilized?

- Clearly define the problem and delineate the reasons why child labor is unjust.

- What can be done to discourage this practice? Include a call to action so that listeners can help prevent this injustice.

Compare Poems

Compare and contrast the perspectives of the poems from *Songs of Innocence* and *Songs of Experience*, using the following criteria:

- **Word choice:** Look for descriptive words and note how they are used to emphasize characteristics of a subject.

- **Ideas:** Identify common or contrasting ideas expressed in the poems.

- **Tone:** Notice the speaker's attitude toward the subject.

As you read, you may use a chart like this one to record similarities and differences between each linked pair of poems.

A	"The Lamb"	B "The Tyger"
Word Choice		
Ideas		
Tone		

Analyze the Texts

Discuss these questions in your group.

1. **COMPARE** "The Lamb" and "The Tyger" develop around questions posed at the beginning of each poem. How do the speakers' different responses to these questions reflect the contrast between innocence and experience?

2. **CRITIQUE** Does Blake use symbols effectively to help convey his themes? Why or why not?

3. **INTERPRET** Is Blake's view of innocence and experience essentially the same as the idea of good versus evil? Explain your response.

4. **DRAW CONCLUSIONS** Do these poems suggest that innocence is better than experience? Explain your response.

Collaborate and Present

With your group, continue exploring the ideas in the poems by identifying and comparing word choice, symbols, and themes. Follow these steps:

1. **DECIDE ON THE MOST IMPORTANT DETAILS** What words or phrases stood out the most to you? What symbols help convey the theme? Come to a consensus with your group.

2. **DETERMINE A MESSAGE FOR EACH POEM** Use a chart to keep track of the important details your group members identify in each poem. Then, use these details to come up with a message for each poem.

	Details	Message
Songs of Innocence		
Songs of Experience		

3. **COMPARE IDEAS** With your group, compare the ideas in the poems and discuss whether the messages are similar or different. Listen actively to the members of your group and ask them to clarify any points you do not understand.

4. **PRESENT TO THE CLASS** Be sure to include clear statements on the theme for each poem. Discuss whether the messages are similar or different.

Reader's Choice

Continue your exploration of the Essential Questions for this unit by doing some independent reading. Read the titles and descriptions shown. Then mark the texts that interest you.

ESSENTIAL QUESTIONS:
Review the four Essential Questions for this unit on page 515.

Short Reads   Available on

These texts are available in your ebook. Choose one to read and rate. Then defend your rating to the class.

William Blake: Visions and Verses

Explanatory Essay by Rachel Galvin

William Blake was considered eccentric during his life, but he is now hailed as a creative visionary.

Rate It

Frost at Midnight

Poem by Samuel Taylor Coleridge

A father recalls his childhood and expresses hope for his son's future.

Rate It

Walking with Wordsworth

Personal Narrative by Bruce Stutz

A naturalist explores Wordsworth's beloved Lake District.

Rate It

from A Defense of Poetry

Argument by Percy Bysshe Shelley

Shelley argues that poetry has a special role in literature and society.

Rate It

The Skylark

Poem by John Clare

This poem reflects on flight, freedom, and the resourcefulness of animals.

Rate It

Long Reads

Here are a few books that connect to this unit. For additional options, ask your teacher, school librarian, or peers. Which titles spark your interest?

Frankenstein

Novel by **Mary Shelley**

After creating an artificial man, Victor Frankenstein rejects the creature. But he cannot escape the consequences of his scientific experiment.

The Sun Is Also a Star

Novel by **Nicola Yoon**

Natasha—a Jamaican girl whose family is facing deportation—loves science and facts. Daniel, a Korean American, is a poet at heart and believes in true love. Their paths cross just as they face huge changes in their lives. Is it fate?

The Stranger in the Woods

Nonfiction by **Michael Finkel**

This true story documents the solitary life of Christopher Knight. Knight lived in a tent in the Maine woods for 27 years and survived by stealing supplies from nearby cabins.

Extension
↳ **Collaborate & Create**

EMOTION AND EXPERIMENTATION Think about the title of this unit. Are emotions and experiments connected in some way, or are they unrelated concepts? How do these words relate to the text you read? Discuss these questions with a partner.

BOOK REVIEW Write a review of the book you read. Include the following in your review:

- a brief summary of the book
- discussion of its strengths and weaknesses
- personal reactions to the main characters or people profiled in the book
- quotations from the book to support your ideas

 NOTICE AND NOTE

- Pick one of the texts and annotate the Notice & Note signposts you find.
- Then use the **Notice & Note Writing Frames** to help you write about the significance of the signposts.
- Compare your findings with those of other students who read the same text.

Notice & Note Writing Frames

© Houghton Mifflin Harcourt Publishing Company • Image Credits: (l) ©Nomad_Soul/Fotolia; (c) ©oneinchpunch/Shutterstock; (r) ©AVTG/iStockPhoto.com

Write an Explanatory Essay

Writing Prompt

Using information from texts in this unit, write an explanatory essay for your school newspaper about the relationship between humans and nature.

Manage your time carefully so that you can

- review the texts in the unit;
- plan your essay;
- write your essay; and
- revise and edit your essay.

Be sure to

- state and develop a thesis;
- present your ideas in an organized way;
- support ideas with details from your reading; and
- write a conclusion that follows from your essay.

Review the
Mentor Text

For an example of an explanatory essay you can use as a mentor text and a source for your essay, review

- **"Frankenstein: Giving Voice to the Monster"** (pages 563–567)

Make sure you carefully review your notes and annotations about this text. Think about the techniques the author used to explain the relevance of Mary Shelley's novel *Frankenstein*.

Consider Your Sources

Review the list of texts in the unit and choose at least three that you may want to use for your explanatory essay.

As you review the potential sources, consult the notes you made in your **Response Log** that relate to the question "What can nature offer us?" Make additional notes about ideas that might help you write your essay. Include source titles and page numbers in your notes to help you provide accurate text evidence and citations.

UNIT 4 SOURCES

- [ ] **"Lines Composed a Few Miles Above Tintern Abbey"**
- [ ] **"Composed upon Westminster Bridge, September 3, 1802"**
- [ ] **"I Wandered Lonely As a Cloud"**
- [ ] **"Ode on a Grecian Urn"**
- [ ] from **Frankenstein**
- [ ] **"Frankenstein: Giving Voice to the Monster"**
- [ ] **"Ode to the West Wind"**
- [ ] **"Ode to My Mother's Hair"**
- [ ] from **Songs of Innocence**
- [ ] from **Songs of Experience**

Analyze the Prompt

Review the prompt to make sure you understand the assignment.

1. Mark the sentence in the prompt that identifies the topic of your explanatory essay. Rephrase this sentence in your own words.

2. Write sentences identifying the purpose and audience for your essay.

Find a Purpose

Two common purposes of an explanatory essay are

- to **explain** a topic
- to **analyze** information or ideas

What is my topic? What is my writing task?

_____

What is my purpose?

_____

Who is my audience?

_____

Review the Rubric

Your explanatory essay will be scored using a rubric. As you write, focus on the characteristics of a high-scoring essay as described in the chart. You will learn more about these characteristics as you work through the lesson.

Purpose, Focus, and Organization	Evidence and Elaboration	Conventions of Standard English
The response includes: • A strongly maintained controlling idea • Use of transitions to connect ideas • Logical progression of ideas • Appropriate style and tone	The response includes: • Effective use of evidence and sources • Effective use of elaboration • Clear and effective expression of ideas • Appropriate vocabulary • Varied sentence structure	The response may include: • Some minor errors in usage but no patterns of errors • Correct punctuation, capitalization, sentence formation, and spelling • Command of basic conventions

1 PLAN YOUR EXPLANATORY ESSAY

Develop Your Thesis

To develop your **thesis,** review your notes on the Unit 4 texts.

- Look for ideas about **the relationship between humans and nature**.

- Decide on an idea for your **thesis.** What do you want readers to know about your topic?

Thesis Statements

Your **thesis statement** sums up your thinking about the topic. It is the **controlling idea** of your explanatory essay.

Topic	Thesis
the relationship between humans and nature	

Identify Details

To support your thesis, present key ideas with relevant supporting details.

- A **key idea** is your opinion, observation, or claim.
- **Supporting details** are facts, definitions, quotations, and examples from your sources.

In the chart, restate your thesis and identify key ideas and supporting details. Record the title, author, and page number for each detail.

Thesis	
Key Ideas	
Supporting Details	

© Houghton Mifflin Harcourt Publishing Company

Reflect on Your Ideas

In addition to a thesis at the beginning, your essay also needs a conclusion. In your conclusion, include a **reflection** that

- engages readers by sharing intriguing final thoughts on the topic, or
- raises a question as "food for thought."

Review your notes and use them to help you craft a thought-provoking conclusion.

Help with Planning

Consult **Interactive Writing Lesson: Writing Informative Texts.**

My Reflection

Organize Ideas

To develop a **coherent** essay, organize your key ideas and supporting details in a logical way.

Use transitions to

- **identify connections** between the thesis and key ideas, and
- **clarify the relationship** between key ideas and supporting details.

INTRODUCTION	• Introduce your topic and state the thesis. • Engage readers with an interesting fact or detail.
BODY PARAGRAPHS	• Present key ideas and details to support your thesis. • Devote a paragraph to each idea. • Use transitions to reveal the progression of ideas.
CONCLUSION	• Restate your thesis and its significance. • End with a reflection or an intriguing thought.

Structure Your Essay

Here are two suggestions for adding structure to your essay:

- To grab your reader's attention, **begin with the most important idea** and move to the least important.
- To leave a strong impression on your reader, begin with the second most important idea and **conclude with your most important idea.**

2 DEVELOP A DRAFT

Now it is time to draft your essay. Take a look at how professional authors craft effective explanatory essays. Try to use similar techniques in your own writing.

Provide Supporting Details

EXAMINE THE MENTOR TEXT

Notice how the author of "Frankenstein: Giving Voice to the Monster" begins the essay on page 563 with an observation that he supports with details.

Frankenstein:
Giving Voice to
the Monster

The author's **thesis**:
Humans have long been
interested in creating
artificial life.

The possibility that artificial creatures, products of human hands, might achieve sentience and take on an active role in society is an age-old conception in world cultures, the subject of myths, stories, moral fables, and philosophical speculation.

In Greek mythology one finds the tale of Pygmalion who carves a statue named Galatea with whom he falls in love and who eventually comes to life. In Jewish folklore there are stories of the Golem, an artificial creature animated with surprising results.

Two **examples**
support the thesis.

Try It Out

To build support for your ideas:

- State an **observation or opinion**.
- Support it with **details**.
- **Cite the sources** of the details.
- Provide **transitions** between key ideas and details.

APPLY TO YOUR DRAFT

Use this frame to identify your thesis or one of your key ideas. Then provide relevant details to support it.

Thesis or Key Idea	
Supporting Detail #1	
Supporting Detail #2	

Introduce Quotations

To support a key idea or thesis, experts use textual evidence: details, ideas, paraphrases, or quotations from the text.

EXAMINE THE MENTOR TEXT

On page 566 of the essay "Frankenstein: Giving Voice to the Monster," the author introduces a quotation by giving its author and its source and adds some information about the quotation's relevance.

Drafting Online

Check your assignment list for a writing task from your teacher.

The writer introduces the **source** of the quotation.

> In a BBC interview, Stephen Hawking warned, "The development of full artificial intelligence could spell the end of the human race. . . . Humans, limited by slow biological evolution, couldn't compete and would be superseded by AI. . . ."

The quotation **explains** and **elaborates** on the key idea that AI research is risky.

Introduce Your Quotations

Vary the way you integrate quotations into your essay. Here are some ideas:

- In [source], the author states . . .
- According to [paragraph/author] . . .
- The research shows . . .
- As [author/speaker/character] says in [paragraph/line] . . .

APPLY TO YOUR DRAFT

Use this chart to practice selecting quotations to support each of your key ideas.

Introduce

State a reason for using a quotation.

Cite

Identify the name and the source. Include line and paragraph numbers if applicable.

Elaborate

Explain how the quotation supports your key idea.

Write an Explanatory Essay   **611**

3 REVISE YOUR EXPLANATORY ESSAY

Professional writers rework their ideas and language as they revise. Use the guide to help you revise your explanatory essay.

 Ed

Help with Revision

Find a **Peer Review Guide** and **Student Models** online.

REVISION GUIDE

Ask Yourself	Prove It	Revise It
Thesis Does my first paragraph introduce the topic and my thesis in an engaging way?	**Underline** your thesis.	**Add** a surprising observation or arresting quotation. **Reword** or **add** a sentence to introduce the topic and thesis more clearly.
Support Do I develop my thesis with key ideas?	**Underline** sentences that state your key ideas.	**Review** your notes for additional key ideas. **Add** sentences stating key ideas.
Evidence Do I provide at least two details to support each of my key ideas?	Place a **star** (★) next to each sentence containing a supporting detail.	**Add** supporting details from your notes, including examples, facts, and quotations.
Transitions Do I use transitions to link ideas and paragraphs?	Circle the transition words and phrases in your essay.	**Add** transition words and phrases to connect ideas.
Conclusion Does my conclusion restate my thesis and end with an intriguing idea?	**Highlight** the parts of your conclusion that support your thesis and key ideas. **Underline** your intriguing thought.	**Add** or **revise** the conclusion to make sure it supports the information in your essay and leaves the reader with "food for thought."

APPLY TO YOUR DRAFT

Reread your explanatory essay and look for opportunities to improve your writing.

- Consider your use of transitions to connect ideas and show the structure of your essay.
- Avoid the use of informal language.
- Make sure your essay concludes with a reflection that engages your readers.

Peer Review in Action

Once you have finished revising your explanatory essay, you will exchange papers with a partner in a **peer review.** During a peer review you will give suggestions to improve your partner's draft.

Read this conclusion from a student's draft, and examine the comments made by her peer reviewer.

First Draft

From Screens to Leaves of Green
By Leslie Kornfield, Derry Township High School

For centuries, people have interacted with nature. I think nature's a balm for the human race. Based on literature and scientific reports, it's clear that when people go outdoors to experience nature firsthand, their mental health and overall sense of well-being improve. It's also a fact that they have a better understanding of their place in the universe. What's not to love about nature?

Use a stronger "food for thought" sentence for your conclusion. Avoid overused ideas.

Is this the conclusion? Needs a transition. Avoid using "I" and contractions—too informal.

Now read the revised conclusion. Notice how the writer has improved her draft by making revisions based on the peer reviewer's comments.

Revision

From Screens to Leaves of Green
By Leslie Kornfield, Derry Township High School

In conclusion, it is clear that when people take time away from their screens to go outdoors and experience nature, their mental health and overall happiness improve. As literature and scientific reports show, nature is a balm for the human soul. Yet, as cities grow and nature succumbs to devastating disasters like hurricanes and forest fires, how much nature will we have left to savor? If nature becomes a rarified thing, will we all end up staring at screens with pictures of natural settings that are gone forever?

Nice job of adding transitions to show relationships between the ideas.

You added a reflection that will get readers thinking. Great!

APPLY TO YOUR DRAFT

During your peer review, give each other specific suggestions for how you could make your explanatory essay more effective. Use your revision guide to help you.

When receiving feedback from your partner, listen attentively and ask questions to make sure you fully understand the revision suggestions.

4 EDIT YOUR EXPLANATORY ESSAY

Edit your final draft to check for proper use of Standard English conventions and to correct any misspellings or grammatical errors.

 Ed

Interactive Grammar Lesson: Appositives and Appositive Phrases

Watch Your Language!

USE APPOSITIVE PHRASES

An **appositive** is a noun or pronoun that identifies, or renames, another noun or pronoun. An **appositive phrase** is made up of an appositive plus its modifiers. Writers often use appositive phrases to add important details without being wordy.

Read the following sentence from "Frankenstein: Giving Voice to the Monster":

> The possibility that artificial creatures, **products of human hands,** might achieve sentience and take on an active role in society is an age-old conception in world cultures, the subject of myths, stories, moral fables, and philosophical speculation.

The author uses the appositive phrase *products of human hands* to clarify what he means by *artificial creatures* without having to add another sentence.

APPLY TO YOUR DRAFT

Now apply what you've learned about appositive phrases to your own writing.

1. **Read your essay aloud** and circle phrases that identify or provide additional information about a word or phrase in a previous sentence.

2. **Add an appositive phrase** to the previous sentence where appropriate so that you can eliminate the second sentence and avoid wordiness.

3. **Exchange drafts** with a peer and review opportunities for adding appositive phrases in each other's work.

5 PUBLISH YOUR EXPLANATORY ESSAY

Share It!

Format your explanatory essay for publication in your school newspaper. You may also use your essay as inspiration for other projects.

Ways to Share

- **Create a podcast** for students to listen to and respond.

- **Write a documentary film script** based on your essay and film the movie.

- **Make a nature journal** that includes essays from your class as well as art and photographs.

Reflect & Extend

Here are some other ways to show your understanding of the ideas in Unit 4.

Reflect on the Essential Questions

Think about the Essential Question you identified as most intriguing on page 516. Has your answer to the question changed after reading the texts in the unit? Discuss your ideas.

You can use these sentence starters to help you reflect on your learning.

- **My thoughts on the question changed because . . .**
- **I was surprised by . . .**
- **I would like to find out more about . . .**

Project-Based Learning
↳ Create a Photo Essay

Many Romantic works celebrate the beauty of the natural world. Others bemoan the ugliness caused by industrialization. Create a photo essay exploring the contrast between natural beauty and aspects of human life. Follow these steps:

1. Plan your essay by identifying the message you'd like to communicate, choosing a quotation from one of the unit texts, and picking specific images to photograph.
2. Shoot contrasting images, or find images online or in print that will convey your message.
3. Edit your essay and add the quotation. Then share your work in a print or digital display.

Media Projects

To find help with this task online, access **Create a Photo Essay.**

Writing
↳ Write an Argument

Romantics valued individual experience and acceptance of change over reason and tradition. Write an argument about whether this view the world is applicable to the world today. Review texts in the unit and other sources for evidence that supports your view. Be sure to address and refute an opposing claim. Use the chart to take notes before you write your argument.

Ask Yourself	My Notes
What is my claim?	
What evidence supports my claim?	
What opposing claim will I include? How will I refute the opposing claim?	

"The history of England is emphatically the history of progress."
—Thomas Babington Macaulay

The Victorians

An Era of Rapid Change

? As you read the texts in this unit, think about how they explore these **Essential Questions.**

What is a true benefactor?
In Victorian England, there was a wide gap between the haves and the have-nots. Some wealthy people took action to help the poor, but they weren't always motivated by kindness.

How do you view the world?
Although many Victorians embraced new ideas about religion and science, others viewed these changes with dread and looked to the past for comfort.

What brings out cruelty in people?
Victorian readers, like readers today, were often fascinated by cruel, weird, or dangerous literary characters.

Which invention has had the greatest impact on your life?
Technology transformed British life in the 19th century, allowing people to travel and communicate at a speed never imagined before.

ANALYZE THE IMAGE
Which details in this image show developments in transportation and communication? Which details suggest an older way of life?

Explore unit themes and build background.
Stream to Start Video

© Houghton Mifflin Harcourt Publishing Company

617

Spark Your Learning

Here are some opportunities to think about issues related to **Unit 5: An Era of Rapid Change.**

As you read, you can use the **Response Log** (page R5) to track your thinking about the Essential Questions.

?

Think About the **Essential Questions**

Review the Essential Questions on page 617. Which question is most intriguing to you? Perhaps it relates to something you have read or reminds you of a personal experience. Write down your thoughts.

Make the Connection

Think about whether we live in a time of rapid change. What are the most memorable changes in your lifetime? Have these changes made your life significantly better or worse? Discuss your thoughts with a partner.

Prove It!
Use one of the Academic Vocabulary words in a sentence about how people feel about technology today.

Build Academic Vocabulary

You can use these Academic Vocabulary words to write and talk about the topics and themes in the unit. Which of these words do you already feel comfortable using when speaking or writing?

	I can use it!	I understand it.	I'll look it up.
abandon	☐	☐	☐
confine	☐	☐	☐
conform	☐	☐	☐
depress	☐	☐	☐
reluctance	☐	☐	☐

Preview the Texts

Review the images, titles, and descriptions of the texts in the unit. Mark the title of the text that interests you most.

from **Jane Eyre**

Novel by **Charlotte Brontë**

A young girl adjusts to life in a boarding school for poor orphans.

Factory Reform

Documentary by **Timelines.tv**

Learn about a Victorian employer who led a movement to improve working conditions in British industry.

The Lady of Shalott

Narrative Poem by **Alfred, Lord Tennyson**

A beautiful woman, confined to solitude in a tower due to a curse, takes a risk for love.

from **Great Expectations**

Novel by **Charles Dickens**

Pip, an orphan, is brought into a strange, dark house where he meets an equally strange woman.

The Victorians Had the Same Concerns About Technology As We Do

Essay by **Melissa Dickson**

Fears about the harmful effects of new technology are nothing new.

Dover Beach

Poem by **Matthew Arnold**

Waves crashing upon the beach at night bring more than just a sound—they tell a story.

The Darkling Thrush

Poem by **Thomas Hardy**

A man observes a bleak landscape, but the singing of a small bird gives him pause and, perhaps, hope.

My Last Duchess

Poem by **Robert Browning**

A duke tells the disturbing story behind a portrait on his wall.

Blood

Poem by **Natasha Trethewey**

The speaker reflects on how racial identity is represented in a 19th-century painting of field workers.

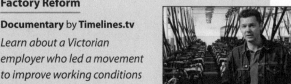

An Era of Rapid Change

"The sun never sets on the British Empire," boasted the Victorians. Around the globe, it was always daytime in some part of the vast territory ruled by Great Britain. During the reign of Queen Victoria, Britain was at the height of its power. Abroad, Britain dominated world politics. At home, the Industrial Revolution was in full swing. For the wealthy, the Victorian era was a time of economic prosperity, but for the working class, life was marked by poverty and hardship, leading many writers to criticize the injustices resulting from rapid industrialization.

A Modern Monarchy

Queen Victoria was just 18 years old when she came to the throne in 1837. She went on to rule for more than 60 years, longer than any English ruler before her. Victoria's devotion to hard work and duty, her insistence on proper behavior, and her support of British imperialism became the hallmarks of the Victorian period.

Victoria knew that previous monarchs had clashed with Parliament, and she realized that the role of royalty had to change. She accepted the concept of a constitutional monarchy in which she gave advice rather

1837
Victoria becomes Queen of Great Britain.

1842
Britain gains control of Hong Kong.

1847
Charlotte Brontë publishes *Jane Eyre*; Emily Brontë publishes *Wuthering Heights*.

1859
Charles Darwin publishes *On the Origin of Species*.

1835

1844
Samuel Morse sends the first long-distance telegraph message.

1845
The Irish Potato Famine begins.

1860
Charles Dickens publishes the first magazine installment of *Great Expectations*.

1861
Prince Albert dies.

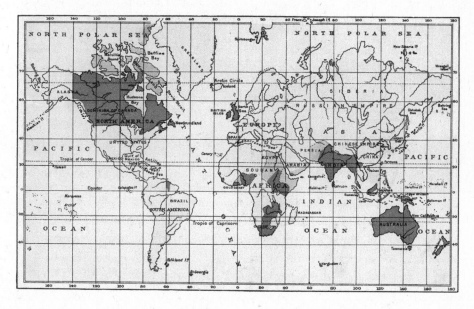

Areas in red show the British Empire in 1880.

than orders, and yielded control of day-to-day governmental affairs to a series of very talented prime ministers. When the queen withdrew from politics after the death of her beloved husband, Prince Albert, the position of prime minister became even more important.

The Price of Progress

The Industrial Revolution had already transformed Britain into a modern industrial state by the time Victoria took the throne. By 1850, England boasted 18,000 cotton mills and produced half of the world's iron. Progress also brought new inventions, such as the telephone, light bulb, radio, and automobile, and advances in science and medicine.

1874
Alexander Graham Bell develops the telephone.

1883
Robert Louis Stevenson publishes the adventure novel *Treasure Island*.

1893
Henry Ford develops the gasoline-powered automobile.

1905

1867
The Second Reform Act extends voting rights to workingmen.

1876
Queen Victoria gains the title Empress of India.

1884
The Third Reform Act allows nearly all adult males to vote.

1901
Queen Victoria dies after nearly 64 years of rule.

Houghton Mifflin Harcourt Publishing Company • Image Credits: (t) ©Chronicle/Alamy; (b) ©De Luan/Alamy

British political leader Benjamin Disraeli introduces the Second Reform Act in Parliament.

Applicants for Admission to a Casual Ward by Luke Fildes depicts people waiting to be allowed into a workhouse.

Some writers expressed enthusiasm for the material advantages afforded by the industrial age. Others were appalled by the materialism of the Victorian upper and middle classes—an attitude they considered tasteless, joyless, and destructive of community.

While the middle class grew more prosperous, conditions for the poor became intolerable. Factory workers, including many children, spent long hours toiling for low wages under harsh and dangerous conditions. In the 1840s, unemployment soared in England, and the Great Famine devastated Ireland. Families without income and starving Irish immigrants crowded into England's already squalid slums.

Though Parliament enacted many important reforms during this period, change came slowly. The Great Reform Act of 1832 expanded suffrage, or the right to vote, to wealthy middle-class men. Before this law, only about 5 percent of Britain's population had the right to vote. In 1833, slavery was abolished in the British Empire, and the first laws restricting child labor were enacted. In the decades that followed, laws were passed establishing public schools, improving sanitation and housing, legalizing trade unions, easing harsh factory conditions, and giving working-class men the right to vote.

From Romanticism to Realism

Confronted with the harsh realities of the Victorian world, many poets followed the lead of the Romantics, focusing on idealized love and the awe-inspiring beauty of nature. But some poets, especially later in the century, addressed contemporary issues such as spiritual doubt and the loss of old customs, traditions, and values due to the pressures of industrialization and scientific discoveries.

While many poets retreated from modern life, novelists embraced the issues of the age. Victorian novels were weighty affairs, quite literally—so weighty that they typically had to be divided into three volumes. Keen-eyed, sharp-witted writers probed every corner of society—from the drawing room to the slums, exposing problems and pretensions. Victorian readers craved this realism. They wanted to meet characters like themselves and the people

© Houghton Mifflin Harcourt Publishing Company • Image Credits: ©Painters/Alamy

they knew; they wanted to learn more about their rapidly changing world. Families often spent evenings reading aloud to each other, laughing at the adventures of Charles Dickens's Mr. Pickwick and his oddball friends or sighing over Heathcliff and Catherine's doomed romance in Emily Brontë's *Wuthering Heights*. In the next century, modernist writers would pick up the torch from their Victorian predecessors and grapple with issues the Victorians could not have imagined.

COLLABORATIVE DISCUSSION

In a small group, review the essay and the timeline. Discuss which events had the greatest effects on everyday life for people in Victorian Britain.

Assessment Practice

Choose the best answer to each question.

1. Which **best** describes the British government during the Victorian era?
   - (A) Conflicts between Victoria and Parliament led to the weakening of the monarchy.
   - (B) Victoria and Parliament agreed to give primary authority to the prime minister.
   - (C) Victoria modified the role of the monarch and strengthened the position of the prime minister.
   - (D) Parliament took Victoria's retirement from politics as an opportunity to establish a constitutional monarchy.

2. The reforms enacted by Parliament primarily affected the lower classes by —
   - (A) increasing the oppression faced by factory workers
   - (B) slowly improving living and working conditions
   - (C) addressing the unemployment crisis that arose in the 1840s
   - (D) contributing to the development of slums

3. What topic in Victorian novels appealed most to readers?
   - (A) stories about ancient myths and legends
   - (B) celebrations of romantic love
   - (C) the awe-inspiring beauty of nature
   - (D) realistic portrayals of everyday people

Test-Taking Strategies

from
Jane Eyre

Novel by **Charlotte Brontë**

ESSENTIAL QUESTION:
What is a true benefactor?

Engage Your Brain

Choose one or more of these activities to start connecting with the text you're about to read.

Seasons of Change

Think about a time of transition you've experienced in your life, such as moving to a new neighborhood or changing schools. Share details about your experience with a partner. Consider these questions in your discussion:

- What were some obstacles you faced at the time?

- Who helped you get used to your new circumstances?

- How did you adjust to your life after the change?

Writing Under Another Name

Charlotte Brontë originally published her works under a pseudonym, or pen name, instead of her original name.

- Do some research to find out what her pseudonym was and why she used it.

- Discuss with a partner some reasons why a writer might choose to use a pseudonym today.

Pass the Burnt Porridge, Please

The food served at the school depicted in *Jane Eyre* does not sound appetizing. Would you eat "thin oaten cakes," burnt porridge, or potatoes with "shreds of rusty meat"?

Imagine you are a critic assigned to review the food in your school cafeteria. Write your own evaluation of the food, using colorful language and vivid details. Explain whether you'd recommend the food to others.

Analyze First-Person Point of View

Stories are told from a narrative perspective, or **point of view**. In *Jane Eyre*, the story is narrated in the **first-person** point of view. The narrator is the character Jane, who uses the personal pronouns *I*, *me*, and *my*. Readers experience everything through her eyes. Jane's thoughts and commentary convey the intensity of her feelings about the Lowood boarding school and its occupants.

As you read, notice how Charlotte Brontë's use of the first-person point of view affects what you learn about the novel's characters, events, setting, and themes.

Focus on Genre
↳ Novel
• is a long work of fiction
• is usually written in the first- or third-person point of view
• can develop characters and conflict more thoroughly than a short story
• often has a complex plot structure, including subplots

Analyze Setting

The **setting** of a novel is the time and place in which the action occurs. This excerpt from *Jane Eyre* is set in a boarding school for girls. During the Victorian period, hundreds of charity schools were established in Britain to provide free education, clothing, lodging, and meals for orphans and poor children. They were funded by contributions from wealthy donors. Some of the people who ran these schools were very idealistic and treated students well. However, many schools were led by harsh disciplinarians and offered only the most basic education. Schools for the poorest children were called "ragged schools," a name inspired by the children's shabby clothing.

As you read, notice how the setting is connected to the novel's plot, characterization, and themes. Use a chart like this one to record details that reveal the historical, economic, and social context of the setting.

Setting Details	Historical, Economic, and Social Context

Annotation in Action

Here is an example of notes a student made about first-person point of view in *Jane Eyre*. As you read, notice how you experience events through the narrator's eyes.

> The refectory was a great, low-ceiled, gloomy room; on two long tables smoked basins of something hot, which, however, to my dismay, sent forth an odor far from inviting. I saw a universal manifestation of discontent when the fumes of the repast met the nostrils of those destined to swallow it. . . .

The narrator uses a formal, restrained tone to describe the awful smell, which suggests she's describing it after time has passed.

Expand Your Vocabulary

Put a check mark next to the vocabulary words that you feel comfortable using when speaking or writing.

- ruddy
- indefatigable
- morose
- vogue
- commence

Then, turn to a partner and talk about why it is important to give help to those who need it. Use as many vocabulary words as you can in your discussion. As you read the excerpt from *Jane Eyre*, use the definitions in the side column to learn the vocabulary words that you don't already know.

Background

Charlotte Brontë (1816–1855) grew up in a rural area of England, the daughter of a clergyman and a mother who died when Charlotte was five. She worked as a governess and teacher before beginning her writing career. Her first book was a collection of poetry that she wrote with two of her sisters, Emily and Anne. *Jane Eyre*, originally published under a pseudonym, was her first novel. It blends the suspense and moody atmosphere of a Gothic novel with a realistic portrayal of the moral, social, and economic pressures faced by a Victorian woman who lacks family support.

from
Jane Eyre

Novel by **Charlotte Brontë**

Pay attention to how Jane reacts to conditions at school and the people she meets there.

NOTICE & NOTE
As you read, use the side margins to make notes about the text.

Orphaned as a young child, Jane Eyre has spent most of her childhood at Gateshead, the home of her wealthy yet heartless aunt, Mrs. Reed. At Gateshead, Jane is tormented by her cousins and repeatedly reminded of her low economic and social status. After a fight with one of her cousins, Jane's aunt decides to send her away to boarding school when she is 10 years old. As this excerpt begins, Jane has left Gateshead and is traveling by coach to the Lowood Institution, a boarding school for orphans and poor girls.

1   The afternoon came on wet and somewhat misty: as it waned into dusk, I began to feel that we were getting very far indeed from Gateshead: we ceased to pass through towns; the country changed; great grey hills heaved up round the horizon: as twilight deepened, we descended a valley, dark with wood, and long after night had overclouded the prospect, I heard a wild wind rushing amongst trees.

ANALYZE FIRST-PERSON
POINT OF VIEW

Annotate: In paragraph 4, mark details about what Jane sees after being lifted from the coach.

Analyze: How does this description give the impression that we see everything through Jane's eyes?

2   Lulled by the sound, I at last dropped asleep: I had not long slumbered when the sudden cessation of motion awoke me; the coach-door was open, and a person like a servant was standing at it: I saw her face and dress by the light of the lamps.

3   "Is there a little girl called Jane Eyre here?" she asked. I answered "Yes," and was then lifted out; my trunk was handed down, and the coach instantly drove away.

4   I was stiff with long sitting, and bewildered with the noise and motion of the coach: gathering my faculties, I looked about me. Rain, wind, and darkness filled the air; nevertheless, I dimly discerned a wall before me and a door open in it. Through this door I passed with my new guide: she shut and locked it behind her. There was now visible a house or houses—for the building spread far—with many windows, and lights burning in some; we went up a broad pebbly path, splashing wet, and were admitted at a door; then the servant led me through a passage into a room with a fire, where she left me alone.

5   I stood and warmed my numbed fingers over the blaze, then looked round; there was no candle, but the uncertain light from the hearth showed, by intervals, papered walls, carpet, curtains, shining mahogany furniture: it was a parlor, not so spacious or splendid as the drawing-room at Gateshead, but comfortable enough. I was puzzling to make out the subject of a picture on the wall, when the door opened, and an individual carrying a light entered; another followed close behind.

6   The first was a tall lady with dark hair, dark eyes, and a pale and large forehead; her figure was partly enveloped in a shawl, her countenance was grave, her bearing erect.

7   "The child is very young to be sent alone," said she, putting her candle down on the table. She considered me attentively for a minute or two, then further added—

8   "She had better be put to bed soon; she looks tired: are you tired?" she asked, placing her hand on my shoulder.

9   "A little, ma'am."

10   "And hungry too, no doubt: let her have some supper before she goes to bed, Miss Miller. Is this the first time you have left your parents to come to school, my little girl?"

11   I explained to her that I had no parents. She inquired how long they had been dead; then how old I was, what was my name, whether I could read, write, and sew a little: then she touched my cheek gently with her forefinger, and saying,

12   "She hoped I should be a good child," dismissed me along with Miss Miller.

13   The lady I had left might be about twenty-nine; the one who went with me appeared some years younger: the first impressed me by her voice, look, and air. Miss Miller was more ordinary; **ruddy** in complexion, though of a careworn countenance; hurried in gait and action, like one who had always a multiplicity of tasks on hand: she looked, indeed, what I afterwards found she really was, an under-teacher. Led by her, I passed from compartment to compartment,

ruddy
(rŭd´ē) *adj.* having a healthy, reddish glow.

from passage to passage, of a large and irregular building; till, emerging from the total and somewhat dreary silence pervading that portion of the house we had traversed, we came upon the hum of many voices, and presently entered a wide, long room, with great deal tables, two at each end, on each of which burnt a pair of candles, and seated all round on benches, a congregation of girls of every age, from nine or ten to twenty. Seen by the dim light of the dips, their number to me appeared countless, though not in reality exceeding eighty; they were uniformly dressed in brown stuff frocks of quaint fashion, and long holland pinafores. It was the hour of study; they were engaged in conning[1] over their tomorrow's task, and the hum I had heard was the combined result of their whispered repetitions.

14   Miss Miller signed to me to sit on a bench near the door, then walking up to the top of the long room, she cried out—

15   "Monitors, collect the lesson-books and put them away!"

16   Four tall girls arose from different tables, and going round, gathered the books and removed them. Miss Miller again gave the word of command—

17   "Monitors, fetch the supper-trays!"

18   The tall girls went out and returned presently, each bearing a tray, with portions of something, I knew not what, arranged thereon, and a pitcher of water and mug in the middle of each tray. The portions were handed round; those who liked took a draught of the water, the mug being common to all. When it came to my turn, I drank, for I was thirsty, but did not touch the food, excitement and fatigue rendering me incapable of eating: I now saw, however, that it was a thin oaten cake, shared into fragments.

19   The meal over, prayers were read by Miss Miller, and the classes filed off, two and two, upstairs. Overpowered by this time with weariness, I scarcely noticed what sort of a place the bedroom was; except that, like the schoolroom, I saw it was very long. Tonight I was to be Miss Miller's bed-fellow; she helped me to undress: when laid down I glanced at the long rows of beds, each of which was quickly filled with two occupants; in ten minutes the single light was extinguished; amid silence and complete darkness, I fell asleep.

20   The night passed rapidly: I was too tired even to dream; I only once awoke to hear the wind rave in furious gusts, and the rain fall in torrents, and to be sensible that Miss Miller had taken her place by my side. When I again unclosed my eyes, a loud bell was ringing: the girls were up and dressing; day had not yet begun to dawn, and a rushlight or two burnt in the room. I too rose reluctantly; it was bitter cold, and I dressed as well as I could for shivering, and washed when there was a basin at liberty, which did not occur soon, as there was but one basin to six girls, on the stands down the middle of the room. Again the bell rang: all formed in file, two and two, and in that order descended the stairs and entered the cold and dimly-lit schoolroom: here prayers were read by Miss Miller; afterwards she called out—

---

[1] **conning:** examining or studying.

ANALYZE SETTING

Annotate: Mark details in paragraph 18 about the supper.

Draw Conclusions: What does this description suggest about living conditions at Lowood?

© Houghton Mifflin Harcourt Publishing Company

"Form classes!"

A great tumult succeeded for some minutes, during which Miss Miller repeatedly exclaimed, "Silence!" and "Order!" When it subsided, I saw them all drawn up in four semi-circles, before four chairs, placed at the four tables; all held books in their hands, and a great book, like a Bible, lay on each table, before the vacant seat. A pause of some seconds succeeded, filled up by the low, vague hum of numbers; Miss Miller walked from class to class, hushing this indefinite sound.

A distant bell tinkled: immediately three ladies entered the room, each walked to a table and took her seat; Miss Miller assumed the fourth vacant chair, which was that nearest the door, and around which the smallest of the children were assembled: to this inferior class I was called, and placed at the bottom of it.

Business now began: the day's Collect was repeated, then certain texts of Scripture were said, and to these succeeded a protracted reading of chapters in the Bible, which lasted an hour. By the time that exercise was terminated, day had fully dawned. The **indefatigable** bell now sounded for the fourth time: the classes were marshalled and marched into another room to breakfast: how glad I was to behold a prospect of getting something to eat! I was now nearly sick from inanition, having taken so little the day before.

The refectory[2] was a great, low-ceiled, gloomy room; on two long tables smoked basins of something hot, which, however, to my dismay, sent forth an odor far from inviting. I saw a universal manifestation of discontent when the fumes of the repast met the nostrils of those destined to swallow it; from the van of the procession, the tall girls of the first class, rose the whispered words—

"Disgusting! The porridge is burnt again!"

"Silence!" ejaculated a voice; not that of Miss Miller, but one of the upper teachers, a little and dark personage, smartly dressed, but of somewhat **morose** aspect who installed herself at the top of one table, while a more buxom lady presided at the other. I looked in vain for her I had first seen the night before; she was not visible: Miss Miller occupied the foot of the table where I sat, and a strange, foreign looking, elderly lady, the French teacher, as I afterwards found, took the corresponding seat at the other board. A long grace was said and a hymn sung; then a servant brought in some tea for the teachers, and the meal began.

Ravenous, and now very faint, I devoured a spoonful or two of my portion without thinking of its taste; but the first edge of hunger blunted, I perceived I had got in hand a nauseous mess: burnt porridge is almost as bad as rotten potatoes; famine itself soon sickens over it. The spoons were moved slowly: I saw each girl taste her food and try to swallow it; but in most cases the effort was soon relinquished. Breakfast was over, and none had breakfasted. Thanks being returned for what we had not got, and a second hymn

---

[2] **refectory:** a room where meals are served in a school or an institution.

ANALYZE SETTING

Annotate: Mark details about books and reading in paragraphs 22–25.

Analyze: What does this passage reveal about education at Victorian charity schools?

indefatigable
(ĭn-dĭ-făt´ĭ-gə-bəl) *adj.* not tiring or relenting.

morose
(mə-rōs´, mô-) *adj.* sullen or gloomy.

chanted, the refectory was evacuated for the schoolroom. I was one of the last to go out, and in passing the tables, I saw one teacher take a basin of the porridge and taste it; she looked at the others; all their countenances expressed displeasure, and one of them, the stout one, whispered—

29 "Abominable stuff! How shameful!"

30 A quarter of an hour passed before lessons again began, during which the schoolroom was in a glorious tumult; for that space of time, it seemed to be permitted to talk loud and more freely, and they used their privilege. The whole conversation ran on the breakfast, which one and all abused roundly. Poor things! it was the sole consolation they had. Miss Miller was now the only teacher in the room: a group of great girls standing about her, spoke with serious and sullen gestures. I heard the name of Mr. Brocklehurst pronounced by some lips; at which Miss Miller shook her head disapprovingly; but she made no great effort to check the general wrath: doubtless she shared in it.

31 A clock in the schoolroom struck nine; Miss Miller left her circle, and standing in the middle of the room, cried—

32 "Silence! To your seats!"

33 Discipline prevailed: in five minutes the confused throng was resolved into order, and comparative silence quelled the Babel clamour of tongues. The upper teachers now punctually resumed their posts: but still, all seemed to wait. Ranged on benches down the sides of the room, the eighty girls sat motionless and erect: a quaint assemblage they appeared, all with plain locks combed from their faces, not a curl visible; in brown dresses, made high and surrounded by a narrow tucker about the throat, with little pockets of holland (shaped something like a Highlander's purse) tied in front of their frocks, and designed to serve the purpose of a work-bag: all too wearing woollen stockings and country-made shoes, fastened with brass buckles. Above twenty of those clad in this costume were full-grown girls, or rather young women; it suited them ill, and gave an air of oddity even to the prettiest.

34 I was still looking at them, and also at intervals examining the teachers—none of whom precisely pleased me; for the stout one was a little coarse, the dark one not a little fierce, the foreigner harsh and grotesque, and Miss Miller, poor thing! looked purple, weather-beaten, and over-worked—when, as my eye wandered from face to face, the whole school rose simultaneously, as if moved by a common spring.

35 What was the matter? I had heard no order given: I was puzzled. Ere I had gathered my wits, the classes were again seated: but as all eyes were now turned to one point, mine followed the general direction, and encountered the personage who had received me last night. She stood at the bottom of the long room, on the hearth; for there was a fire at each end: she surveyed the two rows of girls silently and gravely. Miss Miller approaching, seemed to ask her a question, and having received her answer, went back to her place, and said aloud—

Don't forget to **Notice & Note** as you read the text.

 NOTICE & NOTE
CONTRASTS AND CONTRADICTIONS

When you notice a sharp contrast between what you would expect and what a character actually does, you've found a **Contrasts and Contradictions** signpost.

Notice & Note: Mark statements in paragraph 28 that describe unexpected behavior by students in the school.

Infer: What do these statements suggest about how people are treated at the school?

ANALYZE FIRST-PERSON POINT OF VIEW

Annotate: Mark words and phrases in paragraph 37 that express Jane's admiration for Miss Temple.

Analyze: Which details reveal that Jane has spent time in fashionable society?

vogue
(vōg) *n.* the prevailing fashion, practice, or style.

36 "Monitor of the first class, fetch the globes!"

37 While the direction was being executed, the lady consulted moved slowly up the room. I suppose I have a considerable organ of Veneration, for I retain yet the sense of admiring awe with which my eyes traced her steps. Seen now, in broad daylight, she looked tall, fair, and shapely; brown eyes, with a benignant light in their irids, and a fine penciling of long lashes round, relieved the whiteness of her large front; on each of her temples her hair, of a very dark brown, was clustered in round curls, according to the fashion of those times, when neither smooth bands nor long ringlets were in **vogue**; her dress, also in the mode of the day, was of purple cloth, relieved by a sort of Spanish trimming of black velvet; a gold watch (watches were not so common then as now) shone at her girdle. Let the reader add,

to complete the picture, refined features; a complexion, if pale, clear; and a stately air and carriage, and he will have, at least, as clearly as words can give it, a correct idea of the exterior of Miss Temple— Maria Temple, as I afterwards saw the name written in a prayer-book entrusted to me to carry to church.

38   The superintendent of Lowood (for such was this lady) having taken her seat before a pair of globes placed on one of the tables, summoned the first class round her, and **commenced** giving a lesson in geography; the lower classes were called by the teachers: repetitions in history, grammar, etc., went on for an hour; writing and arithmetic succeeded, and music lessons were given by Miss Temple to some of the elder girls. The duration of each lesson was measured by the clock, which at last struck twelve. The superintendent rose—

39   "I have a word to address to the pupils," said she.

40   The tumult of cessation from lessons was already breaking forth, but it sank at her voice. She went on—

41   "You had this morning a breakfast which you could not eat; you must be hungry—I have ordered that a lunch of bread and cheese shall be served to all."

42   The teachers looked at her with a sort of surprise.

43   "It is to be done on my responsibility," she added, in an explanatory tone to them, and immediately afterwards left the room.

44   The bread and cheese was presently brought in and distributed, to the high delight and refreshment of the whole school. The order was now given "To the garden!" Each put on a coarse straw bonnet, with strings of colored calico, and a cloak of grey frieze. I was similarly equipped, and, following the stream, I made my way into the open air.

45   The garden was a wide enclosure, surrounded with walls so high as to exclude every glimpse of prospect: a covered verandah ran down one side, and broad walks bordered a middle space divided into scores of little beds: these beds were assigned as gardens for the pupils to cultivate, and each bed had an owner. When full of flowers they would doubtless look pretty; but now, at the latter end of January, all was wintry blight and brown decay. I shuddered as I stood and looked round me: it was an inclement day for outdoor exercise; not positively rainy, but darkened by a drizzling yellow fog; all underfoot was still soaking wet with the floods of yesterday. The stronger among the girls ran about and engaged in active games, but sundry pale and thin ones herded together for shelter and warmth in the verandah; and amongst these, as the dense mist penetrated to their shivering frames, I heard frequently the sound of a hollow cough.

Don't forget to
Notice & Note as you
read the text.

commence
(kə-mĕns´) v. to begin or start.

ANALYZE SETTING

Annotate: Mark details in paragraph 45 showing how the students feel about their exercise period.

Analyze: What does this description suggest about the school's attitude toward the students' well-being?

VOCABULARY

Use Context Clues: Mark words and phrases in paragraph 46 that hint at the meaning of the word *isolation*.

Analyze: What is your best guess at the meaning of *isolation*? Check your answer in a dictionary.

46 As yet I had spoken to no one, nor did anybody seem to take notice of me; I stood lonely enough: but to that feeling of isolation I was accustomed; it did not oppress me much. I leant against a pillar of the verandah, drew my grey mantle close about me, and, trying to forget the cold which nipped me without, and the unsatisfied hunger which gnawed me within, delivered myself up to the employment of watching and thinking. My reflections were too undefined and fragmentary to merit record: I hardly yet knew where I was; Gateshead and my past life seemed floated away to an immeasurable distance; the present was vague and strange, and of the future I could form no conjecture. I looked round the convent-like garden, and then up at the house; a large building, half of which seemed grey and old, the other half quite new. The new part, containing the schoolroom and dormitory, was lit by mullioned and latticed windows, which gave it a church-like aspect; a stone tablet over the door, bore this inscription—

47 "Lowood Institution.—This portion was rebuilt A.D.—, by Naomi Brocklehurst, of Brocklehurst Hall, in this county."

48 "Let your light so shine before men that they may see your good works, and glorify your Father which is in heaven."— St. Matt. v. 16.

49 I read these words over and over again: I felt that an explanation belonged to them, and was unable fully to penetrate their import. I was still pondering the signification of "Institution," and endeavoring to make out a connection between the first words and the verse of Scripture, when the sound of a cough close behind me, made me turn my head. I saw a girl sitting on a stone bench near; she had bent over a book, on the perusal of which she seemed intent: from where I stood I could see the title—it was "Rasselas;" a name that struck me as strange, and consequently attractive. In turning a leaf she happened to look up, and I said to her directly—

50 "Is your book interesting?" I had already formed the intention of asking her to lend it to me some day.

51 "I like it," she answered, after a pause of a second or two, during which she examined me.

52 "What is it about?" I continued. I hardly know where I found the hardihood thus to open a conversation with a stranger; the step was contrary to my nature and habits: but I think her occupation touched a chord of sympathy somewhere; for I too liked reading, though of a frivolous and childish kind; I could not digest or comprehend the serious or substantial.

53 "You may look at it," replied the girl, offering me the book.

54 I did so; a brief examination convinced me that the contents were less taking than the title: "Rasselas" looked dull to my trifling taste; I saw nothing about fairies, nothing about genii; no bright variety seemed spread over the closely-printed pages. I returned it to her; she received it quietly, and without saying anything she was about to relapse into her former studious mood: again I ventured to disturb her—

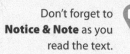
55   "Can you tell me what the writing on that stone over the door means? What is Lowood Institution?"

56   "This house where you are come to live."

57   "And why do they call it Institution? Is it in any way different from other schools?"

58   "It is partly a charity-school: you and I, and all the rest of us, are charity-children. I suppose you are an orphan: are not either your father or your mother dead?"

59   "Both died before I can remember."

60   "Well, all the girls here have lost either one or both parents, and this is called an institution for educating orphans."

61   "Do we pay no money? Do they keep us for nothing?"

62   "We pay, or our friends pay, fifteen pounds a year for each."

63   "Then why do they call us charity-children?"

64   "Because fifteen pounds is not enough for board and teaching, and the deficiency is supplied by subscription."

65   "Who subscribes?"

66   "Different benevolent-minded ladies and gentlemen in this neighborhood and in London."

67   "Who was Naomi Brocklehurst?"

68   "The lady who built the new part of this house as that tablet records, and whose son overlooks and directs everything here."

69   "Why?"

70   "Because he is treasurer and manager of the establishment."

71   "Then this house does not belong to that tall lady who wears a watch, and who said we were to have some bread and cheese."

72   "To Miss Temple? Oh, no! I wish it did: she has to answer to Mr. Brocklehurst for all she does. Mr. Brocklehurst buys all our food and all our clothes."

73   "Does he live here?"

74   "No—two miles off, at a large hall."

75   "Is he a good man?"

76   "He is a clergyman, and is said to do a great deal of good."

77   "Did you say that tall lady was called Miss Temple? "

78   "Yes."

79   "And what are the other teachers called?"

80   "The one with red cheeks is called Miss Smith; she attends to the work, and cuts out—for we make our own clothes, our frocks, and pelisses, and every thing; the little one with black hair is Miss Scatcherd; she teaches history and grammar, and hears the second class repetitions; and the one who wears a shawl, and has a pocket-handkerchief tied to her side with a yellow riband, is Madame Pierrot: she comes from Lisle, in France, and teaches French."

81   "Do you like the teachers?"

82   "Well enough."

83   "Do you like the little black one, and the Madame——?—I cannot pronounce her name as you do."

ANALYZE FIRST-PERSON POINT OF VIEW

Annotate: Mark paragraph 57.

Analyze: Why does Jane ask these questions? What do they indicate about the type of person she is?

ANALYZE FIRST-PERSON
POINT OF VIEW

Annotate: Mark the girl's response to Jane's question about Miss Temple.

Compare: How does the girl's response contrast with Jane's reasons for admiring Miss Temple?

84   "Miss Scatcherd is hasty—you must take care not to offend her; Madame Pierrot is not a bad sort of person."

85   "But Miss Temple is the best—isn't she?"

86   "Miss Temple is very good, and very clever; she is above the rest, because she knows far more than they do."

87   "Have you been long here?"

88   "Two years."

89   "Are you an orphan?"

90   "My mother is dead."

91   "Are you happy here?"

92   "You ask rather too many questions. I have given you answers enough for the present: now I want to read."

93   But at that moment the summons sounded for dinner: all reentered the house. The odor which now filled the refectory was scarcely more appetizing than that which had regaled our nostrils at breakfast: the dinner was served in two huge tin-plated vessels, whence rose a strong steam redolent of rancid fat. I found the mess to consist of indifferent potatoes and strange shreds of rusty meat, mixed and cooked together. Of this preparation a tolerably abundant plateful was apportioned to each pupil. I ate what I could, and wondered within myself whether every day's fare would be like this.

94   After dinner, we immediately adjourned to the schoolroom: lessons recommenced, and were continued till five o'clock.

95   The only marked event of the afternoon was, that I saw the girl with whom I had conversed in the verandah, dismissed in disgrace, by Miss Scatcherd, from a history class, and sent to stand in the middle of the large schoolroom. The punishment seemed to me in a high degree ignominious, especially for so great a girl—she looked thirteen or upwards. I expected she would show signs of great distress and shame; but to my surprise she neither wept nor blushed: composed, though grave, she stood, the central mark of all eyes. "How can she bear it so quietly—so firmly?" I asked of myself. "Were I in her place, it seems to me I should wish the earth to open and swallow me up. She looks as if she were thinking of something beyond her punishment—beyond her situation: of something not round nor before her. I have heard of daydreams—is she in a daydream now? Her eyes are fixed on the floor, but I am sure they do not see it—her sight seems turned in, gone down into her heart: she is looking at what she can remember, I believe; not at what is really present. I wonder what sort of a girl she is—whether good or naughty."

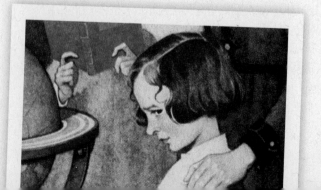

96   Soon after five P.M. we had another meal, consisting of a small mug of coffee and half a slice of brown bread. I devoured my bread and drank my coffee with relish; but I should have been glad of as much more—I was still hungry. Half an hour's recreation succeeded, then study; then the glass of water and the piece of oat-cake, prayers, and bed. Such was my first day at Lowood.

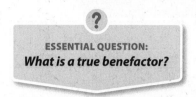

ESSENTIAL QUESTION:
What is a true benefactor?

Review your notes and add your thoughts to your Response Log.

COLLABORATIVE DISCUSSION

Which details about life in the Lowood Institution left a strong impression on you? Discuss your ideas with a partner.

Assessment Practice

Answer these questions before moving on to the **Analyze the Text** section on the following page.

1. What is Miss Temple's reaction when she first meets Jane?

   (A) She is annoyed that Jane has arrived so late.

   (B) She expresses sympathy and concern for Jane.

   (C) She thinks Jane is too young for the school.

   (D) She fears that Jane will misbehave.

2. Why does Miss Temple order bread and cheese to be served on Jane's first day at Lowood?

   (A) She wants to celebrate Jane's arrival.

   (B) Mr. Brocklehurst is coming for a visit.

   (C) The students could not eat their breakfast.

   (D) The school has run out of other food.

3. Who makes the decisions about how Lowood is run?

   (A) Miss Temple

   (B) Miss Miller

   (C) Miss Scatcherd

   (D) Mr. Brocklehurst

Test-Taking Strategies

Analyze the Text

Support your responses with evidence from the text.

1. **COMPARE** Reread the introductory note in italics on page 627. How does Jane's experience at Lowood compare with the life she led at Gateshead?

2. **EVALUATE** England did not have government-funded schools in the period covered by the novel; the children at Lowood must rely on charity for their education. Based on Jane's descriptions of the setting, how well does this system serve the needs of students? Explain.

3. **DRAW CONCLUSIONS** What does the excerpt hint about Mr. Brocklehurst's character?

4. **ANALYZE** In paragraph 95, Jane notes a **Contrast and Contradiction** between the older girl's reaction to being punished and the reaction that Jane expects her to have. What does this incident reveal about Jane's personality?

5. **CRITIQUE** Is the first-person narration of *Jane Eyre* effective, or should Brontë have used the third-person point of view to tell the story? Give reasons for your opinion.

6. **EVALUATE** Review details about the historical, social, and economic context you noted and any other details that stood out to you. What theme does Brontë express? How do your details support that theme?

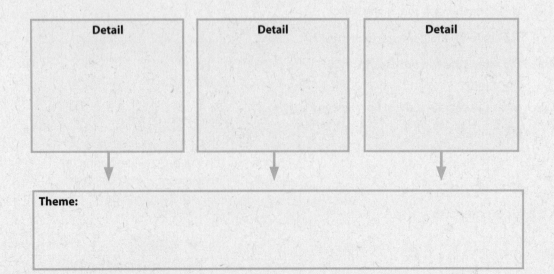

Detail	Detail	Detail

Theme:

Choices

Here are some other ways to demonstrate your understanding of the ideas in this lesson.

Writing
↳ A Diary Entry

In this excerpt, you see all of the events that happen from Jane's perspective. But what would it be like if you knew how another character was feeling?

Write a diary entry from the voice of the older girl whom Jane meets in the garden. You might choose to write about the girl's perspective on one of the following events:

- the burnt porridge in the cafeteria (paragraphs 25–29)
- meeting Jane in the garden (paragraphs 45–92)
- being punished (paragraph 95)

As you write, consider how the older girl's view of events might be different from Jane's.

As you write and discuss, be sure to use the **Academic Vocabulary** words.

| abandon |
| confine |
| conform |
| depress |
| reluctance |

Research
↳ Education in Victorian England

Research "ragged schools" and other charitable education institutions in England during the Victorian era. Address the following questions in your research:

- Why did these schools exist?
- Whom did they serve?
- What impact did they have on pupils?

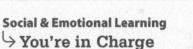

Social & Emotional Learning
↳ You're in Charge

Imagine that you and a group of classmates have been invited to form a committee and suggest changes to Lowood. How will you improve the lives of students?

1. Hold a meeting where your committee brainstorms ideas for improvement. Make sure each committee member is permitted to speak and propose at least one idea.

2. Identify five changes you want to make. Rank them in order of importance from 1 to 5. Provide reasons to justify your recommendations.

3. Create a flyer or poster announcing the changes that you want to implement.

Expand Your Vocabulary

PRACTICE AND APPLY

Choose the situation that best fits with the vocabulary word.

1. If you feel **indefatigable**, are you likely to complete a marathon race or quit early?

2. If your complexion is **ruddy**, have you been exposed to the sun or covered up?

3. If a movie were described as **morose**, would it be sad or funny?

4. If a class is **commencing**, is it beginning or ending?

5. If a woman's outfit is said to be in **vogue**, is it in style or out of style?

Vocabulary Strategy
↳ **Context Clues**

Looking at **context clues** can help you figure out the meaning of an unfamiliar or multiple-meaning word. For example, in this sentence from paragraph 13 of *Jane Eyre*, the words *ruddy, complexion,* and *careworn* help you understand that *countenance* means "facial appearance."

> Miss Miller was more ordinary; ruddy in complexion, though of a careworn countenance. . . .

☺*Ed*

Interactive Vocabulary Lesson: Using Context Clues

PRACTICE AND APPLY

Find the following words in *Jane Eyre*. Identify context clues to each word's meaning, and write down your best guess for the word's definition in the chart. Then, look up each word in a dictionary to check your definition.

Word	Context Clues	Definition
discerned (paragraph 4)		
congregation (paragraph 13)		
redolent (paragraph 93)		
ignominious (paragraph 95)		

Watch Your Language!

Gerunds and Gerund Phrases

A **gerund** is a verb form ending in -*ing* that functions as a noun. **Gerund phrases** include the gerund plus its modifiers and complements. Gerunds and gerund phrases may perform any function that a noun performs and can appear in any part of a sentence where a noun could be used. Gerunds can add a sense of motion or action to a sentence.

Interactive Grammar Lesson: Gerunds and Gerund Phrases

Part of the Sentence	Example
Subject	**Having little food** was a way of life at Lowood.
Direct object	The girls finished **gardening.**
Indirect object	They gave **working** their full attention.
Subject complement	Her best skill is **coping with hardship.**
Object of the preposition	She came home weary from **working all day.**

PRACTICE AND APPLY

Write your own sentences with gerunds or gerund phrases using the sentences above as models.

Factory Reform

Documentary by **Timelines.tv**

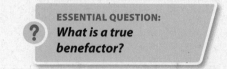

ESSENTIAL QUESTION:
? *What is a true benefactor?*

Engage Your Brain

Get together with a group of classmates, and share stories about difficult places to work. You can discuss your own work experiences or workplaces that you've heard about from friends, relatives, or the media. Consider the following kinds of problems:

- noise
- unsanitary conditions
- dangerous machinery
- long hours
- stressful assignments
- unfriendly supervisors or coworkers

After everyone has shared a story, take a vote on which of the workplaces described was the worst!

Background

"Factory Reform" is an excerpt from the documentary *History of Britain—Changing Lives* on the website Timelines.tv. It depicts manufacturer Titus Salt's advocacy for Britain's lower-class factory workers. In the Industrial Revolution, business owners became wealthy, while average citizens lived in poverty. Workers—men, women, and children—sometimes worked more than 14 hours per day and made very little money. Many were killed or severely injured; accidents ranging from falls to explosions were common in Victorian factories.

Titus Salt

© Houghton Mifflin Harcourt Publishing Company • Image Credits: (t) ©Moviestore Collection ltd/Alamy; (b) ©G. Archive/Alamy

Evaluate Documentaries

A **documentary** is a nonfiction film about social, political, or historical subject matter. A historical documentary usually focuses on a particular time period, person, or event and informs viewers by taking a detailed look at the subject. Documentary filmmakers often rely on visual and sound elements to immerse viewers in the subject and to convey certain viewpoints.

Visual and Sound Elements	• **Footage** is recorded material used to reveal information about a subject. It can include photos, film clips, and even reenactments. • **Illustrations** can be used to help create a storyline by portraying important people and incidents. • **Music** and **sound effects** can be used to set a mood or to capture viewers' attention.
Strategies for Viewing	• Consider the viewpoint of the documentary. Is it **objective**, based strictly on the facts? Or does it make its points in a **subjective** way by sharing only certain views? • Note images used to help you connect ideas. • Think about what the creators emphasize and what impressions they might want to convey.

Learn about a Victorian employer who led a movement to improve working conditions in British industry.

☺ **Ed**

Video

View "**Factory Reform**" in your ebook.

Factory Reform

Documentary by Timelines.tv

Analyze Media

Support your responses with evidence from the documentary.

1. **IDENTIFY** At the start of the documentary, what sounds do you hear as the presenter gives background information? What mental images do these sounds conjure up?

2. **ANALYZE** How does footage of the community of Saltaire help to convey the risk Titus Salt took by moving his factory and investing in living quarters for his workers?

3. **CAUSE/EFFECT** In the graphic organizer, write down improvements that Titus Salt made to address the problems faced by Victorian mill workers.

Problems	Improvements
Air pollution	
Dark, poorly ventilated workplaces	
Exhausted and impoverished workers	

4. **SUMMARIZE** According to the documentary, how did Salt's factory influence future factory owners?

5. **ANALYZE** What does the appearance of a narrator, as well as the use of his voice-over, contribute to the documentary?

6. **COMPARE** "Factory Reform" repeatedly shows illustrations in a notebook that depict life in Victorian factories. How are workers depicted compared to images of the wealthy factory owners?

Choices

Here are some other ways to demonstrate your understanding of the ideas in this lesson.

Writing
↳ Short Story

Create a story about a character who receives support from a benefactor. You may base your story on something that happened to you or someone you know, or you can rely on your imagination.

- Establish the story's setting—where and when it takes place.

- Use a story map to plan the plot of your story. Sequence events so that they build on one another to reach a climax and satisfying conclusion.

- Include sensory language to convey a vivid impression of the main character's experience.

- Reread and edit your narrative. Reorder events or add details as needed.

As you write about and discuss the documentary, be sure to use the **Academic Vocabulary** words.

> abandon

> confine

> conform

> depress

> reluctance

Media
↳ Company Brochure

Do research to learn more details about life in Saltaire in the Victorian era. Then, create a brochure to attract workers to live and work in this model industrial town. Include photos of buildings and homes, along with text that reflects Titus Salt's vision and values.

Speaking & Listening
↳ Group Discussion

In a documentary video, the narrator often conveys a specific point of view or stance on a topic. In a small group, discuss the narrator's point of view in "Factory Reform."

- Identify the narrator's main claim in the video.

- Assess the premises on which his claim is based and how the narrator links his ideas. Does he use transitions to help viewers understand how the ideas fit together?

- Analyze the narrator's tone, including his word choices and points of emphasis. How well does his tone communicate his ideas and convey appropriate emotion?

- Evaluate the narrator's use of rhetoric to persuade listeners.

Get Ready

The Lady of Shalott

Narrative Poem by **Alfred, Lord Tennyson**

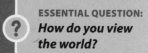

ESSENTIAL QUESTION:
How do you view the world?

Engage Your Brain

Choose one or more of these activities to start connecting with the poem you're about to read.

Solitary Confinement

Many legends and fairy tales depict a character who is confined to a place and shut off from the world. Imagine what it would be like to experience such isolation. Consider the following questions:

- How do you think being cut off from other people would affect you?

- What risks might you take to gain freedom and live among other people?

Write a paragraph in response to these questions.

Curses!

In a small group, share stories from books, films, and TV shows about characters who live under some sort of curse. What situations in real life might make people feel that they are "cursed"?

In Search of Camelot

The poem you are about to read is set around Camelot, where King Arthur held court. With a partner, research information about this legendary castle. Use these questions to guide your research:

- What was life like in Camelot?

- Why did King Arthur and his knights gather at a round table?

- Who was Sir Lancelot, a figure who appears in Tennyson's poem?

© Houghton Mifflin Harcourt Publishing Company • Image Credits: © Colin Paterson/Photodisc/Getty Images

Analyze Allegory

An **allegory** is a story with two levels of meaning—a literal one and a symbolic one. In allegorical fiction and poetry, characters represent abstract qualities or ideas. Like a fable or parable, an allegory may have one or more of the following purposes:

- to convey truths about life
- to teach religious or moral lessons
- to criticize social institutions

Some critics argue that "The Lady of Shalott" is an allegory for the life of an artist, while others believe it represents the plight of women in Victorian society. As you read "The Lady of Shalott," look for symbolic meaning in the poem's setting, objects, and characters.

Focus on Genre
↳ **Narrative Poetry**

- **tells a story**
- **uses elements of fiction, such as character, setting, and plot**
- **is written in poetic form using lines and stanzas**
- **may be written with regular patterns of rhyme and meter or in free verse without a regular structure**

Analyze Mood

Mood is the feeling or atmosphere that a writer creates for the reader. Some examples of words describing mood are *mysterious, somber,* and *joyful*. A poem's mood may change as a poem progresses. Elements that help create a poem's mood include diction, imagery, line length, stanza structure, and sound devices, such as repetition and rhyme.

Read these lines from the beginning of "The Lady of Shalott":

> On either side the river lie
> Long fields of barley and of rye,
> That clothe the wold and meet the sky;
> And through the field the road runs by
>   To many-towered Camelot;

Each line in this passage contains four iambic feet, consisting of an unstressed syllable followed by a stressed syllable. The strong, regular pattern of this meter, the rhyme scheme, and the imagery of King Arthur's mythical realm of Camelot contribute to a tranquil and orderly mood early in the poem. As you read, think about how these elements combine to create that mood or other moods that arise throughout Tennyson's poem.

Annotation in Action

Here are one student's notes about the opening lines of "The Lady of Shalott."
As you read, highlight details that may have symbolic meaning in the poem.

On either side the river lie
Long fields of barley and of rye,
That clothe the wold and meet the sky;
And through the field the road runs by
    To many-towered Camelot;
And up and down the people go,
Gazing where the lilies blow
Round an island there below,
    The island of Shalott.

In this rural setting, Camelot may represent society.

Alfred, Lord Tennyson (1809–1892)

Alfred Tennyson experienced misfortune early in life, but he became the most celebrated poet of his age. The fourth son in a family of 12 children, he grew up in a turbulent household. His father, an educated but embittered clergyman, took out his frustrations on the family. Depressed by his gloomy home life, Tennyson immersed himself in poetry. During his first year at Cambridge University, he won a poetry contest, and his friends believed he was destined for greatness. However, he had to leave Cambridge in 1831 without a degree due to lack of funds.

Melancholy Poet

In 1832, Tennyson published his first significant book of poems, which included an early version of "The Lady of Shalott." It received harsh criticism from reviewers, who objected to its melancholy themes. The next year, he was stunned by the sudden death of his closest friend, Arthur Henry Hallam, who was only 22 years old. Tennyson became engaged to Emily Sellwood in 1836, but he postponed their marriage because of his uncertain financial future. Despite all these difficulties, Tennyson never wavered from his determination to be a poet.

Literary Triumphs

Tennyson's career began to turn around in 1842, when he published a two-volume collection that drew praise from critics. Three years later, the British government granted him an annual pension in recognition of his talent. Although Hallam's death grieved Tennyson deeply, it also inspired some of his finest works, including *In Memoriam A.H.H.*, a poem in 131 sections that pays tribute to Hallam. It was published in 1850 to great success. That same year, Tennyson finally married, and Queen Victoria named him poet laureate. Decades later, he also accepted the title of baron, becoming Alfred, Lord Tennyson.

"'Tis better to have loved and lost / Than never to have loved at all."

—Alfred, Lord Tennyson

The Lady of Shalott

Narrative Poem by **Alfred, Lord Tennyson**

Think about what it would be like to see the world from the Lady of Shalott's perspective.

NOTICE & NOTE
As you read, use the side margins to make notes about the text.

Part I

On either side the river lie
Long fields of barley and of rye,
That clothe the wold and meet the sky;
And through the field the road runs by
5   To many-towered Camelot;
And up and down the people go,
Gazing where the lilies blow
Round an island there below,
        The island of Shalott.

3 **wold:** rolling plain.

7 **blow:** bloom.

ANALYZE MOOD

Annotate: Mark the words or phrases that establish the moods of the first and second stanzas.

Analyze: How does the mood change from the first to the second stanza?

The Lady of Shalott **649**

© Houghton Mifflin Harcourt Publishing Company • Image Credits: ©Chronicle/Alamy

10   Willows whiten, aspens quiver,
Little breezes dusk and shiver
Through the wave that runs forever
By the island in the river
     Flowing down to Camelot.
15   Four gray walls, and four gray towers,
Overlook a space of flowers,
And the silent isle imbowers
     The Lady of Shalott.

By the margin, willow-veiled,
20   Slide the heavy barges trailed
By slow horses; and unhailed
The shallop flitteth silken-sailed
     Skimming down to Camelot:
But who hath seen her wave her hand?
25   Or at the casement seen her stand?
Or is she known in all the land,
     The Lady of Shalott?

Only reapers, reaping early
In among the bearded barley,
30   Hear a song that echoes cheerly
From the river winding clearly,
     Down to towered Camelot;
And by the moon the reaper weary,
Piling sheaves in uplands airy,
35   Listening, whispers "'Tis the fairy
     Lady of Shalott."

Part II

There she weaves by night and day
A magic web with colors gay.
She has heard a whisper say,
40   A curse is on her if she stay
     To look down to Camelot.
She knows not what the curse may be,
And so she weaveth steadily,
And little other care hath she,
45   The Lady of Shalott.

17 **imbowers:** encloses; surrounds.

22 **shallop** (shăl´əp)**:** a small open boat.

25 **casement:** a hinged window that opens outward.

ANALYZE ALLEGORY

Annotate: In lines 19–27, mark details that suggest the Lady of Shalott is invisible or unknown to the citizens of Camelot.

Interpret: How might these details relate to the allegorical meaning of the poem?

© Houghton Mifflin Harcourt Publishing Company • Image Credits: ©Chronicle/Alamy

And moving through a mirror clear
That hangs before her all the year,
Shadows of the world appear.
There she sees the highway near
50   Winding down to Camelot;
There the river eddy whirls,
And there the surly village churls,
And the red cloaks of market girls,
        Pass onward from Shalott.

46–48 Weavers often used mirrors while working from the back of a tapestry to view the tapestry's appearance, but this one is used to view the outside world.

55   Sometimes a troop of damsels glad,
An abbot on an ambling pad,
Sometimes a curly shepherd lad,
Or long-haired page in crimson clad,
        Goes by to towered Camelot;
60   And sometimes through the mirror blue
The knights come riding two and two:
She hath no loyal knight and true,
        The Lady of Shalott.

But in her web she still delights
65   To weave the mirror's magic sights,
For often through the silent nights
A funeral, with plumes and lights
        And music, went to Camelot;
Or when the moon was overhead,
70   Came two young lovers lately wed:
"I am half sick of shadows," said
        The Lady of Shalott.

52 surly village churls: rude members of the lower class in a village.

55 damsels: young, unmarried women.
56 abbot . . . pad: the head monk in a monastery on a slow-moving horse.
58 page: a boy in training to be a knight.

ANALYZE ALLEGORY

Annotate: In lines 64–72, mark the words or phrases that represent the isolation experienced by the main character.

Infer: What does the Lady's statement in line 71 suggest about her character?

Part III

A bowshot from her bower eaves,
He rode between the barley sheaves,
75   The sun came dazzling through the leaves,
And flamed upon the brazen greaves
        Of bold Sir Lancelot.
A red-cross knight forever kneeled
To a lady in his shield,
80   That sparkled on the yellow field,
        Beside remote Shalott.

73 bowshot: the distance an arrow can be shot; **bower** (bouʹər) **eaves:** the part of the roof that extends above the Lady's private room.

76 brazen greaves: metal armor for protecting the legs below the knees.

78–79 A red-cross . . . shield: His shield showed a knight wearing a red cross and kneeling to honor a lady. The red cross was a symbol worn by knights who had fought in the Crusades.

82 **gemmy:** studded with gems.

The gemmy bridle glittered free,
Like to some branch of stars we see
Hung in the golden Galaxy.

85 The bridle bells rang merrily
    As he rode down to Camelot;
And from his blazoned baldric slung
A mighty silver bugle hung,
And as he rode his armor rung,

90   Beside remote Shalott.

87 **blazoned** (blā´zənd) **baldric:** a
decorated leather belt worn across the
chest to support a sword or, as in this
case, a bugle.

All in the blue unclouded weather
Thick-jeweled shone the saddle leather,
The helmet and the helmet-feather
Burned like one burning flame together,

95   As he rode down to Camelot;
As often through the purple night,
Below the starry clusters bright,
Some bearded meteor, trailing light,
    Moves over still Shalott.

100 His broad clear brow in sunlight glowed;
On burnished hooves his war horse trode;
From underneath his helmet flowed
His coal-black curls as on he rode,
    As he rode down to Camelot.

105 From the bank and from the river
He flashed into the crystal mirror,
"Tirra lirra," by the river
    Sang Sir Lancelot.

NOTICE & NOTE
AGAIN AND AGAIN

When you notice certain images
or words being repeated in a
portion of the poem, you've found
an **Again and Again** signpost.

Notice & Note: Mark the
repeated words in lines 109–113.

Infer: What effect does this
repetition have on the stanza?

She left the web, she left the loom,
110 She made three paces through the room,
She saw the water lily bloom,
She saw the helmet and the plume,
    She looked down to Camelot.
Out flew the web and floated wide;
115 The mirror cracked from side to side;
"The curse is come upon me," cried
    The Lady of Shalott.

Part IV

In the stormy east wind straining,
The pale yellow woods were waning,
120 The broad stream in his banks complaining,
Heavily the low sky raining
    Over towered Camelot;
Down she came and found a boat
Beneath a willow left afloat,
125 And round about the prow she wrote
    The Lady of Shalott.

And down the river's dim expanse
Like some bold seër in a trance,
Seeing all his own mischance—
130 With a glassy countenance
    Did she look to Camelot.

ANALYZE MOOD

Annotate: In lines 118–153, mark instances of imagery and sound devices.

Analyze: How do these images and sound devices help convey a tragic mood?

128 **seër** (sē´ər): someone who can see into the future; a prophet.
129 **mischance:** misfortune; bad luck.

The Lady of Shalott **653**

And at the closing of the day
She loosed the chain, and down she lay;
The broad stream bore her far away,
135   The Lady of Shalott.

Lying, robed in snowy white
That loosely flew to left and right—
The leaves upon her falling light—
Through the noises of the night
140   She floated down to Camelot;
And as the boat-head wound along
The willowy hills and fields among,
They heard her singing her last song,
        The Lady of Shalott.

ANALYZE ALLEGORY

Annotate: Mark details about the Lady of Shalott's death in lines 145–153.

Interpret: What idea might be suggested by her death?

150 **ere** (âr): before.

145 Heard a carol, mournful, holy,
Chanted loudly, chanted lowly,
Till her blood was frozen slowly,
And her eyes were darkened wholly,
        Turned to towered Camelot.
150 For ere she reached upon the tide
The first house by the waterside,
Singing in her song she died,
        The Lady of Shalott.

Under tower and balcony,
155 By garden wall and gallery,
A gleaming shape she floated by,
Dead-pale between the houses high,
        Silent into Camelot.
Out upon the wharfs they came,
160 Knight and burgher, lord and dame,
And round the prow they read her name,
        The Lady of Shalott.

160 **burgher:** a middle-class citizen of a town.

Who is this? and what is here?
And in the lighted palace near
165 Died the sound of royal cheer;
And they crossed themselves for fear,
        All the knights at Camelot:
But Lancelot mused a little space;
He said, "She has a lovely face;
170 God in his mercy lend her grace,
        The Lady of Shalott."

© Houghton Mifflin Harcourt Publishing Company • Image Credits: ©Chronicle/Alamy

With a partner, discuss the ending of the poem. What kind of effect do you think Tennyson wanted to have on his readers?

Review your notes and add your thoughts to your Response Log.

Assessment Practice

Answer these questions before moving on to the **Analyze the Text** section on the following page.

1. What will set off the Lady of Shalott's curse?

   (A) viewing the world without looking through her mirror

   (B) falling in love with a loyal knight

   (C) asking forbidden questions

   (D) taking a break from weaving her tapestry

2. Before Lancelot appears in her mirror, the Lady of Shalott —

   (A) feels tormented by her isolation

   (B) enjoys spending her time weaving

   (C) tries to undo the curse placed on her

   (D) yearns to live in Camelot

3. Lines 73–90 show that Lancelot's life is different from the Lady's by —

   (A) contrasting his boldness with her shyness

   (B) contrasting the way people react to him with the way they react to her

   (C) contrasting his freedom with her confinement

   (D) contrasting the appearance of his armor with the appearance of her gown

Test-Taking Strategies

Analyze the Text

Support your responses with evidence from the text.

NOTICE & NOTE

Review what you **noticed and noted** as you read the text. Your annotations can help you answer these questions.

1. **INFER** Why does the Lady of Shalott decide to look down upon Camelot?

2. **DRAW CONCLUSIONS** Is it likely that the Lady's actions would be different if she knew more about the curse? Why or why not?

3. **ANALYZE** The **climax** of a plot is the turning point or moment of greatest intensity. What is the climax of this narrative poem? Explain your answer.

4. **COMPARE** Use the graphic organizer to note details that create a contrast between the Lady of Shalott's life and the lives of the villagers.

Lady of Shalott	Villagers

5. **ANALYZE** Identify the rhyme scheme of the poem. What effect does this rhyme scheme create?

6. **INTERPRET** Which images, objects, or ideas in "The Lady of Shalott" can be seen as symbols that suggest the poem is an allegory for the experience of women in Victorian society?

7. **ANALYZE** Consider the pattern of repetition of words in the fifth and ninth lines of each stanza. Also, note that these lines are indented and usually shorter than the other lines in the stanza. How do these **Again and Again** elements affect the mood of the poem?

Choices

Here are some other ways to demonstrate your understanding of the ideas in this lesson.

Writing
↳ Diary Entry

People who lead isolated lives often keep diaries to express their thoughts. Imagine you are the Lady of Shalott. Write a diary entry about the day she looked directly at Camelot. Before you begin, review your notes about this scene. Consider the following:

- her comment in line 71
- Lancelot's appearance
- the immediate consequences of her action

As you write and discuss, be sure to use the **Academic Vocabulary** words.

- abandon
- confine
- conform
- depress
- reluctance

Media
↳ Graphic Novel Panel

"The Lady of Shalott" is full of vivid descriptions. Create a graphic novel panel showing a scene in the poem.

1. Choose a scene you want to illustrate.

2. Reread the scene, and form mental images of the characters, setting, and events.

3. Decide on text to include in the panel: a descriptive statement, dialogue, or both.

Speaking & Listening
↳ Poetry Recital

With a group, recite part of "The Lady of Shalott" aloud for the class.

- Work with your group to select at least one stanza of the poem.

- Discuss how you will recite the section of the poem you've chosen. Will you recite it together as a choral reading? Will each member of your group speak a different part? Will you sing it like a song?

- Memorize your lines, and rehearse them a few times with your group.

- Present the poem to the class, using appropriate volume, enunciation, and gestures.

from
Great Expectations

Novel by **Charles Dickens**

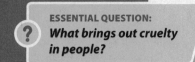

Engage Your Brain

Choose one or more of these activities to start connecting with the text you're about to read.

Can a Broken Heart Ever Heal?

The metaphor of a "broken heart," which describes severe emotional pain, dates back thousands of years. Today, many sad movies, songs, and stories refer to a broken heart. Discuss the following questions with a group of classmates:

- What is the last story you read or saw that refers to a broken heart?

- What event in the story causes the broken heart?

- Does the character whose heart was broken ever recover?

A Youthful Shock

When Charles Dickens was a boy, his life turned upside down after his father fell into debt and Charles had to work in a factory. With a partner, do research to learn more about this experience. Answer the following questions:

- What conditions did Dickens find in the factory?

- How did this experience affect his relationship with his parents?

- How did it influence his writing?

Feeling Out of Place

Think of a time when you went somewhere and felt very awkward or self-conscious. What made you feel that way? Write a diary entry describing this incident. Include vivid, descriptive details of the setting and the people involved.

Analyze Plot

Great Expectations is set in Victorian England following the Industrial Revolution. This social and historical context has an important influence on the **plot**—the series of events that occur in a literary work. During this time, class differences became more pronounced as the middle class grew wealthier while the poor sank deeper into poverty. In the excerpt you are about to read, the main character, Pip, visits the mansion of a wealthy old woman. He feels intimidated in her presence, especially when a girl who lives with her comments negatively about his lower-class background.

A **subplot** is an additional, or secondary, plot in a story. Subplots often concern the backstories of particular characters. The excerpt you will read has a subplot that relates to Miss Havisham, which is revealed in part by the old, yellowing wedding dress she wears. As you read, consider what this detail suggests about Miss Havisham's past and look for other ways the subplot is developed.

Focus on Genre
↳ **Novel**

- **is a long work of fiction**
- **is usually written in the first- or third-person point of view**
- **can develop characters and conflict more thoroughly than a short story**
- **often develops complex plot structures, including subplots**

Analyze Characterization

Characterization is the way a writer creates and develops characters. There are four basic methods of characterization:

- The narrator may comment directly about a character, including discussion of the character's personality, social class, and economic status.

- The writer may describe the character's physical appearance.

- The writer may present the character's own thoughts, speech, and actions.

- The writer may develop the character through the thoughts, speech, and actions of other characters.

As you read, use the chart to keep track of the way Dickens portrays the characters in the text. Note the method of characterization Dickens uses in the descriptions.

Character	Description

Annotation in Action

Here is an example of notes a student made about the author's use of characterization. As you read, notice how Dickens develops characters.

> She seemed much older than I, of course, being a girl, and beautiful and self-possessed; and she was as scornful of me as if she had been one-and-twenty, and a queen.

This character seems self-assured and a bit snobby.

Expand Your Vocabulary

Put a check mark next to the vocabulary words that you feel comfortable using when speaking or writing.

self-possessed	☐
gilded	☐
trinket	☐
dogged	☐
aversion	☐
brooding	☐

Then, write a sentence about a time you were tempted to be unkind toward someone else. As you read the excerpt from *Great Expectations,* use the definitions in the side column to learn the vocabulary words that you don't already know.

Background

Charles Dickens (1812–1870) was born into a middle-class family in England. After his father went to prison, Dickens had to withdraw from school and work in a factory, an experience that deeply influenced his writing. *Great Expectations* is considered one of his finest works. The main character, Pip, is an orphan raised by his sister. In this excerpt, a relative named Mr. Pumblechook takes him to play at the house of Miss Havisham, a wealthy and eccentric old woman.

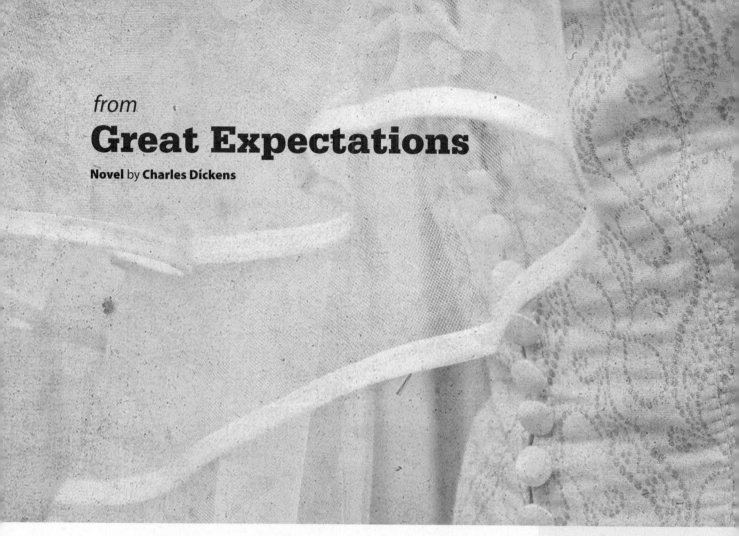

from
Great Expectations

Novel by **Charles Dickens**

Note imagery that helps you visualize the scenes and characters as they are described.

© Houghton Mifflin Harcourt Publishing Company • Image Credits: ©Angyalosi Beata/Shutterstock

NOTICE & NOTE

As you read, use the side margins to make notes about the text.

1   Mr. Pumblechook and I breakfasted at eight o'clock in the parlor behind the shop, while the shopman took his mug of tea and hunch of bread-and-butter on a sack of peas in the front premises. I considered Mr. Pumblechook wretched company. Besides being possessed by my sister's idea that a mortifying and penitential character ought to be imparted to my diet—besides giving me as much crumb as possible in combination with as little butter, and putting such a quantity of warm water into my milk that it would have been more candid to have left the milk out altogether—his conversation consisted of nothing but arithmetic. On my politely bidding him Good morning, he said, pompously, "Seven times nine, boy?" And how should I be able to answer, dodged in that way, in a strange place, on an empty stomach! I was hungry, but before I had swallowed a morsel, he began a running sum that lasted all through the breakfast. "Seven?" "And four?" "And eight?" "And six?" "And two?" "And ten?" And so on. And after each figure was disposed of,

ANALYZE CHARACTERIZATION

Annotate: Mark details in paragraph 1 that reveal aspects of Mr. Pumblechook's character.

Analyze: Which methods of characterization does Dickens use to portray him?

it was as much as I could do to get a bite or a sup, before the next
came; while he sat at his ease guessing nothing, and eating bacon
and hot roll, in (if I may be allowed the expression) a gorging and
gormandising manner.

2   For such reasons I was very glad when ten o'clock came and
we started for Miss Havisham's; though I was not at all at my ease
regarding the manner in which I should acquit myself under that
lady's roof. Within a quarter of an hour we came to Miss Havisham's
house, which was of old brick, and dismal, and had a great many iron
bars to it. Some of the windows had been walled up; of those that
remained, all the lower were rustily barred. There was a courtyard in
front, and that was barred; so, we had to wait, after ringing the bell,
until some one should come to open it. While we waited at the gate,
I peeped in (even then Mr. Pumblechook said, "And fourteen?" but
I pretended not to hear him), and saw that at the side of the house
there was a large brewery. No brewing was going on in it, and none
seemed to have gone on for a long time.

3   A window was raised, and a clear voice demanded "What name?"
To which my conductor replied, "Pumblechook." The voice returned,
"Quite right," and the window was shut again, and a young lady came
across the courtyard, with keys in her hand.

4   "This," said Mr. Pumblechook, "is Pip."

5   "This is Pip, is it?" returned the young lady, who was very pretty
and seemed very proud; "come in, Pip."

ANALYZE CHARACTERIZATION

Annotate: Mark words and
phrases Dickens uses to describe
Mr. Pumblechook's feelings in
paragraphs 6–10.

Infer: What character traits does
he reveal in this interaction?

6   Mr. Pumblechook was coming in also, when she stopped him
with the gate.

7   "Oh!" she said. "Did you wish to see Miss Havisham?"

8   "If Miss Havisham wished to see me," returned Mr. Pumblechook,
discomfited.

9   "Ah!" said the girl; "but you see she don't."

10   She said it so finally, and in such an undiscussible way, that Mr.
Pumblechook, though in a condition of ruffled dignity, could not
protest. But he eyed me severely—as if *I* had done anything to him!—
and departed with the words reproachfully delivered: "Boy! Let
your behavior here be a credit unto them which brought you up by
hand!" I was not free from apprehension that he would come back to
propound through the gate, "And sixteen?" But he didn't.

11   My young conductress locked the gate, and we went across the
courtyard. It was paved and clean, but grass was growing in every
crevice. The brewery buildings had a little lane of communication
with it; and the wooden gates of that lane stood open, and all the
brewery beyond stood open, away to the high enclosing wall; and all
was empty and disused. The cold wind seemed to blow colder there,
than outside the gate; and it made a shrill noise in howling in and out
at the open sides of the brewery, like the noise of wind in the rigging
of a ship at sea.

© Houghton Mifflin Harcourt Publishing Company

12   She saw me looking at it, and she said, "You could drink without hurt all the strong beer that's brewed there now, boy."

13   "I should think I could, miss," said I, in a shy way.

14   "Better not try to brew beer there now, or it would turn out sour, boy, don't you think so?"

15   "It looks like it, miss."

16   "Not that anybody means to try," she added, "for that's all done with, and the place will stand as idle as it is, till it falls. As to strong beer, there's enough of it in the cellars already, to drown the Manor House."

17   "Is that the name of this house, miss?"

18   "One of its names, boy."

19   "It has more than one, then, miss?"

20   "One more. Its other name was Satis; which is Greek, or Latin, or Hebrew, or all three—or all one to me—for enough."

21   "Enough House!" said I: "that's a curious name, miss."

22   "Yes," she replied; "but it meant more than it said. It meant, when it was given, that whoever had this house, could want nothing else. They must have been easily satisfied in those days, I should think. But don't loiter, boy."

23   Though she called me "boy" so often, and with a carelessness that was far from complimentary, she was of about my own age. She seemed much older than I, of course, being a girl, and beautiful and **self-possessed**; and she was as scornful of me as if she had been one-and-twenty, and a queen.

24   We went into the house by a side door—the great front entrance had two chains across it outside—and the first thing I noticed was, that the passages were all dark, and that she had left a candle burning there. She took it up, and we went through more passages and up a staircase, and still it was all dark, and only the candle lighted us.

25   At last we came to the door of a room, and she said, "Go in."

26   I answered, more in shyness than politeness, "After you, miss."

27   To this, she returned: "Don't be ridiculous, boy; I am not going in." And scornfully walked away, and—what was worse—took the candle with her.

28   This was very uncomfortable, and I was half afraid. However, the only thing to be done being to knock at the door, I knocked, and was told from within to enter. I entered, therefore, and found myself in a pretty large room, well lighted with wax candles. No glimpse of daylight was to be seen in it. It was a dressing-room, as I supposed from the furniture, though much of it was of forms and uses then quite unknown to me. But prominent in it was a draped table with a **gilded** looking-glass, and that I made out at first sight to be a fine lady's dressing-table.

29   Whether I should have made out this object so soon, if there had been no fine lady sitting at it, I cannot say. In an arm-chair, with an elbow resting on the table and her head leaning on that hand, sat the strangest lady I have ever seen, or shall ever see.

ANALYZE CHARACTERIZATION

Annotate: Mark details in paragraphs 12–23 that characterize the girl.

Draw Conclusions: What does this passage suggest about her personality?

self-possessed
(sĕlf′pə-zĕst′) *adj.* having calm and self-assured command of one's faculties, feelings, and behavior.

gilded
(gĭl′dĭd) *adj.* covered with or having the appearance of being covered with a thin layer of gold.

30   She was dressed in rich materials—satins, and lace, and silks—all of white. Her shoes were white. And she had a long white veil dependent from her hair, and she had bridal flowers in her hair, but her hair was white. Some bright jewels sparkled on her neck and on her hands, and some other jewels lay sparkling on the table. Dresses, less splendid than the dress she wore, and half-packed trunks, were scattered about. She had not quite finished dressing, for she had but one shoe on—the other was on the table near her hand—her veil was but half arranged, her watch and chain were not put on, and some lace for her bosom lay with those **trinkets**, and with her handkerchief, and gloves, and some flowers, and a Prayer-book, all confusedly heaped about the looking-glass.

31   It was not in the first few moments that I saw all these things, though I saw more of them in the first moments than might be supposed. But, I saw that everything within my view which ought to be white, had been white long ago, and had lost its luster and was faded and yellow. I saw that the bride within the bridal dress had withered like the dress, and like the flowers, and had no brightness left but the brightness of her sunken eyes. I saw that the dress had been put upon the rounded figure of a young woman, and that the figure upon which it now hung loose, had shrunk to skin and bone. Once, I had been taken to see some ghastly waxwork at the Fair, representing I know not what impossible personage lying in state. Once, I had been taken to one of our old marsh churches to see a skeleton in the ashes of a rich dress, that had been dug out of a vault under the church pavement. Now, waxwork and skeleton seemed to have dark eyes that moved and looked at me. I should have cried out, if I could.

32   "Who is it?" said the lady at the table.

33   "Pip, ma'am."

34   "Pip?"

35   "Mr. Pumblechook's boy, ma'am. Come—to play."

36   "Come nearer; let me look at you. Come close."

37   It was when I stood before her, avoiding her eyes, that I took note of the surrounding objects in detail, and saw that her watch had stopped at twenty minutes to nine, and that a clock in the room had stopped at twenty minutes to nine.

38   "Look at me," said Miss Havisham. "You are not afraid of a woman who has never seen the sun since you were born?"

39   I regret to state that I was not afraid of telling the enormous lie comprehended in the answer "No."

40   "Do you know what I touch here?" she said, laying her hands, one upon the other, on her left side.

41   "Yes, ma'am." (It made me think of the young man.)

42   "What do I touch?"

43   "Your heart."

44   "Broken!"

ANALYZE CHARACTERIZATION

Annotate: In paragraphs 30 and 31, mark repeated words used to describe Miss Havisham and her dress.

Analyze: What does Dickens emphasize through the use of repetition in this description?

trinket
(trĭng´kĭt) *n.* a small ornament, such as a piece of jewelry.

Annotate: Mark details in paragraph 45 that describe how Miss Havisham delivers her remark about her heart.

Predict: Based on this remark and the way Miss Havisham is dressed, what do you predict the novel will reveal about her past?

dogged

(dô´gĭd, dŏg´ĭd) *adj.* stubbornly persevering; tenacious.

45   She uttered the word with an eager look, and with strong emphasis, and with a weird smile that had a kind of boast in it. Afterwards, she kept her hands there for a little while, and slowly took them away as if they were heavy.

46   "I am tired," said Miss Havisham. "I want diversion, and I have done with men and women. Play."

47   I think it will be conceded by my most disputatious reader, that she could hardly have directed an unfortunate boy to do anything in the wide world more difficult to be done under the circumstances.

48   "I sometimes have sick fancies," she went on, "and I have a sick fancy that I want to see some play. There, there!" with an impatient movement of the fingers of her right hand; "play, play, play!"

49   For a moment, with the fear of my sister's working me before my eyes, I had a desperate idea of starting round the room in the assumed character of Mr. Pumblechook's chaise-cart. But, I felt myself so unequal to the performance that I gave it up, and stood looking at Miss Havisham in what I suppose she took for a **dogged** manner, inasmuch as she said, when we had taken a good look at each other:

50   "Are you sullen and obstinate?"

51   "No, ma'am, I am very sorry for you, and very sorry I can't play just now. If you complain of me I shall get into trouble with my sister, so I would do it if I could; but it's so new here, and so strange, and so fine—and melancholy—" I stopped, fearing I might say too much, or had already said it, and we took another look at each other.

52   Before she spoke again, she turned her eyes from me, and looked at the dress she wore, and at the dressing-table, and finally at herself in the looking-glass.

53   "So new to him," she muttered, "so old to me; so strange to him, so familiar to me; so melancholy to both of us! Call Estella."

54   As she was still looking at the reflection of herself, I thought she was still talking to herself, and kept quiet.

55   "Call Estella," she repeated, flashing a look at me. "You can do that. Call Estella. At the door."

56   To stand in the dark in a mysterious passage of an unknown house, bawling Estella to a scornful young lady neither visible nor responsive, and feeling it a dreadful liberty so to roar out her name, was almost as bad as playing to order. But, she answered at last, and her light came along the dark passage like a star.

57   Miss Havisham beckoned her to come close, and took up a jewel from the table, and tried its effect upon her fair young bosom and against her pretty brown hair. "Your own, one day, my dear, and you will use it well. Let me see you play cards with this boy."

58   "With this boy! Why, he is a common laboring-boy!"

59   I thought I overheard Miss Havisham answer—only it seemed so unlikely—"Well? You can break his heart."

60   "What do you play, boy?" asked Estella of myself, with the greatest disdain.

61   "Nothing but beggar my neighbor, miss."

62   "Beggar him," said Miss Havisham to Estella. So we sat down to cards.

63   It was then I began to understand that everything in the room had stopped, like the watch and the clock, a long time ago. I noticed that Miss Havisham put down the jewel exactly on the spot from which she had taken it up. As Estella dealt the cards, I glanced at the dressing-table again, and saw that the shoe upon it, once white, now yellow, had never been worn. I glanced down at the foot from which the shoe was absent, and saw that the silk stocking on it, once white, now yellow, had been trodden ragged. Without this arrest of everything, this standing still of all the pale decayed objects, not even the withered bridal dress on the collapsed form could have looked so like grave-clothes, or the long veil so like a shroud.

64   So she sat, corpse-like, as we played at cards; the frillings and trimmings on her bridal dress, looking like earthy paper. I knew nothing then of the discoveries that are occasionally made of bodies buried in ancient times, which fall to powder in the moment of being distinctly seen; but, I have often thought since, that she must have looked as if the admission of the natural light of day would have struck her to dust.

65   "He calls the knaves, Jacks, this boy!" said Estella with disdain, before our first game was out. "And what coarse hands he has! And what thick boots!"

66   I had never thought of being ashamed of my hands before; but I began to consider them a very indifferent pair. Her contempt for me was so strong, that it became infectious, and I caught it.

67   She won the game, and I dealt. I misdealt, as was only natural, when I knew she was lying in wait for me to do wrong; and she denounced me for a stupid, clumsy laboring-boy.

68   "You say nothing of her," remarked Miss Havisham to me, as she looked on. "She says many hard things of you, yet you say nothing of her. What do you think of her?"

69   "I don't like to say," I stammered.

70   "Tell me in my ear," said Miss Havisham, bending down.

71   "I think she is very proud," I replied, in a whisper.

72   "Anything else?"

73   "I think she is very pretty."

74   "Anything else?"

75   "I think she is very insulting." (She was looking at me then with a look of supreme **aversion**.)

76   "Anything else?"

77   "I think I should like to go home."

78   "And never see her again, though she is so pretty?"

79   "I am not sure that I shouldn't like to see her again, but I should like to go home now."

80   "You shall go soon," said Miss Havisham aloud. "Play the game out."

81   Saving for the one weird smile at first, I should have felt almost sure that Miss Havisham's face could not smile. It had dropped into a

Don't forget to
Notice & Note as you
read the text.

NOTICE & NOTE
AHA MOMENT

When you notice a sudden realization that shifts a character's understanding, you've found an **Aha Moment** signpost.

Notice & Note: Underline the sentence in paragraph 63 that reveals a shift in Pip's understanding.

Draw Conclusions: What does this shift help you understand about the subplot involving Miss Havisham?

aversion
(ə-vûr´zhən) n. a fixed, intense dislike; repugnance.

brooding
(broo´dĭng) *adj.* thinking about
something moodily.

watchful and **brooding** expression—most likely when all the things about her had become transfixed—and it looked as if nothing could ever lift it up again. Her chest had dropped, so that she stooped; and her voice had dropped, so that she spoke low, and with a dead lull upon her; altogether, she had the appearance of having dropped, body and soul, within and without, under the weight of a crushing blow.

82   I played the game to an end with Estella, and she beggared me. She threw the cards down on the table when she had won them all, as if she despised them for having been won of me.

83   "When shall I have you here again?" said Miss Havisham. "Let me think."

84   I was beginning to remind her that today was Wednesday, when she checked me with her former impatient movement of the fingers of her right hand.

85   "There, there! I know nothing of days of the week; I know nothing of weeks of the year. Come again after six days. You hear?"

86   "Yes, ma'am."

87   "Estella, take him down. Let him have something to eat, and let him roam and look about him while he eats. Go, Pip."

88   I followed the candle down, as I had followed the candle up, and she stood it in the place where we had found it. Until she opened the side entrance, I had fancied, without thinking about it, that it must necessarily be nighttime. The rush of the daylight quite confounded me, and made me feel as if I had been in the candlelight of the strange room many hours.

89   "You are to wait here, you boy," said Estella; and disappeared and closed the door.

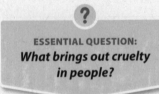

ESSENTIAL QUESTION:
What brings out cruelty in people?

Review your notes and add your thoughts to your Response Log.

COLLABORATIVE DISCUSSION

What is the most memorable detail you recall about one of the characters in the text? Share your ideas with a partner.

Assessment Practice

Answer these questions before moving on to the **Analyze the Text** section on the following page.

1. What surprises Mr. Pumblechook when he arrives with Pip at Miss Havisham's house?

   (A) Pip shows poor manners when Estella greets them.

   (B) Estella doesn't want him to come inside the house.

   (C) Miss Havisham doesn't come down to say hello.

   (D) Estella is not how he remembers her.

2. What does Pip find most strange about Miss Havisham when he meets her?

   (A) She is very thin.

   (B) She is only wearing one shoe.

   (C) She is dressed in a wedding gown.

   (D) She doesn't seem to recognize him.

3. Why is Estella scornful toward Pip?

   (A) He is unable to play by himself.

   (B) He stares too much at Miss Havisham.

   (C) He is very shy and quiet.

   (D) He comes from a lower-class family.

Test-Taking Strategies

Analyze the Text

Support your responses with evidence from the text.

NOTICE & NOTE

Review what you **noticed and noted** as you read the text. Your annotations can help you answer these questions.

(1) **INTERPRET** In paragraph 10, Mr. Pumblechook says to Pip, "Let your behavior here be a credit unto them which brought you up by hand!" What does this remark suggest about why Pip's family agreed to send him to visit Miss Havisham?

(2) **INTERPRET** Complete the chart with examples of imagery that Dickens uses to describe the courtyard and buildings in paragraph 11. What **mood,** or atmosphere, does this imagery help create?

Sight:
Hearing:
Touch:

(3) **EVALUATE** What method does Dickens rely on most in his characterization of Miss Havisham? Is his use of this method effective? Explain why or why not.

(4) **DRAW CONCLUSIONS** Dickens introduces the subplot involving Miss Havisham's past through clues such as the yellowed wedding dress and her comment about her broken heart. How might this subplot relate to the events of this excerpt? Cite details in your response.

(5) **ANALYZE** In paragraph 66, Pip says that for the first time he feels ashamed of his hands. What **Aha Moment** does Pip have because of his experience in this wealthy household?

(6) **PREDICT** Miss Havisham tells Pip to return in six days. What do you predict will happen on his future visits to her house?

Choices

Here are some other ways to demonstrate your understanding of the ideas in this lesson.

Writing
↳ Create a Character

Think about the most unusual person you have ever met. Write a paragraph that brings this person to life for readers. Consider using these methods of characterization:

- Describe what the person looks like.

- Show an action that reveals the person's character traits.

- Use dialogue to show what the person is like or how other people react to that person.

As you write and discuss, be sure to use the **Academic Vocabulary** words.

| abandon |
| confine |
| conform |
| depress |
| reluctance |

Research
↳ Investigate the Historical Context

Class differences are an important topic of *Great Expectations*. Conduct research on the class structure of Victorian England, and note how this is reflected in the text. Share what you learn in a group discussion.

Social & Emotional Learning
↳ Make Rules . . . or Break Them?

Individuals who behave outside of the social norms of the day (as Miss Havisham does) may be considered eccentric. In a small group, have a discussion about behavior that is considered peculiar or unusual.

- Discuss what defines "normal" behavior in your school or community.

- Ask yourself: What happens when someone breaks the rules of accepted behavior? What is an appropriate reaction when this happens?

- Share your ideas on the positive or negative consequences of behaving in a way that others consider strange or unique.

- Make sure all members of your group have a chance to share their thoughts.

Expand Your Vocabulary

PRACTICE AND APPLY

Mark the boldfaced word that best completes each sentence.

1. At Laura's church, the ceilings were **gilded/dogged**.

2. James found a(n) **aversion/trinket** at the antique store.

3. When Janine met Eric, he was **self-possessed/brooding** over a book in the library.

Vocabulary Strategy
↳ **Heteronyms**

Words that are spelled the same but have different pronunciations and meanings are called **heteronyms.** The vocabulary word *dogged* is an example of a heteronym.

⊙ **Ed**

Interactive Vocabulary Lesson: Using Reference Sources

- As used in *Great Expectations, dogged* is an adjective meaning "stubborn or tenacious" and is pronounced (dô´gĭd) in two syllables.

- *Dogged* can also be the past tense of the verb *dog*, meaning "to follow or track persistently," which is pronounced (dôgd) in one syllable.

When you come across a heteronym, examine the context to find clues for the pronunciation and meaning.

PRACTICE AND APPLY

Write down two definitions for each heteronym in the chart. Discuss with a partner how the word's pronunciation changes depending on the definition. Consult a dictionary to check your definitions and pronunciations.

Heteronym	Definition 1	Definition 2
alternate		
converse		
contest		
moderate		
produce		

Watch Your Language!

Repetition

Dickens uses **repetition** in his writing to reveal or emphasize character traits, convey ideas, and develop humor. For example, in the opening paragraph, Dickens shows a comically annoying side of Mr. Pumblechook by having him repeatedly ask Pip multiplication questions:

> "Seven times nine, boy?" . . .
> "Seven?" "And four?" "And eight?"
> "And six?" "And two?"

The chart shows examples of repetition in the novel and their effects.

Type of Repetition	Example	Purpose or Effect
Single Words	Pip repeatedly calls Estella "miss," while Estella repeatedly calls him "boy." (paragraphs 12–22)	These terms of address reveal Pip's politeness and Estella's snobbishness and rudeness.
Phrases	The phrases "I saw" and "Once, I had been taken" are repeated in paragraph 31.	The repeated phrases emphasize how strange everything appears in Miss Havisham's room and help create a compelling rhythm in the sentences.
Grammatical Structures	"'So new to him,' she muttered, 'so old to me; so strange to him, so familiar to me; so melancholy to both of us!'" (paragraph 53)	Dickens repeatedly uses the same grammatical structure to emphasize how different Pip is from Miss Havisham, but also to show one way in which they are similar.

PRACTICE AND APPLY

Review a piece of your own writing and look for places where you could add repetition. Try to use the three types of repetition from the chart.

The Victorians Had the Same Concerns About Technology As We Do

Essay by **Melissa Dickson**

ESSENTIAL QUESTION:
Which invention has had the greatest impact on your life?

Engage Your Brain

Choose one or more of these activities to start connecting with the essay you're about to read.

Tech Talk

Take a poll about digital technology. Respond to each statement with a number from 1 to 5, with 1 meaning that you strongly disagree and 5 meaning that you strongly agree. As a class, tally up the responses and calculate the average response to each statement.

- Technology sometimes makes me feel isolated from others.

- I am overwhelmed by the amount of information I get from social media.

- I worry about how technology is affecting our society.

Worrying Writers

The essay you are about to read mentions three writers who had concerns about technological developments in their time:

- Thomas Carlyle

- Nicholas Carr

- John Stuart Mill

With a small group, conduct research to learn about their views on technology. Then, present the group's research by having someone role-play each of these writers as if they are on a panel sharing their views with the class.

Fashion Statement

Design a T-shirt that expresses how you feel about one type of digital technology. You might choose tech that plays a big role in your life or something that you avoid. Use brief text and one or more images to create a fun and eye-catching T-shirt.

Integrate and Evaluate Information

Nonfiction writers do not need to rely only on text to communicate meaning. **Graphic features** such as images, charts, and maps can provide information that would be difficult to express in words. Readers of nonfiction with graphic features must integrate and evaluate visual and verbal information to fully understand the writer's message.

Melissa Dickson reproduces two Victorian-era images in her essay, commenting directly on one of them. As you read, think about how effectively Dickson uses these images to support her ideas.

Focus on Genre
↳ **Essay**

- **has an introduction that identifies a specific topic and hooks the audience**
- **contains a thesis statement that offers insight on the topic**
- **contains well-developed body paragraphs, each with a main idea related to the writer's thesis statement or position, and evidence that supports those ideas**
- **has a conclusion that summarizes the topic and leaves the audience with something to think about**

Analyze Compare-and-Contrast Essay

A **thesis** is an expression of the main idea or claim of an essay. In this essay, the thesis is articulated in the title. To convince readers to accept this thesis, Melissa Dickson structures her essay as a **point-by-point comparison** of the similarities between Victorian and contemporary concerns about technology. She compares both periods one point at a time, instead of discussing the Victorian period first and then the contemporary period. As you read, use a chart like the one below to keep track of the main points presented and Dickson's supporting details related to both Victorian and current perspectives on this issue.

Point 1	Point 2
Victorian:	Victorian:
Current:	Current:

Evaluate the essay's organizational pattern and consider whether this structure effectively serves the author's intended purpose.

Annotation in Action

Here is a note one student made about a passage from "The Victorians Had the Same Concerns About Technology As We Do." As you read the essay, highlight words and phrases the author uses to make comparisons.

> Many of us struggle with the bombardment of information we receive and experience anxiety as a result of new media, which we feel threaten our relationships and "usual" modes of human interaction.
>
> Though the technologies may change, these fears actually have a very long history: more than a century ago our forebears had the same concerns.

sets up comparison between the problems of people today and people in Victorian times

Expand Your Vocabulary

Put a check mark next to the vocabulary words that you feel comfortable using when speaking or writing.

forebear	
underpin	
pervasive	
cacophony	
sea change	
posit	
immersion	
Luddite	

Turn to a partner, and talk about the vocabulary words that you already know. Then, write a few sentences about technology, using as many of the words as you can. As you read the essay, use the definitions in the side column to learn the vocabulary words that you don't already know.

Background

"Old technologies were once new."

—Melissa Dickson

Melissa Dickson is a researcher at the University of Birmingham in England. In her doctoral thesis, she wrote about the tales of the *Arabian Nights,* exploring how these Middle Eastern folktales influenced British drama, fiction, poetry, travel writing, and children's literature. "The Victorians Had the Same Concerns About Technology As We Do" grew out of her involvement in a project called "Diseases of Modern Life," which investigates 19th-century cultural, literary, and medical understandings of stress, overwork, and other disorders.

The Victorians Had the Same Concerns About Technology As We Do

Essay by **Melissa Dickson**

Fears about the harmful effects of new technology are nothing new.

NOTICE & NOTE
As you read, use the side margins to make notes about the text.

1   We live, we are so often told, in an information age. It is an era obsessed with space, time and speed, in which social media inculcates[1] virtual lives that run parallel to our "real" lives and in which communications technologies collapse distances around the globe. Many of us struggle with the bombardment of information we receive and experience anxiety as a result of new media, which we feel threaten our relationships and "usual" modes of human interaction.

2   Though the technologies may change, these fears actually have a very long history: more than a century ago our **forebears** had the same concerns. Literary, medical and cultural responses in the Victorian age to the perceived problems of stress and overwork anticipate many of the preoccupations of our own era to an extent that is perhaps surprising.

ANALYZE COMPARE-AND-CONTRAST ESSAY

Annotate: Mark details in paragraph 2 about Victorian issues that also concern people today.

Connect: What are some recent complaints about the harmful effects of new technology that you have heard about?

forebear
(fôr´bâr) *n.* a person from whom one is descended; an ancestor.

---

[1] **inculcate:** to impress (something) upon someone's mind by frequent instruction or repetition; instill.

© Houghton Mifflin Harcourt Publishing Company • Image Credits: ©oneinchpunch/Shutterstock

3   This parallel is well illustrated by the following 1906 cartoon from *Punch*, a satirical British weekly magazine:

FORECASTS FOR 1907.

IV.—Development of Wireless Telegraphy. Scene in Hyde Park.
[These two figures are not communicating with one another. The lady is receiving an amatory message, and the gentleman some racing results.]

Worrying trends, 1906.

© Houghton Mifflin Harcourt Publishing Company • Image Credits: ©Punch Limited

underpin
(ŭn-dər-pĭn´) *v.* to give support or substance to.

pervasive
(pər-vā´sĭv,-zĭv) *adj.* having the quality or tendency to pervade or permeate.

4   The caption reads: "These two figures are not communicating with one another. The lady is receiving an amatory[2] message, and the gentleman some racing results." The development of the "wireless telegraph" is portrayed as an overwhelmingly isolating technology.

5   Replace these strange contraptions with smartphones, and we are reminded of numerous contemporary complaints regarding the stunted social and emotional development of young people, who no longer hang out in person, but in virtual environments, often at great physical distance. Different technology, same statement. And it's **underpinned** by the same anxiety that "real" human interaction is increasingly under threat from technological innovations that we have, consciously or unconsciously, assimilated into daily life. By using such devices, so the popular paranoia would have it, we are somehow damaging ourselves.

Cacophony of voices

6   The 19th century witnessed the rapid expansion of the printing industry. New techniques and mass publishing formats gave rise to a far more **pervasive** periodical press, reaching a wider readership than ever before. Many celebrated the possibility of instant news and greater communication. But concerns were raised about the

[2] **amatory:** of, relating to, or expressive of love, especially romantic love.

overwhelmed middle-class reader who, it was thought, lacked the discernment to judge the new mass of information critically, and so read everything in a superficial, erratic manner.

7 　The philosopher and essayist Thomas Carlyle, for example, lamented the new lack of direct contact with society and nature caused by the intervention of machinery in every aspect of life. Print publications were fast becoming the principal medium of public debate and influence, and they were shaping and, in Carlyle's view, distorting human learning and communications.

8 　The philosopher and economist John Stuart Mill heartily agreed, expressing his fears in an essay entitled "Civilisation". He thought that

John Orlando Parry, *A London Street Scene,* 1835. © Alfred Dunhill Collection

the **cacophony** of voices supposedly overwhelming the general public was creating:

> *A state of society where any voice, not pitched in an exaggerated key, is lost in the hubbub. Success in so crowded a field depends not upon what a person is, but upon what he seems: mere marketable qualities become the object instead of substantial ones, and a man's capital and labor are expended less in doing anything than in persuading other people that he has done it. Our own age has seen this evil brought to its consummation.*

9   Individual authors and writers were becoming disempowered, lost in a glutted marketplace of ideas, opinions, adverts and quacks.

Old complaints

10   The parallels with the concerns of our own society are striking. Arguments along not at all dissimilar lines have been advanced against contemporary means of acquiring information, such as Twitter, Facebook, and our constant access to the internet in general.

11   In his 2008 article, "Is Google Making Us Stupid?", journalist Nicholas Carr speculated that "we may well be in the midst of a **sea change** in the way we read and think". Reading online, he **posits,** discourages long and thoughtful **immersion** in texts in favor of a form of skipping, scanning and digressing via hyperlinks that will ultimately diminish our capacity for concentration and contemplation.

12   Writers, too, have shared Carr's anxieties. Philip Roth and Will Self, for example, have both prophesied these trends as contributing to the death of the novel, arguing that people are increasingly unused to and ill-equipped to engage with its characteristically long, linear form.

13   Of course, all old technologies were once new. People were at one point genuinely concerned about things we take for granted as perfectly harmless now. In the later decades of the 19th century it was thought that the telephone would induce deafness and that sulphurous vapors were asphyxiating passengers on the London Underground. These then-new advancements were replacing older still technologies that had themselves occasioned similar anxieties on their introduction. Plato, as his oral culture began to transition to a literary one, was gravely worried that writing itself would erode the memory.

14   While we cannot draw too strict a line of comparison between 19th-century attitudes to such technologies as the telegraph, train, telephone, and newspaper and our own responses as a culture to the advent of the internet and the mobile phone, there are parallels that almost argue against the **Luddite** position. As dramatically as technology changes, we, at least in the way we regard it, remain surprisingly unchanged.

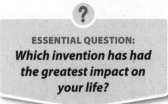

COLLABORATIVE DISCUSSION

With a partner, talk about your reactions to the essay. Did Melissa Dickson's comparison of Victorian and contemporary concerns influence your opinion about new technology?

ESSENTIAL QUESTION:
Which invention has had the greatest impact on your life?

Review your notes and add your thoughts to your Response Log.

Assessment Practice

Answer these questions before moving on to the **Analyze the Text** section on the following page.

1. The role of the graphic features in the essay is to —

   (A) emphasize the ideas expressed by the author

   (B) illustrate how distracted people can be

   (C) show how pervasive technology is today

   (D) suggest that technology has always been in the news

2. Based on the details in the essay, the 21st century is often referred to as the Information Age because people —

   (A) always share information

   (B) are continually distracted by new information

   (C) have access to overwhelming amounts of information

   (D) are unsure which information is accurate

3. The author refers to Plato in paragraph 13 to —

   (A) suggest that he believed technology should be banned

   (B) show that he had concerns about technology

   (C) dismiss the opinions of those who fear technology

   (D) contrast ancient ideas about technology with current ones

Test-Taking Strategies

Analyze the Text

Support your responses with evidence from the text.

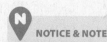

NOTICE & NOTE

Review what you **noticed and noted** as you read the text. Your annotations can help you answer these questions.

(1) **INFER** Reread paragraph 1. Does Dickson agree with the contemporary concerns she summarizes here, or does she seem skeptical of them? Cite details from anywhere in the essay to support your response.

(2) **SUMMARIZE** Use the graphic organizer to summarize comparisons that Dickson makes in her essay.

Topic	Victorian Concerns	Contemporary Concerns
Personal Communication		
Reading		

(3) **EVALUATE** Is point-by-point comparison an effective format for the essay, or should Dickson have discussed the Victorian elements first and then discussed contemporary elements? Explain your response.

(4) **EVALUATE** How do the images Dickson included with the essay support her thesis? What features could she have added to make the essay more effective?

(5) **CRITIQUE** Reread paragraph 14. Does Dickson's comparison of Victorian and contemporary fears offer a convincing reason not to worry about current technological changes? Explain your opinion.

(6) **ANALYZE** How do the **Quoted Words** from Nicholas Carr in paragraph 11 support the author's ideas?

Choices

Here are some other ways to demonstrate your understanding of the ideas in this lesson.

Writing
↳ Opinion Statement

Reread the discussion of Nicholas Carr's ideas about online reading in paragraph 11. Write a paragraph expressing your opinion of whether online reading is any different from reading a print book or article.

As you write and discuss, be sure to use the **Academic Vocabulary** words.

- abandon
- confine
- conform
- depress
- reluctance

Social & Emotional Learning
↳ Group Discussion

In a small group, discuss the role of social media and other digital technology in your lives. Consider

- how much time you spend using social media
- how you interact with friends and relatives through phones and other devices
- how digital technology affects your health and sense of well-being

Create a list of three to five recommendations to help teenagers use digital technology in a positive way.

Media
↳ Historical Timeline

With a partner, create a timeline showing recent advancements in digital technology.

1. Identify important developments in social media and other digital technology over the past 20 years.

2. Gather images to include in your timeline, such as photos of tech leaders and devices.

3. Assemble your timeline and share it with the class.

Expand Your Vocabulary

PRACTICE AND APPLY

Fill in the blanks with the correct words.

forebear	underpin	pervasive	cacophony
sea change	posit	immersion	Luddite

1. Micah's concentration was often interrupted by a(n) _____ of voices and laughter coming from downstairs.

2. Brenda considered her grandfather a(n) _____ ; her _____ always complained about technology.

3. Increased access to tutoring will _____ academic success in our school.

4. The authors _____ that the _____ use of social media causes people to feel less connected to others.

5. Some people believe video gaming will go through a(n) _____ because we will soon be able to create total _____ in virtual reality environments.

Vocabulary Strategy

↳ **Use a Thesaurus**

Reference tools help writers understand the precise meaning of words so they can use them correctly. A **thesaurus**, for example, is used to find **synonyms**, or words with similar meanings, and **antonyms**, words that have opposite meanings. Take a look at this example of a thesaurus entry for the vocabulary word *pervasive*.

☺ *Ed*

Interactive Vocabulary Lesson: Synonyms and Antonyms

pervasive *adjective*
  synonyms: *prevalent, permeating, extensive, ubiquitous*
  antonyms: *limited, narrow, restricted*

PRACTICE AND APPLY

For each vocabulary word, follow these steps:

1. Look up each word in a print or digital thesaurus. Identify the synonyms appropriate to the meaning of each term as it is used in the selection.

2. Write a sample sentence using each word.

3. In each sentence, replace the vocabulary word with one of your synonyms. Make sure that the sentences make sense by having a partner check your work.

Watch Your Language!

Sentence Structure

Good writers use a variety of sentence structures to avoid monotony and to effectively articulate their ideas. The simplest structure has one **clause,** a group of words that contains a subject and a verb. More complex sentence structures include more than one clause. Study the examples in the chart.

Sentence Structure	Example
A **simple sentence** has one independent clause and no subordinate clauses.	We live in the Information Age.
A **compound sentence** has two or more independent clauses joined by a comma and a coordinating conjunction, such as *and, or,* or *but.*	People love using social media, but some worry about its effect on our relationships.
A **complex sentence** has an independent clause and one or more subordinate clauses. The subordinate clause begins with a subordinating conjunction, such as *after, although, because, though, when,* or *while.*	Though the technologies may change, these fears actually have a very long history.
A **compound-complex** sentence has two or more independent clauses and at least one subordinate clause.	Teenagers are constantly bombarded by information, but they understand the need to think critically when it comes to online sources.

Notice how the conjunctions in the example sentences connect the ideas in the clauses. Without the conjunctions, each sentence would be a **run-on,** or multiple sentences written as if they were one. The writer's meaning would also be less clear without conjunctions.

Run-on example: Teenagers are constantly bombarded by information they understand the need to think critically when it comes to online sources.

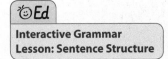

Interactive Grammar Lesson: Sentence Structure

PRACTICE AND APPLY

Write a paragraph about an invention you believe you cannot live without. Then, go back and review the paragraph to look for simple sentences that can be combined to avoid monotony or to clarify relationships among ideas. Use coordinating or subordinating conjunctions to combine these sentences.

Collaborate & Compare

Compare Themes

As you read, notice how the speakers in these poems use observations of nature as a springboard to discussing their ideas and feelings about the times they live in.

A Dover Beach

Poem by **Matthew Arnold**
pages 690–693

B The Darkling Thrush

Poem by **Thomas Hardy**
pages 694–695

After you have read the poems, you will collaborate with a small group to explore their themes. You will follow these steps:

- Decide on the most important details
- Determine a theme
- Compare themes
- Present to the class

Dover Beach

Poem by **Matthew Arnold**

The Darkling Thrush

Poem by **Thomas Hardy**

Engage Your Brain

Choose one or more of these activities to start connecting with the poems you're about to read.

Birdsong

Find a video or audio recording of a thrush singing. Write a paragraph describing the sounds you hear, comparing them to sounds made by human voices or instruments. Note down any emotions that come to mind as you listen to the recording, or draw an image that expresses these emotions through the use of color or other elements.

Half Full or Half Empty?

Our personal perspectives have a strong influence on how we react to things. With a group of students, identify three important issues that affect your community, the country, or the world. Then, explore the different ways an optimist and a pessimist might view these issues by holding a "Pessimists vs. Optimists" debate in which each person supports their point of view.

White Cliffs of Dover

Thomas Hardy's poem is set in one of England's most famous landmarks. Team up with a classmate to create a tourism brochure promoting Dover Beach and the white cliffs that soar above it.

- Write a description for the brochure, using precise details to point out distinctive features of the landscape.

- Include one or more images in your brochure.

Analyze Extended Metaphors

Like any metaphor, an **extended metaphor** is a comparison between two essentially unlike things that nevertheless have something in common. In an extended metaphor, however, the figurative comparison is made at length and in various ways throughout a stanza, a paragraph, or an entire literary work. An extended metaphor is similar to a metaphysical conceit, but the comparison is not as surprising.

Both of the poems you will read in this lesson contain extended metaphors. In "Dover Beach," for example, Matthew Arnold develops a metaphor comparing the sea to traditional religious faith. The poet first offers some specific observations about the sea, then connects these details to his ideas about faith.

As you read each poem, consider how the extended metaphor helps to convey a theme about the period when the poem was written.

Focus on Genre
↳ Lyric Poetry

- expresses strong feelings or thoughts
- has a musical quality
- deals with intense emotions surrounding events like death, love, or loss
- includes forms such as ode, elegy, and sonnet

Analyze Sound Devices

The earliest poetry was composed to be sung in performance. Poets still use sound devices to create musical effects and to help unify lines and stanzas. The most common sound devices are rhyme and meter. Here are some other types of sound devices.

- **Alliteration**—the repetition of a consonant sound at the beginning of words (*His crypt the cloudy canopy*)

- **Assonance**—the repetition of a vowel sound in two or more stressed syllables that do not end with the same consonant (*The tide is full, the moon lies fair*)

- **Consonance**—the repetition of consonant sounds within and at the end of words (*Like strings of broken lyres*)

- **Onomatopoeia**—the use of words whose sounds echo their meanings (*grating*)

After you read these poems the first time, read them again aloud and notice how the sound devices appeal to your sense of hearing and add to the beauty of the language. Also, consider how sound devices support each poem's mood, tone, and theme.

Annotation in Action

Here is an example of notes a student made about these lines from
"Dover Beach." As you read both poems, mark examples of sound devices
that each poet uses.

> The sea is calm tonight.
> The tide is full, the moon lies fair
> Upon the straits—on the French coast the light
> Gleams and is gone; the cliffs of England stand,
> Glimmering and vast, out in the tranquil bay.
> Come to the window, sweet is the night air!

"G" sound alliteration. Gives it a peaceful mood.

Background

Matthew Arnold (1822–1888) was one of the leading poets and essayists of the Victorian era. In his youth, he struggled to live up to the expectations of his father, a famous headmaster of Rugby School. Arnold attended Rugby and then Oxford University; he later held teaching positions at both schools. While at Oxford, he began to gain recognition for his poetry. Arnold's poems are contemplative, often addressing serious themes of isolation and religious doubt.

Thomas Hardy (1840–1928) was born in a small village in southwestern England, the setting of many of his novels and poems. As a young man, he wrote poems and stories in his spare time while working as an architect. Hardy became famous for his novels, although their pessimism and controversial subject matter were often criticized. He published "The Darkling Thrush" just a few days before the end of the 19th century.

Dover Beach

Poem by **Matthew Arnold**

Note how Arnold uses figurative language to convey his perspective on the world.

N NOTICE & NOTE

As you read, use the side margins to make notes about the text.

3 **straits:** the Strait of Dover, a narrow channel separating England and France, located at the northern end of the English Channel.

8 **moon-blanched:** shining palely in the moonlight.

Close Read Screencast

Listen to a modeled close read of this text.

13 **tremulous cadence** (trĕm´yə-ləs kād´ns): trembling rhythm.

The sea is calm tonight.
The tide is full, the moon lies fair
Upon the straits—on the French coast the light
Gleams and is gone; the cliffs of England stand,
5   Glimmering and vast, out in the tranquil bay.
Come to the window, sweet is the night air!
Only, from the long line of spray
Where the sea meets the moon-blanched land,
Listen! you hear the grating roar
10 Of pebbles which the waves draw back, and fling,
At their return, up the high strand,
Begin, and cease, and then again begin,
With tremulous cadence slow, and bring
The eternal note of sadness in.

Don't forget to
Notice & Note as you
read the text.

15   Sophocles long ago
     Heard it on the Aegean, and it brought
     Into his mind the turbid ebb and flow
     Of human misery; we
     Find also in the sound a thought,
20   Hearing it by this distant northern sea.

     The Sea of Faith
     Was once, too, at the full, and round earth's shore
     Lay like the folds of a bright girdle furled.
     But now I only hear
25   Its melancholy, long, withdrawing roar,
     Retreating, to the breath
     Of the night wind, down the vast edges drear
     And naked shingles of the world.

15 **Sophocles** (sŏf´ə-klēz): an ancient Greek writer of tragic plays.

16 **Aegean** (ĭ-jē´ən): the Aegean Sea, the portion of the Mediterranean Sea between Greece and Turkey.

17 **turbid:** in a state of turmoil; muddled.

21 **Sea of Faith:** traditional religious beliefs about God and the world, long viewed as true and unshakable.

23 **girdle:** a belt or sash worn around the waist.

27 **drear:** dreary.

28 **shingles:** pebbly beaches.

ANALYZE SOUND DEVICES

Annotate: Read lines 29–37 aloud. Mark sound devices you notice.

Analyze: What mood do the sound devices help create?

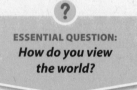

ESSENTIAL QUESTION:
How do you view the world?

Review your notes and add your thoughts to your Response Log.

Ah, love, let us be true
30 To one another! for the world, which seems
To lie before us like a land of dreams,
So various, so beautiful, so new,
Hath really neither joy, nor love, nor light,
Nor certitude, nor peace, nor help for pain;
35 And we are here as on a darkling plain
Swept with confused alarms of struggle and flight,
Where ignorant armies clash by night.

COLLABORATIVE DISCUSSION

With a partner, share your reaction to the speaker's thoughts about the world.

Assessment Practice

Answer these questions about "Dover Beach" before moving on to the next selection.

1. In the poem, the speaker is —

    (A) looking out to sea from the English coast

    (B) sailing on a ship in the English Channel

    (C) swimming in the Aegean Sea

    (D) fighting in a war in France

2. What does the speaker compare to waves pulling back from the shore?

    (A) armed conflict

    (B) ships sailing into the channel

    (C) loss of religious faith

    (D) lovers parting

3. The speaker takes comfort in —

    (A) his spirituality

    (B) nature's beauty

    (C) social progress

    (D) personal relationships

Test-Taking Strategies

B

The Darkling Thrush

Poem by **Thomas Hardy**

Notice the poet's word choices in describing a landscape.

1 **coppice** (kŏp´ĭs) **gate:** a gate leading to a coppice, a small wood or thicket.

2 **specter-gray:** ghost-gray.

5 **bine-stems scored:** twining stems cut across.

6 **lyres:** harp-like musical instruments.

7 **nigh:** near.

10 **outleant:** outstretched.

13 **germ:** seed; bud.

19 **evensong:** evening song.

20 **illimited:** unlimited.

22 **blast-beruffled plume:** wind-ruffled feathers.

I leant upon a coppice gate
    When Frost was specter-gray,
And Winter's dregs made desolate
    The weakening eye of day.
5 The tangled bine-stems scored the sky
    Like strings of broken lyres,
And all mankind that haunted nigh
    Had sought their household fires.

The land's sharp features seemed to be
10   The Century's corpse outleant,
His crypt the cloudy canopy,
    The wind his death-lament.
The ancient pulse of germ and birth
    Was shrunken hard and dry,
15 And every spirit upon earth
    Seem'd fervorless as I.

At once a voice arose among
    The bleak twigs overhead
In a full-hearted evensong
20   Of joy illimited;
An aged thrush, frail, gaunt, and small,
    In blast-beruffled plume,
Had chosen thus to fling his soul
    Upon the growing gloom.

25 So little cause for carollings
     Of such ecstatic sound
Was written on terrestrial things
     Afar or nigh around,
That I could think there trembled through
30   His happy good-night air
Some blessed Hope, whereof he knew
     And I was unaware.

ESSENTIAL QUESTION:
How do you view the world?

Review your notes and add your thoughts to your Response Log.

COLLABORATIVE DISCUSSION

Turn to a partner and discuss your impressions of the speaker.

Assessment Practice

Answer these questions before moving on to the **Analyze the Texts** section on the following page.

1. What is the poem's setting?

(A) sunrise on a mountain slope

(B) an open snowy field

(C) a lake's frozen shore

(D) the edge of the woods in winter

2. The lines "Had chosen thus to fling his soul / Upon the growing gloom" suggest that the thrush —

(A) shares the speaker's sense of hopelessness

(B) is defying the grimness of its surroundings

(C) probably won't live much longer

(D) has flown down from the tree branch

3. The speaker says in lines 29–32 that —

(A) the thrush may have some unknown reason to be happy

(B) he understands why the thrush sings joyfully

(C) he mistook the thrush's singing as a sign of hope

(D) the singing has plunged him even deeper into despair

Test-Taking Strategies

Analyze the Texts

Support your responses with evidence from the texts.

NOTICE & NOTE

Review what you **noticed and noted** as you read the texts. Your annotations can help you answer these questions.

1 **ANALYZE** In "Dover Beach," how does Arnold use details about the sea to develop his extended metaphor about faith?

2 **INFER** Arnold refers to Sophocles in lines 15–20 of "Dover Beach." What idea does he suggest through this allusion to the ancient Greek playwright?

3 **INTERPRET** Reread lines 29–37 of "Dover Beach." How does the speaker's description of the world connect to his plea that he and his love "be true / To one another"?

4 **ANALYZE** How does Hardy's use of alliteration and assonance in lines 1–4 of "The Darkling Thrush" support the poem's theme?

5 **ANALYZE** Use the graphic organizer to identify details in lines 9–16 of "The Darkling Thrush" that compare the landscape to the century. What idea does Hardy express through this extended metaphor?

The Landscape	The Century

6 **DRAW CONCLUSIONS** In "The Darkling Thrush," why did Hardy choose to describe the bird as an "aged thrush, frail, gaunt, and small"?

Choices

Here are some other ways to demonstrate your understanding of the ideas in this lesson.

Writing
↳ **Poem**

In "Dover Beach," the speaker expresses his thoughts to his beloved as they look out a window at the ocean. Write a poem in which she expresses her thoughts in response. Consider:

- Does she share his pessimistic outlook on life, or is she more hopeful?

- Is she ready to put all her faith in their personal relationship, or does she want to stay engaged in the world?

As you write and discuss, be sure to use the **Academic Vocabulary** words.

> abandon

> confine

> conform

> depress

> reluctance

Media
↳ **Poster**

The speaker of "The Darkling Thrush" finds hope in the singing of an old bird. Create a poster that expresses your own idea of hope.

1. Choose a computer application for designing your poster, or gather materials such as poster board and markers.

2. Identify your audience and the message you want to send.

3. Combine text and one or more images in an eye-catching design.

Social & Emotional Learning
↳ **Group Discussion**

Matthew Arnold wrote "Dover Beach" in response to scientific and political developments of his time. With a group of students, discuss recent developments or events that make you worried about the future.

- Explain how these developments or events might impact your lives.

- Discuss how they are presented in the media.

- Suggest actions you can take to feel better about the future.

Compare Themes

A poem's **theme** is the message the author conveys to the reader. Although even a short poem may express several ideas, the theme is the major idea that the poet communicates. Themes are developed through word choice, imagery, figurative language, and other elements.

In both "Dover Beach" and "The Darkling Thrush," the poets use their descriptions of nature to express themes about disillusionment and hopelessness.

Poets seldom directly state their themes, so you must infer them from a close reading of a poem. As you read to understand each poem's message, consider the following:

- **Key statements**—ideas stated directly by the speaker
- **Imagery**—details that appeal to the reader's senses
- **Figurative language**—language that communicates ideas beyond the literal meaning of the words

With your group, complete the chart with details from both poems.

	A "Dover Beach"	B "The Darkling Thrush"
Key Statements		
Imagery		
Figurative Language		

Analyze the Texts

Discuss these questions in your group:

1. **ANALYZE** Both poems start out with descriptions of nature. What literary elements does each poet rely on to develop his description?

2. **COMPARE** How are these two poems similar or different in mood?

3. **DRAW CONCLUSIONS** Which poem expresses a more hopeful view of the world? Explain.

4. **ANALYZE** Both poems include extended metaphors comparing something in nature with an abstract idea. How does this technique help the poets develop their poems?

Collaborate and Present

Now, with your group, continue exploring the ideas in the poems by identifying and comparing their themes. Follow these steps:

1. **DECIDE ON THE MOST IMPORTANT DETAILS** With your group, review your chart to identify the most important details from each poem. Identify points on which you agree, and resolve disagreements by identifying evidence from the poems that support your ideas.

2. **DETERMINE A THEME** Based on the word choices, figurative language, sound devices, and feelings evoked in each poem, determine a theme for each. You may use a chart to keep track of the themes your group members suggest.

	Details	Theme
"Dover Beach"		
"The Darkling Thrush"		

3. **COMPARE THEMES** Compare the two poems' themes with your group, discussing similarities and differences. Listen actively to the members of your group, and ask them to clarify any points you do not understand.

4. **PRESENT TO THE CLASS** Next, present your ideas to the class. Be sure to include clear statements on the theme for each poem. Discuss whether the themes are similar or different. You may add other visuals or diagrams to help convey information to the class.

Collaborate & Compare

Compare Themes

As you read "My Last Duchess" and "Blood," notice how each poem uses a work of art to reveal how a woman has experienced injustice.

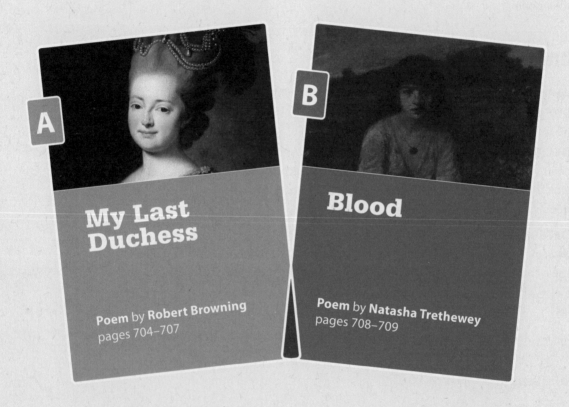

A

My Last Duchess

Poem by **Robert Browning**
pages 704–707

B

Blood

Poem by **Natasha Trethewey**
pages 708–709

After you have read the poems, you will collaborate with a small group to compare their themes. You will follow these steps:

- Decide on the most important details
- Determine themes
- Compare themes
- Develop your ideas
- Present to the class

My Last Duchess

Poem by **Robert Browning**

Blood

Poem by **Natasha Trethewey**

Engage Your Brain

Choose one or more of these activities to start connecting with the poems you're about to read.

A Nagging Feeling

The speaker of "My Last Duchess" is unusually alert to flaws in other people. You probably know someone who tends to criticize friends or family members. What is the danger of being overly critical in your interactions with others? Discuss this question with a small group of classmates.

Fascinating Villains

Think of some unpleasant, even horrible characters that you've enjoyed reading about or watching in movies. Choose one example and create a social media profile of the character. Include details that show why the character is so fascinating.

The Art of Poetry

The poem "Blood" comments on a well-known 19th-century painting. There's a long tradition of poems inspired by paintings and sculptures. Write a short poem about one of your favorite artworks.

- Express an idea about the artwork.

- Explore how it makes you feel.

- Include vivid imagery to help readers visualize the artwork.

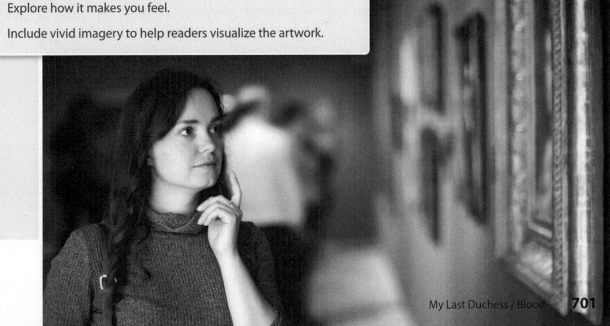

Draw Conclusions About Speakers

Every poem has a speaker, the voice that addresses the reader. In some poems the speaker is a detached observer. Other speakers are more directly involved in the experience described in the poem.

A **dramatic monologue** is a poem in which the speaker addresses a silent or absent listener during an intense or emotionally complex moment. Browning's "My Last Duchess," a famous monologue, is set in 16th-century Italy. The speaker is a duke who negotiates with an agent in order to marry a count's daughter. Notice how Browning begins the poem in the middle of their conversation:

> That's my last Duchess painted on the wall,
> Looking as if she were alive.

Dramatic monologues require readers to make inferences: the speakers reveal themselves by dropping clues that the reader must piece together. Sometimes the clues leave matters uncertain, and readers should understand that their inferences are only guesses.

As you read "My Last Duchess," gather evidence and draw conclusions about the speaker's character and actions. Then, as you read "Blood," see what you can conclude about the speaker based on thoughts expressed in the poem.

Focus on Genre
↳ **Lyric Poetry**

- is usually written in the first person
- expresses the feelings and thoughts of the speaker, who may be a fictional character
- uses sound devices, such as rhythm and repetition, to create a musical quality
- often deals with intense emotions surrounding events like death, love, or loss

Analyze Imagery

Imagery refers to words and phrases that create vivid sensory experiences for the reader. Most imagery is visual, but imagery can also appeal to the senses of smell, hearing, taste, and touch. Imagery appears in all literary forms, but it is especially important in poetry for establishing a mood or tone, expressing emotions, and conveying ideas.

The two poems in this lesson, which describe paintings, are rich in visual imagery. As you read, notice how each poet uses an image or group of images to support the poem's theme. Use a chart like this one to help you analyze ideas and feelings associated with the imagery.

Example of Imagery	Ideas or Feelings Linked to Image
"the faint / Half-flush that dies along her throat"	The duchess blushes easily.

Annotation in Action

Here is an example of notes a student made about these lines from "My Last Duchess." As you read both poems, highlight details that help you draw conclusions about the speakers.

That's my last Duchess painted on the wall,
Looking as if she were alive. I call
That piece a wonder, now: Frà Pandolf's hands
Worked busily a day, and there she stands.
Will't please you sit and look at her?

A cold way to refer to his dead wife. But, the painting seems important to him.

Background

Robert Browning (1812–1889) showed intellectual brilliance at a young age. When his first book of poetry was harshly criticized for its personal content, he decided to write poems about people and characters other than himself. Browning married the poet Elizabeth Barrett in 1846; they lived happily together in Italy until her death 15 years later. After decades of obscurity, Browning began to gain recognition during the 1860s for his dramatic monologues. He is widely considered one of the most important poets of the Victorian era.

Natasha Trethewey (1966–) was born in Gulfport, Mississippi. Her father was a white Canadian immigrant who wrote poetry, and her mother was an African American social worker. Because interracial marriage was still illegal in Mississippi, they had to cross over into Ohio to get married. Trethewey often addresses issues of racial identity and African American history in her poems. She won the Pulitzer Prize in Poetry in 2007 and served as U.S. Poet Laureate from 2012 to 2014. In addition to her books of poetry, Trethewey has published a widely acclaimed memoir of her mother, Gwendolyn Turnbough, who was murdered when Trethewey was 19.

NOTICE & NOTE

As you read, use the side margins to make notes about the text.

My Last Duchess

Poem by **Robert Browning**

Note how Browning reveals the speaker's thoughts and feelings about his late wife.

3 **Frà Pandolf's:** of Brother Pandolf, a fictitious friar-painter.

DRAW CONCLUSIONS ABOUT SPEAKERS

Annotate: Mark the phrases in lines 5–13 that hint at the character of the speaker.

Infer: What can you infer about the duke? What details support your inference?

11 **durst:** dared.

16 **mantle:** cloak.

That's my last Duchess painted on the wall,
Looking as if she were alive. I call
That piece a wonder, now: Frà Pandolf's hands
Worked busily a day, and there she stands.
5 Will't please you sit and look at her? I said
"Frà Pandolf" by design, for never read
Strangers like you that pictured countenance,
The depth and passion of its earnest glance,
But to myself they turned (since none puts by
10 The curtain I have drawn for you, but I)
And seemed as they would ask me, if they durst,
How such a glance came there; so, not the first
Are you to turn and ask thus. Sir, 'twas not
Her husband's presence only, called that spot
15 Of joy into the Duchess' cheek: perhaps
Frà Pandolf chanced to say "Her mantle laps
Over my lady's wrist too much," or "Paint

Must never hope to reproduce the faint
Half-flush that dies along her throat": such stuff
20   Was courtesy, she thought, and cause enough
For calling up that spot of joy. She had
A heart—how shall I say?—too soon made glad,
Too easily impressed; she liked whate'er
She looked on, and her looks went everywhere.
25   Sir, 'twas all one! My favor at her breast,
The dropping of the daylight in the West,
The bough of cherries some officious fool
Broke in the orchard for her, the white mule
She rode with round the terrace—all and each
30   Would draw from her alike the approving speech,
Or blush, at least. She thanked men—good! but thanked
Somehow—I know not how—as if she ranked
My gift of a nine-hundred-years-old name
With anybody's gift. Who'd stoop to blame
35   This sort of trifling? Even had you skill
In speech—(which I have not)—to make your will
Quite clear to such an one, and say, "Just this
Or that in you disgusts me; here you miss,
Or there exceed the mark"—and if she let
40   Herself be lessoned so, nor plainly set
Her wits to yours, forsooth, and made excuse

© Houghton Mifflin Harcourt Publishing Company • Image Credits: ©Album/Alamy

ANALYZE IMAGERY

Annotate: Mark images and other details in lines 21–34 that describe what the duchess was like.

Compare: How does her character differ from that of the duke?

27 officious: offering unwanted services; meddling.

35 trifling: actions of little importance.

41 forsooth: in truth; indeed.

—E'en then would be some stooping; and I choose
Never to stoop. Oh sir, she smiled, no doubt,
Whene'er I passed her; but who passed without
45 Much the same smile? This grew; I gave commands;
Then all smiles stopped together. There she stands
As if alive. Will't please you rise? We'll meet
The company below, then. I repeat,
The Count your master's known munificence
50 Is ample warrant that no just pretense
Of mine for dowry will be disallowed;
Though his fair daughter's self, as I avowed
At starting, is my object. Nay, we'll go
Together down, sir. Notice Neptune, though,
55 Taming a sea horse, thought a rarity,
Which Claus of Innsbruck cast in bronze for me!

49 **munificence** (myoo-nĭf´ĭ-səns): generosity.

50 **just pretense:** legitimate claim.

51 **dowry** (dou´rē): payment given to a groom by the bride's father.

54 **Neptune:** in Roman mythology, the god of the sea.

DRAW CONCLUSIONS ABOUT SPEAKERS

Annotate: Mark the words in lines 43–56 that reveal the duke's sense of his own authority and power.

Interpret: What is the duke's motivation for telling the listener the story of his late wife? Has he revealed more than he intended? Explain.

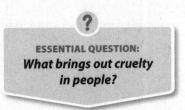

ESSENTIAL QUESTION:
What brings out cruelty in people?

Review your notes and add your thoughts to your Response Log.

COLLABORATIVE DISCUSSION

Get together with a partner or small group, and discuss the duke's comments about his late wife. What surprised you about this poem?

Assessment Practice

Answer these questions about "My Last Duchess" before moving on to the next selection.

1. In the discussion of the duchess's portrait, the duke focuses on the —

   (A) value of the painting

   (B) style of the painter

   (C) duchess's beauty

   (D) expression on her face

2. The duke thinks that he should be admired because of his —

   (A) social status

   (B) intelligence

   (C) appearance

   (D) eloquence

3. Why didn't the duke tell his late wife that she was offending him?

   (A) He was worried she would leave him.

   (B) He was too proud to complain.

   (C) He wanted her to figure it out on her own.

   (D) He knew she would die soon.

Test-Taking Strategies

© Houghton Mifflin Harcourt Publishing Company • Image Credits: The Quadroon (1880), George Fuller/Gift of George A. Hearn, 1910/Metropolitan Museum of Art

Blood

After George Fuller's The Quadroon, *1880*

Poem by **Natasha Trethewey**

Quadroon: a term, now considered offensive, that describes a person of one-quarter Black ancestry.

 NOTICE & NOTE

As you read, use the side margins to make notes about the text.

ANALYZE IMAGERY

Annotate: Mark details about the painting in lines 6–14.

Identify: Which phrases highlight the difference between the main subject of the painting and the other figures?

9 gleaner: someone who gathers grain or other produce left behind in a field.

10 undine: a water spirit.

12 *Mezzo:* Italian word for "middle."

Note the speaker's interpretation of details in the painting.

It must be the gaze of a benevolent viewer
upon her, framed as she is in the painting's
romantic glow, her melancholic beauty
meant to show the pathos of her condition:
5   *black blood*—that she cannot transcend it.
In the foreground she is shown at rest, seated,
her basket empty and overturned beside her
as though she would cast down the drudgery
to which she was born. A gleaner, hopeless
10 undine—the bucolic backdrop a dim aura
around her—she looks out toward us as if
to bridge the distance between. *Mezzo,*
intermediate, how different she's rendered
from the dark kin working the fields behind her.
15 If not for the ray of light appearing as if from beyond
the canvas, we might miss them—three figures
in the near distance, small as afterthought.

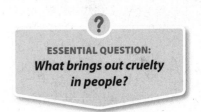

ESSENTIAL QUESTION:
What brings out cruelty in people?

Review your notes and add your thoughts to your Response Log.

COLLABORATIVE DISCUSSION

With a partner, compare the speaker's comments about the painting with your own reaction to it.

Assessment Practice

Answer these questions before moving on to the **Analyze the Texts** section on the following page.

1. Why does the speaker conclude that the painter of *The Quadroon* had the gaze of a "benevolent viewer"?

   A The woman stares directly at the viewer.

   B The painting conveys the woman's beauty and sadness.

   C The painter decided to show her at rest instead of working.

   D Portraits of African Americans were rare in the 19th century.

2. What does the phrase "pathos of her condition" in line 4 refer to?

   A the painting's romantic setting

   B the hardship of working in the fields

   C the woman's isolation from other workers

   D the woman's racial classification as a "quadroon"

3. Which statement is best supported by the poem?

   A The painting shows a woman's rebellion against authority.

   B The speaker believes that *The Quadroon* is a great painting.

   C Racial categories create senseless divisions between people.

   D The subject of the painting felt superior to the other workers.

Test-Taking Strategies

Analyze the Texts

Support your responses with evidence from the texts.

(1) ANALYZE Which images does Browning use repeatedly in "My Last Duchess"? What does this repetition reveal about the speaker's personality?

(2) DRAW CONCLUSIONS What do the following lines suggest about the reason for the duke's "disgust" at his wife's behavior?

- "she liked whate'er / She looked on, and her looks went everywhere" (lines 23–24)

- "all and each / Would draw from her alike the approving speech, / Or blush, at least" (lines 29–31)

- "as if she ranked / My gift of a nine-hundred-years-old name / With anybody's gift" (lines 32–34)

(3) INTERPRET In lines 45–46 of "My Last Duchess," the speaker says, "I gave commands; / Then all smiles stopped together." How do you interpret this statement? Why might Browning have chosen to leave the results of the duke's commands uncertain?

(4) ANALYZE What is ironic about the duke's attempt to impress the count's agent?

(5) ANALYZE Trethewey ends "Blood" with a description of field workers in the background of the painting. What idea does she convey through these visual images?

(6) DRAW CONCLUSIONS What can you conclude about the speaker's attitude toward the way George Fuller represented the mixed-race woman and the other figures in his painting?

(7) CRITIQUE Trethewey chose to discuss Fuller's painting in "Blood" instead of addressing 19th-century racial categories more directly. Do you think that her approach to this subject is effective? Explain why or why not.

Choices

Here are some other ways to demonstrate your understanding of the ideas in this lesson.

Writing
↳ Monologue

John Keats ends his famous poem "Ode on a Grecian Urn" with these mysterious lines:

> *"Beauty is truth, truth beauty,"—that is all*
> *Ye know on earth, and all ye need to know.*

Imagine that you are one of the speakers of the poems in this lesson. Write a prose or verse monologue in which you respond to Keats's idea about beauty and art.

As you write and discuss, be sure to use the **Academic Vocabulary** words.

| abandon |
| confine |
| conform |
| depress |
| reluctance |

Research
↳ Playlist

Feelings of jealousy have been expressed by human beings throughout the ages and across societies. Research songs that address the topic of jealousy and its consequences. Then, create a playlist of your top five songs. Try to find examples of songs from different periods and in different styles. With a partner, share your playlists and discuss what the songs have in common with the poems you read in this lesson.

Speaking & Listening
↳ Oral Presentation

"My Last Duchess" and "Blood" present contrasts in tone and language. The speaker in "My Last Duchess" is a fictional character who expresses his feelings using diction that reflects the Renaissance period. "Blood," on the other hand, has a more detached, contemporary speaker. Choose which poem you would like to read aloud, and prepare an oral presentation.

- Mark the text to indicate shifts in thought or feeling that you want to convey to your audience.

- Note the pronunciation of any difficult words, and look them up in a dictionary if needed.

- Plan appropriate gestures to accompany your reading.

Compare Themes

"My Last Duchess" and "Blood" both discuss paintings, and they also feature women who are treated unjustly. Still, the poems express different messages about human nature.

With your group, discuss each aspect of the poems listed in the chart and record your observations.

	A "My Last Duchess"	B "Blood"
Subject		
Setting		
Injustice revealed		
Speaker's perspective		

Analyze the Texts

Discuss these questions in your group.

1. **COMPARE** What similarities and differences do you see in the situations of the duchess in Browning's poem and the mixed-race woman in "Blood"?

2. **ANALYZE** In each poem, what is the speaker's attitude toward the artist's ability to capture reality?

3. **CONNECT** How does the title of each poem hint at an injustice that the poem reveals?

Collaborate and Present

In your group, continue exploring the ideas in the poems by identifying and comparing their themes. Follow these steps:

1. **DECIDE ON THE MOST IMPORTANT DETAILS** As a group, review the information you gathered in the previous chart. Determine which points you agree on, and resolve disagreements by identifying evidence from the poems that supports your ideas.

2. **DETERMINE THEMES** Write theme statements, or statements that express each poem's message about life or human nature. Use the chart below to help you track your group's ideas and identify possible themes.

	Notes	Possible Themes
"My Last Duchess"		
"Blood"		

3. **COMPARE THEMES** Work together as a group to determine similarities and differences between the themes.

4. **DEVELOP YOUR IDEAS** Organize your ideas around your points of comparison, and provide evidence and explanations for each.

5. **PRESENT TO THE CLASS** Determine how you will present your comparison, who will present it, and if the use of any visuals or diagrams would help clarify your points. Consider using technology as a presentation tool.

Reader's Choice

Continue your exploration of the Essential Questions for this unit by doing some independent reading. Read the titles and descriptions shown. Then mark the texts that interest you.

ESSENTIAL QUESTION:
? *Review the four Essential Questions for this unit on page 617.*

Short Reads Available on ☺Ed

These texts are available in your ebook. Choose one to read and rate. Then defend your rating to the class.

Sonnet 43
Poem by
Elizabeth Barrett Browning

The breadth and depth of love are explored in this passionate sonnet.

Rate It

Remembrance
Poem by **Emily Brontë**

Must one mourn forever to be faithful to a dead lover?

Rate It

Song
Poem by **Christina Rossetti**

The speaker contemplates what will happen after she dies.

Rate It

The Great Exhibition
Article by **Lara Kriegel**

The first world's fair brought visitors to London from all over the globe.

Rate It

Evidence of Progress
Essay by
Thomas Babington Macaulay

During times of turmoil, how can you tell whether a nation is taking steps toward a better future?

Rate It

Long Reads

Here are three recommended books that connect to this unit. For additional options, ask your teacher, school librarian, or peers. Which titles spark your interest?

Great Expectations

Novel by **Charles Dickens**

Pip has little chance for advancement until a mysterious benefactor allows him to escape the Kent marshes for a more promising life in London.

The Eyre Affair

Novel by **Jasper Fforde**

In an alternate reality, literary detective Thursday Next pursues a criminal guilty of kidnapping Jane Eyre from the novel's pages.

While the Locust Slept

Memoir by **Peter Razor**

Abandoned as an infant, Peter has suffered abuse at the hands of those caring for him. He dreams of another, better life.

Extension

↳ Connect & Create

DIALOGUE Write a brief dialogue in which you respond to an idea or feeling expressed in one of the texts. In the dialogue, you can have a discussion with the speaker of one of the poems, a character in a novel, or the author of a nonfiction text.

LESSONS FROM ADVERSITY In a small group, discuss the personal struggles portrayed in the book you chose. Consider the following questions:

- How was the character or author affected by these struggles?

- What lessons can you draw from the experiences portrayed in the book?

 NOTICE & NOTE

- Pick one of the texts and annotate the Notice & Note signposts you find.

- Then, use the **Notice & Note Writing Frames** to help you write about the significance of the signposts.

- Compare your findings with those of other students who read the same text.

Notice & Note Writing Frames

Write a Research Report

Writing Prompt

Review the texts that show the impact of technological developments on the lives of Victorians. Then consult outside sources to write a report about a modern invention that changed the way people live today.

Manage your time carefully so that you can

- consult sources and develop research questions;
- plan your research report;
- write your research report; and
- revise and edit your research report.

Be sure to

- choose credible sources for your report;
- introduce your topic and thesis statement;
- develop your ideas with relevant information;
- end with a concluding paragraph; and
- cite each outside source used in your text.

> ### Review the
> ### Mentor Text
>
> For one example of a well-written essay that uses outside sources, which you can use as a mentor text as well as a source for your report, review
>
> - **"The Victorians Had the Same Concerns About Technology As We Do"** (pages 677–681)
>
> Make sure to carefully review your notes and annotations about this text. Think about the sources the author uses to support her thesis about the impact of technology.

Consider Your Sources

Review the list of Unit 5 texts and consider which ones might provide ideas, information, or examples that can help you plan your research report.

As you review the selections, consult the notes you made in your **Response Log** that relate to the question "Which invention has had the greatest impact on your life?" Make additional notes about ideas that might help you develop research questions and find appropriate sources of information.

UNIT 5 SOURCES

- [ ] *from* **Jane Eyre**
- [ ] **"Factory Reform"** MEDIA
- [ ] **"The Lady of Shalott"**
- [ ] *from* **Great Expectations**
- [ ] **"The Victorians Had the Same Concerns About Technology As We Do"**
- [ ] **"Dover Beach"**
- [ ] **"The Darkling Thrush"**
- [ ] **"My Last Duchess"**
- [ ] **"Blood"**

Analyze the Prompt

Analyze the prompt to make sure you understand the assignment.

1. Underline the sentence in the prompt that identifies the topic of your research report. Rephrase this sentence in your own words.

2. Circle words or phrases that identify your writing task. Rephrase the task in your own words.

3. Look for words that tell you the purpose and audience of your research report. Write a sentence describing each.

Consider Your Audience

Ask yourself these questions:

- Who will read my report?
- What do readers already know about my topic?
- What do readers need to know?

What is my topic? What is my writing task?

What is my purpose?

Who is my audience?

Review the Rubric

Your research report will be scored using a rubric. As you write, focus on the characteristics of a high-scoring essay as described in the chart. You will learn more about these characteristics as you work through the lesson.

Purpose, Focus, and Organization	Evidence and Elaboration	Conventions of Standard English
The response includes: • A strongly maintained controlling idea • Use of transitions to connect ideas • Logical progression of ideas • Appropriate style and tone	The response includes: • Effective use of evidence and sources • Effective use of elaboration • Clear and effective expression of ideas • Appropriate vocabulary • Varied sentence structure	The response may include: • Some minor errors in usage but no patterns of errors • Correct punctuation, capitalization, sentence formation, and spelling • Command of basic conventions

1 PLAN YOUR RESEARCH REPORT

Develop Research Questions

Research questions will guide your research. Try to create three questions about the impact of technology that you can explore in a modern context.

Research Questions

Research questions should be focused and specific. Use the basic question words—*who, what, where, why, when,* and *how*—to develop your research questions.

Topic	Research Questions
One technological invention that has had an impact on people today	1. 2. 3.

Identify Sources and Information

Consult print and online sources for relevant, accurate information that answers your questions.

 Help with Planning

Consult **Interactive Writing Lesson: Conducting Research.**

- **Sources** include reliable and authoritative books, articles, encyclopedia entries, and websites.
- **Relevant information** includes facts, statistics, examples, definitions, and quotations.

Use the chart to identify your sources. Include the author, title, date, page number, and other publication information.

Sources	
Source(s) for Question 1	Information
Source(s) for Question 2	Information
Source(s) for Question 3	Information

Develop Your Thesis

Your thesis identifies your topic and answers an important question about it. You can support your thesis with solid key ideas. Use the chart below to write your thesis and at least three key ideas from your sources that support it.

Thesis:
Key Ideas:

Organize Ideas

Next you will need to organize your ideas in a logical way and use transitions to show relationships among ideas. Use the table below to help you structure your research report.

Structure

Arrange your key ideas in order of importance. Here are two options:

- Begin with your most important key idea and end with your least important key idea.
- Begin with the least important key idea and build up to the most important one.

INTRODUCTION	• Introduce your topic and state your thesis. • Include an interesting observation, quotation, or detail to "hook" readers.
BODY PARAGRAPHS	• Present key ideas that support your thesis, devoting a paragraph to each key idea. • Cite and paraphrase or quote your sources. • Use transition words to link ideas.
CONCLUSION	• Restate your thesis and state its significance. • Summarize your key ideas.
WORKS CITED	• List your sources using an appropriate formatting style.

2 DEVELOP A DRAFT

Now it is time to draft your research report. You can improve your writing by learning from the experts. Read about the techniques professional writers use to introduce and present their research.

Write an Introduction

EXAMINE THE MENTOR TEXT

Notice how Melissa Dickson, the author of "The Victorians Had the Same Concerns About Technology As We Do," clearly states her thesis at the beginning of her essay.

The Victorians Had the Same Concerns About Technology As We Do

Essay by Melissa Dickson

The author begins by providing needed **background information.**

> Many of us struggle with the bombardment of information we receive and experience anxiety as a result of new media, which we feel threaten our relationships and "usual" modes of human interaction. . . . More than a century ago our forebears had the same concerns. Literary, medical and cultural responses in the Victorian age to the perceived problems of stress and overwork anticipate many of the preoccupations of our own era to an extent that is perhaps surprising.

The author states her **thesis.**

APPLY TO YOUR DRAFT

As you write your introduction, make sure you

- introduce your topic;
- include an observation, detail, or quotation that grabs readers' attention;
- add relevant background information; and
- present your thesis statement.

Practice writing a sentence for each element. Be sure to use formal language.

Topic	
Observation, Detail, or Quotation	
Background Information	
Thesis	

Cite Sources

EXAMINE THE MENTOR TEXT

Here, notice how Melissa Dickson introduces a key idea about similar Victorian and modern views. She then cites a source to support her analysis.

Drafting Online

Check your assignment list for a writing task from your teacher.

> Arguments along not at all dissimilar lines have been advanced against contemporary means of acquiring information. . . . In his 2008 article, "Is Google Making Us Stupid?", journalist Nicholas Carr speculated that "we may well be in the midst of a sea change in the way we read and think". Reading online, he posits, discourages long and thoughtful immersion in texts. . . .

The author **paraphrases** additional content from the source to integrate it into her discussion.

The author quotes from a source to support the idea, providing a specific citation for the **quotation.**

APPLY TO YOUR DRAFT

You can use different signal phrases to show that you are citing from a source. Try these out:

- In [Title of Source], the author states . . .
- According to paragraph [#], . . .
- The study/statistic proves . . .

Use this frame to practice citing a source from your draft. Then apply this technique to other sources in your report.

Using Direct Quotations

Your research report should include **direct quotations** from sources to support your key ideas.

- Quotation marks indicate exact words taken from the source.
- The quotation marks let readers know the information is an idea that you are crediting to a particular author.
- Other ideas in your report may be **paraphrases** of ideas borrowed from sources.

Introduce State one key idea that supports your thesis.	
Cite Cite the source that supports the key idea.	
Elaborate Explain how your source supports your idea.	

3 REVISE YOUR RESEARCH REPORT

Professional writers rework their language as they write to make sure they are communicating their ideas effectively. Use the guide to help you revise your report.

Help with Revision

Find a **Peer Review Guide** and **Student Models** online.

REVISION GUIDE		
Ask Yourself	**Prove It**	**Revise It**
Introduction Does the introduction engage the reader, provide background information, and clearly state the thesis?	**Circle** the engaging introduction. **Underline** the background information. **[Bracket]** the thesis statement.	**Add** a quotation or interesting detail to engage readers. **Add** necessary background information. **Add** a thesis statement.
Key Ideas and Support Do my body paragraphs include only relevant key ideas and information from sources?	**Highlight** the key ideas. **Number** (1, 2, 3 . . .) the supporting information for each key idea.	**Delete** irrelevant key ideas and information. **Add** information that supports key ideas.
Citing Sources Are sources introduced and credited correctly?	**Place check marks** (✔) next to material that is or should be cited.	**Introduce** the source material by identifying its author or publication. **Add** signal phrases. **Add** information from additional sources.
Conclusion Does the conclusion restate the thesis and explain its significance?	**Underline** the restatement of the thesis. **[Bracket]** the statement of the thesis's significance.	**Add** a restatement of the thesis. **Add** a sentence or two that explains the significance of the thesis.
Style Have I maintained a formal style?	**Circle** words and phrases that are too informal.	**Replace** informal language with formal language.

APPLY TO YOUR DRAFT

Reread your research report and look for opportunities to improve your writing.

- Consider whether your information is relevant to your key ideas.
- Use transitions that establish relationships among ideas.
- Make sure you identify and introduce your sources using signal phrases.

Peer Review in Action

Once you have finished revising your research report, you will exchange papers with a partner in a **peer review.** During a peer review, you will give suggestions to improve your partner's draft.

Read the beginning of a student's report draft and examine the comments made by his peer reviewer.

First Draft

Who Put the "I" in iPhone?
By Oscar Pelletier, Hanover Academy

The idea that we experience "anxiety as a result of new media" is pretty much washed out by the fact that there are like millions of cell phones in the world. And where do all these cell phones end up when they are suddenly obsolete? In landfills. But before they get there, they are in use everywhere and every minute of the day. That's why it's kind of too late to wonder what kind of effect they have on us.

Good idea to start with a quote. Could you introduce and cite the source?

Words like "pretty much" and "kind of" are informal. Try using more formal language.

This information doesn't really relate to your earlier point. Add a relevant fact, example, or detail here instead.

Now read the revised paragraph below. Notice how the writer has improved his draft by making revisions based on the peer reviewer's comments.

Revision

Who Put the "I" in iPhone?
By Oscar Pelletier, Hanover Academy

The idea that we experience what Melissa Dickson calls "anxiety as a result of new media" is negated by the fact that almost everyone has a cell phone. For example, when a sports arena can be lit up almost entirely by the tiny blue glowing rectangles of fans' mobile phone screens, it is long past time to consider whether cell phone technology is bad for us.

You replaced irrelevant information with a relevant example. Nice!

Good job introducing your source and making your language more formal.

APPLY TO YOUR DRAFT

During your peer review, give each other specific suggestions for how you could make your source citations more effective and your language more formal. Use the revision guide to help you.

When receiving feedback from your partner, listen attentively and ask questions to make sure you fully understand the revision suggestions.

4 EDIT YOUR RESEARCH REPORT

Edit your final draft to check for proper use of standard English conventions and to correct any misspellings or grammatical errors.

Watch Your Language!

COMBINING SENTENCES

Writers connect ideas by using coordinating and subordinating conjunctions to combine sentences.

Read the following sentences from "The Victorians Had the Same Concerns About Technology As We Do."

> [1] Print publications were fast becoming the principal medium of public debate and influence, [2] **and** they were shaping and, in Carlyle's view, distorting human learning and communications.

The numbers [1] and [2] label the two ideas that are connected. The coordinating conjunction *and* connects two independent clauses.

> [1] **Though** the technologies may change, [2] these fears actually have a very long history . . .

The subordinating conjunction *though* introduces a subordinate clause—one that cannot stand by itself as a complete sentence.

APPLY TO YOUR DRAFT

Now apply what you've learned about sentence combining to your own writing.

1. **Read your report aloud** and underline all the short sentences.

2. **Combine** some short sentences by using coordinating or subordinating conjunctions.

3. **Exchange drafts** with a peer and review the combined sentences in each other's drafts.

5 PUBLISH YOUR REPORT

Share It!

Finalize your report for your writing portfolio. You may also use your report as inspiration for other projects.

Use Conjunctions

Here are some common conjunctions to use in combining sentences:

- **Coordinating Conjunctions:** *and, but, so, or, nor, for, yet*

- **Subordinating Conjunctions:** *when, as, before, after* (**time**); *although, though, even if, while* (**contrast**); *because, if, unless* (**cause/effect**)

Ways to Share

- **Create a website** devoted to how teens use the latest technology in their daily lives.

- **Have a debate** about the impact of technology on young people.

- **Give a multimedia presentation** on the topic. See the Speaking and Listening Task.

Present Your Report

You will now adapt your research report as a multimedia presentation for your classmates. You will also watch your classmates' presentations and help them improve their work.

Plan a Multimedia Presentation

As you review your research report, think about how you can use slides and other presentation materials to present your ideas. Follow these steps:

- Plan the content and order of your slides.
- Choose engaging graphics, images, animation, music, audio clips, or sound effects.
- Create a consistent, appealing design.
- Prepare notes to guide you as you narrate the presentation.

Images and Sounds

Make sure the images, graphics, and audio you use come from reliable sources and are appropriate for the classroom.

Use the chart to take notes. Then create a draft of your multimedia presentation.

Ask Yourself	Answers and Notes
How will I convey my thesis and key ideas on the slides?	
What supporting information will I include?	
What images or graphics will best support that information?	
What music or sound effects will help enhance my ideas?	
What software should I use to create my presentation?	

Practice Your Presentation

Once you have completed a draft of your multimedia presentation, practice with a partner or group to improve your presentation and delivery.

Use the checklist to help you respond to the delivery and presentation of your partner or group members. Give specific suggestions for improvement.

Active Listening

When you are listening to your partner or group member, remember to

- give each presenter your attention
- paraphrase each presenter's thesis and key ideas to confirm understanding
- give clear and thoughtful feedback

Checklist	Suggestions for Improvement
Presentation: ☐ Each slide is clear and easy to read and understand. ☐ Music, animation, or other effects support your main points. ☐ The slides are presented in a logical sequence. **Delivery:** ☐ You speak slowly and clearly so that your listeners can understand you. ☐ You make eye contact with your audience.	

Deliver Your Presentation

Use the advice you received during practice to make any final changes. Do a final run-through of your presentation to make sure the images and audio appear at the correct time. Then deliver your multimedia presentation.

Share It!

- **Record your presentations.** With your teacher, plan how to combine and store the presentations.
- **Have a group discussion** about the images, graphics, and animation used in each presentation. Share your favorites.
- **Create a list** of the pros and cons of modern technology.

ⓔ **Ed**

Interactive Speaking & Listening Lesson: Giving a Presentation

Reflect & Extend

Here are some other ways to show your understanding of the ideas in Unit 5.

Reflect on the Essential Questions

Think about the Essential Question you identified as the most intriguing on page 618. Has your answer to the question changed after reading the texts in this unit? Discuss your ideas.

You can use these sentence starters to help you reflect on your learning.

- **My thoughts about this question changed because . . .**
- **I was surprised to learn that . . .**
- **I made a connection between this question and . . .**

Project-Based Learning
↳ **Create a Documentary**

You have read about the rapid social and technological changes that took place during the Victorian period. With a group of classmates, choose one social or technological change and create a research question about it. Then, create a documentary that answers the question.

Here are some questions to answer as you get started:

- What details about this topic will most interest a modern audience?
- What reliable sources can I use to answer my research question and write the narration?
- What images, video clips, and music will help me present the information in a compelling way?

 Ed

Media Projects

To find help with this task online, access **Create a Documentary.**

Writing
↳ **Write a Short Story**

Write a science fiction short story about someone who travels back in time to bring a current technological invention to the Victorian era. Use the chart to note your ideas. Then, write your story.

Ask Yourself	My Notes
• What technological invention will you write about?	
• How will the characters react to this technology?	
• What is the main conflict in the story?	
• What details will you include to help readers understand people, places, and events?	

"The English language is nobody's special property. It is the property of the imagination . . . the property of the language itself."

— Derek Walcott

Modern and Contemporary Literature

New Ideas, New Voices

? As you read the texts in this unit, think about how they explore these **Essential Questions.**

What makes people feel insecure?
The modern world has many technologies and systems devoted to security. Yet people continue to experience insecurity in their daily lives, their relationships, and even their sense of self.

Why is it hard to resist social pressure?
The company you keep can influence your thoughts and actions for better or worse. Social pressure affects us all, whether it comes from friends, relatives, or the community.

What is the power of symbols?
Symbols are a powerful form of communication. They create multiple levels of meaning by connecting ideas to objects and images.

How do you measure a person's worth?
"How much are you worth?" is a common way to ask about wealth. With a wide gap between the rich and everyone else, many object to using money to measure the value of a person.

ANALYZE THE IMAGE
What does this image suggest about contemporary life in London?

Explore unit themes and build background.

Stream to Start Video

Spark Your Learning

Here are some opportunities to think about issues related to **Unit 6: New Ideas, New Voices.**

As you read, you can use the **Response Log** (page R6) to track your thinking about the Essential Questions.

Think About the Essential Questions

Review the Essential Questions on page 729. Which question is most intriguing to you? Perhaps it relates to something you have read or reminds you of a personal experience. Write down your thoughts.

Make the Connection

Think about the quotation by Derek Walcott on page 728.

- What idea do you think Walcott is reacting against in this statement?

- What issues involving language and cultural diversity exist in your community?

Discuss your ideas with a partner.

Build Academic Vocabulary

You can use these Academic Vocabulary words to write and talk about the topics and themes in the unit. Which of these words do you already feel comfortable using when speaking or writing?

Prove It!
Use one of the academic vocabulary words in a sentence about a personal experience.

	I can use it!	I understand it.	I'll look it up.
arbitrary			
controversy			
convince			
denote			
undergo			

Preview the Texts

Review the images, titles, and descriptions of the texts in the unit. Mark the title of the text that interests you most.

A Village After Dark

Short Story by **Kazuo Ishiguro**

A disgraced leader returns to an English village where he was once admired.

A Cup of Tea

Short Story by **Katherine Mansfield**

Find out what happens when a wealthy woman decides to help a stranger.

Shooting an Elephant

Essay by **George Orwell**

A British colonial officer is tested when an elephant goes on a rampage.

My Daughter the Racist

Short Story by **Helen Oyeyemi**

A free-spirited girl draws her mother and herself into conflict with her community.

The Love Song of J. Alfred Prufrock

Poem by **T. S. Eliot**

The indecisive, self-conscious speaker of this poem struggles to ask a woman an "overwhelming question."

The Second Coming

Poem by **William Butler Yeats**

This poem presents a vision of the chaos and destruction that will precede a new cycle of civilization.

Symbols? I'm Sick of Symbols

Poem by **Fernando Pessoa**

The speaker of this poem weighs the value of abstract symbols against the beauty and sadness of the real world.

The Threat of Inequality

Speech by **Sadiq Khan**

A politician argues that inequality harms Britain's economy and society.

The Inequality Bogeyman

Editorial by **Thomas Sowell**

An economist looks on the bright side of inequality.

New Ideas, New Voices

At the turn of the 20th century, Great Britain was a nation at its peak. Under the reign of Edward VII, much of Britain was a land of prosperity, stability, and world dominance. However, vast changes were on the horizon. Over the next hundred years, Britain would become embroiled in wars, experience economic depression, and face the end of its once-massive empire—upon which, it was said, the sun never set.

From Distant Trenches to War at Home

In 1914 a Serbian nationalist assassinated Archduke Franz Ferdinand, heir to the throne of Austria-Hungary. Austria declared war on Serbia, and like a line of dominoes, alliances fell into place: Austria and Germany on one

1900

1901
Queen Victoria dies and is succeeded by her son Edward VII.

1914
Assassination of Archduke Franz Ferdinand sparks World War I.

1918
World War I ends.

1921
Irish Free State is established; Northern Ireland remains part of Great Britain.

1921
T. S. Eliot writes his groundbreaking poem *The Waste Land*.

1929
United States stock market crash causes global economic depression.

1939
Germany invades Poland and World War II begins.

1945
World War II ends; British losses total 360,000.

1947
India and Pakistan are given independence from Great Britain.

side; Russia, France, and Britain on the other. Both sides became locked in bloody trench warfare. The Great War, as the conflict was known, dragged on, devastating Europe, killing or wounding virtually an entire generation of young men, and bringing a profound sense of disillusionment. In 1917 the United States entered the war, leading to Germany's capitulation the following year and an uneasy peace.

Britain had lost nearly 750,000 men, and those who survived came home to unemployment and economic depression. War-torn European nations turned to the United States for loans, but in 1929 the United States stock market crashed, causing a worldwide depression. In the economic and political chaos of the 1920s and early 1930s, dictators seized power in Italy, Russia, and Germany. In 1939 German dictator Adolf Hitler invaded Poland, prompting Britain and France to declare war on Germany. Italy and Japan allied themselves with Germany, and World War II began.

Terrible as the Great War had been, for most British citizens it was a distant tragedy on foreign battlefields. World War II was different. After the fall of France in 1940, German planes began to attack Britain. Bombs rained down on London, and the entire population mobilized to defend the home front. Britain held out against Germany until the United States entered the war in 1941, and Hitler was finally defeated in 1945.

The coronation of Queen Elizabeth II in 1953

EXTEND

Think of a question you have about a topic, event, or person from the historical period. Then, research the answer and add it as an entry to the timeline.

1952
Elizabeth II ascends the throne after the death of her father, George VI.

2007
British Indian author Salman Rushdie is awarded a knighthood from Queen Elizabeth II.

2020
Britain formally leaves the European Union, an event known as Brexit.

Present

1949
George Orwell publishes *1984*, a nightmarish vision of a totalitarian England.

1979
Margaret Thatcher becomes the first female prime minister.

2005
Bombs explode on the London Underground and a bus, killing 56.

© Houghton Mifflin Harcourt Publishing Company • Image credits: (t) ©Hulton–Deutsch Collection/Corbis/Getty Images; (b) ©STR/AFP/Getty Images

After 155 years of colonial rule, Britain handed over control of Hong Kong to China in 1997, an event that is considered to mark the end of the British Empire.

The Fall of the British Empire

After World War II, Britain was financially drained, burdened by debt and the need to rebuild its cities. Everything was rationed. Determined to provide at least the basic necessities, the government transformed Britain with a new national health care system and public education. Concerned with domestic issues, leaders had little desire to cling to colonies that were all too eager for self-rule. After World War I, Britain's grasp on its empire had begun to loosen as the spirit of nationalism swept Europe and its colonial empires. Britain granted greater degrees of self-determination to its colonies, eventually making some of these lands partners in the British Commonwealth of Nations rather than continuing to treat them as possessions. Soon after World War II, Britain gave India its independence. In the decades that followed, Britain yielded to nationalistic and economic pressures and relinquished control of most of its remaining colonies.

A New World in Literature

After World War I, Europe was a place of uncertainty and upheaval. In England, the previously stable social order based on community and class distinctions was giving way to the anonymity of urban life. In the arts, modernism was a way of trying to make sense of this new, fragmented world. Visual artists, composers, and writers rejected traditional forms and experimented with new styles that better reflected the realities and values of modern life.

New narrative styles rejected traditional linear plot and character development, and instead placed the reader inside the character's mind. Many writers felt a sense of alienation from their own society after witnessing the horrors of war, and as a result, explored themes of isolation, human relationships and vulnerabilities, and disillusionment.

The end of the British Empire also shaped and continues to shape literature. Writers from former colonies explore issues related to their countries' colonial past, while writers who have immigrated to England often address cultural tensions in their works. The multicultural perspective these writers bring has broadened the horizons of contemporary British literature.

COLLABORATIVE DISCUSSION

In a small group, discuss how global events during this period have influenced British politics and literature.

Assessment Practice

Choose the best answer to each question.

1. Which most directly caused the outbreak of World War II?

- (A) Italy's and Japan's alliance with Germany
- (B) the crash of the United States stock market
- (C) Hitler's seizure of power in Germany
- (D) the invasion of Poland by Germany

2. British politicians after World War II —

- (A) wanted to hold the British Empire together for as long as possible
- (B) believed that strengthening the colonies would help Britain recover from the war
- (C) placed less emphasis on the empire and focused more on domestic issues
- (D) immediately granted independence to all former British colonies

3. Which was a primary aspect of modernism?

- (A) focus on nationalistic perspectives in the arts and literature
- (B) rejection of traditional forms in the arts and literature
- (C) focus on war recovery and domestic affairs in politics
- (D) rejection of colonialism and empire building in politics

Test-Taking Strategies

A Village After Dark

Short Story by **Kazuo Ishiguro**

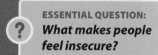

Engage Your Brain

Choose one or more of these activities to start connecting with the short story you're about to read.

Leadership Survey

The narrator of this story is a leader who has lost his influence. With a partner, conduct a survey about the qualities that are important in a leader. Ask classmates or friends to rank the following qualities from 1 to 5, with 1 representing the most important:

- compassion
- eloquence
- honesty
- intelligence
- charisma

When you are finished with your survey, write a summary of the results.

Long and Winding Road

Traveling may sound glamorous, but it can wear you out physically and mentally. With a group of students, share stories of difficult travel experiences. Consider

- whether you had enough sleep or food
- how the experience affected your mood and judgment

Evaluate an Unreliable Narrator

An **unreliable narrator** tells a story in a way that cannot be trusted. This type of narrator is usually found in stories told from the first-person point of view. Some unreliable narrators deliberately exaggerate, withhold information, or try to deceive the reader. Others misunderstand events, often because they are naive or mentally ill.

Authors may use an unreliable narrator for a variety of purposes, including to amuse or surprise readers. The technique is popular with modern writers as a means of conveying a complex and ambiguous view of reality.

To recognize an unreliable narrator, you need to be an active reader. Look for details that contradict what the narrator says or statements by other characters that seem to conflict with the narrator's perspective. As you read "A Village After Dark," ask yourself these questions to evaluate the narrator's reliability:

- What does the narrator tell himself?
- What does the narrator say to the other characters?
- How do the other characters respond to the narrator?
- What information is unclear or withheld from the reader?

Focus on Genre
↳ **Short Story**

- includes the basic elements of fiction, such as plot, character, and setting
- centers on a particular moment or event or follows the life of a character
- expresses a theme related to the story's outcome

Analyze Mood

Mood is the feeling or atmosphere that a writer creates for the reader. For example, a story about a haunted house might have a frightening and suspenseful mood. Writers create mood through setting, imagery, descriptive details, and word choice. Sometimes the mood of a story changes as the plot progresses. Here is an example of mood created by a description of the story's setting at the beginning of "A Village After Dark."

Setting	Mood
There was nothing I recognized, and I found myself walking forever around twisting, badly lit streets hemmed in on both sides by the little stone cottages characteristic of the area.	confused, claustrophobic

Annotation in Action

Here is an example of notes a student made about a paragraph from "A Village After Dark." As you read, mark sentences that suggest that the narrator is unreliable.

I thumped the door again, this time quite ferociously. At last it opened, throwing warmth and light out into the street. An old man was standing in the doorway. He looked at me carefully, then asked, "It's not Fletcher, is it?"

"Yes, and I've just got into the village. I've been travelling for several days."

He thought about this for a moment, then said, "Well, you'd better come in."

Fletcher seems to expect a bigger welcome than he gets.

Expand Your Vocabulary

Put a check mark next to the vocabulary words that you feel comfortable using when speaking or writing.

disoriented	☐
procrastinate	☐
impressionable	☐
lethargy	☐
incessantly	☐

Turn to a partner and talk about the vocabulary words you already know. Then, write a dialogue between two friends who get lost while hiking in the mountains, using as many of the vocabulary words as you can.

As you read "A Village After Dark," use the definitions in the side column to help you learn the vocabulary words you don't already know.

Background

Japanese-born **Kazuo Ishiguro** (b. 1954) moved to England with his family in 1960 when he was five. As a young man, Ishiguro had hoped to become a musician. He said that writing songs was "good preparation for the kind of fiction I went on to write." According to Ishiguro, this meant leaving "a lot of meaning underneath the surface." Among his works are *The Remains of the Day*, a portrait of a butler in post-World War II England, and *Never Let Me Go*, a dystopian science fiction novel. Both of these novels were adapted into popular movies. Ishiguro received the Nobel Prize for Literature in 2017.

A Village After Dark

Short Story by **Kazuo Ishiguro**

A disgraced leader returns to an English village where he was once admired.

NOTICE & NOTE

As you read, use the side margins to make notes about the text.

1   There was a time when I could travel England for weeks on end and remain at my sharpest—when, if anything, the travelling gave me an edge. But now that I am older I become **disoriented** more easily. So it was that on arriving at the village just after dark I failed to find my bearings at all. I could hardly believe I was in the same village in which not so long ago I had lived and come to exercise such influence.

2   There was nothing I recognized, and I found myself walking forever around twisting, badly lit streets hemmed in on both sides by the little stone cottages characteristic of the area. The streets often became so narrow I could make no progress without my bag or my elbow scraping one rough wall or another. I persevered nevertheless, stumbling around in the darkness in the hope of coming upon the village square—where I could at least orient myself—or else of encountering one of the villagers. When after a while I had done neither, a weariness came over me, and I decided my best course was just to choose a cottage at random, knock on the door, and hope it would be opened by someone who remembered me.

disoriented
(dĭs-ôr´ē-ĕnt´əd) *adj.* having lost one's sense of direction, position, or relationship with one's surroundings.

3   I stopped by a particularly rickety-looking door, whose upper beam was so low that I could see I would have to crouch right down to enter. A dim light was leaking out around the door's edges, and I could hear voices and laughter. I knocked loudly to insure that the occupants would hear me over their talk. But just then someone behind me said, "Hello."

4   I turned to find a young woman of around twenty, dressed in raggedy jeans and a torn jumper, standing in the darkness a little way away.

5   "You walked straight past me earlier," she said, "even though I called to you."

6   "Did I really? Well, I'm sorry. I didn't mean to be rude."

7   "You're Fletcher, aren't you?"

8   "Yes," I said, somewhat flattered.

9   "Wendy thought it was you when you went by our cottage. We all got very excited. You were one of that lot, weren't you? With David Maggis and all of them."

10   "Yes," I said, "but Maggis was hardly the most important one. I'm surprised you pick him out like that. There were other, far more important figures." I reeled off a series of names and was interested to see the girl nodding at each one in recognition. "But this must have all been before your time," I said. "I'm surprised you know about such things."

Don't forget to
Notice & Note as you
read the text.

11   "It was before our time, but we're all experts on your lot. We know more about all that than most of the older ones who were here then. Wendy recognized you instantly just from your photos."

12   "I had no idea you young people had taken such an interest in us. I'm sorry I walked past you earlier. But you see, now that I'm older, I get a little disoriented when I travel."

13   I could hear some boisterous talk coming from behind the door. I banged on it again, this time rather impatiently, though I was not so eager to bring the encounter with the girl to a close.

14   She looked at me for a moment, then said, "All of you from those days are like that. David Maggis came here a few years ago. In '93, or maybe it was '94. He was like that. A bit vague. It must get to you after a while, travelling all the time."

15   "So Maggis was here. How interesting. You know, he wasn't one of the really important figures. You mustn't get carried away with such an idea. Incidentally, perhaps you could tell me who lives in this cottage." I thumped the door again.

16   "The Petersons," the girl said. "They're an old house. They'll probably remember you."

17   "The Petersons," I repeated, but the name meant nothing to me.

18   "Why don't you come to our cottage? Wendy was really excited. So were the rest of us. It's a real chance for us, actually talking to someone from those days."

© Houghton Mifflin Harcourt Publishing Company • Image Credits: ©Ann Moore/Alamy

NOTICE & NOTE
AGAIN AND AGAIN

When you notice certain events, images, or words recurring over a portion of the story, you've found an **Again and Again** signpost.

Notice & Note: In paragraphs 14 and 15, mark the sentences containing a name that has also appeared earlier in the story.

Infer: Why might the author bring up this name again and again?

19   "I'd very much like to do that. But first of all I'd better get myself settled in. The Petersons, you say."

20   I thumped the door again, this time quite ferociously. At last it opened, throwing warmth and light out into the street. An old man was standing in the doorway. He looked at me carefully, then asked, "It's not Fletcher, is it?"

21   "Yes, and I've just got into the village. I've been travelling for several days."

22   He thought about this for a moment, then said, "Well, you'd better come in."

23   I found myself in a cramped, untidy room full of rough wood and broken furniture. A log burning in the fireplace was the only source of light, by which I could make out a number of hunched figures sitting around the room. The old man led me to a chair beside the fire with a grudgingness that suggested it was the very one he had just vacated. Once I sat down, I found I could not easily turn my head to see my surroundings or the others in the room. But the warmth of the fire was very welcome, and for a moment I just stared into its flames, a pleasant grogginess drifting over me. Voices came from behind me, inquiring if I was well, if I had come far, if I was hungry, and I replied as best I could, though I was aware that my answers were barely adequate. Eventually, the questions ceased, and it occurred to me that my presence was creating a heavy awkwardness, but I was so grateful for the warmth and the chance to rest that I hardly cared.

24   Nonetheless, when the silence behind me had gone unbroken for several minutes, I resolved to address my hosts with a little more civility, and I turned in my chair. It was then, as I did so, that I was suddenly seized by an intense sense of recognition. I had chosen the cottage quite at random, but now I could see that it was none other than the very one in which I had spent my years in this village. My gaze moved immediately to the far corner—at this moment shrouded in darkness—to the spot that had been *my* corner, where once my mattress had been and where I had spent many tranquil hours browsing through books or conversing with whoever happened to drift in. On summer days, the windows, and often the door, were left open to allow a refreshing breeze to blow right through. Those were the days when the cottage was surrounded by open fields and there would come from outside the voices of my friends, lazing in the long grass, arguing over poetry or philosophy. These precious fragments of the past came back to me so powerfully that it was all I could do not to make straight for my old corner then and there.

25   Someone was speaking to me again, perhaps asking another question, but I hardly listened. Rising, I peered through the shadows into my corner, and could now make out a narrow bed, covered by an old curtain, occupying more or less the exact space where my mattress had been. The bed looked extremely inviting, and I found myself cutting into something the old man was saying.

© Houghton Mifflin Harcourt Publishing Company

ANALYZE MOOD

Annotate: Mark phrases used to describe the room in the first two sentences of paragraph 23.

Analyze: What mood do these descriptive details create?

Don't forget to
Notice & Note as you
read the text.
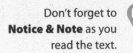

26   "Look," I said, "I know this is a bit blunt. But, you see, I've come such a long way today. I really need to lie down, close my eyes, even if it's just for a few minutes. After that, I'm happy to talk all you like."

27   I could see the figures around the room shifting uneasily. Then a new voice said, rather sullenly, "Go ahead then. Have a nap. Don't mind us."

28   But I was already picking my way through the clutter toward my corner. The bed felt damp, and the springs creaked under my weight, but no sooner had I curled up with my back to the room than my many hours of travelling began to catch up with me. As I was drifting off, I heard the old man saying, "It's Fletcher, all right. God, he's aged."

29   A woman's voice said, "Should we let him go to sleep like that? He might wake in a few hours and then we'll have to stay up with him."

30   "Let him sleep for an hour or so," someone else said. "If he's still asleep after an hour, we'll wake him."

31   At this point, sheer exhaustion overtook me.

32   It was not a continuous or comfortable sleep. I drifted between sleep and waking, always conscious of voices behind me in the room. At some point, I was aware of a woman saying, "I don't know how I was ever under his spell. He looks such a ragamuffin now."

33   In my state of near-sleep, I debated with myself whether these words applied to me or, perhaps, to David Maggis, but before long sleep engulfed me once more.

34   When I next awoke, the room appeared to have grown both darker and colder. Voices were continuing behind me in lowered tones, but I could make no sense of the conversation. I now felt embarrassed at having gone to sleep in the way I had, and for a few further moments remained motionless with my face to the wall. But something about me must have revealed that I was awake, for a woman's voice, breaking off from the general conversation, said, "Oh, look, look." Some whispers were exchanged, then I heard the sound of someone coming toward my corner. I felt a hand placed gently on my shoulder, and looked up to find a woman kneeling over me. I did not turn my body sufficiently to see the room, but I got the impression that it was lit by dying embers, and the woman's face was visible only in shadow.

35   "Now, Fletcher," she said. "It's time we had a talk. I've waited a long time for you to come back. I've thought about you often."

36   I strained to see her more clearly. She was somewhere in her forties, and even in the gloom I noticed a sleepy sadness in her eyes. But her face failed to stir in me even the faintest of memories.

37   "I'm sorry," I said. "I have no recollection of you. But please forgive me if we met some time ago. I do get very disoriented these days."

EVALUATE AN UNRELIABLE NARRATOR

Annotate: Reread paragraphs 26–29. Mark details and comments that suggest how people in the cottage view the narrator, Fletcher.

Analyze: What do they seem to think of the narrator? How does their reaction to him conflict with his perspective of himself?

© Houghton Mifflin Harcourt Publishing Company

38   "Fletcher," she said, "when we used to know one another, I was young and beautiful. I idolized you, and everything you said seemed like an answer. Now here you are, back again. I've wanted to tell you for many years that you ruined my life."

39   "You're being unfair. All right, I was mistaken about a lot of things. But I never claimed to have any answers. All I said in those days was that it was our duty, all of us, to contribute to the debate. We knew so much more about the issues than the ordinary people here. If people like us **procrastinated**, claiming we didn't yet know enough, then who was there to act? But I never claimed I had the answers. No, you're being unfair."

40   "Fletcher," she said, and her voice was oddly gentle, "you used to make love to me, more or less every time I wandered in here to your room. In this corner, we did all kinds of beautifully dirty things. It's odd to think how I could have once been so physically excited by you. And here you're just a foul-smelling bundle of rags now. But look at me—I'm still attractive. My face has got a bit lined, but when I walk in the village streets I wear dresses I've made specially to show off my figure. A lot of men want me still. But you, no woman would look at you now. A bundle of stinking rags and flesh."

41   "I don't remember you," I said. "And I've no time for sex these days. I've other things to worry about. More serious things. Very well, I was mistaken about a lot in those days. But I've done more than most to try and make amends. You see, even now I'm travelling. I've never stopped. I've travelled and travelled trying to undo what damage I may once have caused. That's more than can be said of some others from those days. I bet Maggis, for instance, hasn't worked nearly as hard to try and put things right."

42   The woman was stroking my hair.

43   "Look at you. I used to do this, run my fingers through your hair. Look at this filthy mess. I'm sure you're contaminated with all sorts of parasites." But she continued slowly to run her fingers through the dirty knots. I failed to feel anything erotic from this, as perhaps she wished me to do. Rather, her caresses felt maternal. Indeed, for a moment it was as though I had finally reached some cocoon of protectiveness, and I began once more to feel sleepy. But suddenly she stopped and slapped me hard on the forehead.

44   "Why don't you join the rest of us now? You've had your sleep. You've got a lot of explaining to do." With that she got up and left.

45   For the first time, I turned my body sufficiently to survey the room. I saw the woman making her way past the clutter on the floor, then sitting down in a rocking chair by the fireplace. I could see three other figures hunched around the dying fire. One I recognized to be the old man who had opened the door. The two others—sitting together on what looked like a wooden trunk—seemed to be women of around the same age as the one who had spoken to me.

46 The old man noticed that I had turned, and he indicated to the others that I was watching. The four of them proceeded to sit stiffly, not speaking. From the way they did this, it was clear that they had been discussing me thoroughly while I was asleep. In fact, as I watched them I could more or less guess the whole shape their conversation had taken. I could see, for instance, that they had spent some time expressing concern for the young girl I had met outside, and about the effect I might have on her peers.

47 "They're all so **impressionable**," the old man would have said. "And I heard her inviting him to visit them."

48 To which, no doubt, one of the women on the trunk would have said, "But he can't do much harm now. In our time, we were all taken in because all his kind— they were young and glamorous. But these days the odd one passing through from time to time, looking all decrepit and burned out like that—if anything, it goes to demystify all that talk about the old days. In any case, people like him have changed their position so much these days. They don't know themselves what they believe."

49 The old man would have shaken his head. "I saw the way that young girl was looking at him. All right, he looks a pitiful mess over there just now. But once his ego's fed a little, once he has the flattery of the young people, sees how they want to hear his ideas, then there'll be no stopping him. It'll be just like before. He'll have them all working for his causes. Young girls like that, there's so little for them to believe in now. Even a stinking tramp like this could give them a purpose."

50 Their conversation, all the time I slept, would have gone something very much like that. But now, as I observed them from my corner, they continued to sit in guilty silence, staring at the last of their fire. After a while, I rose to my feet. Absurdly, the four of them kept their gazes averted from me. I waited a few moments to see if any of them would say anything. Finally, I said, "All right, I was asleep earlier, but I've guessed what you were saying. Well, you'll be interested to know I'm going to do the very thing you feared. I'm going this moment to the young people's cottage. I'm going to tell them what to do with all their energy, all their dreams, their urge to achieve something of lasting good in this world. Look at you, what a pathetic bunch. Crouching in your cottage, afraid to do anything, afraid of me, of Maggis, of anyone else from those times. Afraid to do anything in the world out there, just because once we made a few mistakes. Well, those young people haven't yet sunk so low, despite all the **lethargy** you've been preaching at them down the years. I'll talk to them. I'll undo in half an hour all of your sorry efforts."

51 "You see," the old man said to the others. "I knew it would be this way. We ought to stop him, but what can we do?"

52 I crashed my way across the room, picked up my bag, and went out into the night.

impressionable
(ĭm-prĕsh´ə-nə-bəl) *adj.* readily or easily influenced; suggestible.

VOCABULARY STRATEGY

Analyze Prefixes: The word *demystify* in paragraph 48 contains the prefix *de-*, meaning "reduce" or "reverse." Recognizing the word's prefix can help you figure out its meaning.

Analyze: In this imagined conversation, why does the woman think that Fletcher's appearance will demystify him?

EVALUATE AN UNRELIABLE NARRATOR

Annotate: Reread paragraphs 50–51. Mark the narrator's observations about how the people in the cottage are behaving toward him.

Evaluate: What assumption does the narrator make about the others? Do you agree or disagree with it? Explain.

lethargy
(lĕth´ər-jē) *n.* a lack of interest or enthusiasm; apathy.

Don't forget to **Notice & Note** as you read the text.

© Houghton Mifflin Harcourt Publishing Company

A Village After Dark **745**

Annotate: Mark the phrases in paragraph 54 that describe the night and the cottages.

Compare: How does the mood created by these descriptive details compare with the girl's attitude toward Fletcher?

53 The girl was still standing outside when I emerged. She seemed to be expecting me and with a nod began to lead the way.

54 The night was drizzly and dark. We twisted and turned along the narrow paths that ran between the cottages. Some of the cottages we passed looked so decayed and crumbling that I felt I could destroy one of them simply by running at it with all my weight.

55 The girl kept a few paces ahead, occasionally glancing back at me over her shoulder. Once she said, "Wendy's going to be so pleased. She was sure it was you when you went past earlier. By now, she'll have guessed she was right, because I've been away this long, and she'll have brought the whole crowd together. They'll all be waiting."

56 "Did you give David Maggis this sort of reception, too?"

57 "Oh, yes. We were really excited when he came."

58 "I'm sure he found that very gratifying. He always had an exaggerated sense of his own importance."

59 "Wendy says Maggis was one of the interesting ones, but that you were, well, important. She thinks you were really important."

60 I thought about this for a moment.

61 "You know," I said, "I've changed my mind on very many things. If Wendy's expecting me to say all the things I used to all those years ago, well, she's going to be in for a disappointment."

62 The girl did not seem to hear this, but continued to lead me purposefully through the clusters of cottages.

63 After a little while, I became aware of footsteps following a dozen or so paces behind us. At first, I assumed this was just some villager out walking and refrained from turning round. But then the girl halted under a street lamp and looked behind us. I was thus obliged also to stop and turn. A middle-aged man in a dark overcoat was coming toward us. As he approached, he held out his hand and shook mine, though without smiling.

64 "So," he said, "you're here."

65 I then realized I knew the man. We had not seen each other since we were ten years old. His name was Roger Button, and he had been in my class at the school I had attended for two years in Canada before my family returned to England. Roger Button and I had not been especially close, but, because he had been a timid boy, and because he, too, was from England, he had for a while followed me about. I had neither seen nor heard from him since that time. Now, as I studied his appearance under the street lamp, I saw the years had not been kind to him. He was bald, his face was pocked and lined, and there was a weary sag to his whole posture. For all that, there was no mistaking my old classmate.

66 "Roger," I said, "I'm just on my way to visit this young lady's friends. They've gathered together to receive me. Otherwise I'd have come and looked you up straightaway. As it was, I had it in my mind as the next thing to do, even before getting any sleep tonight. I was just thinking to myself, However late things finish

at the young people's cottage, I'll go and knock on Roger's door afterward."

67   "Don't worry," said Roger Button as we all started to walk again. "I know how busy you are. But we ought to talk. Chew over old times. When you last saw me —at school, I mean—I suppose I was a rather feeble specimen. But, you know, that all changed when I got to fourteen, fifteen. I really toughened up. Became quite a leader type. But you'd long since left Canada. I always wondered what would have happened if we'd come across each other at fifteen. Things would have been rather different between us, I assure you."

68   As he said this, memories came flooding back. In those days, Roger Button had idolized me, and in return I had bullied him **incessantly**. However, there had existed between us a curious understanding that my bullying him was all for his own good; that when, without warning, I suddenly punched him in the stomach on the playground, or when, passing him in the corridor, I impulsively wrenched his arm up his back until he started to cry, I was doing so in order to help him toughen up. Accordingly, the principal effect such attacks had on our relationship was to keep him in awe of me. This all came back to me as I listened to the weary-looking man walking beside me.

69   "Of course," Roger Button went on, perhaps guessing my train of thought, "it might well be that if you hadn't treated me the way you did I'd never have become what I did at fifteen. In any case, I've often wondered how it would have been if we'd met just a few years later. I really was something to be reckoned with by then."

70   We were once again walking along the narrow twisted passages between cottages. The girl was still leading the way, but she was now walking much faster. Often we would only just manage to

incessantly
(ĭn-sĕs´ənt-lē) *adv.* continuing without interruption.

EVALUATE AN UNRELIABLE NARRATOR

Annotate: Reread paragraphs 68–69. Mark phrases that describe how the narrator treated Roger at school.

Evaluate: Do Roger's statements in paragraph 69 support the narrator's claim in paragraph 68 that "there had existed between us a curious understanding that my bullying him was all for his own good"? Explain why or why not.

© Houghton Mifflin Harcourt Publishing Company · Image Credits: ©Andy Kerry/Alamy; (inset) ©Graciela Vilagudin/Moment/Getty Images

catch a glimpse of her turning some corner ahead of us, and it struck me that we would have to keep alert if we were not to lose her.

71   "Today, of course," Roger Button was saying, "I've let myself go a bit. But I have to say, old fellow, you seem to be in much worse shape. Compared with you, I'm an athlete. Not to put too fine a point on it, you're just a filthy old tramp now, really, aren't you? But, you know, for a long time after you left I continued to idolize you. Would Fletcher do this? What would Fletcher think if he saw me doing that? Oh, yes. It was only when I got to fifteen or so that I looked back on it all and saw through you. Then I was very angry, of course. Even now, I still think about it sometimes. I look back and think, Well, he was just a thoroughly nasty so-and-so. He had a little more weight and muscle at that age than I did, a little more confidence, and he took full advantage. Yes, it's very clear, looking back, what a nasty little person you were. Of course, I'm not implying you still are today. We all change. That much I'm willing to accept."

72   "Have you been living here long?" I asked, wishing to change the subject.

73   "Oh, seven years or so. Of course, they talk about you a lot around here. I sometimes tell them about our early association. 'But he won't remember me,' I always tell them. 'Why would he remember a skinny little boy he used to bully and have at his beck and call?' Anyway, the young people here, they talk about you more and more these days. Certainly, the ones who've never seen you tend to idealize you the most. I suppose you've come back to capitalize on all that. Still, I shouldn't blame you. You're entitled to try and salvage a little self-respect."

74   We suddenly found ourselves facing an open field, and we both halted. Glancing back, I saw that we had walked our way out of the village; the last of the cottages were some distance behind us. Just as I had feared, we had lost the young woman; in fact, I realized we had not been following her for some time.

75   At that moment, the moon emerged, and I saw we were standing at the edge of a vast grassy field—extending, I supposed, far beyond what I could see by the moon.

76   Roger Button turned to me. His face in the moonlight seemed gentle, almost affectionate.

77   "Still," he said, "it's time to forgive. You shouldn't keep worrying so much. As you see, certain things from the past will come back to you in the end. But then we can't be held accountable for what we did when we were very young."

78   "No doubt you're right," I said. Then I turned and looked around in the darkness. "But now I'm not sure where to go. You see, there were some young people waiting for me in their cottage. By now they'd have a warm fire ready for me and some hot tea. And some home-baked cakes, perhaps even a good stew. And the moment I entered, ushered in by that young lady we were following just now, they'd all have burst into applause. There'd be smiling, adoring faces all around me. That's what's waiting for me somewhere. Except I'm not sure where I should go."

79   Roger Button shrugged. "Don't worry, you'll get there easily enough. Except, you know, that girl was being a little misleading if she implied you could walk to Wendy's cottage. It's much too far. You'd really need to catch a bus. Even then, it's quite a long journey. About two hours, I'd say. But don't worry, I'll show you where you can pick up your bus."

80　　With that, he began to walk back toward the cottages. As I followed, I could sense that the hour had got very late and my companion was anxious to get some sleep. We spent several minutes walking around the cottages again, and then he brought us out into the village square. In fact, it was so small and shabby it hardly merited being called a square; it was little more than a patch of green beside a solitary street lamp. Just visible beyond the pool of light cast by the lamp were a few shops, all shut up for the night. There was complete silence and nothing was stirring. A light mist was hovering over the ground.

81　　Roger Button stopped before we had reached the green and pointed.

82　　"There," he said. "If you stand there, a bus will come along. As I say, it's not a short journey. About two hours. But don't worry, I'm sure your young people will wait. They've so little else to believe in these days, you see."

83　　"It's very late," I said. "Are you sure a bus will come?"

84　　"Oh, yes. Of course, you may have to wait. But eventually a bus will come." Then he touched me reassuringly on the shoulder. "I can see it might get a little lonely standing out here. But once the bus arrives your spirits will rise, believe me. Oh, yes. That bus is always a joy. It'll be brightly lit up, and it's always full of cheerful people, laughing and joking and pointing out the window. Once you board it, you'll feel warm and comfortable, and the other passengers will chat with you, perhaps offer you things to eat or drink. There may even be singing—that depends on the driver. Some drivers encourage it, others don't. Well, Fletcher, it was good to see you."

85　　We shook hands, then he turned and walked away. I watched him disappear into the darkness between two cottages.

86　　I walked up to the green and put my bag down at the foot of the lamppost. I listened for the sound of a vehicle in the distance, but the night was utterly still. Nevertheless, I had been cheered by Roger Button's description of the bus. Moreover, I thought of the reception awaiting me at my journey's end—of the adoring faces of the young people—and felt the stirrings of optimism somewhere deep within me.

ANALYZE MOOD

Annotate: In paragraph 84, mark phrases Roger uses to describe the bus he says will come.

Compare: How does the mood Roger evokes contrast with the overall mood of the story up to this point?

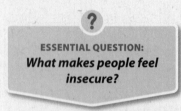

ESSENTIAL QUESTION:
What makes people feel insecure?

Review your notes and add your thoughts to your Response Log.

COLLABORATIVE DISCUSSION

Get together with a partner and discuss the ending of the story. Do you trust what Roger tells Fletcher about the bus ride? Why or why not?

Assessment Practice

Answer these questions before moving on to the **Analyze the Text** section on the following page.

1. Which sentence best describes how the people in the cottage react to Fletcher?

   (A) They are bored by his conversation.

   (B) They are openly hostile toward him.

   (C) They grudgingly tolerate his presence.

   (D) They feel sorry for him now that he's old.

2. Fletcher's defense of his past actions is that —

   (A) his ideas were always correct

   (B) he never tried to influence anyone

   (C) he had suffered from mental illness

   (D) he was right to inspire others to act

3. As a young teenager, Roger Button most likely saw Fletcher as —

   (A) a coward

   (B) a tormentor

   (C) an inspiration

   (D) a companion

 Ed

Test-Taking Strategies

© Houghton Mifflin Harcourt Publishing Company • Image Credits: ©Dave Knibbs/Shutterstock; (bg) ©Graciela Vilagudin/ Moment/Getty Images

Analyze the Text

Support your responses with evidence from the text.

NOTICE & NOTE

Review what you **noticed and noted** as you read the text. Your annotations can help you answer these questions.

1. **ANALYZE** The narrator describes himself as "disoriented" several times. Which aspects of the story might lead readers to share this feeling?

2. **ANALYZE** How does referring to David Maggis **Again and Again** help the author develop Fletcher's character?

3. **COMPARE** In the graphic organizer below, list phrases that Fletcher uses to describe himself and comments about him from people in the village. How does Fletcher's view of himself conflict with the ways that others view him?

Fletcher's Descriptions of Himself	Villagers' Comments

4. **DRAW CONCLUSIONS** How do you explain the different reactions to Fletcher from the young people and the older people in the village?

5. **EVALUATE** Do you think that the narrator seeks to mislead or confuse readers, or is he in denial about his flaws and past actions? Explain your response.

6. **ANALYZE** In the last sentence of paragraph 86, Fletcher says that he feels "the stirrings of optimism somewhere deep within me." Do you think that the mood at the end of the story is optimistic? Explain why or why not.

Choices

Here are some other ways to demonstrate your understanding of the ideas in this lesson.

Writing
↳ **Social Media Post**

Imagine that you are one of the villagers who knew Fletcher in the past. Write a social media post about his return to the village. Consider

- your past experiences with Fletcher
- what has changed about him
- ways in which he hasn't changed
- your suspicions about why he has returned

As you write and discuss, be sure to use the **Academic Vocabulary** words.

| arbitrary |
| controversy |
| convince |
| denote |
| undergo |

Media
↳ **Video Trailer**

With a partner, create a video trailer to draw readers to "A Village After Dark." Combine words and visuals to capture the mysterious atmosphere of the story.

1. Brainstorm ideas for the video.
2. Create a storyboard indicating text, images, and voice-over in each shot.
3. Go online to find images and background music you wish to use in the video.
4. Shoot and edit the video. Then, post it online for classmates to view.

Speaking & Listening
↳ **Mock Trial**

With a group of students, hold a mock trial of Fletcher to determine whether he should be punished for his past actions. Draw on evidence from the story in your role-playing.

1. Choose one person to act as a prosecutor and another to defend Fletcher.
2. Other students can play the roles of Fletcher and characters who testify for or against him.
3. Perform the trial in front of other students in the class, ending with closing statements from the prosecution and the defense.
4. At the end of the trial, have the class vote to convict or acquit Fletcher.

Expand Your Vocabulary

PRACTICE AND APPLY

Answer the questions to show your understanding of the vocabulary
words. Use a dictionary or thesaurus as needed.

1. If I become **disoriented** while walking on an unfamiliar, unlit road at night, am I confused
   or confident? Why?

2. Do people who tend to **procrastinate** tackle a task immediately or put off doing it? Why?

3. Which would suggest that someone is **impressionable**: being easily influenced or being
   unreceptive to new ideas? Why?

4. Which would be an indication of **lethargy:** being excited and interested in a social cause
   or being uninterested and unconcerned about it? Why?

5. If I talk **incessantly,** am I talking constantly, or am I talking very little? Why?

Vocabulary Strategy
↳ Prefixes

A **prefix** is a word part attached before a word's root or stem. Recognizing
a word's prefix can help you understand the word. In the word *disorient,*
for example, the prefix *dis-* means "opposite." Using that knowledge, you
can figure out that *disorient* means the opposite of *orient,* which means "to
become familiar with new surroundings."

**Interactive Vocabulary
Lesson: Common Roots,
Prefixes, Suffixes**

Here are some common prefixes and their definitions:

Prefix	Meaning	Example
ab-	from; away from	abnormal
co-	together	cooperate
mis-	wrong; bad	miscalculate
re-	again; back	recall
un-	not	unhappy

PRACTICE AND APPLY

Locate these words in the story: *uneasily* (paragraph 27), *misleading*
(paragraph 79), and *reassuringly* (paragraph 84). Identify the prefix in each
word, and use it to figure out the word's meaning. Use the words in a brief
dialogue between two of the characters in the story.

Watch Your Language!

Adjectives and Adverbs

Adjectives and adverbs both modify, add, or emphasize information.

- **Adjectives** modify nouns and pronouns by telling *which one, what kind, how many,* or *how much.*

- **Adverbs** modify verbs, adjectives, or other adverbs by telling *when, where, how,* or *to what extent.* Many adverbs are formed by adding *-ly* to adjectives.

In the examples from the story below, note the writer's use of an adjective and adverb. Consider how the descriptive modifiers enhance the information in the sentences.

> I could hear some <u>boisterous</u> talk coming from behind the door.
> (*Boisterous* modifies the noun *talk* and tells *what kind* of talk.)
>
> I banged on it again, this time rather <u>impatiently</u>, though I was not so eager to bring the encounter with the girl to a close.
> (*Impatiently* modifies the verb *banged* and tells *how* he banged.)

PRACTICE AND APPLY

Now, use what you have learned about adjectives and adverbs to write a paragraph describing the setting of "A Village After Dark." Keep the following tips in mind:

- Use vivid adjectives and adverbs that appeal to the senses.

- Be precise in your choice of adjectives and adverbs to make sure they convey exactly what you mean.

- To make your sentences concise and powerful, avoid using a series of adjectives and adverbs.

Interactive Grammar Lesson: Parts of Speech

A Cup of Tea

Short Story by **Katherine Mansfield**

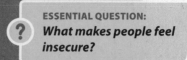

ESSENTIAL QUESTION:
What makes people feel insecure?

Engage Your Brain

Choose one or more of these activities to start connecting with the short story you're about to read.

Can You Spare Any Change?

The story you're about to read involves a common experience: a stranger coming up to you in the street asking for money. With a partner, discuss your thoughts about this type of situation.

- How do you generally respond when asked for money to buy food?

- How should you respond to such requests?

Welcome! ¡Bienvenidos!

The Spanish expression *Mi casa es su casa,* or "My house is your house," is used to put guests at ease. What makes you feel at home when you visit someone else's house? What can make you uncomfortable? Write a brief reflective essay in response to these questions. Consider

- how well you know the people you are visiting

- the reason for your visit

- how similar their home is to your own

Analyze Third-Person Point of View

When a writer uses the **third-person point of view**, the narrator is not a character in the story but an outside observer. Sometimes a third-person narrator is **omniscient** and can describe what all the characters are thinking and feeling. In modern fiction, authors more commonly use a **limited third-person narrator**, describing the thoughts, feelings, and observations of only one character. Readers may feel like they are looking over the shoulder of that character as the story's action unfolds. This technique often helps readers become more emotionally involved with the chosen character, but it can also lead to surprises because the narration is limited by the character's awareness and understanding of events.

In "A Cup of Tea," Mansfield's use of the third-person limited point of view influences character development. The narrator starts off describing the protagonist, Rosemary Fell, from a distance, as if discussing her with a friend. But soon the narrator focuses in on Rosemary, using slang and exaggeration to mimic her speech and suggest how she perceives the world around her. As you read the story, notice how the narrator's conversational tone subtly reveals Rosemary's perspective.

Focus on Genre
↳ Short Story

- includes the basic elements of fiction—setting, characters, plot, conflict, and theme
- centers on a particular moment or event or follows the life of one character
- can be read in one sitting
- may be told by a first-person narrator who is a character in the story or a third-person narrator outside the story

Evaluate a Character

Most complex characters are not entirely good or bad, and readers need to take various factors into account when evaluating them. A character's motivation may influence how you view his or her behavior; for example, a charitable donation may be motivated by compassion, vanity, or a combination of both. When evaluating a character, you should also consider the story's historical, social, and economic context. "A Cup of Tea" is set in London in the early 1900s, a time when rigid class distinctions would have made it seem improper for a wealthy woman to socialize with an impoverished one. This context influences the story's plot and theme, as well as Mansfield's characterization of the protagonist, Rosemary.

As you read "A Cup of Tea," use a chart like this one to help you evaluate Rosemary.

Action	Motivation	Outcome

© Houghton Mifflin Harcourt Publishing Company

Annotation in Action

Here is an example of notes a student made about the opening of "A Cup of Tea." As you read, mark details that show how Mansfield uses a third-person narrator to develop Rosemary's character.

Rosemary Fell was not exactly beautiful. No, you couldn't have called her beautiful. Pretty? Well, if you took her to pieces . . . But why be so cruel as to take anyone to pieces? She was young, brilliant, extremely modern, exquisitely well dressed, amazingly well read in the newest of the new books, and her parties were the most delicious mixture of the really important people and . . . artists—quaint creatures, discoveries of hers, some of them too terrifying for words, but others quite presentable and amusing.

The narrator's tone is conversational and intimate, as if talking about a friend.

Expand Your Vocabulary

Put a check mark next to the vocabulary words that you feel comfortable using when speaking or writing.

- presentable ☐
- tactfully ☐
- listless ☐
- vile ☐
- engagement ☐

Turn to a partner and talk about the vocabulary words you already know. Then, write a few sentences about a social event, using as many of the vocabulary words as you can.

As you read "A Cup of Tea," use the definitions in the side column to learn the vocabulary words you don't already know.

Background

Katherine Mansfield (1888–1923) was born in New Zealand. She disliked her native country and was eager to leave home at 19 to settle in London, where she had attended school several years earlier. Mansfield struggled to earn a living in England, but within a few years she published her first book of short stories. When she was 29, she contracted tuberculosis. In the last year of her life, Mansfield wrote some of her finest stories. By the end of her brief career, she gained recognition as a master of the modern short story, emphasizing psychological realism over dramatic action.

A Cup of Tea

Short Story by Katherine Mansfield

Find out what happens when a wealthy woman decides to help a stranger.

NOTICE & NOTE

As you read, use the side margins to make notes about the text.

1   Rosemary Fell was not exactly beautiful. No, you couldn't have called her beautiful. Pretty? Well, if you took her to pieces . . . But why be so cruel as to take anyone to pieces? She was young, brilliant, extremely modern, exquisitely well dressed, amazingly well read in the newest of the new books, and her parties were the most delicious mixture of the really important people and . . . artists— quaint creatures, discoveries of hers, some of them too terrifying for words, but others quite **presentable** and amusing.

2   Rosemary had been married two years. She had a duck[1] of a boy. No, not Peter—Michael. And her husband absolutely adored her. They were rich, really rich, not just comfortably well off, which is odious and stuffy and sounds like one's grandparents. But if Rosemary wanted to shop she would go to Paris as you and I would go to Bond Street.[2] If she wanted to buy flowers, the car

> **presentable**
> (prĭ-zĕn´tə-bəl) *adj.* fit for introduction to others.

---

[1] **duck:** a British expression for a darling person or thing.
[2] **Bond Street:** a London street famous for its fashionable shops.

pulled up at that perfect shop in Regent Street, and Rosemary inside the shop just gazed in her dazzled, rather exotic way, and said: "I want those and those and those. Give me four bunches of those. And that jar of roses. Yes, I'll have all the roses in the jar. No, no lilac. I hate lilac. It's got no shape." The attendant bowed and put the lilac out of sight, as though this was only too true; lilac was dreadfully shapeless. "Give me those stumpy little tulips. Those red and white ones." And she was followed to the car by a thin shopgirl staggering under an immense white paper armful that looked like a baby in long clothes. . . .

3   One winter afternoon she had been buying something in a little antique shop in Curzon Street. It was a shop she liked. For one thing, one usually had it to oneself. And then the man who kept it was ridiculously fond of serving her. He beamed whenever she came in. He clasped his hands; he was so gratified he could scarcely speak. Flattery, of course. All the same, there was something . . .

4   "You see, madam," he would explain in his low respectful tones, "I love my things. I would rather not part with them than sell them to someone who does not appreciate them, who has not that fine feeling which is so rare. . . ." And, breathing deeply, he unrolled a tiny square of blue velvet and pressed it on the glass counter with his pale fingertips.

ANALYZE THIRD-PERSON
POINT OF VIEW

Annotate: Mark the sentence in paragraph 5 that suggests what the shopkeeper may be thinking about Rosemary's hands.

Evaluate: Does this suggestion reflect his thoughts or Rosemary's? Explain.

5   Today it was a little box. He had been keeping it for her. He had shown it to nobody as yet. An exquisite little enamel box with a glaze so fine it looked as though it had been baked in cream. On the lid a minute creature stood under a flowery tree, and a more minute creature still had her arms around his neck. Her hat, really no bigger than a geranium petal, hung from a branch; it had green ribbons. And there was a pink cloud like a watchful cherub[3] floating above their heads. Rosemary took her hands out of her long gloves. She always took off her gloves to examine such things. Yes, she liked it very much. She loved it; it was a great duck. She must have it. And, turning the creamy box, opening and shutting it, she couldn't help noticing how charming her hands were against the blue velvet. The shopman, in some dim cavern of his mind, may have dared to think so too. For he took a pencil, leaned over the counter, and his pale bloodless fingers crept timidly towards those rosy, flashing ones, as he murmured gently: "If I may venture to point out to madam, the flowers on the little lady's bodice."[4]

6   "Charming!" Rosemary admired the flowers. But what was the price? For a moment the shopman did not seem to hear. Then a murmur reached her. "Twenty-eight guineas,[5] madam."

---

[3] **cherub** (chĕr´əb): an angel depicted as a chubby child with wings.

[4] **bodice** (bŏd´ĭs): the part of a dress above the waist.

[5] **guineas** (gĭn´ēz): units of British money equal to one pound and one shilling, used mainly for pricing luxury items.

Don't forget to
Notice & Note as you
read the text.
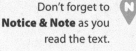

7   "Twenty-eight guineas." Rosemary gave no sign. She laid the little box down; she buttoned her gloves again. Twenty-eight guineas. Even if one is rich . . . She looked vague. She stared at a plump teakettle like a plump hen above the shopman's head, and her voice was dreamy as she answered: "Well, keep it for me—will you? I'll . . ."

8   But the shopman had already bowed as though keeping it for her was all any human being could ask. He would be willing, of course, to keep it for her forever.

9   The discreet door shut with a click. She was outside on the step, gazing at the winter afternoon. Rain was falling, and with the rain it seemed the dark came too, spinning down like ashes. There was a cold bitter taste in the air, and the new-lighted lamps looked sad. Sad were the lights in the houses opposite. Dimly they burned as if regretting something. And people hurried by, hidden under their hateful umbrellas. Rosemary felt a strange pang.[6] She pressed her muff to her breast; she wished she had the little box, too, to cling to. Of course, the car was there. She'd only to cross the pavement. But still she waited. There are moments, horrible moments in life, when one emerges from shelter and looks out, and it's awful. One oughtn't to give way to them. One ought to go home and have an extra-special tea. But at the very instant of thinking that, a young girl, thin, dark, shadowy—where had she come from?—was standing at Rosemary's elbow and a voice like a sigh, almost like a sob, breathed: "Madam, may I speak to you a moment?"

10   "Speak to me?" Rosemary turned. She saw a little battered creature with enormous eyes, someone quite young, no older than herself, who clutched at her coat-collar with reddened hands, and shivered as though she had just come out of the water.

11   "M-madam," stammered the voice. "Would you let me have the price of a cup of tea?"

12   "A cup of tea?" There was something simple, sincere in that voice; it wasn't in the least the voice of a beggar. "Then have you no money at all?" asked Rosemary.

13   "None, madam," came the answer.

14   "How extraordinary!" Rosemary peered through the dusk, and the girl gazed back at her. How more than extraordinary! And suddenly it seemed to Rosemary such an adventure. It was like something out of a novel by Dostoyevsky,[7] this meeting in the dusk. Supposing she took the girl home? Supposing she did do one of those things she was always reading about or seeing on the stage, what would happen? It would be thrilling. And she heard herself saying afterwards to the amazement of her friends: "I simply took her home

---

EVALUATE A CHARACTER

Annotate: Mark words and phrases in paragraph 14 that reveal Rosemary's thoughts about this encounter.

Evaluate: What is Rosemary's motivation for inviting the girl to her home?

---

[6] **pang** (păng): a sudden sharp pain or feeling.

[7] **Dostoyevsky** (dŏs-tə-yĕf´skē): Feodor Dostoyevsky, a 19th-century Russian author who wrote a number of novels and stories dealing with the lives of the poor.

with me," as she stepped forward and said to that dim person beside her: "Come home to tea with me."

15   The girl drew back startled. She even stopped shivering for a moment. Rosemary put out a hand and touched her arm. "I mean it," she said, smiling. And she felt how simple and kind her smile was. "Why won't you? Do. Come home with me now in my car and have tea."

16   "You—you don't mean it, madam," said the girl, and there was pain in her voice.

17   "But I do," cried Rosemary. "I want you to. To please me. Come along."

18   The girl put her fingers to her lips and her eyes devoured Rosemary. "You're—you're not taking me to the police station?" she stammered.

19   "The police station!" Rosemary laughed out. "Why should I be so cruel? No, I only want to make you warm and to hear—anything you care to tell me."

20   Hungry people are easily led. The footman[8] held the door of the car open, and a moment later they were skimming through the dusk.

21   "There!" said Rosemary. She had a feeling of triumph as she slipped her hand through the velvet strap. She could have said, "Now I've got you," as she gazed at the little captive she had netted. But of course she meant it kindly. Oh, more than kindly. She was going to prove to this girl that—wonderful things did happen in life, that—fairy godmothers were real, that—rich people had hearts, and that women *were* sisters. She turned impulsively, saying: "Don't be frightened. After all, why shouldn't you come back with me? We're both women. If I'm the more fortunate, you ought to expect . . ."

22   But happily at that moment, for she didn't know how the sentence was going to end, the car stopped. The bell was rung, the door opened, and with a charming, protecting, almost embracing movement, Rosemary drew the other into the hall. Warmth, softness, light, a sweet scent, all those things so familiar to her she never even thought about them, she watched that other receive. It was fascinating. She was like the little rich girl in her nursery with all the cupboards to open, all the boxes to unpack.

23   "Come, come upstairs," said Rosemary, longing to begin to be generous. "Come up to my room." And, besides, she wanted to spare this poor little thing from being stared at by the servants; she decided as they mounted the stairs she would not even ring for Jeanne, but take off her things by herself. The great thing was to be natural!

24   And "There!" cried Rosemary again, as they reached her beautiful big bedroom with the curtains drawn, the fire leaping on her wonderful lacquer furniture, her gold cushions and the primrose and blue rugs.

© Houghton Mifflin Harcourt Publishing Company

---

[8] **footman:** a household servant, here functioning as Rosemary's chauffeur.

ANALYZE THIRD-PERSON POINT OF VIEW

Annotate: Mark words and phrases in paragraphs 21–22 that describe Rosemary's thoughts about her treatment of the girl.

Evaluate: How do these statements conflict with the impression of Rosemary that this passage conveys to the reader?

Don't forget to
Notice & Note as you
read the text.

25   The girl stood just inside the door; she seemed dazed. But Rosemary didn't mind that.

26   "Come and sit down," she cried, dragging her big chair up to the fire, "in this comfy chair. Come and get warm. You look so dreadfully cold."

27   "I daren't, madam," said the girl, and she edged backwards.

28   "Oh, please,"—Rosemary ran forward—"you mustn't be frightened, you mustn't, really. Sit down, and when I've taken off my things we shall go into the next room and have tea and be cozy. Why are you afraid?" And gently she half pushed the thin figure into its deep cradle.

29   But there was no answer. The girl stayed just as she had been put, with her hands by her sides and her mouth slightly open. To be quite sincere, she looked rather stupid. But Rosemary wouldn't acknowledge it. She leaned over her, saying: "Won't you take off your hat? Your pretty hair is all wet. And one is so much more comfortable without a hat, isn't one?"

30   There was a whisper that sounded like "Very good, madam," and the crushed hat was taken off.

31   "Let me help you off with your coat, too," said Rosemary.

32   The girl stood up. But she held on to the chair with one hand and let Rosemary pull. It was quite an effort. The other scarcely helped her at all. She seemed to stagger like a child, and the thought came

© Houghton Mifflin Harcourt Publishing Company • Image Credits: ©The Artchives/Alamy

ANALYZE THIRD-PERSON POINT OF VIEW

Annotate: In paragraph 32, mark Rosemary's thoughts about the girl's behavior and also mark the girl's dialogue.

Analyze: How does the use of third-person limited point of view create irony here?

and went through Rosemary's mind, that if people wanted helping they must respond a little, just a little, otherwise it became very difficult indeed. And what was she to do with the coat now? She left it on the floor, and the hat too. She was just going to take a cigarette off the mantelpiece when the girl said quickly, but so lightly and strangely: "I'm very sorry, madam, but I'm going to faint. I shall go off, madam, if I don't have something."

33   "Good heavens, how thoughtless I am!" Rosemary rushed to the bell.

34   "Tea! Tea at once! And some brandy immediately!"

35   The maid was gone again, but the girl almost cried out. "No, I don't want no brandy. I never drink brandy. It's a cup of tea I want, madam." And she burst into tears.

36   It was a terrible and fascinating moment. Rosemary knelt beside her chair.

37   "Don't cry, poor little thing," she said. "Don't cry." And she gave the other her lace handkerchief. She really was touched beyond words. She put her arm round those thin, birdlike shoulders.

38   Now at last the other forgot to be shy, forgot everything except that they were both women, and gasped out: "I can't go on no longer like this. I can't bear it. I shall do away with myself. I can't bear no more."

39   "You shan't have to. I'll look after you. Don't cry anymore. Don't you see what a good thing it was that you met me? We'll have tea and you'll tell me everything. And I shall arrange something. I promise. *Do* stop crying. It's so exhausting. Please!"

40   The other did stop just in time for Rosemary to get up before the tea came. She had the table placed between them. She plied the poor little creature with everything, all the sandwiches, all the bread and butter, and every time her cup was empty she filled it with tea, cream and sugar. People always said sugar was so nourishing. As for herself she didn't eat; she smoked and looked away **tactfully** so that the other should not be shy.

41   And really the effect of that slight meal was marvelous. When the tea table was carried away a new being, a light, frail creature with tangled hair, dark lips, deep, lighted eyes, lay back in the big chair in a kind of sweet languor,[9] looking at the blaze. Rosemary lit a fresh cigarette; it was time to begin.

42   "And when did you have your last meal?" she asked softly.

43   But at that moment the door-handle turned.

44   "Rosemary, may I come in?" It was Philip.

45   "Of course."

46   He came in. "Oh, I'm so sorry," he said, and stopped and stared.

47   "It's quite all right," said Rosemary smiling. "This is my friend, Miss—"

tactfully
(tăkt´fəl-lē) *adv.* considerately and discreetly.

---

[9] **languor** (lăng´gər): a dreamy, lazy state.

EVALUATE A CHARACTER

Annotate: Mark references to the girl's name in paragraphs 47–49.

Evaluate: What does it suggest about Rosemary that she hasn't asked for her name until now?

48   "Smith, madam," said the languid figure, who was strangely still and unafraid.

49   "Smith," said Rosemary. "We are going to have a little talk."

50   "Oh, yes," said Philip. "Quite," and his eye caught sight of the coat and hat on the floor. He came over to the fire and turned his back to it. "It's a beastly[10] afternoon," he said curiously, still looking at that **listless** figure, looking at its hands and boots, and then at Rosemary again.

51   "Yes, isn't it?" said Rosemary enthusiastically. "**Vile**."

52   Philip smiled his charming smile. "As a matter of fact," said he, "I wanted you to come into the library for a moment. Would you? Will Miss Smith excuse us?"

53   The big eyes were raised to him, but Rosemary answered for her. "Of course she will." And they went out of the room together.

54   "I say," said Philip, when they were alone. "Explain. Who is she? What does it all mean?"

55   Rosemary, laughing, leaned against the door and said: "I picked her up in Curzon Street. Really. She's a real pick-up. She asked me for the price of a cup of tea, and I brought her home with me."

56   "But what on earth are you going to do with her?" cried Philip.

listless
(lĭst′lĭs) *adj.* lacking energy or disinclined to exert effort; lethargic.

vile
(vīl) *adj.* unpleasant or objectionable.

---

10 beastly: awful; unpleasant.

57 "Be nice to her," said Rosemary quickly. "Be frightfully nice to her. Look after her. I don't know how. We haven't talked yet. But show her—treat her—make her feel—"

58 "My darling girl," said Philip, "you're quite mad, you know. It simply can't be done."

59 "I knew you'd say that," retorted Rosemary. "Why not? I want to. Isn't that a reason? And besides, one's always reading about these things. I decided—"

60 "But," said Philip slowly, and he cut the end of a cigar, "she's so astonishingly pretty."

61 "Pretty?" Rosemary was so surprised that she blushed. "Do you think so? I—I hadn't thought about it."

62 "Good Lord!" Philip struck a match. "She's absolutely lovely. Look again, my child. I was bowled over when I came into your room just now. However . . . I think you're making a ghastly mistake. Sorry, darling, if I'm crude and all that. But let me know if Miss Smith is going to dine with us in time for me to look up *The Milliner's Gazette*."[11]

63 "You absurd creature!" said Rosemary, and she went out of the library, but not back to her bedroom. She went to her writing-room and sat down at her desk. Pretty! Absolutely lovely! Bowled over! Her heart beat like a heavy bell. Pretty! Lovely! She drew her checkbook towards her. But no, checks would be no use, of course. She opened a drawer and took out five pound notes, looked at them, put two back, and holding the three squeezed in her hand, she went back to her bedroom.

64 Half an hour later Philip was still in the library, when Rosemary came in.

65 "I only wanted to tell you," said she, and she leaned against the door again and looked at him with her dazzled exotic gaze, "Miss Smith won't dine with us tonight."

66 Philip put down the paper. "Oh, what's happened? Previous **engagement**?"

67 Rosemary came over and sat down on his knee. "She insisted on going," said she, "so I gave the poor little thing a present of money. I couldn't keep her against her will, could I?" she added softly.

68 Rosemary had just done her hair, darkened her eyes a little, and put on her pearls. She put up her hands and touched Philip's cheeks.

69 "Do you like me?" said she, and her tone, sweet, husky, troubled him.

70 "I like you awfully," he said, and he held her tighter. "Kiss me."

71 There was a pause.

72 Then Rosemary said dreamily, "I saw a fascinating little box today. It cost twenty-eight guineas. May I have it?"

[11] ***The Milliner's Gazette:*** an imaginary newsletter for working-class women. A milliner is a maker of women's hats.

NOTICE & NOTE
AHA MOMENT

When you notice a sudden realization that shifts a character's actions or understandings, you've found an **Aha Moment** signpost.

Notice & Note: Mark the sentence in paragraph 63 that describes how Philip's comments have affected Rosemary.

Infer: Why is Rosemary rushing to give money to Miss Smith?

engagement
(ĕn-gāj´mənt) *n.* a promise or agreement to be at a particular place at a particular time.

73   Philip jumped her on his knee. "You may, little wasteful one," said he.

74   But that was not really what Rosemary wanted to say.

75   "Philip," she whispered, and she pressed his head against her bosom, "am I *pretty?*"

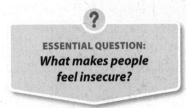

ESSENTIAL QUESTION:
What makes people feel insecure?

Review your notes and add your thoughts to your Response Log.

COLLABORATIVE DISCUSSION

Turn to a partner and discuss your reaction to the story's ending. Does it change your understanding of Rosemary or just confirm what you already thought about her?

Assessment Practice

Answer these questions before moving on to the **Analyze the Text** section on the following page.

1. In paragraphs 3–5, what can you infer about the shopkeeper?

    (A) He has a secret crush on Rosemary.

    (B) He uses flattery to sell expensive things to rich people.

    (C) He isn't very interested in money.

    (D) He wishes he didn't have to sell his things.

2. In paragraphs 10–14, which sentence suggests Rosemary's motivation for taking Miss Smith home with her?

    (A) *"M-madam," stammered the voice. "Would you let me have the price of a cup of tea?"*

    (B) *There was something simple, sincere in that voice; it wasn't in the least the voice of a beggar.*

    (C) *It was like something out of a novel by Dostoyevsky, this meeting in the dusk.*

    (D) *And she heard herself saying afterwards to the amazement of her friends: "I simply took her home with me...."*

3. How does Rosemary's husband convince her to send the girl away?

    (A) He plays on Rosemary's insecurity about her looks.

    (B) He embarrasses her for not reading the paper.

    (C) He scolds her about money.

    (D) He flatters her need to feel superior.

Test-Taking Strategies

Analyze the Text

Support your responses with evidence from the text.

NOTICE & NOTE

Review what you **noticed and noted** as you read the text. Your annotations can help you answer these questions.

1. **ANALYZE** **Foreshadowing** is a writer's use of hints or clues to indicate events that will occur later in a story. Reread paragraph 9. How does Rosemary's reaction to the rainy afternoon foreshadow events later in the story? Consider

   - her emotional response to the weather
   - her hesitation to cross the street to the car waiting for her
   - her wish to escape from discomfort

2. **ANALYZE** How does the third-person limited point of view affect your reaction to Rosemary and her plan to help Miss Smith? How might the story have been different if told by an omniscient narrator?

3. **INFER** Reread paragraphs 60–62. Why does Philip speak so enthusiastically to his wife about Miss Smith's attractiveness? Explain.

4. **ANALYZE** What theme about wealthy people does Mansfield convey in "A Cup of Tea"? How do Rosemary's actions and motivation in trying to help Miss Smith relate to this theme?

5. **DRAW CONCLUSIONS** Rosemary abandons her plan after Philip makes her aware of Miss Smith's beauty. Has this **Aha Moment** changed Rosemary? Why or why not?

6. **CONNECT** "A Cup of Tea" is set in a time when wealthy women did not have professions and were expected to appear fashionable. How does this context influence your evaluation of Rosemary's character?

Choices

Here are some other ways to demonstrate your understanding of the ideas in this lesson.

Writing
↳ **Fictional Scene**

We know that Rosemary goes back to her bedroom and gives Miss Smith some money before asking her to leave, but the scene is not in the story. Write this scene from Miss Smith's perspective, using the third-person limited point of view.

- Create dialogue that is consistent with how the characters speak to each other earlier in the story.

- Remember that the third-person narrator is a voice outside of the story.

- The narrator should relate only Miss Smith's thoughts and feelings.

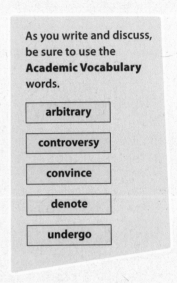

As you write and discuss, be sure to use the **Academic Vocabulary** words.

arbitrary
controversy
convince
denote
undergo

Social & Emotional Learning
↳ **Paired Discussion**

Rosemary tells herself that she "was going to prove to this girl that—wonderful things did happen in life, that—fairy godmothers were real. . . ." Yet she ends up sending Miss Smith away abruptly with only a small amount of cash.

1. Get together with a partner, and look up the definitions of *empathy* and *pity*. Which of these feelings motivates Rosemary to help Miss Smith?

2. Go online and find websites for three organizations that raise funds to relieve hunger or poverty. Determine whether each website appeals primarily to viewers' sense of empathy or pity.

3. Discuss whether arousing empathy or pity is a better way to motivate people to help others.

Media
↳ **Podcast**

With a group of students, create a podcast performance of a scene in "A Cup of Tea."

- Write a script for the performance, removing any dialogue tags (phrases such as *he said*) and descriptions that can be replaced with sound effects.

- Choose actors to perform the characters and one actor to read aloud the narration.

- Use an appropriate accent for each character as you rehearse the script.

- Record audio of your performance, and upload it to the internet.

Expand Your Vocabulary

PRACTICE AND APPLY

Complete the sentences with vocabulary words.

| presentable | tactfully | listless | vile | engagement |

1. The baby is so pale and _____. She must be sick!

2. I'm sorry to cancel our plans, but I have another _____.

3. If I'd known I was having visitors, I'd have tried to look _____ instead of wearing sweatpants.

4. I need to _____ remind her that she owes me money.

5. I won't tolerate such _____ language just because you are angry with me.

Vocabulary Strategy
↳ **Clarify Precise Meaning**

Many words have several meanings, so it may not be immediately clear how they are used in a sentence. You can often clarify a word's precise meaning by using a dictionary and looking for context clues—hints about the word in surrounding words, phrases, and sentences.

In paragraph 66, Philip asks Rosemary if Miss Smith left because she had a previous engagement. The vocabulary word *engagement* has multiple definitions, including "a pledge or obligation" and "a period of employment." In this case, Philip's earlier sarcastic remarks about Miss Smith's social status indicate that the precise meaning of *engagement* here is "a promise or agreement to be at a particular place at a particular time."

> **⚆Ed**
> **Interactive Vocabulary Lesson: Using Reference Sources**

PRACTICE AND APPLY

Use a dictionary as well as context clues to define each of the underlined words in these sentences from the story.

1. "They were rich, really rich, not just <u>comfortably</u> well off...." (paragraph 2)

2. "'If I may <u>venture</u> to point out to madam, the flowers on the little lady's bodice.'" (paragraph 5)

3. "She <u>plied</u> the poor little creature with everything, all the sandwiches, all the bread and butter, and every time her cup was empty she filled it with tea, cream and sugar." (paragraph 40)

4. "'It's a <u>beastly</u> afternoon,' he said curiously...." (paragraph 50)

5. "'However ... I think you're making a <u>ghastly</u> mistake.'" (paragraph 62)

Watch Your Language!

Precise Details

In order to engage the reader, authors use precise details to illustrate or suggest key ideas. A good writer does not provide details arbitrarily, but rather makes very deliberate choices in using details to develop characters and themes.

> She had a feeling of triumph as she slipped her hand through the <u>velvet strap</u>.

In this sentence, the velvet strap reminds the reader that Rosemary lives a life of luxury and comfort.

> There was a whisper that sounded like "Very good, madam," and the <u>crushed hat</u> was taken off.

In this sentence, the "crushed hat" gives the reader a sense of the girl's poverty and misfortune.

PRACTICE AND APPLY

In the passages below from "A Cup of Tea," mark the precise details the author uses to develop the characters and theme.

> "Don't cry, poor little thing," she said. "Don't cry." And she gave the other her lace handkerchief. She really was touched beyond words. She put her arm round those thin, birdlike shoulders.
>
> When the tea table was carried away a new being, a light, frail creature with tangled hair, dark lips, deep, lighted eyes, lay back in the big chair in a kind of sweet languor, looking at the blaze.

How do these details contribute to the reader's understanding of the characters and the theme of the story?

Interactive Writing Lesson: The Language of Narrative

Shooting an Elephant

Essay by **George Orwell**

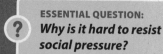

Engage Your Brain

Choose one or more of these activities to start connecting with the essay you're about to read.

Doing as You're Told

There are times in our lives when a family member, a teacher, or someone close to us asks us to do an assignment or a chore that we really don't want to do.

With a partner, discuss an instance when this has happened to you. How did you feel while you were doing what was asked of you? Do you wish you could have reacted differently in retrospect?

Create a Timeline

Between the 1600s and the 1800s, Great Britain built a vast empire that included colonies in parts of Asia, Australia, Africa, and North America. This essay is set in the 1920s in Burma, a country in Southeast Asia that is now called Myanmar. Do some research on the dates listed, and create a timeline of significant events about the relationship and conflicts between Burma and Great Britain.

- 1825
- 1885
- 1937
- 1948
- 1989

What Is Colonialism?

Colonialism refers to the rule of one nation over a group of people in a geographically distant land—usually for the purpose of maintaining control of that land's resources.

- Think about impressions of British colonialism from your knowledge of history, from books you have read, or from movies you have seen. (Remember—the United States once consisted of British colonies.)

- Make a list of some of these impressions.

- Then, based on your list, write a few sentences about your view of the ideals, principles, or beliefs behind British colonialism.

Analyze Reflective Essay

In a **reflective essay,** the author examines a personal experience and reveals what he or she learned from it. A good reflective essay

- offers insight into the author's personal growth.
- connects a specific observation to some larger idea about life or society.

In "Shooting an Elephant," Orwell reflects on an incident he experienced as a young police officer in British-ruled Burma in the 1920s. By exploring this experience, Orwell allows readers to understand what he learned about the true nature of colonialism. As you read, pay attention to the thoughts and feelings that Orwell expresses as he describes the incident.

Focus on Genre
↳ **Essay**

- a short piece of nonfiction
- offers an opinion on a subject
- formal essays have a serious and impersonal tone
- informal essays are loosely structured and have a conversational tone
- a reflective essay examines an experience in the author's life

Analyze Cause-and-Effect Relationships

In "Shooting an Elephant," Orwell describes events leading up to an unfortunate ending. Many of these events have a **cause-and-effect relationship.**

- A **cause** is an event or action that directly results in another event or action.
- An **effect** is the consequence of an earlier event or action.

By revealing a chain or sequence of causes and effects, a writer can help explain a complex situation. Note that a cause can have multiple effects, and a single effect can have more than one cause.

As you read the essay, notice how events interact and develop in the course of the text. Use a graphic organizer like this one to trace the cause-and-effect relationships.

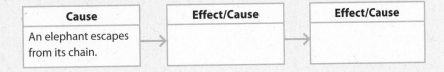

Cause	Effect/Cause	Effect/Cause
An elephant escapes from its chain.		

Annotation in Action

Here are one student's notes about the reflective essay. As you read, notice the cause-and-effect relationship between events described in the essay.

In Moulmein, in Lower Burma, I was hated by large numbers of people—the only time in my life that I have been important enough for this to happen to me. I was subdivisional police officer of the town, and in an aimless, petty kind of way anti-European feeling was very bitter. No one had the guts to raise a riot, but if a European woman went through the bazaars alone somebody would probably spit betel juice over her dress. As a police officer I was an obvious target and was baited whenever it seemed safe to do so.

Orwell's attitude toward the Burmese people must have been affected by this experience of being targeted.

Expand Your Vocabulary

Put a check mark next to the vocabulary words that you feel comfortable using when speaking or writing.

imperialism	☐
cowed	☐
supplant	☐
prostrate	☐
despotic	☐
labyrinth	☐
garish	☐
senility	☐

Turn to a partner and discuss a time when you experienced peer pressure, using as many of the vocabulary words as you can. As you read, use the definitions in the side-column to learn the vocabulary words you don't already know.

Background

George Orwell (1903–1950) was born in India. When he was 19, he joined the Indian Imperial police and left to serve in Burma, which at the time was ruled by Britain. Disillusioned with imperialism, he resigned in 1928 and decided to become a writer. In 1936 Orwell went to Spain to fight with antifascist forces in the Spanish Civil War, an experience that greatly influenced his political views. Throughout his life, Orwell spoke out against injustice. His most famous novels, *Animal Farm* and *1984*, reflect his dedication to political freedom.

Shooting an Elephant

Essay by **George Orwell**

Note details that tell you how Orwell feels about
his role as a colonial officer.

 NOTICE & NOTE
As you read, use the side
margins to make notes
about the text.

1 In Moulmein, in Lower Burma,[1] I was hated by large numbers
of people—the only time in my life that I have been important
enough for this to happen to me. I was subdivisional police officer
of the town, and in an aimless, petty kind of way anti-European
feeling was very bitter. No one had the guts to raise a riot, but if a
European woman went through the bazaars alone somebody would
probably spit betel juice[2] over her dress. As a police officer I was
an obvious target and was baited whenever it seemed safe to do so.
When a nimble Burman tripped me up on the football[3] field and the
referee (another Burman) looked the other way, the crowd yelled

ANALYZE REFLECTIVE ESSAY

Annotate: Mark details that
tell you about the relationship
between the Burmans and the
Europeans.

Interpret: How would you
describe the relationship between
the Burmans and the Europeans?

---

[1] **Moulmein** (mo͞ol-mān´), **in Lower Burma:** the main city of British-controlled Burma, now
the independent Asian nation of Myanmar. Moulmein is now usually called Mawlamyine.
[2] **betel** (bēt´l) **juice:** the saliva created when chewing a mixture of betel palm nuts, betel
palm leaves, and lime.
[3] **football:** soccer.

with hideous laughter. This happened more than once. In the end the sneering yellow faces of young men that met me everywhere, the insults hooted after me when I was at a safe distance, got badly on my nerves. The young Buddhist priests were the worst of all. There were several thousands of them in the town and none of them seemed to have anything to do except stand on street corners and jeer at Europeans.

2   All this was perplexing and upsetting. For at that time I had already made up my mind that **imperialism** was an evil thing and the sooner I chucked up[4] my job and got out of it the better. Theoretically—and secretly, of course—I was all for the Burmese and all against their oppressors, the British. As for the job I was doing, I hated it more bitterly than I can perhaps make clear. In a job like that you see the dirty work of Empire at close quarters. The wretched prisoners huddling in the stinking cages of the lock-ups, the gray, **cowed** faces of the long-term convicts, the scarred buttocks of the men who had been flogged with bamboos—all these oppressed me with an intolerable sense of guilt. But I could get nothing into perspective. I was young and ill-educated and I had had to think out my problems in the utter silence that is imposed on every Englishman in the East. I did not even know that the British Empire is dying, still less did I know that it is a great deal better than the younger empires that are going to **supplant** it. All I knew was that I was stuck between my hatred of the empire I served and my rage against the evil-spirited little beasts who tried to make my job impossible. With one part of my mind I thought of the British Raj[5] as an unbreakable tyranny, as something clamped down, *in saecula saeculorum*,[6] upon the will of **prostrate** peoples; with another part I thought that the greatest joy in the world would be to drive a bayonet into a Buddhist priest's guts. Feelings like these are the normal by-products of imperialism; ask any Anglo-Indian official, if you can catch him off duty.

3   One day something happened which in a roundabout way was enlightening. It was a tiny incident in itself, but it gave me a better glimpse than I had had before of the real nature of imperialism—the real motives for which **despotic** governments act. Early one morning the subinspector at a police station the other end of the town rang me up on the phone and said that an elephant was ravaging the bazaar. Would I please come and do something about it? I did not know what I could do, but I wanted to see what was happening and I got on to a pony and started out. I took my rifle, an old 44 Winchester and much too small to kill an elephant, but I thought the noise might be useful *in terrorem*.[7] Various Burmans stopped me on the way and told me about the elephant's doings. It was not, of course, a wild elephant,

---

imperialism
(ĭm-pîr´ē-ə-lĭ´z əm): *n.* the extension of a nation's authority by territorial acquisition or by the establishment of economic and political dominance over other nations.

cowed
(koud): *adj.* frightened or subdued with threats or a show of force.

supplant
(sə-plănt´): *tr.v.* to take the place of or substitute for (another).

prostrate
(prŏs´trāt): *adj.* lying face down, as in submission or adoration.

despotic
(dĭ-spŏt´ĭk): *adj.* of or relating to a person who wields power oppressively, or a tyrant.

---

[4] **chucked up:** threw off; gave up.
[5] **British Raj:** India and adjoining areas (such as Burma) controlled by Britain in the 19th and early 20th centuries. *Raj* is the word for "kingdom" or "rule" in Hindi, a chief language of India.
[6] *in saecula saeculorum* (ĭn sĕk´yə-lə sĕk-yə-lôr´əm) *Latin:* forever and ever.
[7] *in terrorem* (ĭn tĕ-rôr´əm) *Latin:* for terror.

but a tame one which had gone "must."[8] It had been chained up as tame elephants always are when their attack of "must" is due, but on the previous night it had broken its chain and escaped. Its mahout,[9] the only person who could manage it when it was in that state, had set out in pursuit, but had taken the wrong direction and was now twelve hours' journey away, and in the morning the elephant had suddenly reappeared in the town. The Burmese population had no weapons and were quite helpless against it. It had already destroyed somebody's bamboo hut, killed a cow and raided some fruit-stalls and devoured the stock; also it had met the municipal rubbish van, and, when the driver jumped out and took to his heels, had turned the van over and inflicted violences upon it.

4   The Burmese subinspector and some Indian constables[10] were waiting for me in the quarter where the elephant had been seen. It was a very poor quarter, a **labyrinth** of squalid bamboo huts, thatched with palm-leaf, winding all over a steep hillside. I remember that it was a cloudy stuffy morning at the beginning of the rains. We began questioning the people as to where the elephant had gone, and, as usual, failed to get any definite information. That is invariably the case in the East; a story always sounds clear enough at a distance, but the nearer you get to the scene of events the vaguer it becomes. Some of the people said that the elephant had gone in one direction, some said that he had gone in another, some professed not even to have heard of any elephant. I had almost made up my mind that the whole story was a pack of lies, when we heard yells a little distance away. There was a loud, scandalized cry of "Go away, child! Go away this instant!" and an old woman with a switch in her hand came round the corner of a hut, violently shooing away a crowd of naked children. Some more women followed, clicking their tongues and exclaiming; evidently there was something there that the children ought not to have seen. I rounded the hut and saw a man's dead body sprawling in the mud. He was an Indian, a black Dravidian coolie,[11] almost naked, and he could not have been dead many minutes. The people said that the elephant had come suddenly upon him round the corner of the hut, caught him with its trunk, put its foot on his back and ground him into the earth. This was the rainy season and the ground was soft, and his face had scored a trench a foot deep and a couple of yards long. He was lying on his belly with arms crucified and head sharply twisted to one side. His face was coated with mud, the eyes wide open, the teeth bared and grinning with an expression of unendurable agony. (Never tell me, by the way, that the dead look peaceful. Most of the corpses I have seen looked devilish.) The friction of the great beast's foot had stripped the skin from his back as neatly as one skins a rabbit. As soon as I saw the dead man I sent an

labyrinth
(lăb´ə-rĭnth): *n.* an intricate structure of interconnecting passages through which it is difficult to find one's way; a maze.

ANALYZE REFLECTIVE ESSAY

Annotate: Mark Orwell's description of the corpse in paragraph 4.

Draw Conclusions: Why might he have chosen to include such precise details about the corpse?

---

[8] **gone "must":** had an attack of must, a dangerous frenzy that periodically seizes male elephants.

[9] **mahout** (mə-hout´)**:** an elephant keeper.

[10] **constables:** police officers.

[11] **Dravidian** (drə-vĭd´ē-ən) **coolie:** a dark-skinned menial laborer from the south of India.

British troops patrolling a city in Burma

orderly[12] to a friend's house nearby to borrow an elephant rifle. I had already sent back the pony, not wanting it to go mad with fright and throw me if it smelled the elephant.

5   The orderly came back in a few minutes with a rifle and five cartridges, and meanwhile some Burmans had arrived and told us that the elephant was in the paddy fields[13] below, only a few hundred yards away. As I started forward practically the whole population of the quarter flocked out of the houses and followed me. They had seen the rifle and were all shouting excitedly that I was going to shoot the elephant. They had not shown much interest in the elephant when he was merely ravaging their homes, but it was different now that he was going to be shot. It was a bit of fun to them, as it would be to an

ANALYZE CAUSE-AND-EFFECT RELATIONSHIPS

Annotate: Mark details in paragraph 5 that describe the Burmans.

Analyze: What causes the Burmans to behave this way?

---

[12] **orderly:** a military aide.
[13] **paddy fields:** rice fields.

English crowd; besides, they wanted the meat. It made me vaguely uneasy. I had no intention of shooting the elephant—I had merely sent for the rifle to defend myself if necessary—and it is always unnerving to have a crowd following you. I marched down the hill, looking and feeling a fool, with the rifle over my shoulder and an ever-growing army of people jostling at my heels. At the bottom, when you got away from the huts, there was a metalled road and beyond that a miry waste of paddy fields a thousand yards across, not yet ploughed but soggy from the first rains and dotted with coarse grass. The elephant was standing eighty yards from the road, his left side towards us. He took not the slightest notice of the crowd's approach. He was tearing up bunches of grass, beating them against his knees to clean them and stuffing them into his mouth.

6   I had halted on the road. As soon as I saw the elephant I knew with perfect certainty that I ought not to shoot him. It is a serious matter to shoot a working elephant—it is comparable to destroying

a huge and costly piece of machinery—and obviously one ought not to do it if it can possibly be avoided. And at that distance, peacefully eating, the elephant looked no more dangerous than a cow. I thought then and I think now that his attack of "must" was already passing off; in which case he would merely wander harmlessly about until the mahout came back and caught him. Moreover, I did not in the least want to shoot him. I decided that I would watch him for a little while to make sure that he did not turn savage again, and then go home.

7   But at that moment I glanced round at the crowd that had followed me. It was an immense crowd, two thousand at the least and growing every minute. It blocked the road for a long distance on either side. I looked at the sea of yellow faces above the **garish** clothes—faces all happy and excited over this bit of fun, all certain that the elephant was going to be shot. They were watching me as they would watch a conjurer[14] about to perform a trick. They did not like me, but with the magical rifle in my hands I was momentarily worth watching. And suddenly I realized that I should have to shoot the elephant after all. The people expected it of me and I had got to do it; I could feel their two thousand wills pressing me forward, irresistibly. And it was at this moment, as I stood there with the rifle in my hands, that I first grasped the hollowness, the futility of the white man's dominion in the East. Here was I, the white man with his gun, standing in front of the unarmed native crowd—seemingly the leading actor of the piece; but in reality I was only an absurd puppet pushed to and fro by the will of those yellow faces behind. I perceived in this moment that when the white man turns tyrant it is his own freedom that he destroys. He becomes a sort of hollow, posing dummy, the conventionalized figure of a sahib.[15] For it is the condition of his rule that he shall spend his life in trying to impress the "natives," and so in every crisis he has got to do what the "natives" expect of him. He wears a mask, and his face grows to fit it. I had got to shoot the elephant. I had committed myself to doing it when I sent for the rifle. A sahib has got to act like a sahib; he has got to appear resolute, to know his own mind and do definite things. To come all that way, rifle in hand, with two thousand people marching at my heels, and then to trail feebly away, having done nothing—no, that was impossible. The crowd would laugh at me. And my whole life, every white man's life in the East, was one long struggle not to be laughed at.

8   But I did not want to shoot the elephant. I watched him beating his bunch of grass against his knees, with that preoccupied grandmotherly air that elephants have. It seemed to me that it would be murder to shoot him. At that age I was not squeamish about killing animals, but I had never shot an elephant and never wanted to. (Somehow it always seems worse to kill a *large* animal.) Besides, there

garish
(gâr´ĭsh, găr´): *adj.* overly bright or ornamented, especially in a vulgar or tasteless way; gaudy.

NOTICE & NOTE
AHA MOMENT

When you notice a sudden realization that shifts the writer's actions or understandings, you've found an **Aha Moment** signpost.

Notice & Note: In paragraph 7, mark statements expressing Orwell's realization about his role as a colonial officer.

Analyze: What is ironic about these statements?

---

[14] **conjurer** (kŏn´jər-ər): a magician.
[15] **sahib** (sä´hĭb): a title of respect formerly used by native Indians to address a European gentleman.

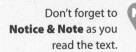
was the beast's owner to be considered. Alive, the elephant was worth at least a hundred pounds; dead, he would only be worth the value of his tusks—five pounds, possibly. But I had got to act quickly. I turned to some experienced-looking Burmans who had been there when we arrived, and asked them how the elephant had been behaving. They all said the same thing: he took no notice of you if you left him alone, but he might charge if you went too close to him.

9   It was perfectly clear to me what I ought to do. I ought to walk up to within, say, twenty-five yards of the elephant and test his behavior. If he charged I could shoot, if he took no notice of me it would be safe to leave him until the mahout came back. But also I knew that I was going to do no such thing. I was a poor shot with a rifle and the ground was soft mud into which one would sink at every step. If the elephant charged and I missed him, I should have about as much chance as a toad under a steam-roller. But even then I was not thinking particularly of my own skin, only of the watchful yellow faces behind. For at that moment, with the crowd watching me, I was not afraid in the ordinary sense, as I would have been if I had been alone. A white man mustn't be frightened in front of "natives"; and so, in general, he isn't frightened. The sole thought in my mind was that if anything went wrong those two thousand Burmans would see me pursued, caught, trampled on and reduced to a grinning corpse like that Indian up the hill. And if that happened it was quite probable that some of them would laugh. That would never do. There was only one alternative. I shoved the cartridges into the magazine[16] and lay down on the road to get a better aim.

10   The crowd grew very still, and a deep, low, happy sigh, as of people who see the theater curtain go up at last, breathed from innumerable throats. They were going to have their bit of fun after all. The rifle was a beautiful German thing with cross-hair sights. I did not then know that in shooting an elephant one should shoot to cut an imaginary bar running from ear-hole to ear-hole. I ought, therefore, as the elephant was sideways on, to have aimed straight at his ear-hole; actually I aimed several inches in front of this, thinking the brain would be further forward.

11   When I pulled the trigger I did not hear the bang or feel the kick—one never does when a shot goes home—but I heard the devilish roar of glee that went up from the crowd. In that instant, in too short a time, one would have thought, even for the bullet to get there, a mysterious, terrible change had come over the elephant. He neither stirred nor fell, but every line of his body had altered. He looked suddenly stricken, shrunken, immensely old, as though the frightful impact of the bullet had paralyzed him without knocking him down. At last, after what seemed a long time—it might have been five seconds, I dare say—he sagged flabbily to his knees. His mouth slobbered. An enormous **senility** seemed to have settled upon

ANALYZE REFLECTIVE ESSAY

Annotate: In paragraph 9, mark Orwell's explanation of what he ought to have done in this situation.

Draw Conclusions: What idea does this paragraph convey about how imperialism affects the individuals who serve it?

senility
(sĭ-nĭl´ĭ-tē): *n.* relating to or having diminished cognitive function, as when memory is impaired, because of old age.

---

16 magazine: the compartment from which cartridges are fed into the rifle's firing chamber.

him. One could have imagined him thousands of years old. I fired again into the same spot. At the second shot he did not collapse but climbed with desperate slowness to his feet and stood weakly upright, with legs sagging and head drooping. I fired a third time. That was the shot that did for him. You could see the agony of it jolt his whole body and knock the last remnant of strength from his legs. But in falling he seemed for a moment to rise, for as his hind legs collapsed beneath him he seemed to tower upwards like a huge rock toppling, his trunk reaching skyward like a tree. He trumpeted, for the first and only time. And then down he came, his belly towards me, with a crash that seemed to shake the ground even where I lay.

ANALYZE CAUSE-AND-EFFECT RELATIONSHIPS

Annotate: Mark descriptions of the elephant's dying in paragraph 12.

Analyze: What effect does the elephant's slow death have on Orwell?

12   I got up. The Burmans were already racing past me across the mud. It was obvious that the elephant would never rise again, but he was not dead. He was breathing very rhythmically with long rattling gasps, his great mound of a side painfully rising and falling. His mouth was wide open—I could see far down into caverns of pale pink throat. I waited a long time for him to die, but his breathing did not weaken. Finally I fired my two remaining shots into the spot where I thought his heart must be. The thick blood welled out of him like red velvet, but still he did not die. His body did not even jerk when the shots hit him, the tortured breathing continued without a pause. He was dying, very slowly and in great agony, but in some world remote from me where not even a bullet could damage him further. I felt that I had got to put an end to that dreadful noise. It seemed dreadful to see the great beast lying there, powerless to move and yet powerless to die, and not even to be able to finish him. I sent back for my small rifle and poured shot after shot into his heart and down his throat. They seemed to make no impression. The tortured gasps continued as steadily as the ticking of a clock.

13   In the end I could not stand it any longer and went away. I heard later that it took him half an hour to die. Burmans were arriving with dahs[17] and baskets even before I left, and I was told they had stripped his body almost to the bones by the afternoon.

14   Afterwards, of course, there were endless discussions about the shooting of the elephant. The owner was furious, but he was only an Indian and could do nothing. Besides, legally I had done the right thing, for a mad elephant has to be killed, like a mad dog, if its owner fails to control it. Among the Europeans opinion was divided. The older men said I was right, the younger men said it was a damn shame to shoot an elephant for killing a coolie, because an elephant was worth more than any damn Coringhee[18] coolie. And afterwards I was very glad that the coolie had been killed; it put me legally in the right and it gave me a sufficient pretext for shooting the elephant. I often wondered whether any of the others grasped that I had done it solely to avoid looking a fool.

---

[17] **dahs:** large knives.
[18] **Coringhee:** coming from a port in southeastern India.

How did Orwell's role as an officer affect him? Discuss your ideas with a partner.

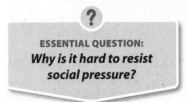

ESSENTIAL QUESTION:
Why is it hard to resist social pressure?

Review your notes and add your thoughts to your Response Log.

Assessment Practice

Answer these questions before moving on to the **Analyze the Text** section on the following page.

1. What annoyed the narrator?

- Ⓐ The elephant's destruction of trees
- Ⓑ How the Burmans mocked soldiers
- Ⓒ The weather in Asia
- Ⓓ His small gun

2. When Orwell finally sees the elephant, it is —

- Ⓐ wild
- Ⓑ ravenous
- Ⓒ tame
- Ⓓ gentle

3. The narrator had to shoot the elephant because —

- Ⓐ so many people were watching
- Ⓑ the elephant was charging toward him
- Ⓒ his job was to protect the village people
- Ⓓ the elephant was already injured

Test-Taking Strategies

Analyze the Text

Support your responses with evidence from the text.

NOTICE & NOTE

Review what you **noticed and noted** as you read the text. Your annotations can help you answer these questions.

1. **ANALYZE** Which sequence of actions and events caused Orwell to feel that his only choice was to shoot the elephant?

2. **EVALUATE** Orwell describes the shooting and slow death of the elephant in excruciating detail. How does this description support his reflections in the essay?

3. **DRAW CONCLUSIONS** At the end of the essay, Orwell wonders whether other Europeans realized that he shot the elephant "solely to avoid looking a fool." Why was it so important for him to keep up appearances before the Burmans?

4. **CRITIQUE** Do you think Orwell provides a reliable account of how the Burmans viewed him? Explain why or why not.

5. **ANALYZE** Orwell describes an **Aha Moment** when he says that this experience taught him that "when the white man turns tyrant it is his own freedom that he destroys." In what ways did his role as a colonial policeman end his freedom?

6. **EVALUATE** Discuss whether the elephant is an effective symbol for colonialism. Consider the following in your response:

   - details for the description of the elephant
   - the effect of colonialism on the young Orwell
   - the effect of colonialism on the Burmese

Choices

Here are some other ways to demonstrate your understanding of the ideas in this lesson.

Writing

↳ Explain an Injustice

Write about a social injustice that is occurring today. Describe the toll that this injustice takes on all the individuals involved in the circumstances.

- Begin your essay with a hook—a stirring incident or anecdote.

- Create an effective transitional sentence between the hook and the next section of your essay.

- Use evidence and examples from news stories you research and what you may know from your own experience.

- Express why you are concerned about this injustice.

- Create a memorable theme or message to share an insight.

As you write and discuss, be sure to use the **Academic Vocabulary** words.

| arbitrary |
| controversy |
| convince |
| denote |
| undergo |

Speaking & Listening

↳ Words to Dwell On

Review Orwell's essay, and find one passage that you think is especially important, controversial, or even upsetting. With a partner, discuss the passage and explain why it stands out to you. Share your response to the passage, and state whether you think it relates to any situation in today's society.

Social & Emotional Learning

↳ Facing Peer Pressure

In retrospect, Orwell regrets his behavior. But at the time, the younger Orwell finds it hard to fight back against the feeling that he should act a certain way. With a group, discuss how you can identify and address peer pressure constructively.

- What are some situations in which peer pressure takes place?

- How does it feel when someone is putting peer pressure on you?

- What are some strategies you can use to resist peer pressure?

Expand Your Vocabulary

PRACTICE AND APPLY

Choose the words that best complete each sentence.

imperialism	cowed	supplant	prostrate
despotic	labyrinth	garish	senility

1. The economic interests of _____ led the British to seize control of local governments and _____ local officials.

2. As the elephant wove through the _____ of the village, the _____ residents sent word to the police of the event.

3. In his _____, he would dress in _____ costumes and relive the scene for any who would stop and listen.

4. As he gazed at the _____ form of the dead man, he felt the _____ expectation of the crowd pushing him toward an action he did not want to take.

Vocabulary Strategy
↳ **Etymology**

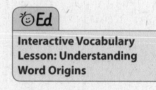

Interactive Vocabulary Lesson: Understanding Word Origins

Etymology is the history of a word. Most dictionary entries include etymologies that identify which language the word came from and what the original word meant. The etymology also traces the route by which a word passed into the English language.

The entry below gives the history of the vocabulary word *labyrinth*. It shows that *labyrinth* comes from the ancient Greek *laburinthos,* which refers to the Minotaur's maze in the Greek myth of Jason and the Argonauts.

lab•y•rinth (lăb´ə-rĭnth): *n.* an intricate structure of interconnecting passages through which it is difficult to find one's way; a maze. [Middle English *laberinthe,* from Latin *labyrinthus,* from Greek *laburinthos;* possibly akin to *labrus,* double-headed axe used as a ritual weapon and a sign of authority in Minoan civilization, so that Greek *laburinthos* may originally have designated a Minoan palace as "the house of the double-headed axe."]

PRACTICE AND APPLY

Look up the remaining vocabulary words in a college-level dictionary, and trace their etymology. Discuss with a partner how closely the original meaning resembles the usage of the word today.

Watch Your Language!

Prepositional Phrases

A **prepositional phrase** consists of a preposition (such as *in* or *with*), its object, and any modifiers of the object. Prepositional phrases can act as adjectives or adverbs. If a prepositional phrase describes a noun or pronoun (telling *what kind* or *how many*), it is an **adjectival phrase.** If a prepositional phrase describes a verb, an adverb, or an adjective (telling *where, when, why,* or *how*), it is an **adverbial phrase.** Here are some examples from the essay "Shooting an Elephant."

> It was a very poor quarter, a labyrinth <u>of squalid bamboo huts,</u> thatched <u>with palm-leaf,</u> winding all <u>over a steep hillside.</u>

Notice that "of squalid bamboo huts" describes *what kind* of labyrinth, so it is an adjectival phrase. The phrase "with palm-leaf" describes *how* the huts are thatched, so it is an adverbial phrase. Another adverbial phrase is "over a steep hillside," which describes *where* the huts are winding.

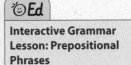

Interactive Grammar Lesson: Prepositional Phrases

PRACTICE AND APPLY

Choose a piece of your own writing, and add or revise at least three prepositional phrases. Include at least one adjectival phrase and one adverbial phrase. Explain to a partner how each added or revised phrase improves the specificity and variety of your sentences.

My Daughter the Racist

Short Story by **Helen Oyeyemi**

Engage Your Brain

Choose one or more of these activities to start connecting with the story you're about to read.

Keeping the Peace

When countries are torn apart by civil war or government collapse, international organizations such as the United Nations (UN) may send in peacekeeping soldiers to help restore order. With a group of students, discuss what you know about peacekeeping operations. Address the following questions:

- Where do peacekeeping soldiers come from?

- Why are they sometimes resented by people they are supposed to help?

Inside or Outside?

Do you tend to look for friends among people with the same background as you, or are you interested in meeting people who come from different backgrounds? Write a paragraph in response to this question. Consider the following:

- How much exposure do you have to people from different backgrounds?

- What other factors may influence your pattern of friendships?

Analyze Setting

Setting is the time and place of the action in a story. Setting also encompasses the culture and customs of the time and place. Religion, historical events, economic conditions, popular beliefs, and political climate are all part of a story's setting. "My Daughter the Racist" takes place in an unnamed country near a desert occupied by foreign troops.

As you read the story, notice how the historical and social context influence the characterization, plot, and theme of the story.

Focus on Genre
↳ **Short Story**

- includes the basic elements of fiction, such as plot, character, and setting
- centers on a particular moment or event or follows the life of a character
- expresses a theme related to the story's outcome

Make Predictions

You can use text clues to make **predictions** about what will happen next in a story. For example, near the beginning of "My Daughter the Racist," the narrator makes the following comment when discussing the tension between people in her village and foreign soldiers:

> **And that girl of mine has really begun to stare at the soldiers, too, . . .**

This remark hints that her daughter will somehow become involved in the tension between villagers and soldiers. As you read this story, try to anticipate what changes will occur in the lives of the main characters. Pay careful attention to the main characters' beliefs about themselves and their way of life, and consider how the events in the story might call these beliefs into question. Use a chart like this one to record your predictions.

Clue from Text	My Prediction	What Happened
"She chopped all her hair off two months ago because she wanted to go around with the local boys. . . ."	Her adventurousness might get her into some trouble.	

Annotation in Action

Here is an example of notes a student made about this paragraph from "My Daughter the Racist." As you read, mark details about the story's setting.

> They fight us and they try to tell us, in our own language, that they're freeing us. Maybe, maybe not. I look through the dusty window (I can never get it clean, the desert is our neighbor) and I see soldiers every day.

Set in a dry area near a desert. Some kind of military conflict going on.

Expand Your Vocabulary

Put a check mark next to the vocabulary words that you feel comfortable using when speaking or writing.

balmy	☐
loftily	☐
brazen	☐
impeccably	☐

Turn to a partner and talk about the vocabulary words you already know. Then, write a description of a person, using as many of the vocabulary words as you can.

As you read "My Daughter the Racist," use the definitions in the side column to learn the vocabulary words you don't already know.

Background

Helen Oyeyemi (b. 1984) was born in Nigeria and raised in London. She has published novels, plays, and a collection of short stories. She says that she was inspired to write fiction as a child after reading Louisa May Alcott's *Little Women*. Oyeyemi wrote her first novel while still attending secondary school. Her story "My Daughter the Racist," which is set in an unnamed Middle Eastern or African country, was a finalist for the 2010 BBC National Short Story Award.

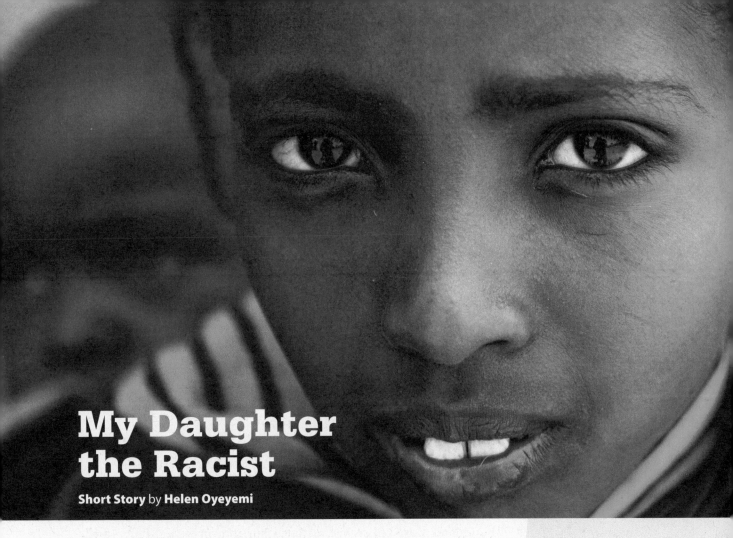

My Daughter
the Racist

Short Story by **Helen Oyeyemi**

A free-spirited girl draws her mother and herself into conflict with her community.

NOTICE & NOTE

As you read, use the side margins to make notes about the text.

1   One morning my daughter woke up and said all in a rush: "Mother, I swear before you and God that from today onwards I am racist." She's eight years old. She chopped all her hair off two months ago because she wanted to go around with the local boys and they wouldn't have her with her long hair. Now she looks like one of them; eyes dazed from looking directly at the sun, teeth shining white in her sunburnt face. She laughs a lot. She plays. "Look at her playing," my mother says. "Playing in the rubble of what used to be our great country." My mother exaggerates as often as she can. I'm sure she would like nothing more than to be part of a Greek tragedy. She wouldn't even want a large part, she'd be perfectly content with a chorus role, warning that fate is coming to make havoc of all things. My mother is a fine woman, all over wrinkles and she always has a clean handkerchief somewhere about her person, but I don't know what she's talking about with her rubble this, rubble that—we live in a village, and it's not bad here. Not peaceful, but not bad. In cities it's worse. In the city center, where we used to live, a bomb took my

MAKE PREDICTIONS

Annotate: Mark details about the narrator's daughter in paragraph 1.

Predict: What expectations do you have about her personality based on these clues?

husband and turned his face to blood. I was lucky, another widow told me, that there was something left so that I could know of his passing. But I was ungrateful. I spat at that widow. I spat at her in her sorrow. That's sin. I know that's sin. But half my life was gone, and it wasn't easy to look at what was left.

2 Anyway, the village. I live with my husband's mother, whom I now call my mother, because I can't return to the one who gave birth to me. It isn't done. I belong with my husband's mother until someone else claims me. And that will never happen, because I don't wish it.

3 The village is hushed. People observe the phases of the moon. In the city I felt the moon but hardly ever remembered to look for it. The only thing that disturbs us here in the village is the foreign soldiers. Soldiers, soldiers, soldiers, patrolling. They fight us and they try to tell us, in our own language, that they're freeing us. Maybe, maybe not. I look through the dusty window (I can never get it clean, the desert is our neighbor) and I see soldiers every day. They think someone dangerous is running secret messages through here; that's what I've heard. What worries me more is the young people of the village. They stand and watch the soldiers. And the soldiers don't like it, and the soldiers point their guns, especially at the young men. They won't bother with the women and girls, unless the woman or the girl has an especially wild look in her eyes. I think there are two reasons the soldiers don't like the young men watching them. The first reason is that the soldiers know they are ugly in their boots and fatigues, they are perfectly aware that their presence spoils everything around them. The second reason is the nature of the watching—the boys and the men around here watch with a very great hatred, so great that it feels as if action must follow. I feel that sometimes, just walking past them—when I block their view of the soldiers these boys quiver with impatience.

4 And that girl of mine has really begun to stare at the soldiers, too, even though I slap her hard when I catch her doing that. Who knows what's going to happen? These soldiers are scared. They might shoot someone. Noura next door says: "If they could be so evil as to shoot children then it's in God's hands. Anyway I don't believe that they could do it."

5 But I know that such things can be. My husband was a university professor. He spoke several languages, and he gave me books to read, and he read news from other countries and told me what's possible. He should've been afraid of the world, should've stayed inside with the doors locked and the blinds drawn, but he didn't do that, he went out. Our daughter is just like him. She is part of his immortality. I told him, when I was still carrying her, that that's what I want, that that's how I love him. I had always dreaded and feared pregnancy, for all the usual reasons that girls who daydream more than they live fear pregnancy. My body, with its pain and mess and hunger—if I could have bribed it to go away, I would have. Then I married my man, and

ANALYZE SETTING

Annotate: Mark words and phrases in paragraph 2 that signal the social context. Mark the phrases in paragraph 3 that signal the historical context.

Infer: What do these details help you understand about the characters and plot?

© Houghton Mifflin Harcourt Publishing Company

I held fast to him. And my brain, the brain that had told me I would never bear a child for any man, no matter how nice he was, that brain began to tell me something else. Provided the world continues to exist, provided conditions remain favorable, or at least tolerable, our child will have a child and that child will have a child and so on, and with all those children of children come the inevitability that glimpses of my husband will resurface, in their features, in the way they use their bodies, a fearless swinging of the arms as they walk. Centuries from now some quality of a man's gaze, smile, voice, way of standing or sitting will please someone else in a way that they aren't completely aware of, will be loved very hard for just a moment, without inquiry into where it came from. I ignore the women who say that my daughter does things that a girl shouldn't do, and when I want to keep her near me, I let her go. But not too far, I don't let her go too far from me.

6   The soldiers remind me of boys from here sometimes. The way our boys used to be. Especially when you catch them with their helmets off, three or four of them sitting on a wall at lunchtime, trying to enjoy their sandwiches and the sun, but really too restless for both. Then you see the rifles beside their lunchboxes and you remember that they aren't our boys.

7   "Mother… did you hear me? I said that I am now a racist."

8   I was getting my daughter ready for school. She can't tie knots but she loves her shoelaces to make extravagant bows.

9   "Racist against whom, my daughter?"

10   "Racist against soldiers."

11   "Soldiers aren't a race."

12   "Soldiers aren't a race," she mimicked. "Soldiers aren't a race."

13   "What do you want me to say?"

14   She didn't have an answer, so she just went off in a big gang with her schoolfriends. And I worried, because my daughter has always seen soldiers—in her lifetime she hasn't known a time or place when the cedars stood against the blue sky without khaki canvas or crackling radio signals in the way.

15   An hour or so later Bilal came to visit. A great honor, I'm sure, a visit from that troublesome Bilal who had done nothing but pester me since the day I came to this village. He sat down with us and mother served him tea.

16   "Three times I have asked this daughter of yours to be my wife," Bilal said to my mother. He shook a finger at her. As for me, it was as if I wasn't there. "First wife," he continued. "Not even second or third—first wife."

17   "Don't be angry, son," my mother murmured. "She's not ready. Only a shameless woman could be ready so soon after what happened."

18   "True, true," Bilal agreed. A fly landed just above my top lip and I let it walk.

19   "Rather than ask a fourth time I will kidnap her…"

MAKE PREDICTIONS

Annotate: Mark details in paragraphs 15–23 that describe Bilal's personality.

Predict: At this point in the story, what can you predict about Bilal's involvement in the story?

20 "Ah, don't do that, son. Don't take the light of an old woman's eyes," my mother murmured, and she fed him honey cake. Bilal laughed from his belly, and the fly fled. "I was only joking."

21 The third time Bilal asked my mother for my hand in marriage I thought I was going to have to do it after all. But my daughter said I wasn't allowed. I asked her why. Because his face is fat and his eyes are tiny? Because he chews with his mouth open?

22 "He has a tyrannical mustache," my daughter said. "It would be impossible to live with." I'm proud of her vocabulary. But it's starting to look as if I think I'm too good for Bilal, who owns more cattle than any other man for miles around and could give my mother, daughter and I everything we might reasonably expect from this life.

23 Please, God. You know I don't seek worldly things. If you want me to marry again, so be it. But please—not Bilal. After the love that I have had…you don't believe me, but I would shatter.

24 My daughter came home for her lunch. After prayers we shared some cold karkedeh,[1] two straws in a drinking glass, and she told me what she was learning, which wasn't much. My mother was there, too, rattling her prayer beads and listening indulgently. She made faces when she thought my daughter talked too much. Then we heard the soldiers coming past as usual, and we went and looked at them through the window. I thought we'd make fun of them a bit, as usual. But my daughter ran out of the front door and into the path of the army truck, yelling: "You! You bloody soldiers!" Luckily the truck's wheels crawled along the road, and the body of the truck itself was slumped on one side, resigned to a myriad of pot holes. Still, it was a very big truck, and my daughter is a very small girl.

25 I was out after her before I knew what I was doing, shouting her name. It's a good name—we chose a name that would grow with her, but she seemed determined not to make it to adulthood. I tried to trip her up, but she was too nimble for me. Everyone around was looking on from windows and the open gates of courtyards. The truck rolled to a stop. Someone inside it yelled: "Move, kid. We've got stuff to do."

26 I tried to pull my daughter out of the way, but she wasn't having any of it. My hands being empty, I wrung them. My daughter began to pelt the soldier's vehicle with stones from her pockets. Her pockets were very deep that afternoon, her arms lashed the air like whips. Stone after stone bounced off metal and rattled glass, and I grabbed at her and she screamed: "This is my country! Get out of here!"

27 The people of the village began to applaud her. "Yes," they cried out, from their seats in the audience, and they clapped. I tried again to seize her arm and failed again. The truck's engine revved up and I opened my arms as wide as they would go, inviting everyone to witness. Now I was screaming too: "So you dare? You really dare?"

28 And there we were, mother and daughter, causing problems for the soldiers together.

---

[1] **karkedeh:** Egyptian drink made from dried hibiscus.

29   Finally a scrawny soldier came out of the vehicle without his gun. He was the scrawniest fighting man I've ever seen—he was barely there, just a piece of wire, really. He walked towards my daughter, who had run out of stones. He stretched out a long arm, offering her chewing gum, and she swore at him, and I swore at her for swearing. He stopped about thirty centimeters away from us and said to my daughter: "You're brave."

30   My daughter put her hands on her hips and glared up at him.

31   "We're leaving tomorrow," the scrawny soldier told her.

32   Whispers and shouts: *the soldiers are leaving tomorrow!*

33   A soldier inside the truck yelled out: "Yeah, but more are coming to take our place," and everyone piped low. My daughter reached for a stone that hadn't fallen far. Who is this girl? Four feet tall and fighting something she knows nothing about. Even if I explained it to her she wouldn't get it. I don't get it myself.

34   "Can I shake your hand?" the scrawny soldier asked her, before her hand met the stone. I thought my girl would refuse, but she said yes. "You're okay," she told him. "You came out to face me."

35   "Her English is good," the coward from within the truck remarked.

36   "I speak to her in English every day," I called out. "So she can tell people like you what she thinks."

37   We stepped aside then, my daughter and I, and let them continue their patrol.

38   My mother didn't like what had happened. But didn't you see everyone clapping for us, my daughter asked. So what, my mother said. People clap at anything. Some people even clap when they're on an airplane and it lands. That was something my husband had told us from his travels—I hadn't thought she'd remember.

39   My daughter became a celebrity amongst the children, and from what I saw, she used it for good, bringing the shunned ones into the inner circle and laughing at all their jokes.

40   The following week a foreigner dressed like one of our men knocked at my mother's door. It was late afternoon, turning to dusk. People sat looking out onto the street, talking about everything as they took their tea. Our people really know how to discuss a matter from head to toe; it is our gift, and such conversation on a **balmy** evening can be sweeter than sugar. Now they were talking about the foreigner who was at our door. I answered it myself. My daughter was

MAKE PREDICTIONS

Annotate: Mark details in paragraphs 29–34 that describe the girl's interaction with the scrawny soldier.

Predict: What do you think might happen if they meet again?

ANALYZE SETTING

Annotate: Mark details in paragraphs 40–51 that reveal more about the social context.

Analyze: How does the setting contribute to the plot at this point in the story?

balmy
(bä´mē) *adj.* mild and pleasant.

at my side and we recognized the man at once; it was the scrawny soldier. He looked itchy and uncomfortable in his djellaba,[2] and he wasn't wearing his keffiyeh[3] at all correctly—his hair was showing.

41   "What a clown," my daughter said, and from her seat on the cushioned floor my mother vowed that clown, or no clown, he couldn't enter her house.

42   "Welcome," I said to him. It was all I could think of to say. See a guest, bid him welcome. It's who we are. Or maybe it's just who I am.

43   "I'm not here to cause trouble," the scrawny soldier said. He was looking to the north, south, east, and west so quickly and repeatedly that for some seconds his head was just a blur. "I'm completely off duty. In fact, I've been on leave since last week. I'm just—I just thought I'd stick around for a little while. I thought I might have met a worthy adversary—this young lady here, I mean." He indicated my daughter, who chewed her lip and couldn't stop herself from looking pleased.

44   "What is he saying?" my mother demanded.

45   "I'll just—go away, then," the soldier said. He seemed to be dying several thousand deaths at once.

46   "He'd like some tea…" my daughter told my mother. "We'll just have a quick cup or two," I added, and we took the tea out onto the verandah, and drank it under the eyes of God and the entire

© Houghton Mifflin Harcourt Publishing Company • Image Credits: ©Boris Stroujko/Alamy

VOCABULARY

Idioms: The phrase *die a thousand deaths* in paragraph 45 is an idiom. The context of this phrase in the story can help you determine its meaning.

Analyze: What details in paragraphs 43–45 can help you figure out that the idiom means "to feel extreme embarrassment or anxiety"?

---

[2] **djellaba** (jə-lä´bə): a long, loose, hooded garment with full sleeves, worn especially in Muslim countries.

[3] **keffiyeh** (kə-fē´ə): a square of cloth, often embroidered, traditionally worn as a headdress by Arab men, either by winding it around the head or by folding it into a triangle, draping it over the head, and securing it with a woven black cord.

neighborhood. The neighborhood was annoyed. Very annoyed, and it listened closely to everything that was said. The soldier didn't seem to notice. He and my daughter were getting along famously. I didn't catch what exactly they were talking about, I just poured the tea and made sure my hand was steady. *I'm not doing anything wrong*, I told myself. *I'm not doing anything wrong.*

47 The scrawny soldier asked if I would tell him my name. "No," I said. "You have no right to use it." He told me his name, but I pretended he hadn't spoken. To cheer him up, my daughter told him her name, and he said: "That's great. A really, really good name. I might use it myself one day."

48 "You can't—it's a girl's name," my daughter replied, her nostrils flared with scorn.

49 "Ugh," said the soldier. "I meant for my daughter…"

50 He shouldn't have spoken about his unborn daughter out there in front of everyone, with his eyes and his voice full of hope and laughter. I can guarantee that some woman in the shadows was cursing the daughter he wanted to have. Even as he spoke someone was saying, May that girl be born withered for the grief people like you have caused us.

51 "Ugh," said my daughter. "I like that sound. Ugh, ugh, ugh."

52 I began to follow the conversation better. The scrawny soldier told my daughter that he understood why the boys lined the roads with anger. "Inside my head I call them the children of Hamelin."[4]

53 "The what?" my daughter asked.

54 "The who?" I asked.

55 "I guess all I mean is that they're paying the price for something they didn't do."

56 And then he told us the story of the Pied Piper of Hamelin[5] because we hadn't heard it before. We had nightmares that night, all three of us—my mother, my daughter and I. My mother hadn't even heard the story, so I don't know why she joined in. But somehow it was nice that she did.

57 On his second visit the scrawny soldier began to tell my daughter that there were foreign soldiers in his country, too, but that they were much more difficult to spot because they didn't wear uniforms and some of them didn't even seem foreign. They seemed like ordinary citizens, the sons and daughters of shopkeepers and dentists and restaurant owners and big businessmen. "That's the most dangerous

---

[4] **Hamelin** (hăm´ə-lĭn): a city in northern Germany on the Weser River southwest of Hanover.

[5] **Pied Piper of Hamelin:** a tale of a piper who led children away from their homes using his music.

kind of soldier. The longer those ones live amongst us, the more they hate us, and everything we do disgusts them…these are people we go to school with, ride the subway with—we watch the same movies and play the same video games. They'll never be with us, though. We've been judged, and they'll always be against us. Always."

58   He'd wasted his breath, because almost as soon as he began with all that I put my hands over my daughter's ears. She protested loudly, but I kept them there. "What you're talking about is a different matter," I said. "It doesn't explain or excuse your being here. Not to this child. And don't say 'always' to her. You have to think harder or just leave it alone and say sorry."

59   He didn't argue, but he didn't apologize. He felt he'd spoken the truth, so he didn't need to argue or apologize.

60   Later in the evening I asked my daughter if she was still racist against soldiers and she said **loftily**: "I'm afraid I don't know what you're referring to." When she's a bit older I'm going to ask her about that little outburst, what made her come out with such words in the first place. And I'm sure she'll make up something that makes her sound cleverer and more sensitive than she really was.

loftily
(lôf´tə·lē) *adv.* arrogantly; haughtily.

MAKE PREDICTIONS

Annotate: Mark details in paragraph 61 that tell how the villagers treated the narrator and her daughter.

Predict: Story plots are driven by conflict. Based on these details about conflict with their neighbors, what might happen to the narrator and her daughter as a result of their friendship with the soldier?

61   We were expecting our scrawny soldier again the following afternoon, my daughter and I. My daughter's friends had dropped her. Even the ones she had helped find favor with the other children forgot that their new position was due to her and urged the others to leave her out of everything. The women I knew snubbed me at market, but I didn't need them. My daughter and I told each other that everyone would come round once they understood that what we were doing was innocent. In fact we were confident that we could convince our soldier of his wrongdoing and send him back to his country to begin life anew as an architect. He'd confessed a love of our minarets.[6] He could take the image of our village home with him and make marvels of it.

62   Noura waited until our mothers, mine and hers, were busy gossiping at her house, then she came to tell me that the men were discussing how best to deal with me. I was washing clothes in the bathtub and I almost fell in.

63   My crime was that I had insulted Bilal with my **brazen** pursuit of this soldier…

brazen
(brā´zən) *adj.* unrestrained by a sense of shame; rudely bold.

64   "Noura! This soldier—he's just a boy! He can hardly coax his beard to grow. How could you believe—"

---

[6] **minaret** (mĭn´ə-rĕt´): a tall slender tower attached to a mosque, having one or more projecting balconies from which a muezzin or a recording of a muezzin summons the people to prayer.

65   "I'm not saying I believe it. I'm just saying you must stop this kind of socializing. And behave **impeccably** from now on. I mean—angelically."

66   Three months before I had come to the village, Noura told me, there had been a young widow who talked back all the time and looked haughtily at the men. A few of them got fed up, and they took her out to the desert and beat her severely. She survived, but once they'd finished with her she couldn't see out of her own eyes or talk out of her own lips. The women didn't like to mention such a matter, but Noura was mentioning it now, because she wanted me to be careful.

67   "I see," I said. "You're saying they can do this to me?"

68   "Don't smile; they can do it. You know they can do it! You know that with those soldiers here our men are twice as fiery. Six or seven of them will even gather to kick a stray dog for stealing food…"

69   "Yes, I saw that yesterday. Fiery, you call it. Did they bring this woman out of her home at night or in the morning, Noura? Did they drag her by her hair?"

70   Noura averted her eyes because I was asking her why she had let it happen and she didn't want to answer.

71   "You're not thinking clearly. Not only can they do this to you but they can take your daughter from you first, and put her somewhere she would never again see the light of day. Better that than have her grow up like her mother. Can't you see that that's how it would go? I'm telling you this as a friend, a true friend…my husband doesn't want me to talk to you anymore. He says your ideas are wicked and bizarre."

72   I didn't ask Noura what her husband could possibly know about my ideas. Instead I said: "You know me a little. Do you find my ideas wicked and bizarre?"

73   Noura hurried to the door. "Yes. I do. I think your husband spoilt you. He gave you illusions…you feel too free. We are not free."

74   I drew my nails down my palm, down then back up the other way, deep and hard. I thought about what Noura had told me. I didn't think for very long. I had no choice—I couldn't afford another visit from him. I wrote him a letter. I wonder if I'll ever get a chance to take back all that I wrote in that letter; it was hideous from beginning to end. Human beings shouldn't say such things to each other. I put the letter into an unsealed envelope and found a local boy who knew where the scrawny soldier lived. Doubtless Bilal read the letter before the soldier did, because by evening everyone but my daughter knew what I had done. My daughter waited for the soldier until it was fully dark, and I waited with her, pretending that I was still expecting our friend. There was a song she wanted to sing

impeccably
(ĭm·pĕk´kə·blē) *adv.* in accordance with having no flaws; perfectly.

to him. I asked her to sing it to me instead, but she said I wouldn't appreciate it. When we went inside at last, my daughter asked me if the soldier could have gone home without telling us. He probably hated goodbyes.

75   "He said he would come…I hope he's alright…" my daughter fretted.

76   "He's gone home to build minarets."

77   "With matchsticks, probably."

78   And we were both very sad.

79   My daughter didn't smile for six days. On the seventh she said she couldn't go to school.

80   "You have to go to school," I told her. "How else will you get your friends back again?"

81   "What if I can't," she wailed. "What if I can't get them back again?"

82   "Do you really think you won't get them back again?"

83   "Oh, you don't even care that our friend is gone. Mothers have no feelings and are enemies of progress."

84   (I really wonder who my daughter has been talking to lately. Someone with a sense of humor very like her father's…)

85   I tickled the sole of her foot until she shouted.

86   "Let this enemy of progress tell you something," I said. "I'm never sad when a friend goes far away, because whichever city or country that friend goes to, they turn the place friendly. They turn a suspicious-looking name on the map into a place where a welcome can be found. Maybe the friend will talk about you sometimes, to other friends that live around him, and then that's almost as good as being there yourself. You're in several places at once! In fact, my daughter, I would even go so far as to say that the further away your friends are, and the more spread out they are, the better your chances of going safely through the world…"

87   "Ugh," my daughter said.

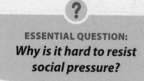

ESSENTIAL QUESTION:
Why is it hard to resist social pressure?

Review your notes and add your thoughts to your Response Log.

COLLABORATIVE DISCUSSION

Get together with a partner or group, and discuss the story's ending. Do you think the narrator handled this situation well? Why or why not?

Assessment Practice

Answer these questions before moving on to the **Analyze the Text** section on the following page.

1. Why does the narrator's daughter cut her hair?

   (A) She wants to look pretty.

   (B) She wants the boys to notice her.

   (C) She wants to be able to play with the boys.

   (D) She wants to blend in with the soldiers.

2. Why is the narrator currently unmarried?

   (A) She is a widow.

   (B) She hasn't found a suitor.

   (C) She has to take care of her mother.

   (D) She isn't allowed to marry.

3. What can be inferred about the role of women in the society in which the story is set?

   (A) Women protect each other from men.

   (B) Women are leaders in the community.

   (C) Women have a limited role in society.

   (D) Women are not allowed in public spaces.

Test-Taking Strategies

Analyze the Text

Support your responses with evidence from the text.

1. **INFER** Why does the soldier come to visit the narrator and her daughter? Consider the following:

   - his initial encounter with the daughter
   - what he says about his home country

2. **ANALYZE** What tone does the narrator generally use in descriptions of her daughter? Provide examples of words and phrases to support your response.

3. **COMPARE** In what ways is the narrator different from Noura? What do they have in common? Use the graphic organizer to record your response.

Differences	Similarities

4. **ANALYZE** What is the theme of the story? How does this theme relate to the cultural and historical setting?

5. **PREDICT** How might relations between the villagers and the narrator change after the conclusion of the story? Explain the reasons for your prediction.

6. **DRAW CONCLUSIONS** At the end of the story, the narrator tries to console her daughter with **Words of the Wiser** about how absent friends enrich our lives, which the daughter undercuts with the comical exclamation "Ugh." How has the daughter's life been enriched by her brief friendship with the foreign soldier?

Choices

Here are some other ways to demonstrate your understanding of the ideas in this lesson.

Writing
↳ Letter

The narrator wonders "if I'll ever get a chance to take back all that I wrote in that letter" sent to the soldier. Suppose she found out his home address. Write a letter from the narrator to the soldier, asking for forgiveness. Include the following:

- an explanation of why she wrote the first letter

- how she felt after sending the first letter to him

- how her daughter felt when he never returned to visit them

As you write and discuss, be sure to use the **Academic Vocabulary** words.

| arbitrary |
| controversy |
| convince |
| denote |
| undergo |

Speaking & Listening
↳ Group Discussion

With a group of students, discuss the choices Helen Oyeyemi made in writing her short story. Think about the following questions:

- Why do you think Oyeyemi never clearly identifies the setting?

- What aspects of the story do you find thought provoking?

- What social attitudes toward women are reflected in the story?

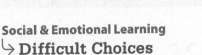

Social & Emotional Learning
↳ Difficult Choices

In "My Daughter the Racist," the narrator faces a dilemma: she and her daughter may be harmed if they continue to socialize with the soldier, but if she publicly denounces him, she risks destroying her daughter's ideals. Write a brief essay about a difficult decision you have made.

- Write about a decision that has had an impact on your life.

- Identify the factors that went into the decision, such as your values, the potential consequences, and your physical and emotional well-being.

- Discuss how you feel about the decision and what you learned from this experience.

Expand Your Vocabulary

PRACTICE AND APPLY

Choose the vocabulary word that completes the sentence.

balmy	loftily	brazen	impeccably

1. Alice's _____ speech made the audience uncomfortable.

2. When the weather turned _____, Hillary went for a walk.

3. Sid behaved _____ at work because he wanted a promotion.

4. Darryl spoke passionately and _____ about his political views.

Vocabulary Strategy
↳ **Idioms**

🙂Ed

Interactive Vocabulary Lesson: Using Context Clues

An **idiom** is a commonly used figure of speech whose meaning is different from the literal meaning of its words. An example of an idiom in "My Daughter the Racist" appears in paragraph 24: "She made faces when she thought my daughter talked too much." *Made faces* does not mean that the grandmother literally drew or crafted a face. This idiom means she tried to communicate her disapproval of her granddaughter's talking through facial expressions.

To determine the meaning of an idiom, you might consult a dictionary. There are also specialized dictionaries that provide more detailed lists of idioms and explain their origins.

PRACTICE AND APPLY

Complete each sentence with the idiom in the diagram that makes the most sense. Use context to help you choose the correct idiom. When you are finished, try to explain the meaning of each idiom you used. Consult a dictionary to verify the meaning.

1. This was the first time that Carly and Mo met _____.

2. Jill had to _____ when she was caught cheating on an exam.

3. If you _____ all afternoon, you won't be hungry for dinner.

4. If you continue to act foolishly, you'll end up with _____.

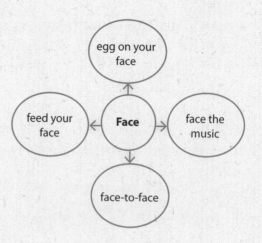

Watch Your Language!

Syntax

Syntax refers to the order of words or phrases in a sentence. The author of "My Daughter the Racist" varies the syntax throughout the story to create variety, to add emphasis, and to establish a conversational tone.

For example, in paragraph 4, the narrator uses a combination of short and long sentences to call attention to the soldiers:

> And that girl of mine has really begun to stare at the soldiers, too, even though I slap her hard when I catch her doing that. Who knows what's going to happen? These soldiers are scared. They might shoot someone. Noura next door says: "If they could be so evil as to shoot children then it's in God's hands. Anyway I don't believe that they could do it."

The varied structure of the sentences places emphasis on the girl's boldness and suggests that something could happen between the daughter and the soldiers. By posing the question "Who knows what's going to happen?" the author draws readers in and prompts them to anticipate how the plot will unfold.

In paragraph 58, the narrator uses a sentence fragment in saying:

> "It doesn't explain or excuse your being here. Not to this child. And don't say 'always' to her. . . ."

The sentence fragment—following a longer, complete sentence—emphasizes the narrator's protectiveness toward her child and stresses how she wants the soldier to behave. The fragment in this dialogue also mirrors the way people naturally speak. The effect is realistic-sounding dialogue.

 Ed
Interactive Grammar Lesson: Sentence Structure

PRACTICE AND APPLY

Reread a short story or personal essay that you wrote recently, paying attention to the length and structure of the sentences. As you revise your writing, vary the syntax to make your writing more engaging, to emphasize ideas, or to make dialogue sound realistic.

The Love Song of J. Alfred Prufrock

Poem by **T. S. Eliot**

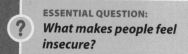

ESSENTIAL QUESTION:
What makes people feel insecure?

Engage Your Brain

Choose one or more of these activities to start connecting with the poem you're about to read.

Losing Faith in Yourself

Some people appear confident in any situation, while others are filled with self-doubt. What circumstances can diminish a person's confidence?

- Write a paragraph in response to this question.

- Then, discuss your ideas with a partner.

Poetry Predictions

With a group of students, discuss the title of T. S. Eliot's poem. What predictions can you make about the poem's style and subject matter? Use the following questions to spark your discussion:

- What expectations do you have about a "love song"?

- What thoughts or images does the name *J. Alfred Prufrock* bring to mind?

When you have finished reading the poem, gather with the same group and decide whether any of your predictions were accurate.

Understand Modernist Poetry

Modernist poets such as T. S. Eliot abandoned traditional verse forms and experimented with literary techniques to better reflect the social and technological changes of their times. Eliot's poetry can be difficult to understand because he presents a patchwork of images, symbols, and allusions that readers must connect for themselves. Consider using the following strategies to help you interpret "The Love Song of J. Alfred Prufrock":

- Read the poem aloud, pausing between sections and lingering over striking images.
- Reread the poem more than once.
- Annotate the text by marking difficult lines and passages and paraphrasing or summarizing them.
- Consult the side notes for explanations of literary allusions.

Focus on Genre
↳ **Lyric Poetry**

- expresses strong feelings or thoughts
- has a musical quality
- often deals with intense emotions surrounding events like death, love, or loss
- includes forms such as ode, elegy, and sonnet

Analyze Stream of Consciousness

One of the most radical breaks from convention in modernist literature was the development of **stream of consciousness.** This writing technique, used by poets and fiction writers, presents the random flow of thoughts, emotions, memories, and associations running through the mind of a character or speaker. The goal is to re-create states of mind instead of describing them.

"The Love Song of J. Alfred Prufrock" is a dramatic monologue in which Prufrock addresses a silent listener with a tumble of thoughts, allusions, and figurative language, as in the following stanza:

> Shall I part my hair behind? Do I dare to eat a peach?
> I shall wear white flannel trousers, and walk upon the beach.
> I have heard the mermaids singing, each to each.

As you read the poem, try not to be put off by the seemingly nonsensical nature of the stream-of-consciousness verse, but be alert to any feelings or ideas that the images seem to suggest.

Make Inferences

In his poetry, Eliot rarely expresses ideas in a straightforward manner. To understand and appreciate these poems, readers must make **inferences,** logical guesses based on clues found in the text. Making inferences is sometimes called "reading between the lines" because you come to an understanding of something that the author has not explicitly stated. For example, we can infer from the following lines that the speaker is going to a social gathering where he thinks he must hide his true personality or feelings from the other guests:

> There will be time, there will be time
> To prepare a face to meet the faces that you meet;

As you read "The Love Song of J. Alfred Prufrock," look for images that suggest thoughts and feelings.

Annotation in Action

Here is an example of notes a student made about the opening lines of "The Love Song of J. Alfred Prufrock." As you read, mark details that help you make inferences about the speaker.

> Let us go then, you and I,
> When the evening is spread out against the sky
> Like a patient etherised upon a table;
> Let us go, through certain half-deserted streets,
> The muttering retreats
> Of restless nights in one-night cheap hotels
> And sawdust restaurants with oyster-shells:

Prufrock seems to be thinking about a seedy side of town.

Background

T. S. Eliot (1888–1965) was one of the most influential poets and literary critics of the 20th century. He grew up in a cultured household in St. Louis, Missouri. While pursuing his graduate studies, he became involved with a circle of avant-garde writers and settled down in London. He published his first collection of poems, *Prufrock and Other Observations,* in 1917. The book baffled some reviewers but was hailed by modernists. Eliot followed it up in 1922 with *The Waste Land,* which made him internationally famous. The poem expresses the sense of alienation and spiritual loss felt by many in his generation.

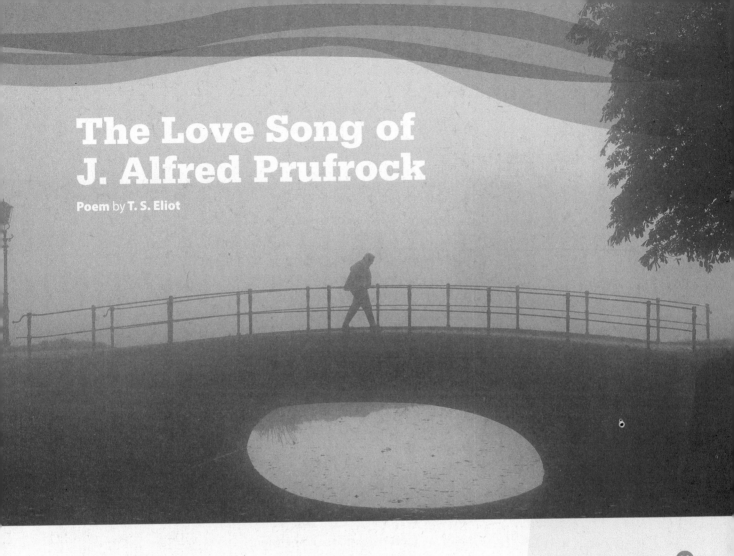

The Love Song of J. Alfred Prufrock

Poem by **T. S. Eliot**

Notice what the images and figurative language
in the poem suggest about the speaker.

NOTICE & NOTE

As you read, use the side
margins to make notes
about the text.

S'io credessi che mia risposta fosse
a persona che mai tornasse al mondo,
questa fiamma staria senza più scosse.
Ma per ciò che giammai di questo fondo
non tornò vivo alcun, s'i'odo il vero,
senza tema d'infamia ti rispondo.

Let us go then, you and I,
When the evening is spread out against the sky
Like a patient etherised upon a table;
Let us go, through certain half-deserted streets,
5   The muttering retreats
Of restless nights in one-night cheap hotels
And sawdust restaurants with oyster-shells:
Streets that follow like a tedious argument
Of insidious intent
10   To lead you to an overwhelming question . . .

S'io credessi . . . ti rispondo:
These lines are from the *Inferno*,
written in the early 14th century
by Italian poet Dante Alighieri.
As Dante visits hell, one of the
damned agrees to speak of his
torment only because he believes
that Dante cannot return to the
living world to repeat the tale.

3 **etherised:** given ether, a liquid used
as an anesthetic.

☺ **Ed**

Close Read Screencast

Listen to a modeled close
read of this text.

9 **insidious** (ĭn-sĭd´e-əs):
more dangerous than it seems.

Oh, do not ask, "What is it?"
Let us go and make our visit.

In the room the women come and go
Talking of Michelangelo.

15   The yellow fog that rubs its back upon the window-panes,
The yellow smoke that rubs its muzzle on the window-panes,
Licked its tongue into the corners of the evening,
Lingered upon the pools that stand in drains,
Let fall upon its back the soot that falls from chimneys,
20   Slipped by the terrace, made a sudden leap,
And seeing that it was a soft October night,
Curled once about the house, and fell asleep.

And indeed there will be time
For the yellow smoke that slides along the street
25   Rubbing its back upon the window-panes;
There will be time, there will be time
To prepare a face to meet the faces that you meet;
There will be time to murder and create,
And time for all the works and days of hands
30   That lift and drop a question on your plate;
Time for you and time for me,
And time yet for a hundred indecisions,
And for a hundred visions and revisions,
Before the taking of a toast and tea.

35   In the room the women come and go
Talking of Michelangelo.

ANALYZE STREAM OF CONSCIOUSNESS

Annotate: Mark interruptions in Prufrock's train of thought in lines 37–46.

Analyze: What connection can you make between Prufrock's thoughts about his appearance and the question he repeatedly asks in this passage?

And indeed there will be time
To wonder, "Do I dare?" and, "Do I dare?"
Time to turn back and descend the stair,
40   With a bald spot in the middle of my hair—
(They will say: "How his hair is growing thin!")
My morning coat, my collar mounting firmly to the chin,
My necktie rich and modest, but asserted by a simple pin—
(They will say: "But how his arms and legs are thin!")
45   Do I dare
Disturb the universe?
In a minute there is time
For decisions and revisions which a minute will reverse.

For I have known them all already, known them all—
50   Have known the evenings, mornings, afternoons,
I have measured out my life with coffee spoons;

I know the voices dying with a dying fall
Beneath the music from a farther room.
        So how should I presume?

55 And I have known the eyes already, known them all—
The eyes that fix you in a formulated phrase,
And when I am formulated, sprawling on a pin,
When I am pinned and wriggling on the wall,
Then how should I begin
60 To spit out all the butt-ends of my days and ways?
        And how should I presume?

And I have known the arms already, known them all—
Arms that are braceleted and white and bare
(But in the lamplight, downed with light brown hair!)
65 Is it perfume from a dress
That makes me so digress?
Arms that lie along a table, or wrap about a shawl.
        And should I then presume?
        And how should I begin?

• • • • •

70 Shall I say, I have gone at dusk through narrow streets
And watched the smoke that rises from the pipes
Of lonely men in shirt-sleeves, leaning out of windows? . . .

I should have been a pair of ragged claws
Scuttling across the floors of silent seas.

• • • • •

75 And the afternoon, the evening, sleeps so peacefully!
Smoothed by long fingers,
Asleep . . . tired . . . or it malingers,
Stretched on the floor, here beside you and me.
Should I, after tea and cakes and ices,
80 Have the strength to force the moment to its crisis?
But though I have wept and fasted, wept and prayed,
Though I have seen my head (grown slightly bald) brought in
        upon a platter,
I am no prophet—and here's no great matter;
I have seen the moment of my greatness flicker,
85 And I have seen the eternal Footman hold my coat, and snicker,
And in short, I was afraid.

And would it have been worth it, after all,
After the cups, the marmalade, the tea,
Among the porcelain, among some talk of you and me,
90 Would it have been worth while,
To have bitten off the matter with a smile,
To have squeezed the universe into a ball

54 **presume:** act overconfidently; dare.

55–58 **And I have . . . on the wall:** Prufrock recalls being scrutinized by women at other parties. He portrays himself as a live insect that has been classified, labeled, and mounted for display.

56 **formulated:** reduced to a formula.

MAKE INFERENCES

Annotate: Mark the metaphors in lines 55–61.

Infer: What do these metaphors suggest about how Prufrock feels among women at parties?

73–74 **I should . . . silent seas:** Here Prufrock presents an image of himself as a crayfish.

77 **malingers** (mə-lĭng´gərz): pretends illness in order to avoid duty or work.

81–83 **But though . . . prophet:** an allusion to the biblical story of John the Baptist, who is imprisoned by King Herod (Matthew 14; Mark 6). At the request of his wife, Herod had the Baptist's head cut off and brought to him on a platter.

To roll it towards some overwhelming question,
To say: "I am Lazarus, come from the dead,
95 Come back to tell you all, I shall tell you all"—
If one, settling a pillow by her head,
Should say: "That is not what I meant at all.
That is not it, at all."

And would it have been worth it, after all,
100 Would it have been worth while,
After the sunsets and the dooryards and the sprinkled streets,
After the novels, after the teacups, after the skirts that trail along
the floor—
And this, and so much more?—
It is impossible to say just what I mean!
105 But as if a magic lantern threw the nerves in patterns on a
screen:
Would it have been worth while
If one, settling a pillow or throwing off a shawl,
And turning toward the window, should say:
"That is not it at all,
110 That is not what I meant, at all."

• • • • •

No! I am not Prince Hamlet, nor was meant to be;
Am an attendant lord, one that will do
To swell a progress, start a scene or two,
Advise the prince; no doubt, an easy tool,
115 Deferential, glad to be of use,
Politic, cautious, and meticulous;
Full of high sentence, but a bit obtuse;
At times, indeed, almost ridiculous—
Almost, at times, the Fool.

120 I grow old . . . I grow old . . .
I shall wear the bottoms of my trousers rolled.

Shall I part my hair behind? Do I dare to eat a peach?
I shall wear white flannel trousers, and walk upon the beach.
I have heard the mermaids singing, each to each.

125 I do not think that they will sing to me.

I have seen them riding seaward on the waves
Combing the white hair of the waves blown back
When the wind blows the water white and black.

105 **magic lantern:** a forerunner of the slide projector.

UNDERSTAND MODERNIST POETRY

Annotate: Mark the literary allusion in lines 111–119.

Summarize: Write a summary of this stanza.

115 **deferential:** yielding to someone else's opinion.

116 **meticulous:** extremely careful and precise about details.

117 **obtuse:** slow to understand; dull.

124–125 **mermaids . . . to me:** In mythology, mermaids attract mortal men by their beauty and their singing, sometimes allowing men to live with them in the sea.

© Houghton Mifflin Harcourt Publishing Company

We have lingered in the chambers of the sea

130 By sea-girls wreathed with seaweed red and brown

Till human voices wake us, and we drown.

ESSENTIAL QUESTION:
What makes people feel insecure?

Review your notes and add your thoughts to your Response Log.

COLLABORATIVE DISCUSSION

Turn to a partner and discuss the poem's style. Does it remind you of any poetry or music you listen to?

Assessment Practice

Answer these questions before moving on to the **Analyze the Text** section on the following page.

1. Which aspect of Prufrock's life is reflected in the simile comparing the evening to "a patient etherised upon a table"?

   Ⓐ his fear of the evening

   Ⓑ an illness he is recovering from

   Ⓒ his profession as a doctor

   Ⓓ his sense of paralysis

2. How does Prufrock feel about the guests at the party he is going to?

   Ⓐ He feels alienated from them.

   Ⓑ He feels hatred toward them.

   Ⓒ He feels kindness from them.

   Ⓓ He feels generosity toward them.

3. Lines 87–98 indicate that the woman Prufrock wants to talk to —

   Ⓐ feels nervous in his presence

   Ⓑ worries that he has gone insane

   Ⓒ isn't interested in what he has to say

   Ⓓ is trying to avoid him

Test-Taking Strategies

Analyze the Text

Support your responses with evidence from the text.

NOTICE & NOTE

Review what you **noticed and noted** as you read the text. Your annotations can help you answer these questions.

(1) **ANALYZE** What does Prufrock compare the fog to in lines 15–22? How does this extended metaphor relate to his situation in the poem?

(2) **INTERPRET** What thought does Prufrock express in line 51 when he says, "I have measured out my life with coffee spoons"?

(3) **ANALYZE** Read the side margin notes about the quotation from Dante's *Inferno* at the beginning of the poem and the allusion to Lazarus in line 94. What do the quotation and the allusion have in common? How are they connected to Prufrock's experience?

(4) **DRAW CONCLUSIONS** Why might Eliot have chosen not to clarify the nature of Prufrock's "overwhelming question" or what he wants to say to the woman at the party?

(5) **INFER** Reread lines 111–125. How does Prufrock eventually resolve his dilemma? How is this resolution related to his image of himself? Use the chart below to record your inference and the details that support it.

My Inference	Details from the Text

(6) **CONNECT** Eliot wrote "The Love Song of J. Alfred Prufrock" at a time when new technology and media were rapidly changing society. How might Eliot's use of stream of consciousness reflect such changes?

Choices

Here are some other ways to demonstrate your understanding of the ideas in this lesson.

Writing
↳ Stream-of-Consciousness Poem

Write a poem using the stream-of-consciousness style that Eliot helped pioneer.

- Write down your thoughts on paper for five minutes, not worrying about grammar, punctuation, or even whether what you are writing makes sense.

- Use different-colored highlighters to identify words and phrases that are related in some way, such as conveying the same feeling.

- Compose a free-verse poem using the words and phrases you have highlighted. The poem will not follow a logical order, but there should be enough connections between ideas and images that a reader can make inferences about the poem's meaning.

- Share your poem with a small group, and exchange thoughts about each other's writing.

> As you write and discuss, be sure to use the **Academic Vocabulary** words.
>
> | arbitrary |
>
> | controversy |
>
> | convince |
>
> | denote |
>
> | undergo |

Social & Emotional Learning
↳ Self-Esteem Advice

With a group of students, create a list of recommendations for boosting Prufrock's self-esteem and confidence. Discuss the following questions to help you develop your advice.

- How does Prufrock view himself, and how does he think other people view him? What connection do you see between his self-image and his relationships with others?

- How does low self-esteem affect people in social situations?

- What steps can someone take to develop a more positive self-image?

Media
↳ Cartoon

"The Love Song of J. Alfred Prufrock" is rich in visual imagery. Create a cartoon based on an image in the poem.

- Review the poem and identify an image that offers insight into Prufrock's personality.

- Create a cartoon illustration inspired by the image.

- Include a phrase or sentence from the poem as a caption for your cartoon.

Collaborate & Compare

ESSENTIAL QUESTION:
What is the power of symbols?

Compare Themes

The poems you are about to read make use of symbols—a type of figurative language. As you read, look for people, places, or objects that seem likely to have a symbolic meaning. Consider how the symbols help convey the poems' themes.

A

The Second Coming

Poem by **William Butler Yeats**
pages 820-821

B

Symbols? I'm Sick of Symbols

Poem by **Fernando Pessoa**
pages 822-823

After you have read the poems, you will collaborate with a small group to explore their themes. You will follow these steps:

- Decide on the most important details
- Create theme statements
- Compare and contrast themes
- Present your ideas to the class

The Second Coming

Poem by **William Butler Yeats**

Symbols? I'm Sick of Symbols

Poem by **Fernando Pessoa**

Engage Your Brain

Choose one or more of these activities to start connecting with the poems you're about to read.

The Power of Symbols

Create a collage based on a symbol or a group of symbols.

1. Look up the definition of *symbol* in a dictionary.

2. Think of one or more symbols you would like to explore in an artwork.

3. Collect images of the symbol or symbols online.

4. Print out the images, and paste them onto paper or cardboard in an interesting composition.

Anticipation

Think about the last time you were expecting something big to happen—something you might have dreaded or something you looked forward to. What did it feel like to wait for it to happen? Share your experience with a partner.

Understand Symbolism

A **symbol** is a person, place, or object that has a concrete meaning in itself and also represents something beyond itself, such as an idea or a feeling. For example, a rose is a traditional symbol of romantic love.

Symbolism is the practice of using symbols, and it is also the name of a literary movement that began in France in the late 19th century. The Symbolists used symbols to suggest states of mind and ideas that cannot be expressed directly. Like many modernist writers, William Butler Yeats was strongly influenced by this literary movement. His poems often feature complex symbols drawn from a wide variety of sources.

Fernando Pessoa was also influenced by symbolism, but nothing about this Portuguese poet's work is easy to pin down. He wrote his poems through multiple personas, which he called "heteronyms." Each heteronym is a character who has his own approach to the art of poetry. The poem "Symbols? I'm Sick of Symbols" was written under the heteronym Álvaro de Campos, a naval engineer who lives in London. While some of Pessoa's heteronyms embrace symbolism, in this poem Campos playfully criticizes the movement.

As you read, consider which people, places, and objects could symbolize ideas or feelings. Also, think about how the poets develop the moods and themes of their poems through the use of symbols.

> **Focus on Genre**
> ↳ **Lyric Poetry**
>
> - **expresses the thoughts and feelings of the speaker**
> - **uses sound devices such as rhyme and rhythm to create a musical quality**
> - **often deals with intense emotions surrounding events such as love, death, or loss**

Analyze Rhythmic Patterns

In poetry, **meter** is a pattern of stressed and unstressed syllables. Each unit of meter, known as a **foot,** consists of a combination of stressed and unstressed syllables. These patterns create rhythm, which brings out the musical quality of language and often serves to unify a work of literature.

- An **iamb** is a foot that contains one unstressed syllable (˘) followed by one stressed syllable (´). For example, the word *apart* is an iamb.

- A **trochee** is a foot that contains one stressed syllable followed by one unstressed syllable, as in the word *falcon*.

Many forms of poetry are written in **iambic pentameter,** with five iambic feet in each line. In "The Second Coming," Yeats primarily uses irregular rhythms, but several of the lines are written in perfect iambic pentameter. When he uses regular metrical lines among lines with irregular meter, he creates a dramatic rhythm that helps support his theme.

Pessoa's poem, on the other hand, is written in **free verse,** which is poetry that does not follow any regular patterns of rhyme or meter. Pessoa creates a unique, irregular rhythm by using conversational language and alternating between long and short lines.

Annotation in Action

Here is an example of notes a student made about these lines from "The Second Coming." As you read, mark examples of symbols in each poem.

> Turning and turning in the widening gyre
> The falcon cannot hear the falconer;
> Things fall apart; the center cannot hold;

"The falcon that cannot hear the falconer" may symbolize loss of control.

Background

William Butler Yeats (1865–1939) is widely considered the finest English language poet of the 20th century. He was born in a suburb of Dublin, Ireland, but he spent much of his childhood with his grandparents in the countryside, where he learned about Irish history and mythology—subjects that would heavily influence his writing. In addition to his poetry, Yeats was a dramatist who helped found Dublin's prestigious Abbey Theatre. In 1923 he was awarded the Nobel Prize for Literature. Yeats wrote "The Second Coming" in 1919, shortly after the Russian Revolution and the end of World War I—events that traumatized Europe.

Fernando Pessoa (1888–1935) was born in Lisbon, Portugal, but spent part of his childhood in South Africa, where he attended an English school. After studying briefly at the University of Lisbon, he worked as a commercial translator while publishing literary criticism, poetry, and prose. Pessoa wrote in English as well as Portuguese. His work was not well known in his lifetime. After he died, thousands of unpublished manuscript pages were discovered, revealing the full extent of his achievement. Today Pessoa is considered one of the masters of modernist poetry.

The Second Coming

Poem by **William Butler Yeats**

Note places and objects in the poem that could be symbols, and consider what they might represent.

Turning and turning in the widening gyre
The falcon cannot hear the falconer;
Things fall apart; the center cannot hold;
Mere anarchy is loosed upon the world,
5   The blood-dimmed tide is loosed, and everywhere
The ceremony of innocence is drowned;
The best lack all conviction, while the worst
Are full of passionate intensity.

Surely some revelation is at hand;
10   Surely the Second Coming is at hand.
The Second Coming! Hardly are those words out
When a vast image out of *Spiritus Mundi*
Troubles my sight: somewhere in sands of the desert
A shape with lion body and the head of a man,
15   A gaze blank and pitiless as the sun,
Is moving its slow thighs, while all about it
Reel shadows of the indignant desert birds.

N NOTICE & NOTE

As you read, use the side margins to make notes about the text.

1 **gyre** (jīr): spiral.

6 **ceremony of innocence:** the rituals (such as the rites of baptism and marriage) that give order to life.

ANALYZE RHYTHMIC PATTERNS

Annotate: Mark the meter in lines 7–10.

Analyze: Where does Yeats vary the rhythm from iambic pentameter? What effect does this have?

10 **Second Coming:** Christ's return to Earth, predicted in the New Testament to be an event preceded by a time of terror and chaos.

12 **Spiritus Mundi** (spîr´ĭ-tŏŏs mŏŏn´dē) *Latin:* Spirit of the World. Yeats used this term to refer to the collective unconscious, a supposed source of images and memories that all human beings share.

14 This image suggests the Great Sphinx in Egypt, built more than 40 centuries ago.

The darkness drops again; but now I know
That twenty centuries of stony sleep
20 Were vexed to nightmare by a rocking cradle,
And what rough beast, its hour come round at last,
Slouches towards Bethlehem to be born?

UNDERSTAND SYMBOLISM

Annotate: Mark the symbol in line 20.

Analyze: What might this object symbolize?

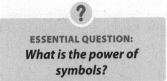

ESSENTIAL QUESTION:
What is the power of symbols?

Review your notes and add your thoughts to your Response Log.

COLLABORATIVE DISCUSSION

Get together with a partner or group, and discuss your reaction to the poem's final set of images in the desert.

Assessment Practice

Answer these questions about "The Second Coming" before moving on to the next selection.

1. What situation is suggested by the phrase "the center cannot hold" in line 3?
   - (A) repressive government
   - (B) political disagreement
   - (C) artistic freedom
   - (D) descent into chaos

2. What is the best interpretation of "The blood-dimmed tide is loosed" in line 5?
   - (A) Violence is everywhere.
   - (B) The tide is receding.
   - (C) Terrible floods are occurring.
   - (D) The ocean is full of blood.

3. Why does the speaker say in line 10 that "the Second Coming is at hand"?
   - (A) People are becoming more religious.
   - (B) The world seems to be falling apart.
   - (C) The speaker has seen a vision of Christ's birth.
   - (D) The speaker has the gift of prophecy.

Test-Taking Strategies

Symbols? I'm Sick of Symbols

Poem by **Fernando Pessoa**

Pay attention to how Pessoa uses symbols and imagery to convey ideas in the poem.

NOTICE & NOTE

As you read, use the side margins to make notes about the text.

UNDERSTAND SYMBOLISM

Annotate: Mark the symbols mentioned in lines 5–7.

Analyze: What idea does the speaker express in his elaboration of these symbols in lines 8–16?

Symbols? I'm sick of symbols . . .
Some people tell me that everything is symbols.
They're telling me nothing.

What symbols? Dreams . . .
5 Let the sun be a symbol, fine . . .
Let the moon be a symbol, fine . . .
Let the earth be a symbol, fine . . .
But who notices the sun except when the rain stops
And it breaks through the clouds and points behind its back
10 To the blue of the sky?
And who notices the moon except to admire
Not it but the beautiful light it radiates?
And who notices the very earth we tread?
We say earth and think of fields, trees and hills,
15 Unwittingly diminishing it,
For the sea is also earth.
Okay, let all of this be symbols.
But what's the symbol—not the sun, not the moon, not the earth—
In this premature sunset amid the fading blue

20 With the sun caught in expiring tatters of clouds
And the moon already mystically present at the other end of the sky
As the last remnant of daylight
Gilds the head of the seamstress who hesitates at the corner
Where she used to linger (she lives nearby) with the boyfriend who
        left her?
25 Symbols? I don't want symbols.
All I want—poor frail and forlorn creature! —
Is for the boyfriend to go back to the seamstress.

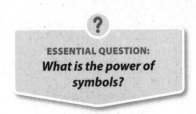

?

ESSENTIAL QUESTION:
What is the power of symbols?

Review your notes and add your thoughts to your Response Log.

COLLABORATIVE DISCUSSION

Turn to a partner and discuss the poem's ending. How does it influence your understanding of the speaker's earlier comments about symbols?

Assessment Practice

Answer these questions about "Symbols? I'm Sick of Symbols" before moving on to the **Analyze the Texts** section on the following page.

1. In lines 8–10, the speaker describes —

   (A) the abstract idea of the sun

   (B) the sun as a symbol of hope

   (C) how the sun appears after a rainfall

   (D) the beauty of a sunset

2. What idea does the speaker convey in line 16 when he says "the sea is also earth"?

   (A) Symbolic language is often too vague.

   (B) The sea and the earth are both symbols.

   (C) The sea is part of the earth.

   (D) Rising seas are diminishing the earth.

3. Why does the seamstress hesitate at the corner?

   (A) She is waiting for the boyfriend to join her.

   (B) She used to spend time there with her boyfriend.

   (C) She doesn't want to walk home in the dark.

   (D) She doesn't want to walk back to work.

☺Ed

Test-Taking Strategies

© Houghton Mifflin Harcourt Publishing Company

Analyze the Texts

Support your responses with evidence from the texts.

NOTICE & NOTE

Review what you **noticed and noted** as you read the text. Your annotations can help you answer these questions.

(1) **INTERPRET** In lines 7–8 of "The Second Coming," what does the speaker mean when he says, "The best lack all conviction, while the worst / Are full of passionate intensity"?

(2) **ANALYZE** What is ironic about the image that comes to the speaker's mind after he declares, "Surely the Second Coming is at hand"?

(3) **CONNECT** What does the sphinx-like image in lines 13–22 of "The Second Coming" symbolize? How might this symbol be related to historical events around the time Yeats wrote this poem, such as the Russian Revolution or World War I? Use the chart below to record your answer.

What the Symbol Represents	Connection to Historical Events

(4) **ANALYZE** Reread lines 5–7 and 8–16 of "Symbols? I'm Sick of Symbols." How does Pessoa change the poem's rhythm when he goes from mentioning common symbols to describing more detailed experiences?

(5) **DRAW CONCLUSIONS** In "Symbols? I'm Sick of Symbols," what does the speaker value in the image of the seamstress that he doesn't find in symbols such as the sun, the moon, and the earth?

(6) **COMPARE** Compare the speaker's **tone**, or attitude, in lines 1–17 of "Symbols? I'm Sick of Symbols" with the tone in lines 18–27. How does this shift in tone support the idea expressed at the end of the poem?

Choices

Here are some other ways to demonstrate your understanding of the ideas in this lesson.

Writing
↳ **Literary Analysis**

Write a three- to five-paragraph analysis of one of the poems in this lesson. Discuss the following elements:

- theme
- rhythm
- symbols
- imagery
- tone

As you write and discuss, be sure to use the **Academic Vocabulary** words.

| arbitrary |
| controversy |
| convince |
| denote |
| undergo |

Research
↳ **Common Symbols**

Objects and images can gain symbolic meaning over time. With a small group, research the history behind these familiar symbols:

- the Statue of Liberty
- the skull and crossbones symbol
- the Bluetooth symbol

Media
↳ **Song Adaptation**

Both of the poems in this lesson have a strong rhythm. With a partner, adapt one of the poems into a song.

1. Agree on which poem you will adapt.

2. Decide on a genre of music for the song.

3. Choose lines from the poem for different parts of the song's verse, chorus, and bridge.

4. Improvise music for the poem, using whatever instruments you have available or just by drumming on a desk.

Compare Themes

Symbols play an important role in both "The Second Coming" and "Symbols? I'm Sick of Symbols." However, the poems are quite different from each other. Yeats uses symbols to express a grand vision, while Pessoa works on a much more modest scale to make a point about symbolism. Compare how the two authors develop their themes. As you consider the themes of the poems, think about

- key statements made by the speaker in each poem
- central images that play important symbolic roles or evoke the theme
- the speaker's tone, or attitude, toward a subject

In a small group, identify similarities and differences between the two poems. Record your thoughts in the chart.

	A "The Second Coming"	B "Symbols? I'm Sick of Symbols"
Key Statements		
Central Images, Symbols		
Tone		

Analyze the Texts

Discuss these questions in your group.

1. **COMPARE** What similarities and differences do you see in how the two poets use imagery and symbols?

2. **ANALYZE** What is the overall tone of each poem? How does the tone reflect the poem's topic?

3. **EVALUATE** Which poet expresses ideas more clearly? How might this relate to their different approaches to symbolism?

4. **CRITIQUE** Yeats's speaker expresses a prophetic view of history, while Pessoa's speaker gets emotional about something he observes on a street corner. Which poem is more likely to appeal to readers today? Explain.

Collaborate and Present

Now your group can continue exploring the ideas in these texts by identifying and comparing their themes. Follow these steps:

1. **DECIDE ON THE MOST IMPORTANT DETAILS** With your group, review the chart you created to identify the most important details, including symbols, from each poem. Identify points you agree on, and resolve disagreements through discussion, basing your decisions on evidence from the texts.

2. **CREATE THEME STATEMENTS** State a theme for each poem, using complete sentences. Remember, it is up to you and your group to infer the themes based on details. Use a chart like the one shown to help determine each poem's theme.

Detail	Detail	Detail

$\downarrow$ $\downarrow$ $\downarrow$

Theme:

3. **COMPARE AND CONTRAST THEMES** With your group, discuss similarities and differences in the themes of the poems. Listen actively to the members of your group, take notes, and ask the group to clarify any points you do not understand. Identify points of agreement or disagreement before you present your ideas.

4. **PRESENT YOUR IDEAS TO THE CLASS** Now it is time to present your ideas. State your conclusions about the themes of the poems. Cite text evidence from the poems to support your ideas. Discuss points of similarity and difference in the themes. You may adapt the charts you created or use other visuals to help convey your ideas to the class.

Collaborate & Compare

ESSENTIAL QUESTION:
How do you measure a person's worth?

Compare Arguments

You are about to read two arguments about the unequal distribution of wealth in modern society. As you read the arguments, notice how each author tries to influence his audience by appealing to reason, emotions, personal values, or the desire to fit in. Then think about how the arguments relate to one another.

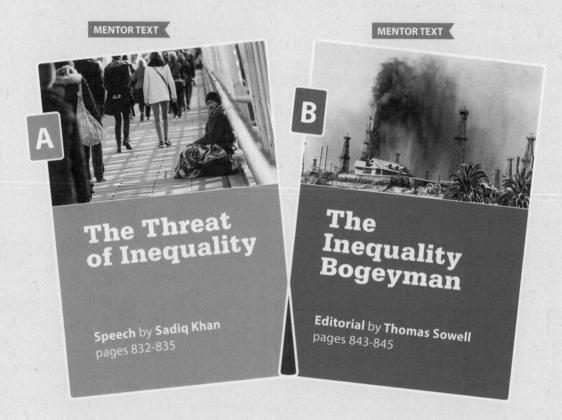

MENTOR TEXT

A

The Threat of Inequality

Speech by **Sadiq Khan**
pages 832-835

MENTOR TEXT

B

The Inequality Bogeyman

Editorial by **Thomas Sowell**
pages 843-845

After you have read both texts, you will collaborate with a group on a project. You will

- Develop questions
- Gather information
- Share research
- Collaborate and create a policy proposal

The Threat of Inequality

Speech by **Sadiq Khan**

Engage Your Brain

Choose one or more of these activities to start connecting with the speech you're about to read.

Prolific Speaker

As a member of Britain's parliament and later the mayor of London, Sadiq Khan has given many public speeches. With a partner, listen to an audio recording or watch a video of one of his speeches, and discuss his speaking style. Do you find him a compelling speaker? Explain why or why not.

Focus on Inequality

Social inequality can involve the opportunities available to people, their status, their wealth, or how they are treated. Discuss the following questions with a group of students:

- What forms of inequality exist in your community?

- Has inequality decreased, increased, or remained the same over the past five years?

- How might inequality pose a threat to the community?

Evaluate Persuasive Techniques

Sadiq Khan delivered the speech you are about to read in 2014, a time when politicians and economists began to pay greater attention to rising inequality between wealthy and ordinary people. He used persuasive techniques to help convince his listeners to accept his position on this issue. **Persuasive techniques** are the methods speakers and writers use to influence others. This chart lists some common ways to appeal to an audience.

Persuasive Technique	Explanation
Logical Appeal	Uses facts and evidence to support a position, appealing to an audience's reasoning or intellect
Ethical Appeal	Invokes shared values and principles to appeal to the audience's sense of right and wrong
Emotional Appeal	Arouses strong feelings in an audience, such as pity or fear
Bandwagon Appeal	Encourages people to support an idea or cause because it is popular

Focus on Genre
↳ **Speech**

- is a talk or public address presented to an audience
- may have one or more purposes, such as to entertain, to explain, or to persuade
- may conclude with a call to action
- may be recorded or transcribed for later reading and analysis

Look for examples of these techniques as you read Khan's speech.

Identify Repetition and Parallelism

Rhetorical devices are often used in speeches to help capture an audience's attention. In his speech, Khan uses the following devices.

- **Repetition** is the technique of repeating words or phrases in a text. Writers often use repetition in speeches to emphasize a point they are making.

- **Parallelism** is the use of similar grammatical constructions to express ideas that are related or equal in importance. This device is a useful way to present contrasting ideas. Parallelism also can make writing more rhythmic and memorable.

As you read "The Threat of Inequality," notice how Khan's use of these devices enhances the power and persuasiveness of his writing.

Annotation in Action

Here is an example of notes a student made about this paragraph from "The Threat of Inequality." As you read, mark examples of persuasive techniques in the speech.

> There are four reasons why inequality matters: Firstly, it causes the cost-of-living crisis which so many people are facing. Secondly, inequality is bad for economic growth. Thirdly, inequality is the most important factor in determining the happiness of society and the cohesiveness of our communities. And finally, a belief in equality and basic moral fairness is a foundation of British society.

Ethical appeal—wants listeners to think about fairness

Expand Your Vocabulary

Put a check mark next to the vocabulary words that you feel comfortable using when speaking or writing.

- disconnect ☐
- cohesiveness ☐
- volatile ☐
- succinctly ☐
- accommodations ☐

Turn to a partner and talk about the vocabulary words you already know. Then, write a few sentences about what you know about inequality, using as many of the vocabulary words as you can.

As you read "The Threat of Inequality," use the definitions in the side column to help you learn the vocabulary words you don't already know.

Background

Sadiq Khan (b. 1970) was born in London. His parents, a bus driver and a seamstress, immigrated to Britain from Pakistan shortly before his birth. He began his career as a human rights lawyer, and later he was elected to Britain's Parliament. In 2016, he became the first Muslim mayor of London. One of Europe's largest and most diverse cities, London has seen rising levels of inequality in wealth and income over the past few decades. Khan delivered his speech "The Threat of Inequality" to a British trade union in 2014.

A

The Threat of Inequality

Speech by **Sadiq Khan**

A politician argues that inequality harms Britain's economy and society.

© Houghton Mifflin Harcourt Publishing Company • Image Credits: ©Meibion/Alamy

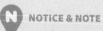

NOTICE & NOTE

As you read, use the side margins to make notes about the text.

disconnect
(dĭs´kə-nĕkt´) *n.* a lack of connection or a gap between two things.

1   I want to talk to you today about an issue that is the single biggest threat to our economy, our society, and to the well-being of the British people today. An issue that is the biggest dividing line in British politics. And a problem that affects all of you and all your members.

2   I want to talk to you about the growing **disconnect** between the wealth of our nation and the finances of working people, and the rise in inequality in Britain which it causes. A rise in inequality of income and wealth, but also in the distribution of power.

3   It's important to start by explaining why this matters so much. We see every day that our economy has stopped working for ordinary people, with the benefits going to those at the top and the rest being left behind. But we must take the time to reflect on exactly why this growing inequality matters if we are to convince Britain that it's the defining issue of our age.

4   There are four reasons why inequality matters: Firstly, it causes the cost-of-living crisis which so many people are facing. Secondly, inequality is bad for economic growth. Thirdly, inequality is the most

important factor in determining the happiness of society and the **cohesiveness** of our communities. And finally, a belief in equality and basic moral fairness is a foundation of British society.

5   I want to explore these reasons in a little more depth. Firstly, the cost-of-living crisis. Every week, government ministers hit the airwaves, claiming the latest set of economic statistics show that our economy is fixed. And there is no doubt that after years of flatlining, the economy is finally growing. But this is just not reflected in day-to-day life for most people. It makes them furious to hear the government claim the crisis is over, when they and their friends and family are all still suffering. When their wages are still frozen. When their job is no more secure. And when earnings are still barely keeping up with outgoings.

6   The vital link between the wealth of the country as a whole and people's family finances has been broken. Quite frankly, our economy is no longer working for most people. The benefits of growth increasingly go only to those at the top. Meaning that despite growth in the economy, the cost-of-living crisis continues to deepen for most people. Ed Miliband[1] summed it up brilliantly at our conference last year when he said: "a rising tide used to lift all boats, now it only seems to lift the yachts."

7   Secondly, inequality actually limits the potential for growth in our economy. And you don't have to take my word for it. The International Monetary Fund said exactly this in a groundbreaking report in February. The report said: "Countries with high levels of inequality suffer lower growth than nations that distribute incomes more evenly." It went on to say: "Inequality can also make growth more **volatile** and create the unstable conditions for a sudden slowdown in growth." In the murky world of economics, it doesn't get more definitive than that. And if the IMF isn't enough to convince you, you should read a speech delivered last week by Mark Carney. He is the governor of that famous left-wing institution—the Bank of England. In a brilliant speech about the dangers of inequality, he summed it up **succinctly**: "Relative equality is good for growth."

8   Thirdly, inequality damages the happiness and well-being of everyone in our society. And threatens the very fabric of our communities. How many of you have heard of a book called *The Spirit Level*?[2] Put your hands up if you have heard of it. It is the book that has had the biggest impact on my views in recent years. The authors comprehensively proved that inequality is bad for the health, happiness, and well-being of everyone in society. From those at the very top, to those at the very bottom.

9   It's worth pausing on that. Inequality is bad for the very wealthy—those who benefit most—just as it is bad for those at the bottom. They proved that inequality causes shorter, unhealthier, and

---

[1] Ed Miliband was the leader of the Labour Party from 2010 to 2015.
[2] *The Spirit Level: Why Greater Equality Makes Societies Stronger* was written by two professors of epidemiology, Richard Wilkinson and Kate Pickett.

cohesiveness
(kō-hē´sĭv-nəs) *n.* the condition of sticking together in a group.

EVALUATE PERSUASIVE TECHNIQUES

Annotate: In paragraph 5, mark the words or phrases that indicate an emotional appeal.

Evaluate: How might this emotional appeal help persuade the audience? Do you consider the appeal effective? Explain.

volatile
(vŏl´ə-tl, -tīl´) *adj.* unstable and prone to extremes.

succinctly
(sək-sĭngkt´lē) *adv.* a way of speaking in a concise or brief manner.

IDENTIFY REPETITION AND PARALLELISM

Annotate: Mark one or more examples of parallelism in paragraph 9.

Analyze: What are the effects of the parallelism?

unhappier lives. It increases the rate of teenage pregnancy, violence, obesity, imprisonment, and addiction. And most importantly, it destroys relationships between individuals born in the same society but into different classes.

NOTICE & NOTE
NUMBERS AND STATS

When you notice the use of specific quantities or comparisons to show amounts, size, or scale, you've found a **Numbers and Stats** signpost.

Notice & Note: In paragraphs 10–12, mark the statistics that the author uses in relation to income equality in Britain.

Evaluate: Why does Khan include these statistics?

10   The final reason that we must fight inequality is because it is rejected by the British people. It offends our most basic sense of fairness and traditional British values. In the most recent polling, 80 percent of British people said the income gap in this country is too high. Eighty percent. And even more—87 percent—think that growing inequality is unfair.

11   The British people are well and truly fed up with inequality. There is no doubt that Britain is becoming a less equal country. And the speed at which inequality is growing is increasing. Over the last year alone, the share of post-tax income of the top 1 percent of taxpayers—that's just 300,000 people—has risen from 8.2 percent to 9.8 percent.

12   Yet at the same time, the bottom 90 percent—a total of 27 million hard-working Britons—have seen their share of income fall from 71.3 percent to 70.4 percent. And it is a problem that is getting worse under the Tories and the Liberal Democrats.[3] The increase in wealth of the richest 100 people in Britain in the last year was 40.1 billion pounds. That's enough to pay a year's rent for nearly half of all renting households. Or to pay the energy bill for all 26.4 million UK households for over a year.

IDENTIFY REPETITION AND PARALLELISM

Annotate: Mark a repeated word in paragraph 13.

Analyze: Why does Khan use this repetition?

13   It is a stain on both their parties that they have refused to recognize inequality as the problem it is. A stain of which I believe even future Tories and Liberal Democrats will be ashamed.

14   In London we see the problems of inequality at their most extreme. Many of the wealthiest people in the world live in London. And they are thriving. They eat in the best restaurants in the world. They enjoy the best arts, theater, and culture in the world. But living side by side with them is the other 99 percent of Londoners. Who work long hard hours—longer than ever before. But for whom life has got more difficult. For whom wages have remained frozen. Who take the bus to work because the tube is now too expensive. Who long ago gave up on the dream of owning their own home. And who live in ever smaller and more overcrowded **accommodations** as the cost of rent goes up and up.

accommodations
(ə-kŏmʹə-dāʹshənz) *n.* lodgings.

15   London really has become a tale of two cities. And our cities' economy no longer works for the majority of Londoners. The gap between the two Londons is growing ever faster. Our job—as the Labour Party and the trade union movement—is to bring the two Londons—and the two Britains—back together. To close the gap between Notting Hill and Newham.[4] And build a true One Nation economy and society.

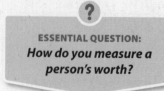

ESSENTIAL QUESTION:
How do you measure a person's worth?

Review your notes and add your thoughts to your Response Log.

---

[3] The Conservative Party (also known as the Tories) and the Liberal Democratic Party formed a coalition government in 2010. It lasted until 2015.
[4] Notting Hill is a wealthy district of London. Newham is a London borough with high rates of poverty and inequality.

Has the author persuaded you that wealth and income equality threaten society? Discuss your thoughts with a partner.

Assessment Practice

Answer these questions before moving on to the **Analyze the Text** section on the following page.

1. Which statement sums up paragraph 5?

   (A) Britain's economy has stalled after years of growth.

   (B) The growing economy does not benefit ordinary people.

   (C) Government ministers have lied about economic statistics.

   (D) Anger has blinded many British people to economic improvement.

2. What is the main persuasive technique that Khan uses in paragraph 10?

   (A) logical appeal

   (B) ethical appeal

   (C) emotional appeal

   (D) bandwagon appeal

3. Which word best describes Khan's tone in discussing the Tory and Liberal Democratic parties?

   (A) scornful

   (B) perplexed

   (C) concerned

   (D) disappointed

 Ed
Test-Taking Strategies

Analyze the Text

Support your responses with evidence from the text.

N NOTICE & NOTE

Review what you **noticed and noted** as you read the text. Your annotations can help you answer these questions.

1) **ANALYZE** In the chart below, provide an example of each type of persuasive technique Khan uses in his speech, and explain how he makes this appeal.

Type of Appeal	Example	Explanation
Logical		
Ethical		
Emotional		
Bandwagon		

2) **ANALYZE** In paragraph 6, Khan quotes another politician who said, "a rising tide used to lift all boats, now it only seems to lift the yachts." How do you interpret this statement? Why does the parallelism of the quotation help make it effective?

3) **ANALYZE** In paragraph 7, how does Khan support his argument that inequality limits the potential growth of the British economy? Did you find this evidence persuasive? Explain your response.

4) **EVALUATE** Review the author's use of **Numbers and Stats** in paragraphs 10–12. How well do these figures support the author's logical appeal?

5) **CRITIQUE** What support could Khan have included to make his argument more effective?

6) **CONNECT** Do you think that Khan's argument about inequality is relevant to the economy of the United States? Explain why or why not.

Choices

Here are some other ways to demonstrate your understanding of the ideas in this lesson.

Writing
↳ Speech

Write a speech in which you express your opinion about a social issue that concerns you.

- Begin your speech with a clear statement of your claim.
- Support your claim with reasons and evidence.
- Use at least two persuasive techniques in your argument.
- Emphasize meaning through the use of parallelism or repetition.

As you write and discuss, be sure to use the **Academic Vocabulary** words.

> arbitrary

> controversy

> convince

> denote

> undergo

Research
↳ Presentation on Inequality

With a group of students, research statistics for wealth and income inequality in your community, and discuss whether inequality is a major problem where you live. Then, present your findings and conclusions to the class.

- Consult reliable sources such as government agencies or university websites.
- Use charts to display data that supports your group's ideas.

Media
↳ Bumper Sticker

Design a bumper sticker to promote one of Khan's ideas about inequality.

- Compose a short, pithy statement to express the idea.
- Create an eye-catching design that combines graphical elements and text.
- Submit your bumper sticker for display in the class.

Expand Your Vocabulary

PRACTICE AND APPLY

Use your understanding of the vocabulary words to answer each question.

| disconnect | cohesiveness | volatile | succinctly | accommodations |

1. Describe your _____ .

2. What happens when you and your friends experience a _____ ?

3. What might cause a crowd to react in a _____ way?

4. Why might you want to _____ give directions to a lost stranger?

5. Give an example of a group that has _____ . How do they show this quality?

Vocabulary Strategy
↳ **Parts of Speech**

Some words can be more than one part of speech. Context clues can help you determine the word's part of speech, even if you know only one meaning of the word. Notice the word's position in a sentence to determine its part of speech and meaning.

I feel a complete <u>disconnect</u> between the world as it is portrayed in the news and my personal experience of it. (*Disconnect* is a noun.)

After you have drained the garden hose, <u>disconnect</u> it from the faucet, roll it up, and store it in the garage. (*Disconnect* is a verb.)

PRACTICE AND APPLY

Use context clues to determine the part of speech of the boldfaced word in each sentence. Then, choose one of the words and write a sentence using the word as a different part of speech. Consult a dictionary as needed.

1. An accountant reviews our family's **finances** and helps us create a yearly budget. _____

2. Every morning the stable worker **ministers** to all the horses, feeding them and cleaning out their stalls. _____

3. The wildfires had a devastating **impact** on the community. _____

☺**Ed**

Interactive Grammar Lesson: Determining Parts of Speech

Watch Your Language!

Who vs. Whom

The pronouns *who* and *whom* are often confused. Read the following sentences from "The Threat of Inequality."

**Interactive Grammar
Lesson: Who and Whom**

> <u>Who</u> work long hard hours—longer than ever before. But for <u>whom</u> life has got more difficult. For <u>whom</u> wages have remained frozen.

- *Who* is used as a subject. Like other subjective pronouns (*she, he, it, I, they,* and *we*), it is often followed by a verb.
- *Whom* is used as the object of either a verb or a preposition. Like other objective pronouns (*him, her, them,* and *us*), it receives an object or action.

> The author is a woman <u>who</u> needs no introduction. (*Who* is a subject followed by a verb.)
>
> The author is a woman <u>whom</u> I have known for years. (*Whom* is the object of the verb have known.)

If you are not certain whether to use *who* or *whom* in a sentence, rearrange the words and replace *who* or *whom* with a subjective or objective pronoun that makes sense.

> The author is a woman. <u>She</u> needs no introduction.
>
> The author is a woman. I have known <u>her</u> for years.

PRACTICE AND APPLY

Look back at an earlier piece of writing that you submitted for class. Do a search for the words *who* and *whom*. Did you use them correctly? Revise your writing as needed to reflect the correct usage of the two pronouns.

MENTOR TEXT

The Inequality Bogeyman

Editorial by **Thomas Sowell**

Engage Your Brain

Choose one or more of these activities to start connecting with the editorial you're about to read.

Bogeyman

The word *bogeyman* refers to an exaggerated or nonexistent threat used to intimidate others. Create a cartoon that exposes a bogeyman.

- Identify a "threat" that you think is exaggerated or doesn't even exist.

- Consider why other people are afraid of this idea, issue, or activity.

- Using techniques such as exaggeration and irony, create a cartoon panel or strip about the bogeyman.

High-Flying Earners

With a group of students, write down the names of five wealthy people who are living today. Answer the following questions:

- How did they become wealthy?

- How have their careers affected you personally?

- Do you think that they deserve their wealth?

Analyze Deductive Reasoning

When writers use **deductive reasoning,** they present a general principle, apply it to a specific situation, and then use reasons and evidence to arrive at a logical conclusion. Use the chart below to help you analyze a deductive argument.

Question	Analysis
Is the general principle stated or implied?	If the author does not state the general principle directly in a deductive argument, identify it for yourself as part of your analysis.
Is the general principle sound?	Instead of assuming that the principle is sound, ask yourself whether it is truly based on evidence.
Is the conclusion valid?	To be valid, a conclusion in a deductive argument must follow logically from the general principle and the specific situation.

As you read "The Inequality Bogeyman," analyze Thomas Sowell's deductive reasoning.

Evaluate a Counterargument

A **counterargument** is an argument made to refute an opposing view. The writer acknowledges the opposing view, and then refutes it using ideas and evidence. "The Inequality Bogeyman" presents a counterargument to the idea that wealth inequality is a major social problem.

In arguing against an opposing view, some writers resort to using **loaded language,** or words with strong connotations that appeal to the audience's biases. For example, the words *freeloader* and *dependent* both describe a person who relies on financial support, but *freeloader* has the negative connotation of someone who takes advantage of others. When you come across loaded language in an argument, be aware that it may disguise logical errors or lack supporting evidence.

Focus on Genre
↳ **Editorial**

- expresses an opinion, often on a controversial topic
- often found on the editorial page of a newspaper
- presents an argument and uses rhetorical techniques to persuade readers

Annotation in Action

Here is an example of notes a student made about a passage in "The Inequality Bogeyman." As you read, mark examples of loaded language in the editorial.

> One of the problems with so many discussions of income and wealth is that the intelligentsia are so obsessed with the money that people receive that they give little or no attention to what causes money to be paid to them in the first place.

Intellectual elite—negative word choice

Expand Your Vocabulary

Put a check mark next to the vocabulary words that you feel comfortable using when speaking or writing.

implication	☐
innate	☐
intelligentsia	☐
zero-sum	☐
innumerable	☐

Turn to a partner and talk about the vocabulary words you already know. Then write a sentence using at least one of the words.

As you read "The Inequality Bogeyman," use the definitions in the side column to help you learn the vocabulary words you don't already know.

Background

Thomas Sowell (b. 1930) is a prize-winning economist and author known for his controversial views. As an advocate of the free-market economy, Sowell believes the government should refrain from interfering in the worlds of commerce, business, and trade. He has written that cultural circumstances cause income inequality and believes statistics related to income inequality can be misleading.

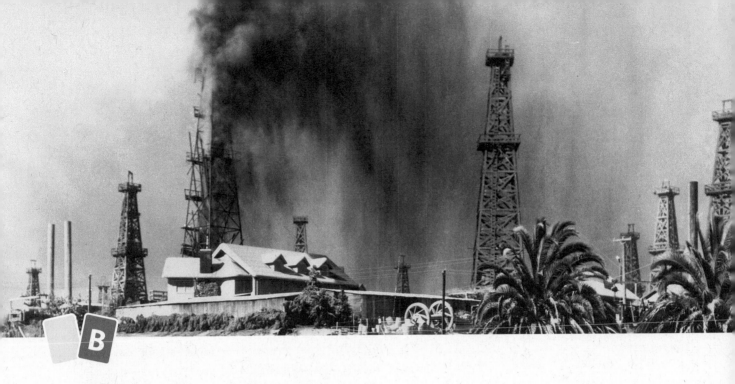

B

The Inequality Bogeyman

The focus on "social justice" ignores the collective wealth that unequal abilities create.

Editorial by **Thomas Sowell**

NOTICE & NOTE **N**
As you read, use the side margins to make notes about the text.

An economist looks on the bright side of inequality.

1   During a recent lunch in a restaurant, someone complimented my wife on the perfume she was wearing. But I was wholly unaware that she was wearing perfume, even though we had been in a car together for about half an hour driving to the restaurant.

2   My sense of smell is very poor. But there is one thing I can smell far better than most people—gas escaping. During my years of living on the Stanford University campus, and walking back and forth to work at my office, I more than once passed a faculty house and smelled gas escaping. When there was nobody home I would leave a note, warning them.

3   When walking past the same house again a few days later, I could see where the utility company had been digging in the yard—and, after that, there was no more smell of gas escaping. But apparently the people who lived in these homes had not smelled anything.

4   These little episodes have much wider **implications**. Most of us are much better at some things than at others, and what we are good at can vary enormously from one person to another. Despite the

N **NOTICE & NOTE**
EXTREME OR ABSOLUTE LANGUAGE

When you notice language that leaves no doubt about a situation or an event, allows no compromise, or seems to exaggerate or overstate a case, you've found an **Extreme or Absolute Language** signpost.

Notice & Note: Mark a word in paragraph 4 that has a negative connotation.

Evaluate: How does this word relate to the author's counterargument?

implication
(ĭm´plĭ-kā´shən) *n.* an implied meaning.

innate

(ĭ-nāt´, ĭn´āt´) *adj.* a quality natural or present from birth rather than learned.

ANALYZE DEDUCTIVE REASONING

Annotate: Mark statements in paragraphs 5–6 that imply a general principle.

Analyze: What general principle do these statements convey?

intelligentsia

(ĭn-tĕl-ə-jĕnt´sē-ə) *n.* the intellectual elite of a society.

EVALUATE A COUNTERARGUMENT

Annotate: Reread paragraphs 7 and 9. Mark phrases that imply an opposing view about inequality.

Infer: What is the opposing view that the author wants to refute?

preoccupation—if not obsession—of intellectuals with equality, we are all very unequal in what we do well and what we do badly.

5   They may not be **innate**, like a sense of smell, but differences in capabilities are inescapable, and they make a big difference in what and how much we can contribute to each other's economic and other kinds of well-being. If we all had the same capabilities and the same limitations, one individual's limitations would be the same as the limitations of the entire human species.

6   We are lucky that we are so different, so that the capabilities of many other people can cover our limitations.

7   One of the problems with so many discussions of income and wealth is that the **intelligentsia** are so obsessed with the money that people receive that they give little or no attention to what causes money to be paid to them in the first place.

8   Money itself is not wealth. Otherwise the government could make us all rich just by printing more of it. From the standpoint of a society as a whole, money is just an artificial device to give us incentives to produce real things—goods and services. Those goods and services are the real "wealth of nations," as Adam Smith[1] titled his treatise on economics in the 18th century.

9   Yet when the intelligentsia discuss such things as the historic fortunes of people like John D. Rockefeller, they usually pay little—if any—attention to what it was that caused so many millions of people to voluntarily turn their individually modest sums of money over to Rockefeller, adding up to his vast fortune.

10   What Rockefeller did first to earn their money was find ways to bring down the cost of producing and distributing kerosene[2] to a fraction of what it had been before his innovations. This profoundly changed the lives of millions of working people.

11   Before Rockefeller came along in the 19th century, the ancient saying "the night cometh, when no man can work" still applied. There were not yet electric lights, and burning kerosene for hours every night was not something that ordinary working people could afford. For many millions of people, there was little to do after dark except go to bed.

12   Too many discussions of large fortunes attribute them to "greed"—as if wanting a lot of money is enough to cause other people to hand it over to you. It is a childish idea when you stop and think about it—but who stops and thinks these days?

zero-sum

(zîr´ō-sŭm) *adj.* a situation in which a gain is offset by an equal loss.

innumerable

(ĭ-noo´mər-ə-bəl) *adj.* too many parts to count.

13   The transfer of money was a **zero-sum** process. What increased the wealth of society was Rockefeller's cheap kerosene that added hundreds of hours of light to people's lives annually.

14   Edison, Ford, the Wright brothers, and **innumerable** others also created unprecedented expansions of the lives of ordinary people. The individual fortunes represented a fraction of the wealth created.

---

[1] Adam Smith was a Scottish philosopher who wrote a pioneering study of economics, *An Inquiry into the Nature and Causes of the Wealth of Nations* (1776).

[2] Kerosene is a fuel used for burning in lamps and for powering jet engines.

15   Even those of us who create goods and services in more mundane ways receive income that may be very important to us, but it is what we create for others with our widely varying capabilities that is the real wealth of nations.

16   Intellectuals' obsession with income statistics—calling envy "social justice"—ignores vast differences in productivity that are far more fundamental to everyone's well-being. Killing the goose that lays the golden egg has ruined many economies.

?

ESSENTIAL QUESTION:
How do you measure a person's worth?

Review your notes and add your thoughts to your Response Log.

COLLABORATIVE DISCUSSION

Do you agree with the author's view that ordinary people benefit from the actions of the very wealthy? Discuss with a partner or small group.

Assessment Practice

Answer these questions before moving on to the **Analyze the Text** section on the following page.

1. This question has two parts. Answer **Part A**, then **Part B**.

    Part A

    The author of "The Inequality Bogeyman" makes the claim that wealthy people have a lot of money because they—

    (A) are obsessed with becoming rich

    (B) have the same limitations as everyone else

    (C) have a natural ability to make money

    (D) create things that people want to buy

    Part B

    How does the author support his claim stated in Part A?

    (A) He offers examples of successful entrepreneurs.

    (B) He provides anecdotes to show how people have different capabilities.

    (C) He quotes from Adam Smith's economic treatise, *The Wealth of Nations*.

    (D) He uses language that engages readers' biases against the poor.

2. What does the author of "The Inequality Bogeyman" mean when he says that attributing large fortunes to "greed" is "a childish idea"?

    (A) He expresses his opinion that greed is a good thing.

    (B) He hints that the idea is one that deserves greater scrutiny.

    (C) He implies that only children would believe this idea.

    (D) He suggests that the idea is not well thought out.

Test-Taking Strategies

Analyze the Text

Support your responses with evidence from the text.

NOTICE & NOTE

Review what you **noticed and noted** as you read the text. Your annotations can help you answer these questions.

1 ANALYZE Use the graphic organizer to identify the elements of Sowell's deductive argument.

General Principle	
Specific Situation	
Logical Conclusion	

2 ANALYZE How do the anecdotes in paragraphs 1–3 relate to the author's general principle? Do you think that this is an effective way to introduce the principle? Why or why not?

3 EVALUATE Is Sowell's conclusion about wealthy individuals valid? Explain why or why not.

4 EVALUATE Does Sowell's use of deductive reasoning make his argument clear, convincing, and engaging? Explain your response.

5 ANALYZE Identify an example of **Extreme or Absolute Language** that the author uses in paragraphs 7 and 9, and explain why it has a negative connotation.

6 EVALUATE Does Sowell provide a strong rebuttal of the "intelligentsia's" view about wealth and inequality? How could he have strengthened his counterargument?

7 CONNECT Which wealthy people in our society today could Sowell have mentioned to add support for his conclusion? Explain why.

Choices

Here are some other ways to demonstrate your understanding of the ideas in this lesson.

Writing
↳ Letter

Write a letter to Sowell in response to his argument.

- Address the support he provides for his claim about the social benefits of inequality. Do you think he offers enough evidence? Explain why or why not.

- Discuss how his conclusion relates to your own experiences and the experiences of people you are close to.

> As you write and discuss, be sure to use the **Academic Vocabulary** words.
>
> | arbitrary |
> | controversy |
> | convince |
> | denote |
> | undergo |

Research
↳ Wealthy Innovators

With a group of students, research the wealthy individuals Sowell discusses in paragraphs 9–14. Answer the following questions:

- How much wealth did they accumulate?

- What innovations led to their wealth?

- How did their innovations affect society?

Speaking & Listening
↳ Paired Discussion

With a partner, discuss how your perception of others is influenced by their levels of wealth and income.

- Do you tend to see wealthy people as more competent than others?

- Is it fair for some people to have extreme wealth?

- Does your perception of wealthy people change if they donate a lot of their money to charities?

Expand Your Vocabulary

PRACTICE AND APPLY

Use your understanding of the vocabulary words to answer each question.

| implication | innate | intelligentsia | zero-sum | innumerable |

1. Which vocabulary word goes with *balanced*? Why?

2. Which vocabulary word goes with *significance*? Why?

3. Which vocabulary word goes with *elites*? Why?

4. Which vocabulary word goes with *natural*? Why?

5. Which vocabulary word goes with *countless*? Why?

Vocabulary Strategy
↳ Compound Adjectives

A **compound adjective** is composed of two words used together to describe a noun. A compound adjective may be a single word, such as *childlike*, but many are hyphenated, like *zero-sum*. Look at the sentence from "The Inequality Bogeyman."

> **The transfer of money was a <u>zero-sum</u> process.**

The word *zero-sum* is a compound adjective. The hyphen between the words *zero* and *sum* helps readers avoid confusion. Without the hyphen, the word—*zerosum*— would be difficult to read and understand.

PRACTICE AND APPLY

Combine words from the two boxes to create four hyphenated compound adjectives. Then, use the compound adjectives in original sentences to show that you understand their meaning.

open	assured
self	behaved
well	confident
	conscious
	dressed
	known
	minded
	possessed
	spoken

Watch Your Language!

Rhetorical Questions

A **rhetorical question** is a question to which no answer is expected. Writers use rhetorical questions for emphasis, to evoke a response in the audience, or to suggest that their claims are so obvious that everyone should agree with them. Employed appropriately, rhetorical questions can enhance an argument.

In "The Inequality Bogeyman," Sowell uses a rhetorical question in paragraph 12:

> **It is a childish idea when you stop and think about it—but who stops and thinks these days?**

Sowell does not expect his readers to have a specific answer to the question he raises. He uses the rhetorical question to achieve two goals:

- to get readers to think critically about the idea that rich people are greedy
- to discredit people who hold a view opposed to his position on the subject

The chart below shows some examples of rhetorical questions and their specific purposes.

Purpose	Examples
Emphasize a point	Who gets to decide such an important issue? Should you? Your parents? Your teachers?
Evoke an emotional response	Don't you and your children and their children deserve a better life?
Inject humor	Seriously? Who knew?
Introduce skepticism or doubt	How could that be right?
Invite critical thinking	Is this the right approach?

PRACTICE AND APPLY

Review a recent piece of argumentative writing you wrote. Look for places where you could add a rhetorical question to emphasize a point, evoke an emotional response, introduce humor, sow doubt, or provoke critical thinking. Revise your writing to include a rhetorical question. Share your work with a partner, and ask whether the rhetorical question improves the piece.

Compare Arguments

When you compare two or more arguments on the same topic, you synthesize the ideas and information in the arguments. This process can help you figure out your own position on the issue.

In a small group, complete the Venn diagram with similarities and differences in the two arguments you read. Consider the claims made about the topic, reasons and evidence provided to support the claims, and rhetorical devices and persuasive techniques used by the authors.

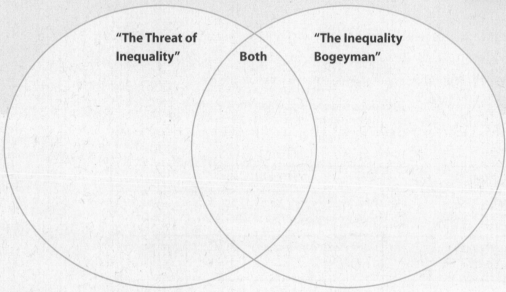

"The Threat of Inequality" **Both** **"The Inequality Bogeyman"**

Analyze the Texts

Discuss these questions in your group.

1. **SUMMARIZE** What topic do both arguments address? In brief, what is each author's claim?

2. **COMPARE** How do the two authors disagree? Cite evidence to support your answer.

3. **CRITIQUE** Identify weaknesses in both arguments. How could they be more effective? Cite evidence to support your answers.

4. **EVALUATE** Which argument employs persuasive techniques and rhetorical devices more effectively? Cite evidence from both texts to support your opinion.

Research and Share

Now your group can continue exploring the ideas in "The Threat of Inequality" and "The Inequality Bogeyman" by collaborating on research and writing a proposal for a public policy that addresses income inequality. Follow these steps:

(1) DEVELOP QUESTIONS With your group, brainstorm questions about the topic of income inequality that came up as you read both texts. Which are the most relevant and interesting? Assign a question to each group member.

(2) GATHER INFORMATION Research the answers to your questions by choosing print and online sources that are credible. Look for sources that are current and published by reliable institutions, such as universities, respected news organizations, and the government.

(3) SHARE RESEARCH Discuss your findings with your group. Take notes about the answer to each question in a chart like the one below.

Research Question	Information	Sources

(4) COLLABORATE AND CREATE A POLICY PROPOSAL As a group, reach an agreement on a public policy proposal that addresses income inequality. Draft a proposal that states your point of view, supports it with facts and evidence from your research, and suggests actions that people can take to deal with the issue. Use a chart to organize your proposal ideas.

We agree that income inequality is _____.
Reason 1:
Evidence:
Reason 2:
Evidence:
Conclusion:

Reader's Choice

Continue your exploration of the Essential Questions for this unit by doing some independent reading. Read the titles and descriptions shown. Then mark the texts that interest you.

? **ESSENTIAL QUESTIONS:** *Review the four Essential Questions for this unit on page 729.*

Short Reads Available on ☺ Ed

These texts are available in your ebook. Choose one to read and rate. Then defend your rating to the class.

Araby
Short Story by **James Joyce**

A poor Irish schoolboy wants to buy a gift to impress a girl.

Rate It ☆☆☆☆☆

Professions for Women
Speech by **Virginia Woolf**

A famous writer relates two strategies she has used to confront obstacles that all women face.

Rate It ☆☆☆☆☆

Do Not Go Gentle into That Good Night
Poem by **Dylan Thomas**

A son pleads with his dying father to hold on for as long as possible.

Rate It ☆☆☆☆☆

Digging
Poem by **Seamus Heaney**

A poet compares his writing to work his family has traditionally done in the fields.

Rate It ☆☆☆☆☆

Marriage Is a Private Affair
Short Story by **Chinua Achebe**

A man tries to heal his relationship with his father after rejecting an arranged marriage.

Rate It ☆☆☆☆☆

Long Reads

Here are a few books that connect to this unit. For additional options, ask your teacher, school librarian, or peers. Which titles spark your interest?

Things Fall Apart

Novel by **Chinua Achebe**

Okonkwo, a wealthy and fearless Igbo warrior in what is now Nigeria, witnesses the painful erosion of his beloved traditions by British colonialism in the late 1800s.

Milkman

Novel by **Anna Burns**

In conflict-scarred Northern Ireland during the 1970s, a young woman endures suspicion and judgment in her town as she is harassed by an older man.

White Teeth

Novel by **Zadie Smith**

A diverse group of characters in London centers around Archie and Samad, two World War II veterans who both marry women significantly younger than themselves.

© Houghton Mifflin Harcourt Publishing Company • Image Credits: (l) ©Peter Horree/Alamy; (c) ©George Munday/Alamy; (r) ©RDImages/Epics/Hulton Archive/Getty Images

Extension
↳ **Collaborate & Create**

NEW VOICES, NEW IDEAS Does the text you chose to read introduce something new to British literature, or is it a continuation of the literary tradition? Write a brief essay in response to this question, comparing the text to at least one selection in an earlier unit.

WHOSE LANGUAGE? Think about the quotation that opens this unit: "The English language is nobody's special property. It is the property of the imagination; it is the property of the language itself." How does this quotation relate to the book you read? Share your ideas with someone who has read the same book.

 NOTICE & NOTE

- Pick one of the texts and annotate the Notice & Note signposts you find.

- Then use the **Notice & Note Writing Frames** to help you write about the significance of the signposts.

- Compare your findings with those of other students who read the same text.

Notice & Note Writing Frames

Write an Argument

Writing Prompt

Think about the selections in this unit that address problems in British society. Then, write an argumentative essay about a social or political issue that affects your community, such as homelessness, school choice, or the environment.

Manage your time carefully so that you can

- choose an issue that is meaningful to you;
- plan your argument;
- write your argument; and
- revise and edit your argument.

Be sure to

- state a clear claim and support it with relevant evidence;
- address opposing claims with counterclaims;
- write a conclusion that supports your argument; and
- use varied syntax and maintain a formal tone.

> ### Review the
> ### Mentor Texts
>
> For two examples of well-written arguments you can use as mentor texts for your own writing, review:
>
> - **"The Threat of Inequality"** (pages 832–835) and
> - **"The Inequality Bogeyman"** (pages 843–845).
>
> Make sure to carefully review your notes and annotations about these texts. Think about the techniques the authors use to make their arguments compelling and convincing.

Consider Your Sources

Review the list of texts in the unit and choose at least three that you may want to use as support for your argument.

As you review potential sources, consult the notes you made in your **Response Log** that relate to the question "Why is it hard to resist social pressure?"

UNIT 6 SOURCES

- [ ] **"A Village After Dark"**
- [ ] **"A Cup of Tea"**
- [ ] **"Shooting an Elephant"**
- [ ] **"My Daughter the Racist"**
- [ ] **"The Love Song of J. Alfred Prufrock"**
- [ ] **"The Second Coming"**
- [ ] **"Symbols? I'm Sick of Symbols"**
- [ ] **"The Threat of Inequality"**
- [ ] **"The Inequality Bogeyman"**

Analyze the Prompt

Review the prompt to make sure you understand the assignment.

1. Mark the sentence in the prompt that identifies the topic of your argument. Rephrase this sentence in your own words.

2. Next, look for words that indicate the purpose and audience of your argument, and write a sentence describing each.

Find a Purpose

Two common purposes for writing an argument are

- to **convince** others to agree with your position.

- to **motivate** others to take action.

What is my topic? What is my writing task?

_____

What is my purpose?

_____

Who is my audience?

_____

Review the Rubric

Your argument will be scored using a rubric. As you write, focus on the characteristics of a high-scoring essay as described in the chart. You will learn more about these characteristics as you work through the lesson.

Purpose, Focus, and Organization	Evidence and Elaboration	Conventions of Standard English
The response includes: • A strongly maintained claim • Effective responses to opposing claims • Use of transitions to connect ideas • Logical progression of ideas • Appropriate style and tone	The response includes: • Effective use of evidence and sources • Effective use of elaboration • Clear and effective expression of ideas • Appropriate vocabulary • Varied sentence structure	The response may include: • Some minor errors in usage but no patterns of errors • Correct punctuation, capitalization, sentence formation, and spelling • Command of basic conventions

1 PLAN YOUR ARGUMENT

Develop a Claim

In an argument, the **claim** is the writer's position on an issue. Choose a political or social issue in your community that interests you, and take a position on it. Use the chart to identify your topic and draft a claim that clearly states your position.

Issue	
Claim	

Identify Support

To build a strong argument, you must have solid **support** for your claim. Support consists of reasons and evidence.

- **Reasons** explain why you have taken a particular position on an issue.
- **Evidence,** such as facts, statistics, examples, interviews, or expert opinions, supports your reasons.

Use the chart below to outline your support. Be sure to cite your sources. Record the title of each source and the page number or person interviewed and the date.

Provide Solid Evidence

Make sure your evidence is

- **relevant**, meaning it is directly related to your claim and reasons.
- **sufficient**, meaning there is enough of it to be convincing.

Reason 1:	
Evidence:	**Source(s):**
Reason 2:	
Evidence:	**Source(s):**
Reason 3:	
Evidence:	**Source(s):**

Address Opposing Claims

Your argument should include an **opposing claim** that reflects a differing view and a **counterclaim** that explains why your position is more valid. Review your notes for ideas that conflict with your position and evidence that you can use to support your view. Then write the opposing claim and counterclaim.

Help with Planning

Consult **Interactive Writing Lesson: Writing Arguments**

Opposing Claim
Counterclaim

Organize Ideas

Now organize your ideas in a **coherent** and convincing way. A coherent argument has a logical, organized progression of ideas and evidence. Transition words and phrases show connections between

- the claim and reasons;
- the reasons and the evidence; and
- opposing claims and counterclaims

Put It In Order

As you organize your ideas, try arranging reasons by order of importance. Here are two options:

- Begin with the most important reason, followed by the second most important reason, and so on.
- Begin with the second most important reason and conclude with the most important reason.

INTRODUCTION	• Clearly introduce your issue and claim. • Include an interesting question, quote, or detail to grab the reader's attention.
BODY PARAGRAPHS	• Present reasons and evidence to support your claim. • Address an opposing claim with a counterclaim. • Use transitional phrases such as "The most important reason for . . ." and "Another compelling reason is. . ." to link ideas.
CONCLUSIONS	• Provide a concluding statement. • Restate your claim and its significance. • End with a final appeal that readers can consider after they finish reading.

2 DEVELOP A DRAFT

Now it is time to draft your essay. You can develop your writing skills by seeing how the experts do it. Read about the techniques professional writers use to craft their arguments.

Introduce Your Topic and Claim

EXAMINE THE MENTOR TEXT

Notice how Sadiq Khan appeals to his audience's emotions before introducing his claim about inequality in Britain.

The Threat of Inequality
Speech by Sadiq Khan

> The author uses an **emotional appeal** to introduce his **topic** and grab his audience's attention.

I want to talk to you today about an issue that is the single biggest threat to our economy, our society, and to the well-being of the British people today. An issue that is the biggest dividing line in British politics. And a problem that affects all of you and all your members.

I want to talk to you about the growing disconnect between the wealth of our nation and the finances of working people, and the rise in inequality in Britain which it causes. A rise in inequality of income and wealth, but also in the distribution of power.

> He states his **claim** clearly and directly, announcing precisely what he will be talking about.

APPLY TO YOUR DRAFT

In the introduction to your argument, use an interesting quotation, surprising fact, or insightful observation to grab your reader's attention. Or consider starting with an ethical or emotional appeal that will support your position.

Rhetorical Appeals

Here are three types of rhetorical appeals you can use to persuade readers:

- **Logical:** Appeal to readers' sense of reason by relying on logic and facts.

- **Emotional:** Appeal to readers' emotions by providing anecdotes or information that makes them feel angry or sympathetic.

- **Ethical:** Appeal to readers' ethics by linking a position to a moral value.

Quotation	Fact	Observation	Appeal

Acknowledge and Refute Opposing Claims

EXAMINE THE MENTOR TEXT

In "The Threat of Inequality," Khan acknowledges an opposing claim with a respectful tone before refuting it with a counterclaim.

Drafting Online

Check your assignment list for a writing task from your teacher.

"But" signals the **contrast** between the statistics and reality.

> I want to explore these reasons in a little more depth. Firstly, the cost-of-living crisis. Every week, government ministers hit the airwaves, claiming the latest set of economic statistics show that our economy is fixed. And there is no doubt that after years of flatlining, the economy is finally growing. But this is just not reflected in day-to-day life for most people. It makes them furious to hear the government claim the crisis is over, when they and their friends and family are all still suffering. When their wages are still frozen. When their job is no more secure. And when earnings are still barely keeping up with outgoings.

The author acknowledges evidence that supports an **opposing claim** about the British economy.

He responds to the opposing claim with a **counterclaim** to strengthen his argument.

APPLY TO YOUR DRAFT

Make sure to include an opposing claim in your draft. Then, include a counterclaim that addresses the opposing claim. Remember to provide evidence that shows why your position is more valid.

Use the chart to guide you as you respectfully refute opposing claims while maintaining a formal tone.

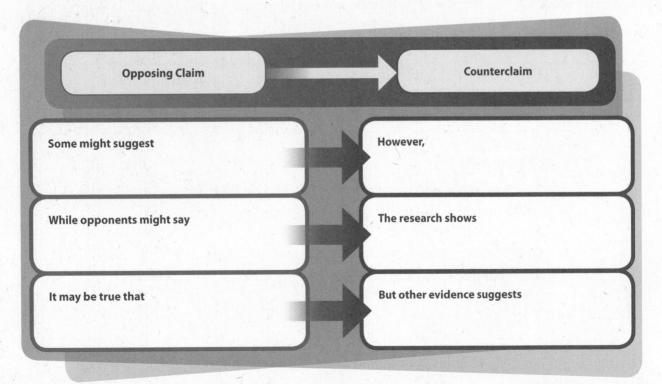

Opposing Claim	→	Counterclaim
Some might suggest	→	However,
While opponents might say	→	The research shows
It may be true that	→	But other evidence suggests

3 REVISE YOUR ARGUMENT

Professional writers rework their ideas and language as they revise to make sure they are communicating effectively. Use the guide to help you revise your argument.

 Ed

Help with Revision

Find a **Peer Review Guide** and **Student Models** online.

REVISION GUIDE		
Ask Yourself	**Prove It**	**Revise It**
Claim Does my introduction contain a claim that clearly states my position?	**Highlight** your claim.	**Add** to or **revise** your claim to clarify or strengthen your position.
Support Do I support my claim with reasons and relevant evidence?	**Highlight** your reasons. **Underline** the supporting evidence.	**Add** reasons or evidence such as a fact, example, or comparison to support each reason.
Counterclaim Have I addressed an opposing claim with a well-supported counterclaim?	**Place a star** (★) next to the opposing claim. **Underline** the counterclaim.	**Add** possible opposing claims and counterclaims.
Organization Do I transition smoothly between ideas, sentences, and paragraphs?	**[Bracket]** the transitional words and phrases.	**Add** transitions that clarify the relationships among ideas, sentences, and paragraphs.
Style Do I maintain a formal tone and style throughout?	**Circle** any informal or inappropriate language.	**Replace** informal language with formal or academic language.
Conclusion Does my conclusion follow from and support my argument?	**[Bracket]** your conclusion.	**Revise** the conclusion so that it follows from the reasoning of your argument.

APPLY TO YOUR DRAFT

Reread your argument and look for opportunities to improve your writing.

- Make sure to use a respectful tone, especially when discussing an opposing claim.
- Avoid using informal language.
- Cite a source when you introduce evidence that supports your claim.

Discuss with a partner how you could make your argument more effective. Give each other specific suggestions for revision.

Peer Review in Action

Once you have finished revising your argument, you will exchange papers with a partner in a **peer review.** During a peer review you will give suggestions to improve your partner's draft.

Read this body paragraph from a student's draft and examine the comments made by her peer reviewer.

First Draft

Homeless People Are Not Lesser
By Teri Albright, Hoover High School

I think that people who believe that homeless people live on the street or in their cars because it's their choice really have no clue. What about kids who are homeless? What choices do they have? They're just kids! It's definitely not fair that these young people should be judged for being homeless when it's not their fault.

You need more evidence to address the opposing claim. Don't forget to cite your source.

Avoid using "I" and think about other ways to make the tone more formal.

Now read the revised body paragraph below. Notice how the writer has improved her draft by making revisions based on the peer reviewer's comments.

Revision

Homeless People Are Not Lesser
By Teri Albright, Hoover High School

Some claim that homeless people have brought their situation on themselves by making bad choices. However, that argument is an oversimplification, especially when it comes to children who don't have permanent housing. Young people are not in a position to make choices because they are dependent on the adults around them. Statistics show that there are many youngsters in this situation. According to the Institute for Children, Poverty, and Homelessness, nearly 1.3 million school-age children are homeless. Many of these children are homeless because their parents experienced an event over which they had no control, such as job loss or illness.

Nicely done! You improved your tone and stated the opposing view clearly and respectfully.

You did a good job here providing a strong statistic, and introducing your source.

APPLY TO YOUR DRAFT

During your peer review, give each other specific suggestions for how you could make your arguments more effective. Use your revision guide to help you.

When receiving feedback from your partner, listen attentively and ask questions to make sure you fully understand the revision suggestions.

4 EDIT YOUR ARGUMENT

Edit your final draft to check for proper use of Standard English conventions and to correct any misspellings or grammatical errors.

Watch Your Language!

USE SYNTAX FOR EFFECT

When you use the same sentence patterns over and over, your writing becomes predictable and boring. You can improve your essay by varying the **syntax,** or word order, of your sentences.

Read the following sentences from "The Inequality Bogeyman" by Thomas Sowell.

> Money itself is not wealth. Otherwise the government could make us all rich just by printing more of it. From the standpoint of a society as a whole, money is just an artificial device to give us incentives to produce real things—goods and services. Those goods and services are the real "wealth of nations," as Adam Smith titled his treatise on economics in the 18th century.

Varied Syntax

Here are two strategies for varying syntax:

- To create a smooth flow, vary sentence structure by combining shorter sentences into compound or complex sentences.

- Shorten sentence lengths to emphasize certain ideas and engage readers.

Sowell varies the structure and length of his sentences. The paragraph begins with a short, simple sentence followed by longer, compound sentences of varying styles. The first two sentences are direct and forceful statements, while the remaining sentences elaborate on his key ideas.

APPLY TO YOUR DRAFT

Now apply what you've learned to your own writing.

1. **Read your essay aloud** and listen for repetitive sentence structures.

2. **Vary your syntax** by combining sentences.

3. **Exchange drafts** with a peer and review each other's writing for varied syntax.

5 PUBLISH YOUR ARGUMENT

Share It!

Finalize your argumentative essay in which you address a social or political issue that affects your community for your writing portfolio. You may also use your essay as inspiration for other projects.

Ways to Share

- **Write a blog post** on a class or school website to let others know about the issue.

- **Give a persuasive multimedia presentation** to a neighborhood or civic group about the issue.

- **Have a debate** with your classmates about the issue. See the next task for tips on how.

Debate an Issue

You will now adapt your argument for a debate with your classmates. You will also listen to other debate teams and prepare to critique their presentations.

Plan Your Debate

Review your written argument. Note that one team will argue for your claim, and the other will argue against it.

- Begin planning by identifying two debate teams with two or three members in each. Assign roles to each member.

Pro:	Con:
1. Introduce team's argument: _____	**1.** Introduce team's argument: _____
2. Refute opposing team: _____	**2.** Refute opposing team: _____
3. Present summary and closing statement: _____	**3.** Present summary and closing statement: _____

- Next, appoint a moderator to introduce the debate and the speakers and to keep the debate orderly.

Moderator: _____

- Complete the chart to plan the content of your debate.

Prepare Briefs	Prepare Rebuttals
Identify your claim:	Identify the opposing claim:
List reasons and evidence that support your claim:	Identify weaknesses in the opposing claim:
Summarize your argument in a closing statement:	Identify possible rebuttals:

Practice with a Team

Once you have prepared your materials, work with your team to improve your presentation by focusing on these techniques. Practice listening and responding respectfully.

Technique	Goal
Voice	Enunciate your words clearly. Use your voice to show enthusiasm and emphasis.
Eye Contact	Let your eyes rest briefly on each member of the audience at least once.
Facial Expression	Smile, frown, or raise an eyebrow to show your feelings or to emphasize points.

Active Listening

Remember to

- give each presenter your attention.
- suggest ways for speakers to improve their tone, rhetoric, and use of evidence.
- point out ways to improve word choices and links between ideas.

Hold the Debate

Set up the classroom for a formal debate, with the team members facing the audience. Review your team roles and follow this format.

Debate Team Member	Task
Pro Speaker 1	Present claim and supporting evidence for the "pro," or supportive side of the argument. (5 minutes)
Con Speaker 2	Ask probing questions that will prompt the other team to address flaws in the argument. (3 minutes)
Pro Speaker 2	Respond to the questions posed by the opposing team and provide counterclaims. (3 minutes)
Con Speaker 1	Present claim and supporting evidence for the "con," or opposing side of the argument. (5 minutes)
Pro Speaker 2	Ask probing questions that will prompt the other team to address flaws in the argument. (3 minutes)
Con Speaker 2	Respond to the questions posed by the opposing team and provide counterclaims. (3 minutes)
Pro Speaker 3	Summarize the claim and evidence for the "pro" side and explain why your claim is more valid. (3 minutes)
Con Speaker 3	Summarize the claim and evidence for the "con" side and explain why your claim is more valid. (3 minutes)

Share It!

- **Have a class discussion** about which debate techniques worked best. Share your favorites.
- **Record your debate for a podcast.** Review the recording and edit out distracting noises or doubletalk.
- **Take a class poll** on which group's claim was the most well-received.

Reflect & Extend

Here are some other ways to show your understanding of the ideas in Unit 6.

Reflect on the Essential Questions

Think about the Essential Question you identified as most intriguing on page 730. Has your answer to the question changed after reading the texts in the unit? Discuss your ideas. You can use these sentence starters to help you reflect on your learning.

- **My thoughts on the question changed because . . .**
- **I was surprised by . . .**
- **I still wonder about . . .**

Project-Based Learning
↳ Create a Book Cover

The texts in this unit are all examples of compelling modern British literature. Choose one of those selections and create a book cover for a new printing of the work that includes the title, author, and reviewer endorsements.

Here are some questions to ask yourself as you get started.

- Who is the audience for this text?
- How can the elements of color, images, and typography work together to create a message about what the text is about?
- What impression should the cover design create to attract potential readers?

Media Projects

To find help with this task online, access **Create a Book Cover.**

Writing
↳ Write an Explanatory Essay

Choose a social issue affecting your community and write an explanatory essay on the causes of the situation and the effect it has on society as a whole. Use the chart below to jot down your ideas. Then, look for information in relevant sources and write your essay.

Ask Yourself	My Notes
What social issue do I want to learn more about? What questions do I have about this issue?	
Where can I find relevant, supporting evidence about this topic?	
What text features should I include in my essay to help convey details? Would charts, graphs, or images be useful?	

Resources

HMH *Into Literature* Resources   Ed

For more instruction and practice, access the *Into Literature* Resources and Interactive Lessons.

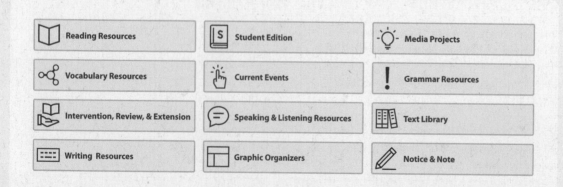

Reading Resources   Student Edition   Media Projects

Vocabulary Resources   Current Events   Grammar Resources

Intervention, Review, & Extension   Speaking & Listening Resources   Text Library

Writing Resources   Graphic Organizers   Notice & Note

Response Log

Use this Response Log to record information
from the texts that relates to or comments on the
Essential Questions in Unit 1.

? Essential Question	Details from Texts
What makes someone a hero?	
What is true chivalry?	
Can we control our fate?	
What happens when a society unravels?	

Response Log

Use this Response Log to record information from the texts that relates to or comments on the **Essential Questions** in Unit 2.

? Essential Question	Details from Texts
What can drive someone to seek revenge?	
How does time affect our feelings?	
What's the difference between love and passion?	
How do you defy expectations?	

Response Log

Use this Response Log to record information from the texts that relates to or comments on the **Essential Questions** in Unit 3.

? Essential Question	Details from Texts
How can satire change people's behavior?	
What's your most surprising friendship?	
What keeps people from reaching their potential?	
Why are plagues so horrifying?	

Response Log

Use this Response Log to record information from the texts that relates to or comments on the **Essential Questions** in Unit 4.

? Essential Question	Details from Texts
What can nature offer us?	
How do you define beauty?	
How can science go wrong?	
What stirs your imagination?	

Response Log

Use this Response Log to record information
from the texts that relates to or comments on the
Essential Questions in Unit 5.

? Essential Question	Details from Texts
What is a true benefactor?	
How do you view the world?	
What brings out cruelty in people?	
What invention has had the greatest impact on your life?	

Response Log

Use this Response Log to record information from the texts that relates to or comments on the **Essential Questions** in Unit 6.

? Essential Question	Details from Texts
What makes people feel insecure?	
Why is it hard to resist social pressure?	
What is the power of symbols?	
How do you measure a person's worth?	

Using a Glossary

A glossary is an alphabetical list of vocabulary words. Use a glossary just as you would a dictionary—to determine the meanings, parts of speech, pronunciation, and syllabification of words. (Some technical, foreign, and more obscure words in this book are defined for you in the footnotes that accompany many of the selections.)

Many words in the English language have more than one meaning. This glossary gives the meanings that apply to the words as they are used in the selections in this book.

The following abbreviations are used to identify parts of speech of words:

adj. adjective   *adv.* adverb   *n.* noun   *v.* verb

Each word's pronunciation is given in parentheses. A guide to the pronunciation symbols appears in the Pronunciation Key below. The stress marks in the Pronunciation Key are used to indicate the force given to each syllable in a word. They can also help you determine where words are divided into syllables.

For more information about the words in this glossary or for information about words not listed here, consult a dictionary.

Pronunciation Key

Symbol	Examples	Symbol	Examples	Symbol	Examples
ă	pat	m	mum	ûr	urge, term, firm, word, heard
ā	pay	n	no, sudden* (sŭd´n)	v	valve
ä	father, hard	ng	thing	w	with
âr	care	ŏ	pot	y	yes
b	bib	ō	toe	z	zebra, xylem
ch	church	ô	caught, paw	zh	vision, pleasure, garage
d	deed, milled	oi	noise	ə	about, item, edible, gallop, circus
ĕ	pet	ŏŏ	took	ər	butter
ē	bee	ōō	boot		
f	fife, phase, rough	ŏŏr	lure		
g	gag	ôr	core		
h	hat	ou	out		
hw	which	p	pop		
ĭ	pit	r	roar		
ī	pie, by	s	sauce		
îr	pier	sh	ship, dish		
j	judge	t	tight, stopped		
k	kick, cat, pique	th	thin		
l	lid, needle* (nēd´l)	*th*	this		
		ŭ	cut		

Sounds in Foreign Words

Symbol	Examples
KH	*German* ich, ach; *Scottish* loch
N	*French* bon (bôN)
œ	*French* feu, œuf; *German* schön
ü	*French* tu; *German* über

*In English the consonants *l* and *n* often constitute complete syllables by themselves.

Stress Marks
The strongest, or primary, stress of a word is indicated by a mark (´). Syllables with weaker stress and words of one syllable show no stress mark.

Glossary of Academic Vocabulary

abandon (ə-băn´dən) *v.* to withdraw one's support or help, especially in spite of duty, allegiance, or responsibility.

ambiguous (ăm-bĭg´yoo-əs) *adj.* open to more than one interpretation.

anticipate (ăn-tĭs´ə-pāt) *v.* to see as a probable occurrence; expect.

appreciate (ə-prē´shē-āt) *v.* to recognize the quality, significance, or magnitude of.

arbitrary (är´bĭ-trĕr-ē) *adj.* determined by chance, whim, or impulse, and not by necessity, reason, or principle.

collapse (kə-lăps´) *v.* to break down or fall apart suddenly and cease to function.

conceive (kən-sēv´) *v.* to understand or form in the mind; to devise.

confine (kən-fīn´) *v.* to keep within bounds; restrict.

conform (kən-fôrm´) *v.* to be similar to or match something or someone; to act or be in accord or agreement.

controversy (kŏn´trə-vûr-sē) *n.* public disagreement; argument.

convince (kən-vĭns´) *v.* persuade or lead to agreement by means of argument.

denote (dĭ-nōt´) *v.* to serve as a symbol for the meaning of; signify.

depress (dĭ-prĕs´) *v.* to cause to be sad or dejected.

displace (dĭs-plās´) *v.* to move, shift, or force from the usual place or position.

drama (drä´mə) *n.* a prose or verse composition intended to be acted out.

encounter (ĕn-koun´tər) *v.* to confront in battle or competition.

exploit (ĭk-sploit´) *v.* to take advantage of; to use for selfish or unethical purposes.

insight (ĭn´sīt) *n.* the ability to discern the true nature of a situation.

integrity (ĭn-tĕg´rĭ-tē) *n.* the quality of being ethically or morally upright.

intensity (ĭn-tĕn´sĭ-tē) *n.* a high degree of concentration, power, or force.

invoke (ĭn-vōk´) *v.* to call on for assistance, support, or inspiration.

military (mĭl´ĭ-tĕr-ē) *n.* the armed forces of a nation considered collectively; *adj.* of, related to, or characteristic of members of the armed forces.

persist (pər-sĭst´) *v.* to hold firmly to a purpose or task in spite of obstacles.

radical (răd´ĭ-kəl) *adj.* departing markedly from the usual or customary; extreme or drastic.

reluctance (rĭ-lŭk´təns) *n.* the state of being reluctant; unwillingness.

subordinate (sə-bôr´dn-ĭt) *adj.* subject to the authority or control of another.

undergo (ŭn-dər-gō´) *v.* to experience or be subjected to.

violate (vī´ə-lāt) *v.* to disregard or act in a manner that does not conform to (a law or promise, for example).

visual (vĭzh´oo-əl) *adj.* seen or able to be seen by the eye; visible.

widespread (wīd´sprĕd´) *adj.* occurring or accepted widely.

Glossary of Critical Vocabulary

abate (ə-bāt´) v. to reduce in amount, degree, or intensity; lessen.

abrogate (ăb´rə-gāt) v. to revoke or nullify.

abyss (ə-bĭs´) n. an immeasurably deep chasm, depth, or void.

accolade (ăk´ə-lād, -läd) n. a special acknowledgment; an award.

accommodations (ə-kŏm-ə-dā´shənz) n. lodgings.

affairs (ə-fârz´) n. personal business.

affliction (ə-flĭk´shən) n. something that causes suffering or pain.

aghast (ə-găst´) adj. struck by shock, terror, or amazement.

algorithm (ăl´gə-rĭth-əm) n. a finite set of unambiguous instructions that, given some set of initial conditions, can be performed in a prescribed sequence to achieve a certain goal and that has a recognizable set of end conditions.

anecdote (ăn´ĭk-dōt) n. a short account of an interesting or humorous incident.

appraise (ə-prāz´) v. 1. to estimate the price or value of: appraise a diamond; appraise real estate. 2. to make a considered judgment about.

ardor (är´dər) n. intensity of emotion, especially strong desire, enthusiasm, or devotion.

artifice (är´tə-fĭs) n. cleverness or ingenuity in making or doing something.

attribute (ə-trĭb´yōot) v. to regard as arising from a particular cause or source; ascribe.

autonomy (ô-tŏn´ə-mē) n. the condition or quality of being autonomous; independence.

aversion (ə-vûr´zhən) n. a fixed, intense dislike; repugnance.

balmy (bä´mē) adj. mild and pleasant.

bequeath (bĭ-kwēth´, -kwēth´) v. to pass (something) on to another; hand down.

bereft (bĭ-rĕft´) adj. 1. deprived of something. 2. lacking something needed or expected.

brazen (brā´zən) adj. unrestrained by a sense of shame; rudely bold.

brooding (brōō´dĭng) adj. thinking about something moodily.

cacophony (kə-kŏf´ə-nē) n. jarring, discordant sound; dissonance.

calamity (kə-lăm´ĭ-tē) n. an event that brings terrible loss, lasting distress, or severe affliction; a disaster.

chafe (chāf) v. to annoy or irritate.

chow (chou) n. food; victuals.

cohesiveness (kō-hē´-sĭv-nəs) n. the condition of sticking together in a group.

collateral (kə-lăt´ər-əl) adj. concomitant or accompanying.

commence (kə-mĕns´) v. to begin or start.

commend (kə-mĕnd´) v. to commit to the care of another; entrust.

compulsory (kəm-pŭl´sə-rē) adj. obligatory; required.

condone (kən-dōn´) v. to overlook, forgive, or disregard (an offense) without protest or censure.

congenial (kən-jēn´yəl) adj. agreeable; sympathetic.

consumption (kən-sŭmp´shən) n. an amount consumed.

cowed (koud) adj. frightened or subdued with threats or a show of force.

curate (kyōor´āt) v. to gather and present to the public.

demonize (dē´mə-nīz) v. to represent as evil or diabolic.

deprivation (dĕp-rə-vā´shən) n. the condition of being deprived; lacking the basic necessities or comforts of life.

despotic (dĭ-spŏt´ĭk) *adj.* of or relating to a person who wields power oppressively, or a tyrant.

disconnect (dĭs´kə-nĕkt) *n.* a lack of connection or a gap between two things.

discourse (dĭs´kôrs) *n.* verbal exchange or conversation.

disoriented (dĭs-ôr´ē-ĕnt´əd) *adj.* having lost one's sense of direction, position, or relationship with one's surroundings.

dissimulation (dĭ-sĭm´yə-lā-shən) *n.* deceit or pretense.

dogged (dô´gĭd, dŏg´ĭd) *adj.* stubbornly persevering; tenacious.

domain (dō-mān´) *n.* a sphere of activity, influence, or knowledge.

dominion (də-mĭn´yən) *n.* rule or power to rule; mastery.

double entendre (dûb´əl än-tän´drə) *n.* an expression having a double meaning.

emulation (ĕm´yə-lā-shən) *n.* competitive imitation.

encumbrance (ĕn-kŭm´brəns) *n.* a burden or impediment.

engagement (ĕn-gāj´mənt) *n.* a promise or agreement to be at a particular place at a particular time.

entail (ĕn-tāl´) *v.* involve as a consequence.

ersatz (ĕr´zäts, ĕr-zäts´) *adj.* being a usually inferior imitation or substitute; artificial.

eschew (ĕ-shōō´, ĕs-chōō´) *v.* to avoid using, accepting, participating in, or partaking of.

esprit de corps (ĕ-sprē´ də kôr´) *n.* a spirit of devotion and loyalty among group members.

evanescent (ĕv-ə-nĕs´ənt) *adj.* vanishing or likely to vanish like vapor.

exorbitant (ĭg-zôr´bĭ-tənt) *adj.* beyond what is reasonable or customary, especially in cost or price.

expound (ĭk-spound´) *v.* to explain in detail; elucidate.

extract (ĭk-străkt´) *v.* to draw or pull out, often with great force or effort.

extremist (ĭk-strē´mĭst) *adj.* advocating or resorting to measures beyond the norm, especially in politics.

feeble (fē´bəl) *adj.* lacking strength.

finite (fī´nīt) *adj.* having bounds; limited.

flotsam (flŏt´səm) *n.* discarded or unimportant things.

forebear (fôr´bâr) *n.* a person from whom one is descended; an ancestor.

forge (fôrj) *v.* to form (metal, for example) by heating in a forge and beating or hammering into shape.

garish (gâr´ĭsh, găr´-) *adj.* overly bright or ornamented, especially in a vulgar or tasteless way; gaudy.

genre (zhän´rə) *n.* a category within an art form, based on style or subject.

gilded (gĭl´dĭd) *adj.* covered with or having the appearance of being covered with a thin layer of gold.

guile (gīl) *n.* clever trickery; deceit.

hierarchy (hī´ə-rär-kē) *n.* a ranking of status within a group.

huddle (hŭd´l) *v.* to crowd together, as from cold or fear.

ignoble (ĭg-nō´bəl) *adj.* not noble in quality, character, or purpose; base or dishonorable.

immersion (ĭ-mûr´zhən, -shən) *n.* the act or instance of engaging in something wholly or deeply.

impeccably (ĭm-pĕk´ə-blē) *adv.* in accordance with having no flaws; perfectly.

imperialism (ĭm-pîr´ē-ə-lĭz-əm) *n.* the extension of a nation's authority by territorial acquisition or by the establishment of economic and political dominance over other nations.

implementation (ĭm-plə-mən-tā´shən) *n.* the process of putting into practical effect; carrying out.

implications (ĭm´plĭ-kā´shənz) *n.* conclusions that are not explicitly stated.

impressionable (ĭm-prĕsh´ə-nə-bəl) *adj.* readily or easily influenced; suggestible.

inanimate (ĭn-ăn´ə-mĭt) *adj.* not having the qualities associated with active, living organisms.

inarticulate (ĭn-är-tĭk´yə-lĭt) *adj.* uttered without the use of normal words or syllables; incomprehensible as speech or language.

incentive (ĭn-sĕn´tĭv) *n.* something, such as the fear of punishment or the expectation of reward, that induces action or motivates effort.

incessantly (ĭn-sĕs´ənt-lē) *adv.* without interruption.

inculcate (ĭn-kŭl´kāt, ĭn´kŭl-) *v.* to impress (something) upon the mind of another by frequent instruction or repetition; instill.

incumbent (ĭn-kŭm´bənt) *adj.* required as a duty or an obligation.

inducement (ĭn-dōōs´mənt, -dyōōs´-) *n.* an incentive.

infantry (ĭn´fən-trē) *n.* the branch of an army made up of units trained to fight on foot.

infuse (ĭn-fyōoz´) *v.* to fill or cause to be filled with something.

innate (ĭ-nāt´, ĭn´āt´) *adj.* natural or present from birth rather than learned.

innumerable (ĭ-nōō´mər-ə-bəl) *adj.* too many to count.

inoculate (ĭ-nŏk´yə-lāt) *v.* to safeguard as if by inoculation; to protect.

intelligentsia (ĭn-tĕl-ə-jĕnt´sē-ə) *n.* the intellectual elite of a society.

labyrinth (lăb´ə-rĭnth) *n.* an intricate structure of interconnecting passages through which it is difficult to find one's way; a maze.

lethargy (lĕth´ər-jē) *n.* a lack of interest or enthusiasm; apathy.

levy (lĕv´ē) *v.* to impose (a tax or fine, for example) on someone.

listless (lĭst´lĭs) *adj.* lacking energy or disinclined to exert effort; lethargic.

loathsome (lōth´səm) *adj.* causing loathing; abhorrent.

loftily (loft´ĭ-lē) *adv.* arrogantly; haughtily.

luddite (lŭd´ĭt) *n.* one who opposes technical or technological change.

malady (măl´ə-dē) *n.* a disease, disorder, or ailment.

manacle (măn´ə-kəl) *v.* to restrain the action or progress of something or someone.

mandatory (măn´də-tôr-ē) *adj.* required or commanded by authority; obligatory.

meme (mēm) *n.* a unit of cultural information, such as a cultural practice or idea, that is transmitted verbally or by repeated action from one mind to another.

mire (mīr) *v.* to hinder, entrap, or entangle.

misdeed (mĭs-dēd´) *n.* a wrong or illegal action; a wrongdoing.

misogyny (mĭ-sŏj´ə-nē) *n.* hatred or mistrust of women.

monetize (mŏn´ĭ-tīz, mŭn´-) *v.* to convert into a source of income.

morose (mə-rōs´, mô-) *adj.* sullen or gloomy.

odious (ō´dē-əs) *adj.* extremely unpleasant; repulsive.

ominous (ŏm´ə-nəs) *adj.* menacing; threatening.

pension (pĕn´shən) *n.* a sum of money paid regularly as a retirement benefit.

pervasive (pər-vā´sĭv,-zĭv) *adj.* having the quality or tendency to pervade or permeate.

plateau (plă-tō´) *v.* to reach a stable level; level off.

plight (plīt) *n.* a situation, especially a bad or unfortunate one.

posit (pŏz´ĭt) *v.* to assume or put forward, as for consideration or the basis of argument.

preamble (prē´ăm-bəl, prē-ăm´-) *n.* a preliminary statement.

precipice (prĕs´ə-pĭs) *n.* an overhanging or extremely steep mass of rock; the brink of a dangerous or disastrous situation.

prerogative (prĭ-rŏg´ə-tĭv) *n.* an exclusive right or privilege held by a person or group, especially a hereditary or official right.

prescient (prĕsh´ənt) *adj.* of or relating to prescience—which means knowledge of actions or events before they occur.

presentable (prĭ-zĕn´tə-bəl) *adj.* fit for introduction to others.

procrastinate (prō-krăs´tə-nāt) *v.* to put off doing something, especially out of habitual carelessness or laziness.

prodigious (prə-dĭj´əs) *adj.* enormous.

prognosis (prŏg-nō´sĭs) *n.* a prediction of the probable course and outcome of a disease.

promiscuously (prə-mĭs´kyōō-əs-lē) *adv.* lacking standards of selection; without careful judgment; indiscriminately.

prostrate (prŏs´trāt) *adj.* lying face down, as in submission or adoration.

pyrrhic victory (pĭr´ĭk vĭk´tə-rē) *n.* a victory that is offset by staggering losses.

quell (kwĕl) *v.* to pacify; quiet.

ransack (răn´săk) *v.* to go through (a place) stealing valuables and causing disarray.

realm (rĕlm) *n.* kingdom.

rebuke (rĭ-byōōk´) *v.* to criticize (someone) sharply; reprimand.

recoil (rĭ-koil´) *v.* to shrink back, as in fear or repugnance.

redress (rĭ-drĕs´) *n.* repayment for a wrong or an injury.

repine (rĭ-pīn´) *v.* to be discontented; complain or fret.

rotation (rō-tā´shən) *n.* regular and uniform variation in a sequence or series.

ruddy (rŭd´ē) *adj.* having a healthy reddish glow.

rudiment (rōō´də-mənt) *n.* fundamental element, principle, or skill.

salutation (săl-yə-tā´shən) *n.* a polite expression of greeting or goodwill.

satire (săt´īr) *n.* a literary work in which human foolishness or vice is attacked through irony, derision, or wit.

scorn (skôrn) *n.* contempt or disdain.

scrounge (skrounj) *v.* to obtain by salvaging or foraging; round up.

scrupulous (skrōō´pyə-ləs) *adj.* conscientious and exact; having scruples.

sea change (sē chānj) *n.* a marked transformation.

self-possessed (sĕlf-pə-zĕst´) *adj.* having calm and self-assured command of one's faculties, feelings, and behavior.

senility (sĭ-nĭl´ĭ-tē) *n.* relating to or having diminished cognitive function, as when memory is impaired, because of old age.

sentient (sĕn´shənt) *adj.* having sense perception; conscious.

smart (smärt) *v.* to suffer acutely, as from mental distress, wounded feelings, or remorse.

sovereignty (sŏv´ər-ĭn-tē, sŏv´rĭn-) *n.* complete independence and self-government.

spoof (spōōf) *n.* a satirical imitation; a parody or send-up.

succinct (sək-sĭngkt´) *adj.* characterized by clear, precise expression in few words; concise and terse.

succinctly (sək-sĭngkt´lē) *adv.* in a concise or brief manner.

superficial (sōō-pər-fĭsh´əl) *adj.* apparent rather than actual or substantial; shallow.

supplant (sə-plănt´) *v.* to take the place of or substitute for (another).

sustenance (sŭs´tə-nəns) *n.* something, especially food, that sustains life or health.

tactfully (tăkt´fəl-lē) *adv.* considerately and discreetly.

theorize (thē´ə-rīz, thîr´īz) *v.* to formulate theories or a theory; speculate.

treachery (trĕch´ə-rē) *n.* an act of betrayal.

trinket (trĭng´kĭt) *n.* a small ornament, such as a piece of jewelry.

tumult (tōō´mŭlt) *n.* a state of agitation of the mind or emotions.

undaunted (ŭn-dôn′tĭd, -dän′-) *adj.* not discouraged or disheartened; resolutely courageous.

underpin (ŭn-dər-pĭn′) *v.* to give support or substance to.

usurp (yo͞o-sûrp′) *v.* to seize unlawfully by force.

Utopian (yo͞o-tō′pē-ən) *adj.* excellent or ideal but impracticable; visionary.

valor (văl′ər) *n.* courage; bravery.

veracity (və-răs′ĭ-tē) *n.* conformity to fact or truth; accuracy.

verandah (və-răn′də) *n.* a porch or balcony.

vexation (vĕk-sā′shən) *n.* a source of irritation or annoyance.

vigilance (vĭj′ə-ləns) *n.* alert watchfulness.

vile (vīl) *adj.* unpleasant or objectionable.

vindication (vĭn-dĭ-kā′shən) *n.* justification.

virtue (vûr′cho͞o) *n. Archaic* chastity, especially in a woman.

visitation (vĭz-ĭ-tā′shən) *n.* a gathering of people in remembrance of a deceased person.

vogue (vōg) *n.* the prevailing fashion, practice, or style.

volatile (vŏl′ə-tl, -tīl′) *adj.* unstable and prone to extremes.

wail (wāl) *v.* to make a long, loud, high-pitched cry, as in grief, sorrow, or fear.

writ (rĭt) *n.* a written order issued by a court, commanding the party to whom it is addressed to perform or cease performing a specified act.

zero-sum (zîr′ō-sŭm) *adj.* of or relating to a situation in which a loss and a gain are balanced.

Index of Skills

A

Academic Vocabulary, 2, 25, 45, 67, 85, 101, 115, 133, 152, 289, 309, 319, 327, 339, 349, 363, 382, 403, 413, 425, 437, 453, 465, 481, 495, 516, 537, 545, 557, 569, 585, 601, 618, 639, 645, 657, 671, 683, 697, 711, 730, 753, 769, 785, 803, 815, 825, 837, 847
active listening, 148, 512, 726, 864
active voice, 146, 405
acts, 160
adjectives, 755
  compound, 848
adverbs, 755
adversity, 715
Again and Again (Notice & Note), 477, 480, 652, 656, 741, 752
agreement, subject-verb, 103
Aha Moment (Notice & Note), 55, 554, 556, 667, 766, 768, 780, 784
allegory, 647, 650, 651, 654
alliteration, 9, 20, 27, 417, 688
allusions, 164
  classical, 290
analogy, 344, 442, 444
analyze
  allegory, 647, 650, 651, 654
  analogy, 444
  Analyze Media, 644
  Analyze the Image, 1, 151, 381, 515, 617, 729
  Analyze the Text, 24, 44, 66, 84, 100, 114, 118, 132, 135, 192, 214, 242, 264, 288, 308, 318, 326, 338, 340, 348, 362, 366, 402, 412, 424, 436, 452, 464, 468, 480, 494, 498, 536, 544, 556, 568, 584, 587, 600, 603, 638, 656, 670, 682, 696, 699, 710, 713, 752, 768, 784, 802, 814, 824, 827, 836, 846, 850
  Analyze the Videos, 294
apostrophe, 540, 542
arguments, 297, 301, 303, 304
author's point of view, 485, 488, 491, 494
author's purpose, 118
cause-and-effect relationships, 773, 778, 782
central ideas, 297, 303, 305
characterization, 71, 73, 76, 77, 82, 659, 661, 662, 664, 665
claims, 452
climax, 656
compare-and-contrast essay, 675, 677

conflict, 49, 52, 53, 55, 56, 61, 63, 163, 198, 201, 227, 253, 273
contradictions, 398
counterarguments, 442, 446
deductive reasoning, 841, 844
diary, 105, 107, 109, 430, 432
diction, 574, 577, 581
dramatic plot, 163, 169, 172, 189, 194, 204, 235, 247, 256, 271, 284
elegy, 417, 419
epic poem, 8–9, 10, 12, 20, 22
essay, 678
extended metaphors, 688
fantasy, 71, 74, 76, 77, 79, 80
first-person point of view, 625, 628, 632, 635, 636
historical context, 344, 346
historical setting, 472, 474, 475, 476, 477
idea development, 407, 410
illustration, 679
imagery, 523, 527, 528, 534, 702, 705, 708
interpretations of drama, 292
lyric poem, 122, 128, 129, 132, 135
memoir, 485, 490
metaphysical conceits, 321, 324
mood, 647, 649, 653, 737, 742, 746, 750
motivation, 547, 550, 551, 552
narrative poem, 29, 41
narrator, 29, 33, 34, 35, 38, 42, 472, 475, 478
ode, 574, 576, 578, 581
Old English poetry, 9, 10, 13, 20, 22
plot, 659, 666
primary sources, 90
pull quotes, 459
reflective essay, 773, 775, 777, 781
repetition, 656
rhetorical devices, 344, 347, 449
rhyme scheme, 539, 542
rhythmic patterns, 818, 820
romance, 49, 53, 61, 63
Romantic poetry, 523, 526, 529, 532
satire, 288, 389, 392, 395, 397, 399
science fiction, 547, 549, 550, 553
setting, 625, 629, 630, 633, 789, 792, 795
social context, 427, 429, 432
soliloquy, 164, 175, 211, 216, 233, 248
sonnets, 313, 315, 318
sound devices, 688, 692
speaker, 330, 336
stanza structure, 539, 542
stream of consciousness, 807, 810
structure, 29, 31

symbols, 590, 593, 596
text features, 353, 357
theme, 417, 420, 421
third-person point of view, 757, 760, 762, 763
tone, 122, 124, 129, 407, 410
vocabulary, 59, 75, 393, 551, 634, 796
writing prompt, 139, 371, 503, 717, 855
Anglo-Saxon culture, 133
annotate. *See* Annotation in Action
Annotation in Action, 106, 298, 314, 322, 331, 345, 354, 390, 408, 418, 428, 443, 458, 473, 486, 524, 540, 548, 562, 575, 591, 626, 648, 660, 676, 689, 703, 738, 758, 774, 790, 808, 819, 831, 842
antithesis, 344, 442
antonyms, 551, 558, 684
apostrophe, 540, 542, 545
appeals
  emotional (pathos), 830, 858
  ethical (ethos), 830, 858
  logical (logos), 830, 858
Apply to Your Draft
  argument, 858, 859, 860, 861, 862
  explanatory essay, 610, 611, 612, 613, 614
  literary analysis, 374, 375, 376, 377, 378
  personal narrative, 506, 507, 508, 509, 510
  research report, 720, 721, 722, 723, 724
  short story, 142, 143, 144, 145, 146
appositive phrases, 87, 614
appositives, 87, 614
  nonrestrictive, 87
  restrictive, 87
argument, write an, 854–862
  address opposing claims, 857, 859
  develop a claim, 856
  develop draft, 858–859
  edit, 862
  mentor text for, 854, 858, 859
  organize ideas, 857
  peer review, 861
  plan, 856–857
  publish, 862
  revise, 860–861
  rubric, 855
  sources for, 854
  student model, 861
  support for, 856
  writing prompt, 854–855
arguments
  analyze, 297, 301, 303, 304
  claims, 297, 372, 452, 856
  compare, 828, 850

Index of Skills

diction, 407, 574, 577, 581

dictionary, consulting, 102

direct object, 641

direct quotations, 378, 467, 510, 721

discussion. *See also* Collaborate and
Present; collaborative discussion
group, 45, 67, 85, 115, 157, 214, 339, 363,
403, 437, 495, 645, 683, 697, 803
paired, 101, 242, 537, 585, 769, 847
roundtable, 327

documentary, 643

domain-specific vocabulary, 310

draft
develop, 142–143, 374–375, 506–507,
610–611, 720–721, 858–859
edit, 146, 378, 510, 614, 724, 862
peer review, 145, 509, 861
revise, 144–145, 376–377, 508–509, 612–
613, 722–723, 860–861

drama
interpretations of, 292–293
Renaissance, 159–160
Shakespearean, 158–161, 163
verse, 161

dramatic irony, 161

dramatic monologue, 702

dramatic plot, analyze, 169, 172, 189, 194,
204, 247, 256, 271, 284

dramatic scene, 101

draw conclusions, 31, 35, 38, 42, 52, 172,
235, 247, 273, 410, 491, 552, 584, 597,
629, 664, 777, 781, 799
Analyze the Text, 24, 44, 66, 84, 100, 114,
132, 192, 214, 264, 288, 308, 318, 338,
348, 362, 402, 412, 424, 436, 452, 464,
480, 494, 536, 544, 556, 587, 600, 603,
638, 656, 670, 696, 699, 710, 752, 768,
784, 802, 814, 824
about author's purpose, 394
about data, 360, 462
Notice & Note, 667
about speakers, 702, 704, 706

E

edit draft
argument, 862
explanatory essay, 614
literary analysis, 378
personal narrative, 510
research report, 724
short story, 146

editorial, genre elements, 407, 841

effect, 773. *See also* cause/effect

elegy
analyze, 417, 419, 424
genre elements, 417

em dash, 365

emotional appeals (pathos), 830, 858

end rhyme, 539

Engage Your Brain, 8, 28, 48, 70, 89, 104,
121, 162, 292, 296, 312, 320, 329, 343,
352, 388, 406, 416, 426, 441, 456, 471,
484, 522, 538, 546, 560, 573, 589, 624,
642, 646, 658, 674, 687, 701, 736, 756,
772, 788, 806, 817, 829, 840

epic poem
genre elements, 9
theme of, determining, 9, 12, 15, 24

epilogue, writing, 481

epitaph, 424, 425

essay
compare-and-contrast, 115, 319, 675, 677
evaluate, 561, 563, 565
explanatory, 149, 606–614, 865
formal, 561
genre elements, 561, 675, 773
informal, 561
photo, 615
reflective, 601, 773, 775, 777, 781
structure, 609
writing, 465, 569

Essential Questions, 1, 2, 8, 23, 28, 42, 48,
64, 70, 83, 88, 98, 104, 113, 120, 127,
130, 136, 149, 151, 152, 162, 190, 212,
240, 262, 286, 292, 294, 296, 306, 312,
317, 320, 324, 328, 337, 347, 360, 368,
379, 381, 382, 388, 400, 406, 411, 416,
423, 426, 434, 440, 450, 463, 470, 479,
492, 500, 513, 515, 516, 522, 535, 538,
543, 546, 555, 560, 566, 572, 579, 582,
594, 598, 604, 615, 617, 618, 624, 637,
642, 646, 655, 658, 668, 674, 681, 686,
692, 695, 700, 707, 709, 714, 727, 729,
730, 736, 750, 756, 767, 772, 783, 788,
800, 806, 813, 816, 821, 823, 828, 834,
845, 852, 865
reflect on, 149, 379, 513, 615, 727, 865

ethical appeals (ethos), 830, 858

etymology, 786

eulogy, 289

evaluate
Analyze the Text, 24, 44, 66, 84, 100, 114,
118, 135, 192, 214, 242, 264, 288, 308,
326, 340, 348, 362, 402, 412, 436, 452,
480, 494, 556, 568, 587, 638, 670, 682,
713, 752, 784, 827, 836, 846, 850
articles, 460, 462
author's point of view, 488
author's purpose, 105, 108, 111
character, 757, 761, 764
conflict, 55
counterarguments, 841, 844
documentaries, 643
dramatic plot, 256
essay, 561, 563, 565
extreme or absolute language, 450
fantasy, 80
information, 675, 678, 679

literary criticism, 302

parody, 402

persuasive techniques, 830, 833

quotations, 566

rhetorical devices, 442, 444, 447, 449

science fiction, 553

short story, 760, 762

speaker, 319

texts, 357, 371

unreliable narrator, 737, 743, 744,
745, 747

evaluative questions, 561

evidence, 297, 373, 856
cite, 348, 366
textual, 375

exaggeration, 389

Expand Your Vocabulary, 10, 26, 30, 46, 50,
68, 72, 86, 91, 102, 106, 116, 298, 310,
345, 350, 354, 364, 390, 404, 414, 428,
438, 443, 454, 458, 466, 473, 482, 486,
496, 548, 558, 562, 570, 626, 640, 660,
672, 676, 684, 738, 754, 758, 770, 774,
786, 790, 804, 831, 838, 842, 848

explanatory essay, 149, 865

explanatory essay, write an, 606–614
draft, 610–611
edit, 614
mentor text for, 606
peer review, 613
plan, 608–609
publish, 614
purpose, 607
revise, 612–613
rubric, 607
sources, 606
writing prompt, 606–607

exposition, 140, 163

extend, 385, 519, 621, 733
Analyze the Text, 100
Reflect & Extend, 149, 379, 513, 615,
727, 865

extended metaphors, 688

external conflict, 49, 51, 163

Extreme or Absolute Language (Notice &
Note), 100, 450, 452, 843, 846

F

falling action, 140, 163

fantasy, 71, 74, 76, 77, 79, 80

fictional scene, 769

figurative language, 27, 322, 455, 698
interpret, 330, 334

figures of speech, 164

film adaptation, 292–293

first-person point of view, 140, 625, 628,
632, 635, 636

flashbacks, 141

Focus on Genre
argument, 442

© Houghton Mifflin Harcourt Publishing Company

Index of Titles and Authors

Acknowledgments

Excerpts from *The American Heritage Dictionary of The English Language, Fifth Edition*. Text copyright © 2016 by Houghton Mifflin Harcourt Publishing Company. Reprinted by permission of Houghton Mifflin Harcourt Publishing Company.

Excerpts from *Beowulf* translated by Seamus Heaney. Translation copyright © 2000 by Seamus Heaney. Reprinted by permission of W. W. Norton & Company, Inc. and Faber & Faber Ltd.

"Blood" from *Thrall: Poems* by Natasha Trethewey. Text copyright © 2012 by Natasha Trethewey. Reprinted by permission of Houghton Mifflin Harcourt Publishing Company. All rights reserved.

"Chivalry" from *Smoke and Mirrors* by Neil Gaiman. Text copyright © 1998 by Neil Gaiman. Reprinted by permission of Writers House, LLC.

"A Cup of Tea" from *The Short Stories of Katherine Mansfield* by Katherine Mansfield. Text copyright © 1923 by Penguin Random House LLC, renewed © by J. Middleton Murry. Reprinted by permission of Alfred A. Knopf, an imprint of the Knopf Doubleday Publishing Group, a division of Penguin Random House LLC. All rights reserved.

Quote from *A Dance with Dragons: A Song of Ice and Fire: Book Five* by George R. R. Martin. Text copyright © 2011 by George R. R. Martin. Reprinted by permission of Bantam Books, an imprint of Random House, a division of Penguin Random House LLC, and HarperCollins Publishers Ltd. All rights reserved.

From "Derek Walcott, the Art of Poetry No. 37." Interview by Edward Hirsch, originally published in *The Paris Review*, Issue 101, Winter 1986. Text copyright © 1986 by The Paris Review, Inc. Reprinted by permission of Wylie Agency LLC.

"Education Protects Women from Abuse" by Olga Khazan as first published in *The Atlantic Magazine*, May 14, 2014. Text copyright © 2014 by The Atlantic Media Co. Reprinted by permission of Tribune Content Agency, LLC. All rights reserved. Distributed by Tribune Content Agency, LLC.

"For Army Infantry's 1st Women, Heavy Packs and the Weight of History" by Dave Philipps from *The New York Times*, May 27, 2017. Text copyright © 2017 by The New York Times. Reprinted by permission of PARS International Corps on behalf of The New York Times. All rights reserved.

Excerpt from "Frankenstein: Giving Voice to the Monster" by Langdon Winner from langdonwinner.com, July 7, 2017. Text copyright © 2017 by Langdon Winner. Reprinted by permission of Langdon Winner.

Excerpt from "Hamlet's Dull Revenge" by René Girard from *Stanford Literature Review 1*, Fall 1984. Text copyright © 1984 by René Girard. Reprinted by permission of Martha Girard.

"The Inequality Bogeyman" by Thomas Sowell from *National Review* January 28, 2014. Text copyright © 2014 by Thomas Sowell. Reprinted by permission of Creators Syndicate on behalf of the author.

Excerpt from *Inferno: A Doctor's Ebola Story* by Steven Hatch. Text copyright © 2017 by Steven Hatch. Reprinted by permission of St. Martin's Press and Blackstone Publishing.

Excerpt from *Le Morte D'Arthur: King Arthur and the Legends of the Round Table* by Sir Thomas Malory, a new rendition by Keith Baines. Text copyright © 1962 by Keith Baines. Text copyright renewed © 1990 by Francesca Evans. Reprinted by permission of New American Library, an imprint of Penguin Publishing Group, a division of Penguin Random House LLC. All rights reserved.

"Loneliness" from *Second Childhood* by Fanny Howe. Text copyright © 2014 by Fanny Howe. Reprinted by permission of The Permissions Company, Inc., on behalf of Graywolf Press, www.graywolfpress.org.

"The Love Song of J. Alfred Prufrock" from *Collected Poems 1909-1962* by T. S. Eliot. Text copyright © 1930, 1940, 1941, 1942, 1943, 1958, 1962, 1963 by T. S. Eliot, renewed © 1970 by Esme Valerie Eliot. Reprinted by permission of Faber & Faber Ltd.

"My Daughter the Racist" from *Mr. Fox* by Helen Oyeyemi. Text copyright © 2010 by Helen Oyeyemi. Reprinted by permission of Riverhead, an imprint of Penguin Publishing Group, a division of Penguin Random House LLC, Wylie Agency LLC, and Penguin Random House Canada Limited.

"My Syrian Diary: Parts 1-3" by Marah from www.NewsDeeply.com. Text copyright © 2014 by Syria Deeply. Reprinted by permission of News Deeply, Inc.

"Ode to My Mother's Hair" from *Imago* by Joseph O. Legapsi. Text copyright © 2007 by Joseph O. Legaspi. Reprinted with permission of The Permissions Company, LLC, on behalf of CavanKerry Press.

Excerpt from *The Pastons: A Family in the War of the Roses* edited by Richard Barber. Text copyright © 1981 by Richard Barber. Reprinted by permission of Boydell & Brewer Ltd.

"Poem III" from *Twenty-One Love Poems* by Adrienne Rich. Text copyright © 2016 by the Adrienne Rich Literary Trust. W. W. Norton & Company, Inc., from *Collected Poems: 1950-2012* by Adrienne Rich. Reprinted by permission of W. W. Norton & Company, Inc. and The Frances Goldin Literary Agency.

Excerpt from "Sadiq Khan's Speech on Inequality" by Sadiq Khan, June 10, 2014. Contains Parliamentary information licensed under the Open Parliament License v3.0.

"Satire is dying—the internet is killing it" by Arwa Mahdawi from theguardian.com, August 19, 2014. Text copyright © 2014 by The Guardian News & Media Ltd. Reprinted by permission of The Guardian News & Media Ltd.

"The Second Coming" from *The Collected Works of W. B. Yeats, Volume I: The Poems, Revised* by W. B. Yeats, edited by Richard J. Finneran. Text copyright 1924 by The Macmillan Company, renewed 1952 by Bertha Georgie Yeats. Reprinted by the permission of Scribner, a division of Simon & Schuster, Inc. All rights reserved.

"Shooting an Elephant" from *Shooting an Elephant and Other Essays* by George Orwell. Text copyright 1950 by Sonig Brownell, renewed © 1978 by Sonig, Pitt-Rivers. Reprinted by permission of Houghton Mifflin Harcourt Publishing Company and Bill Hamilton as the Literary Executor of the Estate of the Late Sonia Brownell Orwell and Penguin Books Ltd.

"Symbols? I'm Sick of Symbols" by Fernando Pessoa from *Fernando Pessoa & Co.: Selected Poems*, edited and translated by Richard Zenith. Translation copyright © 1998 by Richard Zenith. Reprinted by permission of Grove Atlantic, Inc. and SLL/Sterling Lord Literistic, Inc.

"The Victorians Had the Same Concerns About Technology As We Do" by Melissa Dickson from theconversation.com, June 21, 2016. Text copyright © 2016 by Melissa Dickson. Reprinted by permission of Melissa Dickson.

"A Village After Dark" by Kazuo Ishiguro from *The New Yorker Magazine*, May 14, 2001. Text copyright © 2001 by Kazuo Ishiguro. Reprinted by permission of ICM Partners on behalf of the author.

"The Wanderer" from *Poems and Prose from the Old English* translated by Burton Raffel. Text copyright © 1997 by Yale University Press. Reprinted by permission of Yale University Press.

Excerpt from "The Wife of Bath's Tale" from *The Canterbury Tales* by Geoffrey Chaucer, translated by Nevill Coghill. Translation copyright © 1951 by Nevill Coghill. Translation copyright renewed © 1958, 1960, 1975, 1977 by the Estate of Nevill Coghill. Reprinted by permission of Penguin Books Ltd. and Curtis Brown Group Ltd., London on behalf of the Estate of Nevill Coghill.

SAT® is a trademark registered by the College Board, which is not affiliated with, and does not endorse, this product.

ACT® is a trademark registered by Act, Inc., which is not affiliated with, and does not endorse, this product.

Unit Opener Image Credits

Tradition and Reason: graphometer ©Album/Alamy, Roman Forum ruins ©smilemf/Adobe Stock, scroll paper ©Active Museum/Le Pictorium/Alamy, quadrant ©joel zatz/Alamy, 18th-century man Courtesy of Library of Congress Prints & Photographs Division, quadrants/Lavoisier's apparatus/barometer/mathematical instrument Public Domain.

New Ideas, New Voices: boy wearing headphones w/laptop ©Pablo Hidalgo/Dreamstime, girl in hijab listening to music ©Viacheslav Iakobchuk/Adobe Stock, adult & child feeding swans ©Halfpoint/Adobe Stock, soccer players ©Syda Productions/Adobe Stock, child w/kite ©TuiPhotoEngineer/Shutterstock, skateboarder ©Jacob Lund/Adobe Stock, person pointing ©wong yu liang/Adobe Stock, geese flying ©Terrance Emerson/Shutterstock, Big Ben ©caligari/Shutterstock, adult swans ©Mark Bond/Cutcaster, baby swans ©imageportal/Adobe Stock, ferris wheel ©Gallery de Labux/Shutterstock, child feeding swans ©6okean/Adobe Stock.